Business Week Guide to Global Investments Using Electronic Tools

Business Week Guide to Global Investments Using Electronic Tools

Robert Schwabach

Osborne **McGraw-Hill**

Berkeley New York St. Louis San Francisco
Auckland Bogotá Hamburg London Madrid Mexico City
Milan Montreal New Delhi Panama City
Paris São Paulo Singapore Sydney Tokyo Toronto

Osborne **McGraw-Hill**
2600 Tenth Street
Berkeley, California 94710
U.S.A.

For information on software, translations, or book distributors outside of the U.S.A., please write to Osborne **McGraw-Hill** at the above address.

Business Week Guide to Global Investments Using Electronic Tools

1234567890 DOC 9987654

ISBN 0-07-882055-3

Publisher
  Lawrence Levitsky

Acquisitions Editor
  Scott Rogers

Project Editor
  Janet Walden

Copy Editor
  Lunaea Hougland

Proofreader
  Pat Mannion

Indexer
  Matthew Spence

Computer Designer
  Peter F. Hancik

Illustrator
  Lance Ravella

Series Design
  Kris Peterson

Quality Control Specialist
  Joe Scuderi

Cover Design
  Clement Mok Designs

This book is dedicated to the readers, in the hope and expectation that reading it and using the programs will return them many times its price.

Contents at a Glance

Table of Contents

Part One: Same Planet, New World

1

Around the World in 80 Markets 3

2

On-Ramps for the Information
Highway 33

3

The Tools of the Trade: What You Need
to Turn on and Tune in 55

Part Two: A Closed-End View of an Open World

▬▬ 6 ▬▬

South of the Border 133

▬▬ 7 ▬▬

New Lands and Looks 147

8

Bond Funds 165

Part Three: The Information Highway: Roadside Attractions

9

The Big One: CompuServe 191

Part Four: Gentlemen, Choose Your Weapons

15

Telescan 307

16

Metastock: The Power 341

Acknowledgments

Writing a book like this is so much work that I wouldn't have started if I had understood the situation at the beginning. I remember reading a reviewer once who made the comment that he had just written a book himself, and it was so much work that now he could hardly bring himself to criticize anyone else's efforts. I'm a reviewer too, and now I know what he meant.

In fact a book like this cannot get done without the help of many people whose names never appear on the cover. It's astonishing, really, to see how many people are involved.

- David Brown, Richard Ames, and Mark Draud at Telescan.
- Keith Black at Windows On WallStreet (MarketArts).
- Steve Achelis and Bill Forsyth at MetaStock (Equis International).
- Catherine Gillis and Jackie Swift at Morningstar.
- Debra Young and Andy Dickson at CompuServe.
- Maggie Landis and Gerald Tallon at Dow Jones News/Retrieval.
- Glen Zimmerer at Prodigy.
- Nancy Morrisroe at Delphi.

At Osborne/McGraw-Hill: Scott Rogers, Larry Levitsky, Janet Walden, Kelly Vogel, Lance Ravella, Jani Beckwith, and Peter Hancik provided editing, guidance, layout, typesetting, and all that stuff that goes into the actual production of a book.

Still more commentary and error-checking was provided by technical readers and editors at *BusinessWeek*. If there are any errors left—and there probably are—it's not because we weren't trying.

And what about librarians? Nobody ever mentions librarians. I would like to thank the librarians in Wilmette, Winnetka, Evanston, Glencoe, Northwestern University, and the University of Chicago. Good libraries are the treasure houses of our civilization. They're an education in themselves, and the tuition is free.

Introduction

The Sound of One Hand Ringing A Bell

There's an old saying among market professionals when they suspect there's been a shift in direction. It goes: "They don't send a little man around ringing a bell, you know."

It's a rueful saying, meaning of course that it's very hard to tell when a market shifts—nobody comes around ringing a bell to tell you it's time to get in, get out, or just lie down until it all passes. The right course is usually apparent only after the fact. Long after the fact.

Well, there has been a shift in the world economy. The tremendous rise in foreign stock and bond markets in 1993—after years of boredom and frustration—was not some strange one-time event, it was the sound of a little man going around ringing a bell. Twenty years ago the U.S. stock markets represented two-thirds of all the stocks and bonds in the world. If you went back 25 years before that the number would have been closer to 90 percent. Now, in 1994, it's down to one-third. In a few years it will be less than a fourth.

What is happening is what had to happen of course. The chief victor of World War II—the only major economic power with its industrial capacity and infrastructure still intact—was us. We made the most of it. We paid ourselves well to rebuild Europe and Japan, and we reveled in the fact that we didn't have to sell the world on American products, because the customers came to us. They had to. Where else were they going to go?

Last year marked a sea change. Although Singapore, Hong Kong, Taiwan, Malaysia, and Thailand had been doing well for a number of years, we were able to view their progress with something of an uncle's indulgent smile. We knew that their prosperity depended on our willingness to buy their goods. But last year something significant happened: for the first time in nearly all of this century, more than half their trade was with each other and their neighbors, not us. Already we can detect a new attitude in these countries, and in Europe, South America, and Africa as well. It is an attitude of growing impatience with the United States, and an increasing unwillingness to make changes solely to satisfy us. It is an attitude that says the U.S. still matters, but we don't matter as much as we used to, and that we are even becoming something of a nuisance. That is a sea change.

Why We Are All Gathered Here

The assumption of this book is that indeed the world has changed and indeed the U.S. no longer dominates the markets. And furthermore, we're not interested in just crabbing about it but would like to go out there, join the fun, and make a buck or two.

If the U.S. only represents one-third of the world's stock markets, it takes something less than a mathematical genius to figure out the other two-thirds must be somewhere else. Fortunately, we can find out where. Thanks to 50 years as top dog, we still hold a key advantage—the most advanced information system in the world. The ease with which we pick up a phone or turn on the computer whenever we want to know something astonishes people from other lands. In Poland it takes 22 years to get a telephone. Even in France it takes five to seven. Here we get annoyed if it takes more than a day. While that edge lasts, let's use it.

Part 1: Same Planet, New World

The first section of this book explains the situation and tells you what kind of equipment you need to go exploring online. It also describes some of the major information sources, and the software and data services that can be used to analyze both domestic and foreign issues.

We're not going to kid you: this overview is not exhaustive. There are more than 500 programs available for technical and fundamental

analysis of stocks and bonds. If we gave all of them one page, that would be all this book could cover. There are more than 100 information services providing quotes and other investment data. A few words on each would eventually flatten even the most enthusiastic data surfer. And then there's the computer equipment. There are people who love nothing more than to discuss the advantages and limitations of various processors, modem protocols, and memory management systems. But we don't know those people, and are inclined to cross the street when we see them coming.

Part 2: A Closed-End View of an Open World

The second section of the book is potentially controversial and was the subject of some internal debate. The participants in this debate were me, myself, and I. (My next book will be on schizophrenia.)

This section is devoted to an examination of closed-end funds, with much of the information on these provided by Morningstar, the chief mutual fund reporting company. An alternative approach would have been to provide a detailed look at foreign stocks and companies. There are about 1,200 of these traded here on American stock exchanges and another 125,000 traded in their home countries. The problems stack up like this:

> One is sheer numbers; the book would have taken on the size and appearance of a small city phone directory.

> Another consideration is that much company information would have been out of date the minute the book was published. Information on many foreign stocks is difficult to come by and long delayed.

> Still another problem, and a major stumbling block, is that some countries do not permit foreigners to own stock in local companies. Not foreign individuals, at least. Some, like Korea, will permit institutions and corporations to own stock, however.

> Some countries have open markets but buying and selling does not conform to the rules any American investor would be familiar

with. Some stock markets in eastern Europe and Asia, for example, are often open for just a few minutes or an hour a day, and not even every day. Prices are set by market makers at the opening—there is no bidding.

▶ Financial reports, notices to shareholders and other information that may be important to the investor are often written only in the language of the home country for that corporation. Dividends are always issued in the local currency only. Reporting on everything is frequently delayed for months.

For these and other reasons it seems likely that most investors would be safer and even have greater flexibility it they invested in foreign companies through a fund, which would take care of the problems of currency and language translations, as well as dealing with markets not accessible to individuals. The funds selected are for the most part what are called closed-end funds. They carry no sales load and tend to confine their investments to a single country or region. In effect, they are a surrogate for shares in a country.

This does not preclude anybody from investing in individual foreign stocks (this book's appendix contains a list of more than 600 that are actively traded in the United States). Stocks traded only abroad can still be purchased by an individual by going through a bank or on a direct visit to that country. Many foreign countries have branches of their banks in this country. As an example of direct purchase, a friend bought some Singapore Airlines stock (not normally traded here) not long ago on a vacation trip to Singapore.

Part 3: The Information Highway: Roadside Attractions

The third section is devoted to a look at some of the major sources for online information. You can connect to these with your computer and a modem and have libraries of information available in seconds. Of course there is a fee for using these services, and you can go to a regular library for nothing.

In reality you should do both. Very few public libraries would have the extent of information available through services like CompuServe.

What you need is access to a major university library. It's doubtful, however, that any library, even at a leading business school, would have as much information as you can get from connecting to Dow Jones News/Retrieval. If cost is not a significant factor, you can let your fingers do the walking and the talking. If you want to economize you can mix library and online research. One of the things that is much easier to do online is "searches." These are screens that can search through thousands of stocks for earnings growth, dividends, momentum, etc. The computer excels at this sort of thing and can do the work of months in a few minutes. It is a subject in its own right and has been dealt with only lightly in this book.

Part 4: Gentlemen, Choose Your Weapons

Section four discusses programs for analyzing stocks, bonds, commodities, and indexes. This is the most exciting part of the book. Here we see the power of the computer to not only look at information, which is a picture of the past, but project the probable consequences of that information, which is the future.

Four programs are discussed, three of which are on disks at the back of this book. These are not demos but actual working versions of the three best-selling technical and fundamental analysis programs on the market today. It would cost several hundred dollars to buy them, so why are they here for free? They're here because I've known some of these people for years, and have been writing on the market and computers for even longer. They came forward eagerly when they heard about this book, believing it would be in their best interest to include their program here. And in fact I think it is in their best interest. That it happens to also be in your best interest is one of those happy confluences that leaves everyone a winner.

The makers are responsible for these programs. In other words, if you get stuck, don't call us, call them. They want it that way. All three programs require that you make a phone call to someone: to get started, to register the program, to get technical support. They want to hear from you. The numbers are provided in the section of the book titled "About the Disks" and in each chapter that is devoted to the programs (Chapters 15, 16, and 18).

Finally (Really)

I'm setting up a bulletin board so readers can talk with me and each other and share observations and discoveries. As a reporter I found that if you talk to enough people you can find the answer to just about anything. The bulletin board number is 708/733-1380.

SAME PLANET,
NEW WORLD

CHAPTER 1

AROUND THE WORLD IN 80 MARKETS

In 1497, Vasco da Gama found a passage to India. The voyage took two years and earned a return of sixty times on investment. Three years later, he did it again.

Now, as then, there is a belief that great rewards can be gained from ventures in far lands and new markets. Curiously, the people in those lands hold the same view about us. The U.S. has about one-third of the world's stock market valuation, down from two-thirds twenty years ago.

Yet it attracts over half the world's investment. What about the other two-thirds of the world's investment possibilities? If most of the money is here, and most of the growth is there, there must be an imbalance to correct. And money to be made correcting it.

In 1993, the U.S. stock market rose 17 percent. If you had the stocks in the Dow Jones Industrial Average, that is. Not bad. Quite good, in fact, and much better than the long-term average of 9 percent for the past half century. The broader market, as represented by the Standard & Poors 500 Index (see Figure 1-1), advanced 9.8 percent, very close to the long-term average. It was the worst performing stock market in the world. However, foreign markets have performed poorly for the previous four years.

Foreign stock markets are generally more volatile than the U.S., though not as much as recently appears. 1993 was unusual in both directions: not only were overseas markets much more volatile than their long-term history, but the U.S. market was much less volatile. Volatility in the Standard & Poor's 500 Index, for example, was 6.7 percent. Volatility in the Hong Kong market, which is the most volatile of the

Figure 1-1　The course of the Standard & Poors 500 Index for 1993

larger world stock markets, was more than 70 percent. Thus it would appear that the Hong Kong stock market is a dozen times more volatile than the U.S. But looking at the longer term—the past 10 years and more—the average volatility of the S&P 500 is 18 percent, and the average volatility of the Hang Seng Index in Hong Kong is 42 percent. It's obviously much higher, but closer to twice as volatile, not 12 times. Looking at the same period for British stocks, their long-term volatility is around 27 percent, which is roughly half again as volatile as the U.S. market. Volatility isn't necessarily bad, by the way. There is some correlation between a market's volatility and its long-term rate of return. In other words, more volatile markets tend to provide greater returns. But like any roller coaster ride, they can also give you that queasy feeling as you go.

Young Turks

The Turkish stock market was up a rousing 221 percent from low to high in 1993. It was down 50 percent in the first part of 1994. Ah well. Win some, lose some.

You probably didn't know Turkey even had a stock market. Well, they do. As do Colombia, Indonesia, Venezuela, Jordan, and a couple dozen other exotic lands. Which naturally raises the question: "Would you want to invest in a place you were afraid to visit?" (Remember: they feel the same way about Miami.)

Indonesia's market was up 103 percent in 1993, low to high; Pakistan, 92 percent; Brazil, 103 percent; Jordan, 41 percent; New Zealand, 70 percent; Columbia, 68 percent; India, 80 percent. Even in the more sedate world of Europe, the British market was up 32 percent—three times as much as the Standard & Poors 500. France was up 26 percent; Switzerland, 55 percent; Germany, 39 percent. (See Tables 1-1 and 1-2, showing the 1993 range and percentage gains for most of the world's active stock markets.)

These are all in dollar terms, answering the eternal traveler's question: "How much is that in real money?" The change and the range are calculated on the basis of having bought at the low and sold at the high, which in almost every case was buying at or around the beginning of the year and selling at the end. While "buy-low, sell-high" is trite advice, and like most such advice, difficult to follow, the range serves as a ready guide

MARKET	RANGE	1993 RANGE (US $)	% IN $
Australia	321-447	193-270	40
Austria	329-477	749-1,036	38
Belgium	390-508	578-715	24
Canada	363-450	305-365	13
Denmark	591-860	704-963	37
Finland	60-124	44-85	93
France	515-688	520-655	26
Germany	227-329	509-707	20
Hong Kong	3,868-8,206	2,774-5,901	113
Ireland	119-189	114-161	41
Italy	354-539	147-211	44
Japan	735-991	2,128-3,502	65
Malaysia	203-440	195-418	114
Netherlands	336-473	665-896	35
New Zealand	69-110	54-92	70
Norway	554-852	571-819	43
Singapore	786-1,291	1,457-2,481	70
Spain	181-286	110-144	31
Sweden	1,139-1,884	799-1,213	67
Switzerland	250-373	721-1,115	55
U.K. (Great Britain)	814-1,053	498-657	32
U.S.A. (Dow Industrials)	3,242-3,794	3,242-3,794	17
E.A.F.E. (Europe, Australia, Far East Index)	451-591	731-1,005	37

Table 1-1   The performance of major stock markets in 1993 (*Barron's*)

to what we're talking about. Many lists will make their calculation based on the last day of the previous year to the last day of the next, a method of calculation that seems to make sense, but is in fact as arbitrary as any

MARKET	RANGE	% CHANGE
Argentina	879-1,521	73
Brazil	240-488	103
Chile	461-698	51
Colombia	76-128	68
Greece	159-221	39
India	76-137	80
Indonesia	319-648	103
Israel	89-119	34
Jordan	85-120	41
Korea	102-151	48
Mexico	1,035-1,742	68
Pakistan	84-161	92
Peru	74-127	72
Philippines	227-527	132
Portugal	49-70	43
Sri Lanka	83-166	100
Taiwan	141-260	84
Thailand	313-628	101
Turkey	73-234	221
Venezuela	73-100	37

Table 1-2   Emerging markets, 1993; all figures are in U.S. dollars
(*Barron's*)

other, since who would make all their investments on a single day, and then sell exactly one year later?

The calculations are in dollar terms to avoid the distortions that would result from pegging everything in local currencies, without taking account of how the currencies changed during the course of the year. We'll talk more about currencies a little later, but suffice it to say that currency fluctuations against the dollar account for a large part of the return in foreign stock investments. In 1993, the effect of a falling dollar accounted for almost half the gain in many markets. Should that trend reverse and we enter a period of a rising dollar, that would seriously affect the results of foreign stock holdings.

Getting Directions on the Information Highway

Whether in New York or Tokyo, Chicago or Bangkok, you can buy and sell stocks, bonds, commodities, sector funds, country funds, regional funds, real estate, shipping, airlines, whatever; and somebody is surely out there right now hawking rubber plantations and cocoa groves.

Information used to be unreliable and difficult to come by. In some places and times, it still is. But for the most part, solid knowledge is as close as your desktop computer. Belly up to the keyboard and go online with half a hundred data services—some of them listed here for the first time. You can call up closing quotes, volume, options, and a lot more. You can get the latest headline and corporate news, join investment clubs, and even place your orders and receive confirmations without ever leaving the glowing screen. Pull up a comfortable chair and let your fingers do the walking.

The biggest sources are Telescan, CompuServe, and Dow Jones News/ Retrieval. The smallest ones don't even have names, and some are reluctant to have their phone numbers listed.

There are more than two dozen online services that only supply quotes on stocks and commodities. Some of these are so obscure you have to send out the Sherpas to make base camp. Still others provide not only quotes but news, free software, and the companionship of like-minded investors and clubs—special interest groups or SIGs, as they're known in the trade (pronounced as one word "sigs").

Guides to Other People's Money

Figuring out a company's prospects is often confusing, both here and abroad. You can skip individual stocks entirely if you want and just go for managed money—mutual funds and the like. According to *The Economist*, an astonishing $14 trillion is currently being professionally managed, both here and abroad. Even in these days of big numbers, $14 trillion is a very big number. (It was the late Senator Dirksen who said: "A billion here and a billion there, and pretty soon you're talking real money.") In fact, $14 trillion is equal to more than half the world's annual output of goods and services. Over half of that managed money—some $8 trillion—is invested in the United States. We too are part of the "globe" in global.

That $8 trillion is essentially tagging after history. Twenty years ago, as we said, the United States markets represented about two-thirds of the total value of the world's stocks and bonds. If you were to go back 25 years before that, the number would have been close to 90 percent. The world was recovering from five years of global war. If you wanted a truck or a hair dryer, you bought it here. That happy circumstance (for Americans) no longer applies. The world is both large and very busy. Trucks are made in Stuttgart and Seoul as well as Detroit, hair dryers are hawked from pushcarts in Saigon, and Arab nomads have Sony Walkmans.

Today, the U.S. represents about a third of the world's industrial capacity, and a third of the market for stocks and bonds. That percentage is close to exact. Though we like to think that nothing of any consequence goes on beyond the confines of our shores, the facts are that, of the world's 100 largest corporations, only 30 are American (see the list in the section, "Not the New Kids on the Block" later in this chapter). It's still a big number, but not as big as it used to be—and short of another worldwide conflict that leaves this country untouched, unlikely to ever be so again.

So what's a mother to do? as mothers like to say. There are good deals and reliable companies everywhere. Look around, listen to the beat, and keep an eye on the news. Any crisis—a coup in Brazil, unrest in Ghana, or a scandal in Tokyo—can, as the Chinese know so well, represent both danger and opportunity.

Name Dropping

Buying a foreign stock or bond need not be as exotic as finding a contact in Kuala Lumpur or reading the business pages in Papua, New Guinea. Well over a thousand foreign stocks and bonds are traded regularly in the United States and listed every week in standard financial publications, like *Barron's* or the *Wall Street Journal*. Many are traded daily, and obtaining an up-to-the-minute quote for them is as easy for you as obtaining one for General Motors or IBM.

note

It is almost always true that the market is more important than any individual stock. There is an old saying on Wall Street: A rising tide lifts all boats. The reverse is true of a falling tide. That is, if the Chilean market is on a slide, it's likely to take almost everything down with it—the good with the bad.

Some of the names of available foreign stocks are almost as familiar as Coke, and a number of them follow. Many have traded here for years. Look them over, casually or in depth, and get a feel for their motion. The charts are for Sony (see Figure 1-2), Nissan (Figure 1-3), Volvo (Figure l-4), Daimler-Benz, Fiat, Philips, Electrolux, Cadbury-Schweppes ("Cadbury's snack fills the gap," as the ads say in Britain, whose citizens have the highest per capita sugar consumption of any country in the world), Royal Dutch/Shell, NEC (Figure l-5), Japan Air Lines, and others.

The easiest kind of foreign stock to buy is one that has ADRs. This stands for American Depository Receipt and is just what it sounds like—a

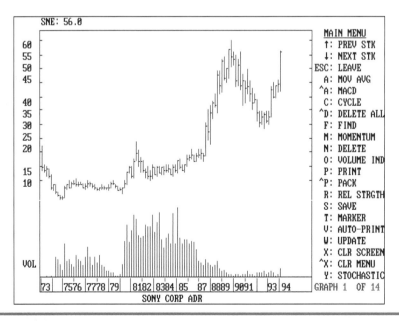

Figure I-2   Sony (Japan) over the past 20 years: a Walkman down memory lane

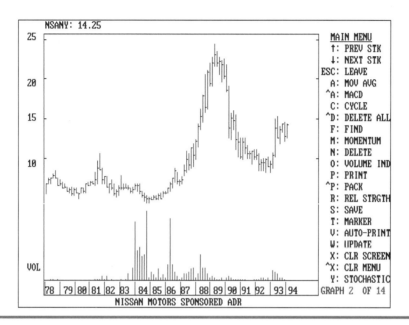

Figure 1-3 On the road with Nissan Motors (Japan), since 1978

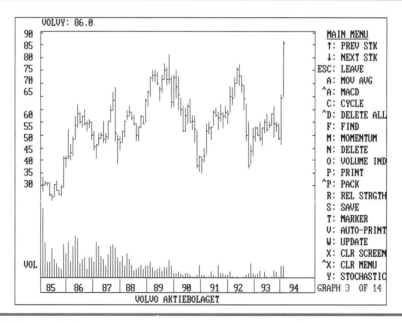

Figure 1-4 On the road with Volvo (Sweden), since 1985

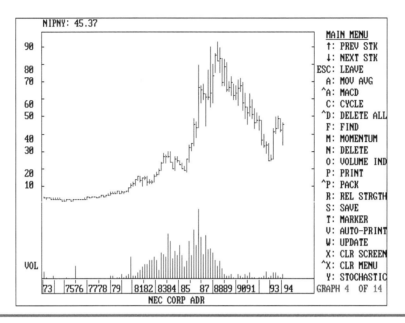

Figure 1-5   NEC (Japan), since 1973 (NEC is about the size of General Electric.)

receipt for stock held somewhere else. But there are other ways to buy foreign stocks, some of them not even foreign.

Some stocks appear to be American companies, but are in fact owned either entirely or in large part by investors and managers of other lands: Reebok (Great Britain, shown in Figure 1-6), Nike (Germany, shown in Figure 1-7), Schlumberger (France), and Zenith Data Systems (France). Many high tech firms are owned in whole or part by overseas investors, though their stock listings show no evidence of that. Creative Technology, for example (shown in Figure 1-8), makers of Sound Blaster, the leading selling computer sound card, which adds speech and music to IBM compatibles, is a Singapore company, though listed in the Over the Counter market in the same way as any other American company.

Another way to play a foreign market is to play its American competitors or its countereffect on our currency. Thus, if there is trouble in the Middle East, the price of oil, and of American oil companies, may rise. If Asian economies are doing well, and their currencies are consequently rising against the dollar, gold may rise as well—because, after all,

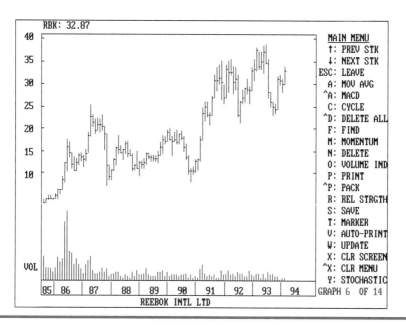

Figure 1-6   Hoofing it with Reebok International (Great Britain), since 1989

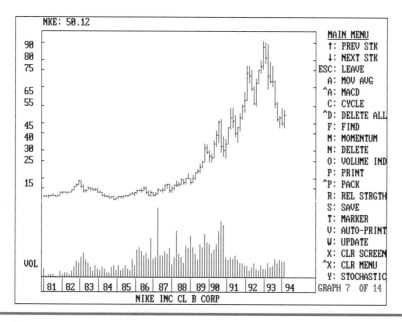

Figure 1-7   Hoofing it with Nike (Germany), since 1981

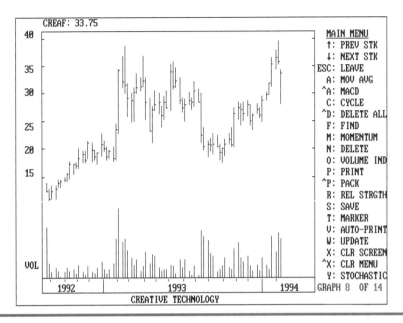

Figure 1-8   Creative Technology (Singapore), since 1992

the price of gold is denominated in dollars, and a weakening currency means it takes more of dollars to buy the same quantity of gold.

Of course, it is in the so-called emerging markets that the hottest action is to be found. None of these is quite so emerging as China. Everybody who makes a product or prints a label has already taken out a pad and pencil and done the arithmetic where they multiply their unit sales by a billion. The result is always a very big number. And while ultimately it seems like a sure thing, it's unlikely to be that simple. China is definitely on the way, however; it recently experienced that most signal of all developed country experiences: several UFO sightings. If that isn't arriving, I don't know what is.

Unfortunately, it is difficult for individual foreigners to purchase stock in Chinese companies. Even the locals have their problems. In 1993, there were riots in front of the Shanghai stock exchange, not because of some fraud, but because investors were unable to buy as much stock as they wanted. Only a handful of Chinese companies are openly traded outside of China. One of those is a new issue here, the China Tire Company (shown in Figure 1-9). This may come as some surprise, but

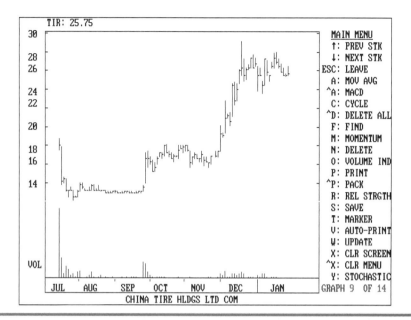

Figure 1-9   Rolling along with China Tire (China), since July of 1993

what the China Tire Company does is make tires. It is, in fact, the largest tire maker in China. The stock rose like a rocket until early 1994, but later dropped like a rock. For the most part, however, investors use sector funds or country funds to spread the risk in emerging markets. In some markets, there is no other way. Korea, for example, does not permit individual foreigners to buy shares in Korean companies. We'll talk about these funds later, in Part II of this book.

Not the New Kids on the Block

Are foreign companies risky? No more than any others. Most of them have been around as long as you have and have been doing pretty well. Glaxo Holdings (Great Britain, shown in Figure 1-10) is one of the two or three largest pharmaceutical companies in Europe, pays a good dividend, sells at a reasonable price-to-earnings ratio (p/e), and has had steadily increasing sales and earnings for more than twenty years. De-Beers controls an estimated 75-85 percent of the world's diamond

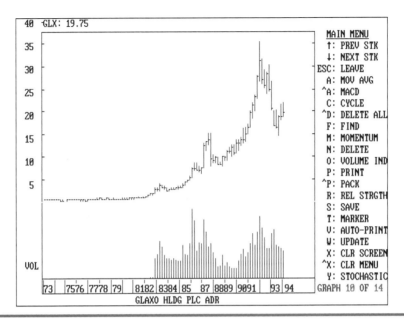

Figure 1-10 Glaxo Holdings (Great Britain), since 1973

trade—a good business to control, you might say. The French firm of Schlumberger is the largest supplier of seismic plotting services in the world. And so on.

Here are just a few of the largest and most established foreign companies, some familiar to you, others not. Whether familiar or strange, they mostly have long histories as well as shares that can be bought and sold. If their product or business is not identified in parentheses, it is because that business is obvious or so well-known as to need no further commentary.

Belgium

Gavert Photo (Film, commercial cameras, reproduction, printing)
Petrofina (Oil and gas)
Societe General (Banking, diverse; a giant)
Union Miniere (Mining. They once owned most of Zaire, called the Congo back then.)

France

Air Liquide (Chemicals and bottled gases)
Club Med (Fun in the sun)
Dessault Avia (Airplanes)
Elf-Aquitaine (Oil and gas)
L'Oreal (Cosmetics)
Machines Bull (The French equivalent of IBM)
Michelin (Tires and guide books)
Peugeot (Cars and trucks)
Rhone-Poulenc (One of the world's largest chemical and pharmaceutical houses—see Figure l-11)
Saint Gobain (The established firm. The world's oldest and perhaps largest glass and industrial materials company—founded in the 15th century.)
Schlumberger (Seismic plotting services)

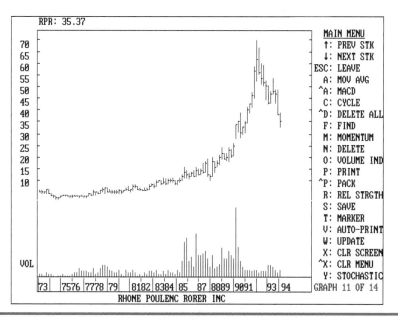

Figure l-11   Rhone-Poulenc Rorer, Inc. (France), since 1973

Germany

AEG (Tools and electrical equipment)
BASF (Recording tape and equipment)
Bayer (Drugs and chemicals, but not Bayer aspirin)
Daimler-Benz (Mercedes-Benz)
Deutsche Bank
Dresdner Bank
Hoescht (Chemicals)
Kloecke Werke (Clocks; don't you just love a language like that?)
Linotype (The world's largest maker of typesetting equipment)
Lufthansa (German Airlines)
Mannesmann (Printers, plotters, computer equipment)
Porsche AG (Autos)
Siemens (One of world's largest makers of electrical and electronic equipment)
Thyssen (Steel and machinery)
Volkswagen (Autos)

Great Britain

Allied-Lyons (Lunch-crowd restaurants)
Barclays (Worldwide banking)
B.A.T. ("British American Tobacco;" tobacco and foods)
The Body Shop (Ecologically conscious cosmetic company)
BP ("British Petroleum;" giant oil and gas company)
British Airways (Love those accents)
Burmah Castrol (Oil and rubber)
Cadbury-Schweppes (Candy and soft drinks)
Forte Group (Classy hotels)
Glaxo (Drugs; one of the largest in Europe)
Guinness (Beer, stout and ale, not just the records book)
Hanson PLC (Giant investment trust, lots of property, etc.)
ICI (Giant chemical company)
Jefferson Smurfitt (Paper and forest products)
Ladbrokes (Chain of bookie joints. It's legal over there.)
Lloyds (The bank, not the insurance group)

Lonrho (Worldwide mining interests)
Lucas (Auto parts, electrical)
Marks & Spencer (Department stores)
National Westminster (Big bank)
P&O (Pacific and Orient lines, shipping)
Pilkington (Glassmaker, holder of the basic patents for window glass)
Racal (Electronics, modems, etc.)
Rank ("J. Arthur;" movies, other holdings)
Reuters (Largest worldwide news service—see Figure 1-12)
Rolls Royce (Cars and aircraft engines)
Rothman's (Tobacco)
Saatchi & Saatchi (World's largest ad agency)
Thorne EMI (Records and music; a biggie)
Vickers (Aircraft, test equipment, machinery, etc.)
Wimpy's (Hamburger joints)

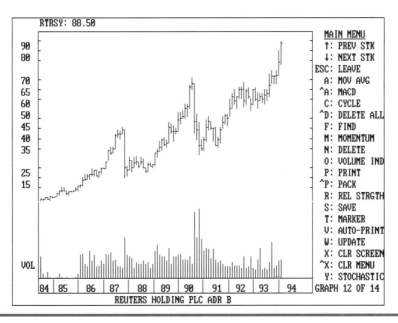

Figure 1-12   Good news from Reuters Holdings (Great Britain), since 1984

Holland

AKZO (Chemicals)
Fokker (Engines, aircraft)
Heineken
Hoogovens (Steel and aluminum)
KLM (Airline)
Philips and Philips Gloeilampen (Norelco, light bulbs, CDs, TVs, etc.; one of the largest electronics companies in the world)
Royal Dutch/Shell (World's fourth largest corporation, and second largest oil company)

Italy

Benetton (Sweaters and controversial ads)
Feruzzi (Pasta and investments; a giant)
Fiat (Autos)
Montecatini-Edison (Giant chemical company, holder of the basic patents on polypropylene)
Olivetti (Computers, printers, typewriters)
Pirelli (Tires, floor coverings)

Spain

Banco de Bilbao
Banco de Santander
Telefonica (Just what it sounds like)

Sweden

Electrolux (Vacuum cleaners, appliances)
Sandvik (High-quality hand tools)
Volvo (Trucks and cars)

Switzerland

Brown Boveri (Construction)
Ciba-Geigy (Giant pharmaceutical house)
Nestles (World's largest food company. They own Stouffers, among other brands.)
Sandoz (Giant; chemicals and pharmaceuticals)
SwissAir (Airline)

South Africa

Anglo American (Gold and diamonds)
DeBeers (Diamonds)
Driefontein (Gold)
Escom (Electric utility)
Impala (Platinum)
Rustenberg (Platinum)
Western Deep Levels (Gold)

Australia

Broken Hill Proprietary (Mining, property, diverse)
Orbital (Two-cycle gasoline engines—very popular in Asia)
Pacific Dunlop (Tires)

Hong Kong

Cathay Pacific (Airlines, banks, shipping)
Hong Kong Land (Largest property company)
Hutchison Whampoa (Trading company, does everything)
Mandarin Oriental (Classy hotels)
Swire Pacific (Trading company, property, diverse)

Japan

The sheer size of these listings, of only large and well-known companies, reflects the fact that the Japanese stock market rivals our own in total valuation and is the second largest in the world.

Asahi (Largest glassmaker)
Bank of Tokyo
Bridgestone (Tires)
Brother (Computer equipment, sewing machines, etc.)
Canon (Cameras, photocopiers, 70 percent of the world's laser printers)
Casio (Gadgets and electronic music keyboards)
Dai-Ichi Bank (A biggie)
Daiwa Securities (The Merrill Lynch of Japan)
Fuji Electric (Heavy equipment)
Fuji Photo (Rivals Kodak)
Fujitsu (Largest computer company in Japan)
Hitachi (Appliances, heavy equipment, diverse)
Honda (Cars, motorcycles, small gasoline engines)
Isuzu (Cars and trucks)
JAL (Japan Airlines)
JVC (Electronics)
Kansai Electric (Heavy equipment, some consumer goods)
Kawasaki (Motorcycles)
Kirin (Beer)
Komatsu (Heavy equipment, earth movers, etc.)
Kyocera (Ceramics; literally: the Kyoto Ceramics Company)
Makita (Small power tools)
Matsushita (Heavy industry, electrical equipment)
Mazda (Light cars and trucks)
Mitsubishi (Autos, heavy industry)
Mitsui (Electrical, heavy equipment)
NEC (The Japanese equivalent of General Electric)
Nikko Securities (Big brokerage house)
Nikon (Lenses, cameras)
Nintendo (Game machines)
Nippon Steel (Japan's largest)
Nissan (Cars and trucks)

NKK (Television, broadcasting)
Nomura Securities (Japan's largest brokerage house)
OKI Electric (Okidata in the United States)
Olympus (Tape recorders, microscopes, cameras)
Pioneer (Stereos, tape decks, CDs)
Ricoh (Printers, electronics)
Sankyo (Electronics, consumer goods)
Sanwa Bank (A biggie)
Sega (Game machines)
Seiko (Watches, printers, computers. Epson is one of their divisions.)
Sharp (Consumer electronics, leader in LCD screens)
Sony (Consumer electronics)
Sumitomo Bank (A biggie)
Sumitomo Chemical (Ditto)
Takeda Chemical (Ditto)
TDK (Recording tape, consumer goods)
Tokio Marine (Insurance)
Tokyo Electric (The electric company)
Toshiba (Computer equipment, electronics)
Toyota (Cars and trucks; fifth largest company in the world)
Yamaha (Music synthesizers pianos, motorcycles)
Yasuda Fire Insurance

Philippines

Benguet (Mining)
Philippine Long Distance (The Philippine phone company. See Figure l-13. All through the 1970s and early 1980s you could have bought this stock for $1 a share. If you had, you would have done even better than Vasco da Gama, making 75 times your investment.)
San Miguel (Beer)

The Dark Side of the Bourse

While insider trading (corporate officers or their friends and family using private information to buy or sell stock in their own company) is a

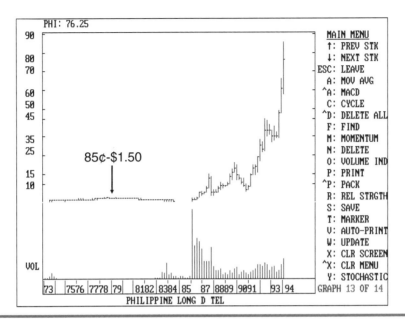

Figure 1-13   Asia calling: Philippine Long Distance (Philippines), since 1973

criminal offense here and in some other countries—Britain, Canada, France, Australia, for example—it is perfectly legal in many others.

The idea that a small group of executives in some small foreign market might buy tons of stock and the next day issue glowing earnings reports, then sell tons of stock and the day after that file for bankruptcy, is entirely thinkable in some parts of the world and would raise only shrugs in the local bars. In other parts of the world, this would raise howls of protest and flights of lawyers. And that's just one of your potential problems.

Of course, the same thing happens here, or things very similar. "I was just selling some stock to raise money to build a new house," said Figby Farthingale, when questioned by a reporter after it was discovered that the company he heads faces a massive deficit next quarter.

"But 90 percent of your holdings, sir?"
"Well, we decided to add an extra bedroom."

Would any American manager do something like that to the stock of your company? Are you kidding? Are frogs waterproof?

Caveat emptor—and then caveat some more.

What Do You Mean *Financial Statement?* We Just Told You What We *Think*

The rules of financial reporting are not a physical constant.

In general, U.S. reporting rules are the most stringent in the world; earn a nickel, log a nickel in the books. In other places, the rules are not so tight. Still, chicanery lurks everywhere, here as well as foreign climes, but there are a few things worth remembering.

First off, reporting rules vary by country and some are not nearly as detailed as ours. Huge amounts of cash, and debt, can be set aside for future balance which may or may not ever come. The financial statement of some European manufacturer may boil down to something like this (exaggerated, of course):

Income: $150,000
Fixed plant: $500,000
Working capital: $50,000
Contingency fund: $3.5 billion

That's some contingency fund but doesn't necessarily mean they are trying to cheat their shareholders. The financial reporting laws in many countries do not require the details of that contingency to be spelled out; it is assumed that the managers of the company know what they are doing. That's an amusing concept, but we'll leave it for the moment.

Similarly, debt can be carried in a number of ways—as a current liability, or as callable against assets or future earnings. So it is, for example, that Volkswagen of Germany, recently listed for trading in the U.S., had a loss of more than $500 million in 1993 under generally accepted U.S. accounting rules, but a profit of over $100 million under German rules. And that's Germany, a place where people don't fool around with the books too much; imagine what the spread can look like someplace where the rules are a little more lax!

Support Your Local Loan Shark

Financing in other countries can be inventive, to say the least, and controlled to say the most. Unless you are a short-term trader playing hourly or daily swings, some attention should be paid to where the business gets the money to stay in business.

In some countries, Taiwan, for example, bank and government lending is inadequate to the demands of a very active and rapidly shifting business community. To put it more bluntly, *The Economist* magazine (formerly the *London Economist*) estimates that normal lending institutions are able to supply less than half the capital needs of business borrowers. For the rest they turn to a myriad of small syndicates and money men, to whom they have to pay interest rates of 35-70 percent a year. Short-term money is 15 percent a month! This could account in large part for the lackluster performance of Taiwanese companies and the Taiwanese stock market for most of the past few years. The government also controls how much foreigners may invest (currently no more than 6 percent of the local stock market) and to a certain extent, where they may invest. The regulations are more complex and difficult to follow than the California Department of Motor Vehicles.

On the other hand, 35 percent interest is the regular bank rate in Poland, about the same as other countries of the former Soviet bloc. As for the Polish infrastructure, if you want a telephone, the average wait is 22 years. You might consider Czechoslovakia instead—oops, the Czech Republic. Bank loan rates are only 15-20 percent, and the wait for a telephone is only 19 years.

The cost of money is a large part of the cost of doing business. Capital is as much an ingredient in the costs of manufacturing or service as salaries, office equipment, or turret lathes. The fact that Japanese interest rates on long-term loans have hovered around 3 percent for many years goes a long way toward explaining that country's phenomenal growth. After all, if you can borrow money at 3 percent, and your competitors have to pay 10 percent, and you both buy the same kind of equipment at similar prices, somebody has a big edge. Figure out who. I don't think we're letting any cats out of the bag here; this is "Econ 101."

The flip side of the equation is that businesses that have to pay 35 percent for their money will find it very difficult to make a profit long-term. While high interest rates are often a sign of a hot economy, lots of demand and hence money to be made by playing the action, there surely comes a day of reckoning—usually sooner rather than later.

note

You can still make money by borrowing at high interest rates, but it's harder. At a certain point, high interest rates will bring down any market. For example, from 1980 to 1982, when interest rates rose to 20 percent, the Dow fell to 786. Point being that rising interest rates can bring any market to its knees.

Money: One Man's Mark Is Another Man's Peseta

This is going to be short, and whether or not it's sweet will depend on which end of the popsicle you're sucking.

The question of "how much is that in dollars?" is more than the irritated cry of a hard-pressed tourist. It is an important question and one that is fundamental to understanding global investments and dealing with them successfully. What follows may be kindergarten stuff to some people, but if it isn't, please go over it until it is engraved on your forehead.

I've Got a Yen for You

Let's say you buy a Japanese stock that sells for 100 yen. If the exchange rate is 100 yen to the dollar, that means you can buy 100 yen for one dollar and therefore that 100-yen stock will cost you $1 a share. Simple enough.

But let's say the dollar falls and the yen rises (see Figure 1-14). In fact, what is meant whenever you hear that the dollar is falling is that it is declining in relation to other major currencies. Most other currencies will rise in value, but there will always be a few that are even weaker than the dollar and will fall even faster.

Let's suppose that after a year or two of a declining dollar, you can only get 50 yen for $1. Meanwhile, that stock you bought hasn't moved a penny, or rather a yen, and still sells for 100. The stock hasn't moved, but you have a 100 percent profit. Because that 100 yen can now be exchanged for two dollars, instead of the dollar it could be exchanged for before.

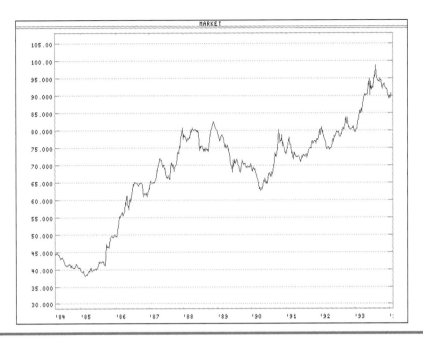

Figure 1-14   The Yen Also Rises

If you think this is a silly, hypothetical example, let me assure you it is not. Here's the same situation in reverse: A few years ago I went to Japan as a tourist. I got 238 yen to the dollar, and that was in the lobby of the Imperial Hotel, where they don't exactly give you the best rate. Today in the same lobby I would get about 110 yen to the dollar—less than half as many as before. My room would now cost me more than double, even if they had not changed the price. So would my breakfast, my dinner—and my stocks. I would have a greater than 50 percent loss.

If things go the other way—a falling yen and a rising dollar—I might be able to get 238 yen for $1 again. In which case, the 100 yen stock we talked about earlier would be worth less than 50 cents a share, showing a big-time loss, even if it had not moved at all in terms of the local currency. To take it step by step, you (or a broker) would sell the share and get 100 yen—just what you paid for it. You would then take that 100 yen to the bank and say, "I'd like this changed into dollars." And they would say, "Okay, that's worth about 40 cents. Have a nice day."

This real-world example is instructive in a number of ways. The Japanese stock market has been falling sharply for a couple of years, though it had a modest gain in 1993. Yet because of the falling dollar, American investors in Japanese stocks actually have a sizable profit for 1993—about 30 percent on average.

This difference in exchange rates—the decline of the dollar versus the yen—also accounts for the improved sales of American cars. The fact that American cars are now cheaper than their Japanese equivalents, when just recently they were considerably more expensive, has little if anything to do with improved management or manufacturing techniques in Detroit and everything to do with the change in the exchange rate of the two currencies. In fact, the price shift in the cars is almost exactly equal to the shift in the exchange rate. What a coincidence.

This is more than a statistical curiosity. What it tells the perceptive global investor is that if the yen is rising against the dollar, not only does that make the Japanese stock market a good investment in dollar terms, but it will also benefit those home industries that compete most directly with the Japanese. In other words, buying American auto stocks is just about as good a way to play the yen as buying Japanese stocks. Others benefit as well. It is no accident that the stock of Caterpillar has risen strongly as the dollar has fallen; Caterpillar makes heavy equipment that competes directly with that of other industrialized countries, especially Japan.

National governments are not ignorant of this basic economic principle, nor should you be. One way they stimulate their own economy is to let their currency fall. Such a fall places an invisible tax on imports—the products of other countries become more expensive in terms of the home currency. So you get a short-term double benefit from a falling currency.

Such a policy has costs, of course. It is, in effect, a devaluation of the currency. Workers paid in the declining currency will for a time appear to be no worse off than before, but in reality their incomes will be falling, since other people (foreigners) will be able to purchase more of their local goods than they can. The return earned by foreign lenders—the purchasers of bonds—will also be falling. It will be more attractive for them to purchase assets (property and machinery) rather than hold debt. Assets of the country with the devalued currency will become bargains for foreigners.

Thus we found ourselves complaining in the past few years about the Japanese buying American real estate, from farmland to expensive homes in Hawaii. It was expensive to us, but cheap to them. These things are consequences of changes in currency exchange rates. We made no complaints when all through the 1950s, 60s and 70s the dollar was high and we took cheap vacations in Europe and bought out the store in Asia. Now the rest of the world takes cheap vacations here. What goes around, comes around, as they say, and along the way it affects your investments.

Watch Out! Great Expectations Ahead

As we move on through the rest of this book and look at the tools available to us in exploring the investments of the world and the world of investments, try to keep this reality in mind: gains of 30, 60, or 100 percent a year cannot be maintained.

Simple arithmetic tells us so. A gain of 75 percent a year, say, when compounded on a regular basis will roughly double your money every 12 months. Do that for 10 years and a $50,000 investment becomes $50 million. Do it for 20 years and it's $50 billion, making you the richest person in the world by far. If it were to continue for 30 years—the life of a standard home mortgage, for example—the total would be $50 trillion, more money than there is on the planet. So you can see, it cannot continue.

Similarly, the growth projections of economies and companies should be looked at with the same arithmetic eye. A company with a growth rate of 35 percent a year (a rate built into the stock price of many companies) will roughly double its sales and earnings every two years. If kept up for 10 years, which is the way many investments are looked at, it means that $50 million company will be doing $1.5 billion a year. Very few companies reach that level.

How did we come up with that "growth rate built into the stock price" philosophy? Well, the rule of thumb in the investment business is that a stock's price-to-earnings multiple will be roughly equal to its annual growth rate. Thus, a company expected to grow 40 percent a year will often sport a 40 to 1 p/e ratio. This is why you will often see the apparently contrary reaction of a high-flying stock falling in price right after reporting higher earnings. It is because the gain, while nice, was not sufficient to justify the lofty price-to-earnings ratio that had been pinned on the stock.

The same thinking should be applied to foreign stocks, with the added modifier of currency valuations. The Japanese stock market sells for an average of 50-60 times earnings, for example, even though the growth rate is less than five percent on average. At that rate, future earnings have been discounted for nearly a century. Looked at in the traditional way of a conservative investment manager, the market would have to double in less than two years, and continue doubling for some time after that. Maybe it will, but it's not likely.

While some overseas markets sell at absurd multiples, many do not. Price-to-earnings ratios of less than 10 to 1 can still be found in some markets; 5 and 6 to 1 can be found in a few.

Will the dollar continue to fall? A lot of foreign observers accept this as a natural concomitant of the American political system. Politically, it is a cheap way out. The people who lose the most are foreign holders of American debt, and they don't vote in U.S. elections. More than 200 years ago, Alexis de Tocqueville, in his classic work *Democracy in America*, noted that it is the nature of popular democracies (ones in which everyone has the right to vote) to devalue their currency. Nothing has proven him wrong so far.

CHAPTER 2

ON-RAMPS FOR THE INFORMATION HIGHWAY

Much like the early days of motoring, there are paved bits and dirt bits. The major domestic financial services, for our purposes, are Dow Jones News/Retrieval, CompuServe, America Online, Prodigy, Genie, and Telescan. Following these is a crowd like the Boston Marathon. Not all are in the same race or even running on the same track. What we're going to do here is provide commentary on the major services and some of the secondary data providers. There is no attempt to be exhaustive; there are far too many data services to list and discuss everybody.

A number of free sign-on coupons for data services discussed in this chapter may be found at the end of this book.

There are a number of companies that provide basic information such as filings with the Securities and Exchange Commission, financial reports, and screening services, and they either provide no current price quotes or this is strictly a sideline service for them. Others specialize in real-time quotes and news bulletins. Aimed at professional traders and brokerage houses, these services are very good and very expensive.

Some provide data by phone lines, some by radio transmission, and quite a few are there only to send you the information on disk—for the more leisurely investor. We'll try to mention them all, though we're bound to offend somebody by failing to give them their full measure of importance in the wide scheme of things.

Some services provide live quotes with a 15-minute delay. Other provide quotes only at the end of the day. Services like CompuServe, Prodigy, and Dow Jones News/Retrieval provide quotes throughout the day. Services that deliver quotes in real time—no delay—charge exchange fees on top of the regular service fee. This is true of all real-time services, whether broadcast or phone line. These fees are charged not by the data service, but by the exchanges themselves—the New York Stock Exchange, the Chicago Board of Options Exchange, etc. If the quotes are delayed 15 minutes or more, there are no exchange charges. Which is why you so often see a 15-minute delay ticker when you turn on CNN Business News or something similar.

Moving on down the food chain there are bulletin board systems—BBSs, in the jargon of the computer world. There are about 50 of these with either a total or heavy emphasis on investing, and new ones spring up almost every month. Some die along the way as well. Some are free, but most charge a small fee for the use of the service and the time and stewardship of the "sysop," which stands for "system operator," and is pronounced "sis-op."

A bulletin board system is always accessed by telephone line and modem. The "host," as it is called, can be as basic as one person with a small computer doing this as a hobby, or it can be a big company with a cast of hundreds. Technically speaking, CompuServe is just a BBS, with 1.5 million members. So is Prodigy, which boasts 2 million users. The point is, just because we later list something as a BBS doesn't necessarily mean there's not much there. Pisces, in Chicago, is probably the biggest "small" BBS devoted to market information and analysis. It provides free software, discounts on major programs, and even lets you download quotes but it is devoted almost entirely to members of its own MetaStock users group.

In all, there are approximately 80,000 bulletin board systems nationwide. Most just serve a local membership—local to their calling area. If the big guys—AT&T, MCI, etc.—are out there busily building the information highway for the next century, it can be honestly said that a lot of little guys have already been out there putting in a network of local roads.

The following list of data providers is by no means exhaustive. In fact, just the opposite, it is restrictive. It is restricted to services that provide daily current and historical data. A majority provide such data in a format that is compatible with the technical analysis program MetaStock.

Why pay particular attention to providers of MetaStock data? For the simple reason that MetaStock is the leading selling market analysis program. And if a data service does not provide data that is compatible with the number one program, you have to question their common sense or how well they understand what they're doing. You would think that everybody knows what they're doing in a business like this, but the fact is, it is very easy to become a data provider. You buy disks of historical data, load them into your computer, update them every day from the newspaper or by calling Dow Jones or some other data provider, and you hang out a shingle or run an ad saying you provide stock and commodity data for a fee. There are few businesses easier to enter, and more people drop in and out of this one than weekend bungee jumpers.

Some of the data providers have commentary after their listing, sometimes extensive commentary. Others have no comments. This doesn't mean they're no good; it just means there was nothing in particular to say. If they're listed here at all, it's because they have proved to be reliable in the past. Many of the services are well known in the industry.

There is also a large group of data services that pay little attention to providing quotes, but focus their energies on doing screens, research, or providing government data like SEC filings. We'll look at those in the next section.

Finally, rather than try to determine a pecking order of who provides the mostest, the fastest, which would be sure to put somebody out of place and their nose out of joint, the names are listed roughly in alphabetical order.

Primary Data Providers

Prices for data services change with remarkable frequency. If you're interested in a provider, call and get their current charges.

> **America Online**
> **8619 Westwood Center Dr.**
> **Vienna, VA 22182**
> **800/827-6364 or 703/448-8700**

This is the successor to The Source, a database service started a decade ago by *Readers Digest* and one that for a while rivaled CompuServe in size and services. It is still quite large and offers a lot of investor services. America Online is covered in more detail in Chapter 11.

You can get daily quotes, both general and business news, financial statements, etc. There is an online brokerage service, and you can maintain a "shadow portfolio" if you want to just do some practice investing or speculation. Everything is recorded as if you actually made the trades. But since it's all just mind bets, if you lose, you only lose your mind. This may appeal to many people, and it certainly would be educational for kids.

Somebody here understands the market, because they also provide daily put/call ratios. Most short-term traders pay attention to these ratios to try and divine when there is too much fear or enthusiasm near-term, which is almost always unlikely to be sustained. There is also a stock watch feature: you can specify a certain trigger point on a stock or an option—a point at which you presumably felt there was a significant breakout rather than mere churning action—and when that price is reached, the system will alert you with a beep and a screen message. Of course, you have to be logged on when that happens.

The charges are $9.95 a month and $3.50 an hour. The first five hours of usage each month are without charge, and you can try America Online with a 30-day free trial that lets you roam the system for 10 hours. Call their 800 number for details.

Bonneville
3 Triad Center, Suite 100
Salt Lake City, UT 84180
800/255-7374 or 801/532-3400

This is one of the leading broadcast data vendors. The data stream is wide and deep. Collection is by satellite.

Commodity Systems, Inc. (CSI)
200 W. Palmetto Park Rd.
Boca Raton, FL 33432
800/274-4727 or 407/392-8663

This is one of the oldest services for commodity quotes, and used to be just commodity quotes. But now they also provide stocks, futures, options, and indices, so they prefer to be known as CSI, to get away from the "commodities only" reputation.

This is a large service and a good one. No particular comments to make either way. Their software is called QuickTrieve, and you will see it advertised in some of the financial papers once in a while.

The startup is $39, and the monthly fee runs $11 and up, depending on whether you want stocks plus commodities, futures, etc.

CompuServe
P.O. Box 20212
5000 Arlington Centre Blvd.
Columbus, OH 43220
800/848-8199 or 614/457-8650

CompuServe is a division of H&R Block. Who would have thought it, as they say. It is also the largest bulletin board system in the known universe. And one of the oldest. This is the established firm, as they say. Chapter 9 is devoted entirely to CompuServe.

Logging on and navigating the system is a snap with the new WinCIM program (Windows CompuServe Information Manager). This is the best communications and database access software we've seen. Gorgeous. And it works. It's essentially free when you sign up. You can download it from CompuServe if you first sign on with some other kind of software.

Access can be either through CompuServe's own network of local phone numbers, available in or near most cities and towns, or through Tymnet, SprintNet, Datapac, Telenet, etc. Using CompuServe's own network is recommended. Not only is it cheaper—no phone line charge to members—but it's usually faster as well. You can connect at any speed up to 14400 baud.

CompuServe's MicroQuote II service carries up to 12 years of price history on more than 125,000 stocks, stock indexes, and bonds. An extra fee service, *Money Magazine's* FundWatch OnLine, has data on close to 2,000 mutual funds.

There are company reports and analysts' earning projections from Standard & Poors, Value Line, and several other services. There are online brokerage services. You can call up Disclosure for SEC filings and insider trading reports. You can also call up a host of newspaper and magazine stories, and they recently added the China News Service. It just goes on and on.

Loading

"Downloading," for the uninitiated, is a term you run into all the time with online services. It simply means getting information from their computer into your computer. You "download" it with your modem. When the information is going the other way—from your computer to their computer—it's an "upload." Of course, from their point of view, the information you are downloading is an upload and your uploading is a download. Is any of this confusing? No? Good. We'll discuss how to download information into several of the investment software programs when they are covered specifically in Part IV of this book.

The charge for Basic Service is $8.95 a month. If you sign up instead for Executive Service, the charge is an extra $10 a month. I recommend taking the Executive Service because of all the extra financial information you get. With Executive Service, there's also an additional use charge of $15 an hour. Think of it as a brokerage commission.

Current quotes (the most recent market day) are 1.5 cents a piece, but downloading historical data costs 5 cents a quote, depending on the level of service you've subscribed to and the time of day you download. A quote is price information for one stock for one day.

The Executive Service gets you a 25 percent discount on downloading historical data and has a number of other useful goodies, such as access to Reuters, Deutsche Press, AP, UPI, the *Washington Post*, etc.

For another $2.50 a month, you can have access to ZiffNet, a database belonging to Ziff Publishing Co. ZiffNet is worth the extra payment because of the large amount of freeware and shareware in its files. Many of these files are also available in other sections of CompuServe, however, like the IBM forum, so what it boils down to is for $2.50 you can try it for a month and if you don't like it, drop it.

A special deal for MetaStock users costs $9.95 a month and lets them download quotes for just one cent each.

The good news is that CompuServe has around 2,000 services, products, and SIGs (special interest groups). Enough to keep anyone off the streets.

The natives are friendly. About 1.5 million people are signed on, and almost all of them will help out; there are very few questions that someone here doesn't know the answer to.

The bad news is that the system has become almost too popular for its own good. Downloading quotes can be next to impossible at some times. A few times, I have had to wait until midnight or later. Calling customer service for technical support or other help is a nearly useless activity. I once tried 42 calls over five days to customer support without getting anything but a busy signal. The way to get any question answered is to send it to customer service through the system itself. Of course, that means you have to be logged on, and if your problem happens to be that you can't log on...well, it's one of those Catch-22s.

This is not the only place to get quotes and other investment data, but it is a good place. There are also numerous other services that can make joining worthwhile, like extensive e-mail, job markets, discount shopping, etc. You can send messages, documents, programs, and pictures to other CompuServe members. CompuServe also provides access to the Internet, the global communications network. The Internet is of little use to investors, but it is available if you want to send a message.

**Data Transmission Network
(a.k.a. DTN Wall Street)
9110 W. Dodge Rd., Suite 200
Omaha, NE 68114
800/779-5000 or 402/390-2328**

Like Signal, this is a broadcast service. Unlike Signal, the transmission is not by FM sub-carrier waves, but is collected either by satellite or a cable TV hookup. This is especially good if you live in a remote location, though it is by no means restricted to that.

They supply the satellite dish. The startup fee is $295, and then it's $38 monthly. For real-time service, the average charge is about $150 a month.

**Delphi
888 Worcester St.
Wellesley, MA 02181
800/695-4005**

Delphi is one of the best known services for research. It also provides current quotes on stocks and commodities, but not historical quotes. What they're really known for in the data surfer world is providing full direct access to the Internet. They charge only $3 a month for this, and the Internet is by far the world's largest information net. Delphi's rate sheet for all services is a model of simplicity: $10 a month for four hours use, or $20 a month for 20 hours use. Delphi is discussed in Chapter 13.

**Dial Data, a division of Track Data Corp.
95 Rockwell Place
Brooklyn, NY 11217
800/275-5544 or 718/522-6886**

This is a nearly pure quote service. Unlike CompuServe and some of the other services here, there are no forums, shopping malls, e-mail systems, etc. Access is through AutoPac, DataPac, Telenet, or direct connection to the service. There is an initial signup fee, which gets you their software, and then a monthly fee of $95 for unlimited access.

They have tens of thousands of stocks, commodities, bonds, mutual funds, indices, and option prices. In addition, they provide information on insider trading, earnings estimates, bond data, economic forecasts, etc.

I used this system for a couple of years a while back and there were occasions when the system would kick me off line or tell me that a symbol they themselves had supplied was incorrect and invalid. Still, overall I was satisfied and would be perfectly willing to sign up again.

A feature of this service and some others for people interested in commodities and futures is the perpetual contract. One of the problems with following futures is that you pick a contract—December wheat, say—and as that time comes closer and closer, the price of the futures declines to match the spot price. Eventually the contract expires, and you have to set up a new one and pick an appropriate month—or follow several months at once.

The perpetual contract is a mathematical construct that continually moves the futures contract out of the current expiration cycle and creates a synthetic price that is an amalgam of the prices of both current and future months. This artificial contract never expires, and so you can have a long-term view of price action. Useful as this seems, some professional traders shun perpetual contracts and maintain that they give a false picture of what's happening in the markets. My impression in looking at such contracts is that this is not true, or at most it is true only in certain very narrow and special circumstances. If you are a commodities and futures person, you will have to make a decision on this yourself.

Dow Jones News/Retrieval
P.O. Box 300
Princeton, NJ 08543
800/522-3567 or 609/520-8349

This is the mother lode—the most extensive list of local and foreign stock prices anywhere in the world. The service is available as end of the day quotes, 15-minute delayed quotes, or real time. The price goes up with each category, and even if you call in during evening hours, it's not cheap. Cost is about 5 cents a quote after hours, 10 cents during business hours—and the way they count time, business hours don't end until well into the evening, no matter what your time zone.

In short, Dow Jones is expensive, but you do have access to an incredible amount of useful information. For $30 a month, you can not only pull quotes on anything this side of yak butter futures, but you can search for articles in the *Wall Street Journal*, the *Washington Post*, *Barron's*, the *Los Angeles Times*, and the *Asian Wall Street Journal*. For a little extra, you can add 1,400 more publications. We'll go into some of them later when we discuss Dow Jones News/Retrieval in Chapter 12. The service is so fast and complete that you can even get company news that is going to be in the *Wall Street Journal* before the *Journal* is published; you can download articles that have been approved and sent on by the copy desk, but have not yet been printed and will not appear for hours.

The bad news is cost, and the fact that historical data only goes back one year. If you want to see the price and volume action on the last three years of IBM, you'll have to get it somewhere else. Further bad news is their connection software and protocols, which are from the digital Stone Age. If you've been using WinCIM to log onto CompuServe, or the graphical menu system for Prodigy, dealing with Dow Jones News/Retrieval will be something of a shock. A lot of the commands are old mainframe commands from 10 or more years ago. They are adequate enough once you get the hang of it, but for new users there will be a lot of initial frustration.

The good news is that the information stream is awesome, and there are no better online sources than this for information on the full range of foreign markets.

Free Financial Network
Microcode Technologies, Inc.
501 Fifth Ave., 22nd floor
New York, NY 10017
800/442-9111 or 212/838-6324

This is a service which allows you to collect daily data at no charge. The cost is $80 per year to belong. (For more information, see Chapter 14.)

Future Link
P.O. Box 6
219 Parkade
Cedar Falls, IA 50613
800/553-2910 or 319/277-7892

Broadcast vendor. Historical and current quotes on stocks, futures, options, etc. Access is by satellite dish.

Genesis Data Service
P.O. Box 49578
Colorado Springs, CO 80949
719/260-6111

Data by direct long-distance phone line connection or on disk. Having a disk mailed to you is obviously slower than downloading the data right when you want it, but if it's a lot of data—you want to look at 100 or more stocks—it is far cheaper.

The startup fee is $85, and the monthly charge is $65. For that you get unlimited access to quotes on everything. So if you're a high volume user, it's a good deal. But if you just want historical quotes on a few stocks or commodities, you can buy a disk with a year's worth for $1.50, so you can see that it's much cheaper to buy by the disk unless you are loading massive amounts.

GEnie
401 N. Washington St.
Rockville, MD 20850
800/638-9636 or 301/340-4442

GEnie is a cute reference to the magical character of Arabian mythology and is close enough to an acronym for "General Electric News and Information Services." It is, like America Online or Prodigy, a large general service aimed at the home user, but it also provides quotes, online brokerage, news services, and portfolio tracking and management.

Minimum charges are $8.95 a month and $3 an hour after four free hours. For extra fees, you can look at investment newsletters online, put questions to registered investment advisors, and get access to the Dow Jones News/Retrieval. The online brokerage connection is to Charles Schwab & Co. (For more information, see Chapter 13.)

Globe Information Services
Marketscan Plus
444 Front Street West
Toronto, Ontario
Canada M5V 2S9
416/585-5250

This is the primary place for Canadian quotes. They have stocks, options, indices, and mutual funds, and provide both daily and weekly data.

Despite the strong Canadian orientation, the coverage of U.S. stocks and markets is extensive, as good as most of the other data services listed here. They cover stocks, options, mutual funds, and indices, but not commodities.

The startup charge is $99, which gives you an hour of free time. After that, it's $3.60 a minute during business hours (based on Ontario's business hours) and 65 cents a minute in the evenings.

This is a very large service, with tons of information from government agencies, SEC filings, and access to other databases in the U.S. and Canada. You can read the feed from the Canadian New Wire and articles from the major Canadian papers. It also covers about 700 Canadian mutual funds. Heaps of stuff, in other words.

IDD Information Services
2 World Trade Center, 18th floor
New York, NY 10048
212/432-0045

I'm not sure if the 18th floor is still there, but IDD is.

This is a service aimed primarily at professionals. But, hey, anybody can play. Fees run all over the lot, depending on what you want and how much of it you want. The company maintains daily updates on 200,000 securities (a staggering number), 2,000 market indices, and covers over 100 foreign exchanges. Impressive.

The historical database goes back 15 years, and that's not just for stocks, but bonds, corporate debt issues, mutual funds, etc. They also do put-and-call option prices and ratios, which any professional service should, and you can check dividends and corporate reports for the last quarter century. Data is available online and by disk and CD-ROM. (When you cover 200,000 stocks, you need a CD-ROM.)

The system is divided into international and domestic coverage, which are called, naturally enough, "Tradeline International" and "Tradeline North America."

They also market a small handheld device called the Tradeline Pocket Stock Guide—$200 to start, $70 for each update. What this little wizard does is carry data for 6,000 stocks and indices, and you can call up charts on any one of them. You can get their relative market strength, price-to-earnings (p/e) ratios, high-low, etc., and you can even screen this database for fundamental and technical data to select groups of stocks you want to examine further. All this in a little gizmo you can bring out on the tablecloth at Delmonico's to impress the Wall Street crowd lunching all around you. Of course, they won't be impressed because they'll all have one, too.

Except for the handheld device, IDD services are also available through Dow Jones News/Retrieval for an extra fee of $30 a month. The two services that matter most are "Tradeline North America" and "Tradeline International." This last is the best available source for information on foreign stocks and indices.

Interactive Data Corporation
95 Hayden Ave.
Lexington, MA 02173
617/863-8100

They provide data for MetaStock, CompuTrac, and AIQ Trading Expert, three of the most popular systems. The feed for CompuTrac covers 56,000 stocks and indices; the feed for MetaStock covers 155,000 stocks, indices, and options.

This is one of the lowest cost services for current quotes—just a penny a quote for many issues, and only three cents a quote for historical data. Not the absolute lowest you can find, but very competitive.

Signup is $25, and there is a fairly wide range of monthly charges, from $10 to $50, depending on what time you connect and how much you're going to download.

Knight-Ridder Financial Services
30 So. Wacker Dr., Suite 1820
Chicago, IL 60606
800/526-3282 or 312/454-1801

This is a division of Knight-Ridder newspapers, the largest newspaper chain in America. They provide data by broadcast, modem, on regular disks, and on CD-ROM. This is a service used almost exclusively by professionals, banks, and brokerage firms.

They have a huge array of data. Basic signup is around $50 a month, and it's worth calling them for a brochure. They provide quotes for just one cent apiece. That's for up to 50,000 quotes a day. If you take more than 50,000 quotes a day, the price drops to only half a cent. Doesn't everybody download 50,000 quotes a day? As you can tell, this is a heavy-duty supplier.

**National Computer Network
(a.k.a. Nite Line)
1929 N. Harlem Ave.
Chicago, IL 60635
312/622-6666**

Offers quotes by phone and historical quotes on disk. Data going back to 1970 on most stocks, and back to 1929 on some. Lots of Canadian stocks.

**PC Quote
401 So. LaSalle St.
Chicago, IL 60605
800/225-5657 or 312/906-3800**

Broadcast vendor of wide range of data that can be accessed by satellite.

**Prodigy
445 Hamilton Ave.
White Plains, NY 10601
800/776-3449**

Prodigy is owned jointly by Sears and IBM. According to their own figures, this is the largest database service in the world. They say they have around 2 million users. That sort of fudges the number on "subscribers," which is the way CompuServe counts it, since you can have several users in a household that would have only one subscriber. But no matter how you nit-pick it, this is a big database.

It is very easy to navigate. In fact, it has the reputation among database hounds of being the easiest of all. It's kind of flashy and heavily graphically oriented, and late last year they put in a new interface that makes it even more so. Getting quick updates on markets throughout the day or after the close is fast and easy—even faster and easier than CompuServe. Major foreign market indices are displayed as well as U.S. Both daily and historical data can be downloaded into all software packages.

Requests for stock quotes are passed through to Dow Jones, and the data you get usually comes from Dow Jones News/Retrieval. This is a cheaper way to get to Dow Jones than using Dow Jones, but you don't get any of the other Dow Jones services.

Prodigy is enormous, and financial services are only a small part. Like CompuServe, there are investor forums and interest groups, conference call and e-mail services, shopping malls, etc.

For $29.95 a month, you can get a package which gives you 25 hours usage. Very few database users ever go over 25 hours a month. Additional hours are $3.60 each. Sending e-mail messages costs 25 cents apiece—cheaper than the Postal Service. (For information, see Chapter 10.)

Prophet Information Services
3350 W. Bayshore, Suite 106
Palo Alto, CA 94303
800/772-8040 or 415/856-1142

This is one of the few services that offer data transmission at 14.4k. That means 14400 baud instead of the typical limit of 9600.

Connection is made through an 800 number that they supply. So the high-speed transfer rate doesn't save you any phone line charges, but it does get you your data much faster. If you're updating a lot of stocks, futures, or whatever, this can be a big convenience. They provide both daily and historical data.

The initial signup is $50, and then regular quotes are a penny apiece. Quotes on futures are 10 cents apiece, however.

Radio Exchange
Telemet America, Inc.
325 First St.
Alexandria, VA 22314
800/368-2078 or 703/548-2042

This is a vendor of broadcast data, by FM or satellite dish. Once again, it's good for remote locations—and also for people who just don't want to have to rely on the phone lines or wait for their turn to download.

There are a variety of services, of which the best known is probably Pocket Quote, which is a handheld device that gives you real-time quotes and business headlines on a tiny display screen. The charge for the gizmo is $395, and then you pay $27.50 a month for the data service. As with others, you also have to pay the fees charged by the various stock, option, and futures exchanges. If you are willing to take the delayed quote service (15 minute delay), there are no exchange fees.

The startup and monthly feed rates are similar for getting the service on your desktop computer as well. The maximum service, in real time, news and everything, costs $600 for the startup and $139 a month. This includes charting software done by them and technical analyst software done by their host computer. Charts are based on real-time data and updated every two minutes. This is mostly for professional traders or the truly dedicated amateur.

Signal, a division of Data Broadcasting Corp.
1900 South Norfolk St., Suite 150
San Mateo, CA 94403
800/367-4670 or 415/571-1800

This is a broadcast service, providing real-time data for the company's own handheld Quotrek device or for the Signal receiver that can be purchased for attachment to your own computer. This service works with the real-time version of MetaStock.

Data is beamed up from San Mateo to the Westar IV satellite in geosynchronous orbit over North America. From there it is bounced back down to FM stations in most large cities, where it is then re-broadcast on an FM sub-carrier wave, a freebie which the FCC has graciously granted to FM radio stations because so many of them are in need. This bit of technical trivia matters because FM is line-of-sight transmission only. In other words, if you're over the horizon, you're literally over the hill as far as collecting Signal data is concerned. So you have to check first on whether you can pick up the signal, so to speak.

The service is fairly expensive, with the cost dependent on how many exchanges you want to receive. If you want options, that's extra; if you want commodities, that's extra; if you want treasury bonds, that's extra, and so on. In practice, it comes to $400-$500 a month for what I would call full service. You better do a lot of trading to justify that. Another way to go with this or any other expensive service is to belong to a club or investment group. Then you can all chip in—if you can all agree on anything.

Stock Data Corp.
905 Bywater Rd.
Annapolis, MD 21401
410/280-5533

Data is provided on disk only. Again, this is the most economical way to build up files of historical data.

Tech Tools
334 State St., Suite 202
Los Altos, CA 94022
800/231-8005 or 415/948-6124

Historical data on disk.

Telescan, Inc.
10550 Richmond Ave., Suite 250
Houston, TX 77042
800/324-8246 or 713/952-1060

A major service, and geared particularly toward the informed individual rather than the professional money manager. Telescan has 80,000 subscribers and offers several software packages for doing technical and fundamental analysis with their huge database and lots of tools for doing screens. Telescan also has a link program for transferring data to MetaStock.

They cover stocks, mutual funds, and options, both domestic and foreign. Connection is through SprintNet at 1200 to 9600 baud. There's lots more on Telescan later in this book in Chapter 15.

Tick Data
720 Kipling St., Suite 115
Lakewood, CO 80215
800/822-8425 or 303/232-3701

This is a first rate data service, for commodities only. Not only do they have a cool address, but you can connect at any speed from 2400 baud up to 19200—the highest in the business.

As the name implies, data is provided trade-by-trade and is extremely reliable. An article in *Futures Magazine* in late 1993 studying various trading systems that use buy and sell signals generated from technical analysis programs examined the profit and loss results changing only one variable—where the data came from. They found that a number of systems that produced losses with other data showed profits when supplied with Tick Data. This is pretty astonishing as nothing else had changed. For investors with a long-term orientation, this kind of data difference is of little or no significance, but if you're an active trader, this would matter a great deal.

The startup fee is $50, and the data feed is $10 a month per commodity. They also provide technical studies and can handle both IBM and Macintosh formats.

Worden Brothers, Inc.
4905 Pine Cone Dr., Suite 12
Durham, NC 27707
800/776-4940

The Worden software package is called TC2000 and provides current and historical data by modem at 1200 to 9600 baud. Connection is through a toll-free number supplied by them.

X Press
4700 So. Syracuse Pkwy, Suite 1050
Denver, CO 80237
800/772-6397 or 303/721-1062

A broadcast vendor of quotes delivered by cable TV systems. Call them for availability in your area.

Overseas Data Providers

The following overseas data vendors were provided through the courtesy of Equis International, the makers of MetaStock and The Technician. Most of these vendors are unknown in the United States and do not appear in any other lists of data providers. Obviously, they have an in-depth view of their local markets not available to most investors here. (Phone numbers include the country code.)

note

The American Association of Individual Investors (AAII) publishes a book listing many more data providers and other useful information. They are an invaluable resource. For more information, contact the AAII in Chicago at 312/280-0170, or write them at 625 North Michigan Avenue, Dept. CI, Chicago, IL 60611.

Australia

Research Technology Corp.
Level 7, 4 O'Connell St.
Sydney, New South Wales 2000
Australia
Phone: 61-2-233-6822

Germany

Sharework
Wachtelforte 26
D-38640
Goslar/Harz
Germany
Phone: 49-05321-279-6

Greece

Profile Systems
7, P.P. Germanou St.
Klathmonos Square
105 61, Athens
Greece
Phone: 30-1-3223-8153

India

DART
31-A Noble Chambers, 4th Floor
4 A-B Lawrence & Mayo House
276 DDN Rd.
Ft. Bombay 400 001
India
Phone: 91-283-5830

The Netherlands

Ed Van der Ende Commodity Consultancy
Engbroekweg 3
Emst, Gld N1-8166 Jm
Holland
Phone: 31-5787-2152

New Zealand

Micom
P.O. Box 25-197
St. Heliers, Auckland
New Zealand
Phone: 64-9-528-3164

Singapore and Malaysia

Key Computers
Block 123, Bukit Merah Lane 1
04-104 Singapore 0315
Phone: 65-271-7075

Sweden

Folkes Data
Hamnvagen 11:5
S-760 49 Herrang
Sweden
Phone: 46-175-13658

Switzerland

Portmann Bureau
47, Chemin de Bezaley
Ch-1247 Geneva-Anieres
Switzerland
Phone: 41-22-732-6040

Thailand

Funtecon
257/19-20 Sukhumvit 71 Road
Bangkok 10110
Thailand
Phone: 662-390 0154

Turkey

Bogazici Data Paralama
Keskin Kalem SK 4/10
Istanbul 80300
Turkey
Phone: 90-1-275 9007

United Kingdom

Penguin Trading Services
Valley View Currant Hill
Westerham Kent TN16 1EN
England
Phone: 44-71-230-3556

CHAPTER 3

THE TOOLS OF THE TRADE: WHAT YOU NEED TO TURN ON AND TUNE IN

You'll need an IBM compatible and a modem. Some people use a Macintosh for financial analysis; Macs work just as well, but you will have a smaller selection of software. On the other hand, if the software you get does what you want done, and you love your Mac, don't worry about it. Let us get to the nuts and bolts of the matter forthwith.

We let the cat out of the bag up there and told you that you should get an IBM compatible; now we'll go into it a little more.

On the most basic level, you can plug into a data service or a bulletin board with almost anything. And I mean almost anything. If you have an old Atari 800 or Commodore 64 or even one of those Sinclair computers that sold for $29, they will all do it. They won't hold any of the software you're going to want (and we're going to talk about in much of the rest of this book), but you will be able to connect to Dow Jones or CompuServe and browse around and get quotes. The reason it is so simple to connect to such services is that the codes and protocols for data transmission have become standardized. Which is why you can even get hand-held devices, like the Quotrek, whose little screen will show you the last trade on Boston Chicken even while you're having lunch at Boston Chicken.

For big money, you can get a dedicated terminal, hooked to a mainframe or mini-computer and plugged into a continuous data feed from Dow Jones, IDD, Reuters, or all of them—and there you are: a broker or a money manager. But let's assume that a desktop computer will do. It can connect to the exact same services—for the same high fees—but it can connect to any other service as well.

Any kind of IBM compatible will do, even those using a 286 processor. These computers are no longer made, but a lot of people still have them on their desks. I used one to connect with financial services until just a couple of years ago and had no complaints.

Computers using 386 processors are faster and 486s are faster yet. The new Pentium processors offer parallel processing, although at present there's no software that needs it. But you can bet that there will be.

Your safest bet: go for the best you can afford and wait for the world to catch up. I want to make it clear once again, if you do not go out and get the latest computer equipment, it will not affect your ability to manipulate the data one whit, nor will you be penalized by being unable to connect to data services. You may not be able to run some of the latest software, but on the other hand, much of the so-called advances in software consist mainly of putting things in windows so they look nicer. Of course, if the computer has helped by making you some money, you'll be able to afford something better. In many situations, it will be a deductible expense. If you use the equipment to manage your own portfolio, for example, it should be as much a deductible expense as transaction fees.

Nuts and Bolts I: The Computer

Obviously, if you want to run Windows programs, you have to get a computer that can run Windows. Microsoft likes to tell the world that you can run Windows on a 286 machine with two megabytes of memory and possibly less—and in fact, I have seen people do it. But as a practical matter, you really should have a 386 or better processor and at least four megabytes of RAM (random access memory) to run Windows. Eight megabytes is even better and will speed things up quite a bit. If you can, get a math co-processor installed; a lot of these programs do heavy calculations and it will go much faster with a co-processor. A video accelerator card helps, too. How much for all this stuff? Around $1,500 to $2,000. The brand? There is very little difference between all the brands; it really has become a commodity kind of business.

Get a good color monitor—super VGA and non-interlaced. While few programs absolutely need color to run, once you start throwing more than a couple of chart lines up on the screen, it gets very difficult to follow what's happening unless you can have those lines in different colors. It's also easier on the eyes in general.

Get a hard drive the size of Cleveland. In other words, get the biggest hard drive you can afford. Programs get bigger every year, and you'll find you will eat up 70 or 80 megabytes with a couple of stock programs, Windows, and a word processor and spreadsheet. A recent market report from 3M calculates that the average hard drive size for new computers is now 180 megabytes and the number is doubling every 18 months. (I now have games that use 20 megabytes!)

This is not holy writ, but I would avoid data compression. But, if you're out of disk space and need more, the big vendors for data compression utilities are Stacker and AddStor. I used Stacker for more than six years and never had any problems with it, but it made me nervous sometimes. The risk of data corruption is always present, though remote, and if you have years of historical stock and commodities data stored on your hard disk, along with valuable programs, you have to decide what it would cost to replace that, in time as well as money, and what your risk tolerance is. Go with the big hard drive first. Compress later if you have to.

Nuts and Bolts II: Modems

You have to have a modem, there's no getting around it. Two cans and a string aren't going to do it.

The standard speed is now around 2400 baud, which means about 2,400 bits of information per second. That's fast, but not as fast as it sounds. Eight bits make a byte, which is what it takes the computer to identify a letter or a number (a "character," in computer terms). So 2,400 bits a second is really 300 characters a second. That's still pretty fast, but you're paying for line time, and for hanging around waiting to download a lot of data. So, like the hard drive and all the other parts of the system, get the fastest modem you can afford.

High speed is 14.4K these days. That's 14400 baud, six times faster than the 2400 baud modem that was considered fast last year. A good 14.4K modem sells for around $200 or less now. A 2400 baud modem can be had for less than $50. It is by no means crucial that you have a high-speed modem, and practical types will point out that many data services cannot yet handle transmission at 14.4K anyway. But the modems are downward compatible, which means they adjust their speed to whatever the other line can receive and send, and as services speed up, you will not have to go out and buy another modem to stay on board.

There are also some savings at high speed. CompuServe charges twice as much per minute for you to connect at 9600 baud as 2400 baud, for example, but the data moves four times faster. Presumably, you are beating the house by two to one in this transaction, but in reality your edge is far less. Part of the connect time is spent waiting for their computer to get ready to send, and for your computer to acknowledge receipt, and you're paying for that waiting time at the higher rate even though nothing is happening. You can roll all this around in your head for a while and see whether the dollar signs come up in your favor or not. As a practical matter, 2400 is fine for doing online research because much of your time is spent writing or waiting for a response. Why pay for the higher speed when you're just twiddling your thumbs?

By the way, many people think the word "baud" is arcane techie shorthand for "bit amplified units" or something like that, but in fact, the word comes from the name of Emile Baud, a French mathematician of the nineteenth century who first proposed transmitting information by sending distinct pulses of electricity over wires.

Nuts and Bolts III: Printers

You gotta have a printer. At some point, you're going to want to print something out, even if it's just to show off to your narcoleptic nephew.

The best bargains these days are ink-jet and bubble-jet printers. You can get a Canon BJ 200 for around $250 and the quality is very close to what you get from a laser printer. In fact, I can't tell the difference.

The best deal in laser printers is the Okidata OL400, which sells for less than $500 as of early 1994. The best high-quality printer I've used is the Lexmark 4039, which sells for around $1,100. Lexmark is the former printer division of IBM, and as far as I know this is the only laser printer made entirely in the U.S. That tells you something about global investing, doesn't it!

I will wrap up this section on hardware purchases by offering two pieces of hard-won advice. The first is never buy anything with a low serial number. The second is, no matter what you get, you'll have to get something else to make it work.

The Software: Getting with the Program

The major programs for analyzing your data are MetaStock, The Technician, Telescan Analyzer, and Windows On WallStreet. We'll discuss each of these (and a few others) briefly at the end of the chapter and take a more detailed look at these four in the last section of the book.

How many programs are there for analyzing the markets—any markets—and otherwise managing your money? More than 500 for the IBM, about 80 for the Macintosh. That includes peripheral programs like Quicken, Microsoft Money, or Managing Your Money, which are useful for portfolio management. They work fine, but are of only marginal interest for investing, and are primarily aimed at household and small business bookkeeping. On the other hand, Pulse, from Equis, is a program designed specifically for portfolio management. In addition, all of the large database services, like CompuServe, have a portfolio management module, which can be automatically maintained by the service.

Large as those numbers are, they exclude whole categories of software, such as spreadsheets, all of which now allow you to create charts and graphs from data entered either manually or by transmission, and with a little effort you can make those same programs perform almost all of the data manipulations of technical analysis. There is in addition a large array of shareware and freeware programs, some devoted to technical and fundamental analysis, many to portfolio management and yield calculations.

For those who are unfamiliar with the terms "freeware" and "shareware," freeware is software that has entered the public domain, either through not having been copyrighted or from being intentionally donated to the commonweal by the programmer. Shareware is software that is being marketed by an individual, almost always without advertising or promotion, at a very low price—typically $25 or less. Because there is no marketing or distribution to speak of, payment is on the honor system. Sending in your money not only gets you virtue points, but typically gets a manual back in the mail and the right to call for technical support. Shareware is commonly available for tryout at no charge through BBSs and large systems like CompuServe (see Chapter 9) and Prodigy (see Chapter 10). We'll talk a lot more about those later. The fact that it is not marketed by a recognized software company does not mean that shareware or freeware is no good, by the way; some of it is very good.

The Heavy Artillery

Working with programs like MetaStock, Telescan, CompuTrac, and SuperCharts, you fairly quickly come to the realization that while they are data dependent, they are also data independent. In other words, while they were all developed to aid in analyzing the movements of the U.S. stock market, they have no country bias, and can just as easily be used to analyze other markets. In fact, the computerized investor should have a bigger advantage there, since so little of what we know as technical and fundamental analysis is done in other parts of the world. In much of the world, it is a complete mystery.

Even here, the power of these programs is little understood by the public at large. It is assumed that we are talking about throwing a chart of the last six months of price action in IBM, or something like that, up on the computer screen and then being able to print it out. Nice, but no big deal. You can buy such charts from several service companies, such as Standard & Poors, Trendlines, or Argus Research, and typically if you use what's called a full-service broker instead of a discounter, they will give them to you for the asking. You can also find them in any decent public library.

What these new programs do is the kind of analysis that used to be the sole preserve of large brokerage and investment banking houses. It was their preserve because it was so expensive to do it. Investment houses like J.P. Morgan, Lazard Freres, Brown Brothers-Harriman, etc., employed staffs of dozens of people whose job was to collect the data and create the charts and indicators that you will do on your personal computer. It took them hundreds of hours; it will take you seconds.

The difference in time means much more than the chance to go out for a cup of coffee or take in the late show on TV. It means that steps that were once put off—left out simply because it took so much time to make another set of calculations—are now done, because they mean only a couple more keystrokes.

Want an example? When was the last time you did a regression from the mean—a commonly used statistical tool to clearly define trends from scattered data? How long would it take you to do one? What if I then asked you to provide a channel of allowable price swings that would encompass two standard deviations from that mean? While you're at it, take the rate of change of a 12-day moving average of the stock or index you're interested in. In calculus, that would be called "taking the derivative" and represents taking a tangent to the curve formed by the moving average. You still on board for all this? Would it take you all night? Well, Telescan, MetaStock, or any of the others will do it in two or three seconds.

The Sorcerer's Apprentice

The main categories of investment software are technical analysis, fundamental analysis, portfolio management, and personal money management.

While almost anyone can understand the function of the last two categories, it is the first two that are the objects of both wonder and scorn. Technical analysis is considered a form of stage magic by some investment advisors, stuff to amuse children and mystify the ignorant, but otherwise of little value. Technicians, as they are called, often hold fundamental analysts in the same low regard, and for pretty much the same reasons. Reality lies in the middle. Some technical indicators are fundamental, and some fundamental information is really just technical in nature.

Technical analysis looks at the motion of the market, the ebb and flow of buying and selling, for clues on appropriate entry and exit points for the purchase or sale of stock or commodities. In other words, the goal is timing.

Fundamental analysis looks at a company's basic business, or the supply and demand for a commodity, and makes estimations of sales, earnings, cash flow, etc., with the aim of determining whether the subject under examination is presently undervalued, overvalued, or fairly valued. The object is to decide whether it's a good time to buy, sell, or do nothing. In other words, the goal is timing.

Both approaches not only have the same goals, they use the same methods. They do what is called "screening." A screen is created through which the stock, commodity, bond, or whatever must pass to be considered an acceptable risk—a kind of modern Sieve of Eratosthenes. We will talk more about screens later on, when we discuss each of the data analysis programs in the last section of the book. First, here's a quick guide to the strengths and weaknesses of some of the major players.

MetaStock (Equis International)

MetaStock (Figure 3-1) is the number one program and justifiably so. The focus is technical analysis of stocks, bonds, and commodities. All the

Figure 3-1   MetaStock is bullish on technical analysis

well-known indicators are represented—Wells Wilder Relative Strength, Stochastics, Commodity Channel Index, Bollinger Bands, etc., along with some of the more obscure ones, like Andrews' Pitchfork and Parabolics.

Like all analytical programs, MetaStock must be fed. There is no data, so data must be entered either manually or through a hookup with one of the data providers such as CompuServe or Dow Jones. Manual entry is extremely time consuming, and downright impractical for some purposes. But it's interesting to note that several of the most successful professional traders prefer to enter their data by hand. I have tried it, and it is true that it does give you a sense of the flow of the market that you do not get when the data flows in at light speed. MetaStock is discussed in detail in Chapter 16. A version of MetaStock is included with this book.

The Technician (Equis International)

Where MetaStock does technical analysis of stocks, The Technician (Figure 3-2) is designed to analyze the overall market. Six indices are used,

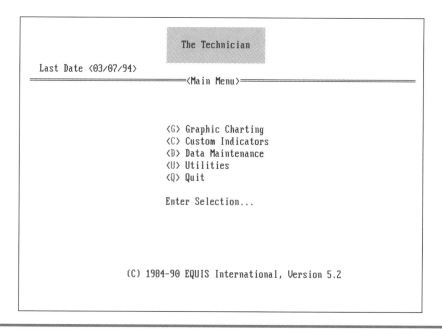

Figure 3-2   The Technician's opening screen is plain vanilla, but inside it's chock full of nuts and raisins

five of which are supplied by exchanges and the sixth supplied by a brokerage house. They are the NYSE (the New York Stock Exchange Composite), SPX (Standard & Poors 500), OEX (S&P 100), VLCI (Value Line Composite), NYFE (New York Futures Exchange Index, commonly called "the knife," in the trade), and the Shearson, Lehman Bond Index. The data is provided by modem by Equis itself, or it can be entered manually.

It should be emphasized that this program was not intended to analyze individual stocks and does not do so. It does accept user-specified categories for data entry, however, and an experienced user can create a stock listing simply by entering the data each day. After all, the program doesn't know what the item is. You can also use this method to enter the indices of foreign markets. The Technician is discussed in detail in Chapter 17.

Telescan Analyzer (Telescan, Inc.)

Telescan (Figure 3-3) is both a software and data provider. The Analyzer works whether or not it's connected to the database in Houston,

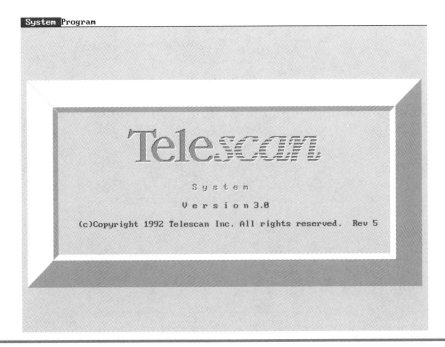

Figure 3-3   Telescan: The solid database

Texas, and you can save money by mostly using it offline. Charges online are by the minute.

Both the database and software are excellent, and the Analyzer even provides some very useful indicators not seen in other programs, like sine wave cycle analysis.

The program does both fundamental and technical analysis. You can call up a stock and chart a technical indicator, such as stochastics, and also chart what is considered a fundamental indicator—the current price of the stock in relation to its historic price-to-earnings ratio. You can also chart other generally considered fundamental indicators, such as cash flow, price-to-sales ratios, insider trading, analyst's earnings estimates, etc. All of this makes the Analyzer extremely useful for doing screens. Telescan is covered in Chapter 15 and a version of the program is included with this book.

Windows On WallStreet (MarketArts)

There is little doubt that this is the future—certainly in the near term. Nearly half of all the PCs in the country were purchased in the past two years, and nearly all of those were sold with Microsoft Windows already installed. There are now millions of users who have never typed in a DOS command, never used DOS, and perhaps don't even know what DOS is. They have become used to a graphical interface, to clicking, double-clicking, and clicking and dragging with the mouse to make things happen and that's the way it's going to be. It's been that way on the Macintosh since that machine first appeared.

MaketArts likes to call Windows On WallStreet (Figure 3-4) "WOW!," and most users will feel that it is a wow. It has a huge number of technical indicators, automatic data collection, and the full version can both read and write data in formats that are understood by other programs. Most of these features will be presented in Chapter 18, and a version of Windows On WallStreet is included with this book.

The Market Analyzer and Market Analyzer Plus (Dow Jones & Co.)

The Market Analyzer Plus adds portfolio management to the technical analysis capabilities of the Market Analyzer. It also comes in a Macintosh version.

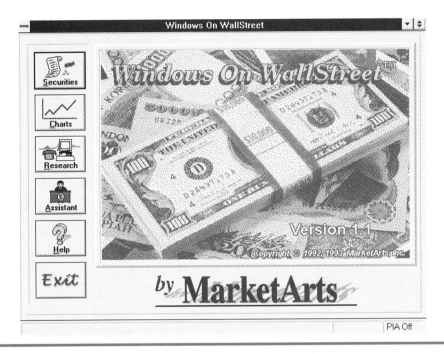

Figure 3-4 Windows On WallStreet: Cash always gets attention

All the standard tools of technical analysis are provided here, and it should be noted that the Macintosh version also displays the Japanese Candlestick method.

The Market Analyzer is one of the earliest programs in this field and is well done. Considering the manufacturer, it should be no surprise that all the Dow Jones programs are set up to automatically connect to the Dow Jones News/Retrieval Service for data collection. You must be a member of the News/Retrieval Service, and data is charged by the item—one stock, one day, is 10 cents, for example; if you pull a lot of data the price goes down. The startup membership charge is provided free with either program.

Intraday Analyst II (CompuTrac Software Inc.)

If there is any granddaddy of computerized technical analysis, this would be it. One of the original programs, it was at first aimed only at brokers and professional money managers. Hence the high price. For

DOS and Windows

Many people are confused by the distinction between Windows and DOS in the IBM compatible operating environment and believe that the main difference is that Windows lets you display windows and use other graphical tools, and DOS does not. Not so. You can have windows in a DOS program, but it takes a little more programming. Windows is not an operating system; DOS is the operating system, and Windows rides on DOS like a rubber ducky in a bathtub. Microsoft is expected to introduce a Windows program that actually is an operating system, independent of DOS, but for now there is no significant advantage in using a Windows program over a DOS program.

The ability to throw several windows onto the screen at once is useful in both technical and fundamental analysis. It is common to want to compare several stocks or commodities against each other, or several indicators, and to want to see them all displayed at once. In earlier versions of MetaStock and similar analysis programs, a shortcoming was that only the last window opened was active. In other words, you could look at gold, silver, and platinum, or the Big Three auto stocks, and display them together on the same screen, but if you then decided to perform some analytical operation on them, you could do that only on the last one brought up. In a Windows environment, all windows are opened simply by moving the cursor into that window and clicking the mouse to perform some action. The same is now true of MetaStock, even though it operates in DOS and not Windows.

many years, it provided those users with an edge that was difficult for the individual investor to match. Once you pay the high initial cost, all further upgrades are provided at no charge.

Other programs now do what CompuTrac does, but that doesn't mean this program is dead. CompuTrac does technical analysis very well, and a much less expensive Windows version of the program is expected to be released some time this year.

SuperCharts (Omega Research)

Omega makes more than SuperCharts, but this is their hot item. They promote it as the next evolutionary stage after MetaStock, the market leader. I don't know about that, but it certainly is a very good program. Because, like Windows On WallStreet, it operates in the

Windows environment, it gains the advantages of being able to overlay a limitless number of indicators onto the same chart, and, perhaps more important to most users, it has the ability to have all windows active.

Now let's take a look at the world.

A CLOSED-END VIEW
OF AN OPEN WORLD

CHAPTER 4

THE EUROPEAN TOUR

As a practical matter, it is difficult for a single U.S. investor to select individual stocks in a foreign company. For that matter, it's not easy even for professional money managers. The problems go from political to legal to ordinary language barriers. The sensible solution would seem to be country funds. For the most part, these are closed-end funds that invest in the companies of specific countries, regions, or industries—a gold fund would be an example of this last type.

High on the list of foreign stock problems is that some countries will not permit individual foreigners to buy stock in their corporations at all, but they will permit minority ownership by institutions, like funds or banks. Others, such as Taiwan, place percentage limits and bureaucratic obstacles in the way of foreign ownership. Until recently, even neighboring Mexico placed severe restrictions on stock ownership by foreigners. Next on the list of problems is information, even with online connections to Dow Jones and other major services that provide foreign company news, the differences in reporting requirements make a reasonable assessment of a company's prospects problematical at best. It's not easy even when you're researching U.S. corporations.

Still, there's no question that a smart or lucky shot in the dark can hit companies that multiply your money 10 or 20 times. They can also provide 90 and 100 percent losses. Traders call such shooters "gunslingers," like in the old west. And, like the old west, they separate into the quick and the dead.

So what's a closed-end fund? It's a fund that is started with a fixed number of shares sold at a stated price. As in: "We're going to raise $10 million for the purpose of investing in Ireland. That will be a million shares at $10 apiece. How many do you want?"

You can then treat that fund and that country as if it were a company. If things go well for Ireland, or Argentina or Germany or Thailand, then things will probably go well for you as an investor. Information is also more generally available on a country than it is on an individual foreign corporation. You can actually go and visit your investment. And it provides an opportunity for history majors and political science types to look at the big picture, so to speak. Peace agreements between Israel and the Palestinians, for example, are good not only for Israeli stocks, but those of neighboring Jordan as well. Trouble in South Africa sends shivers through the gold markets and companies that depend on rare metals. Intermittent warfare among the republics of the former Soviet Union affect the price of oil and gas and consequently the economies of Europe and Japan. It's one world, more or less.

The Closed-End Way of Opening up the World

Closed-end funds can be a surrogate, then, for stock in a single country. There are nearly 100 such funds in the U.S., with more being formed at the rate of two or three a month. Closed-end funds also exist in other countries; on the London Exchange, for example, they're called "Investment Trusts."

Whenever there is strong investor interest in any spot on the globe, the community of investment bankers and fund managers responds to that call by creating new funds to take in the hot money and figure out something to do with it. And they say there are no more humanitarians. Sounding a less cynical note, the formation of a new fund to exploit some emerging market or sector should always be viewed with caution as it is usually a sign of excessive enthusiasm for that particular market.

Closed-end funds are just like open-ended mutual funds except that they're closed. Is that perfectly clear? Okay, a little more explanation: closed-end funds are called such because the number of shares is fixed at the fund's inception, which is not true of a regular mutual fund. Anyone can buy a share in a regular mutual fund, like a Fidelity fund, for example, simply by paying an amount equal to the net asset value of the fund at the close of business that day, plus a sales charge if there is one. If the NAV (net asset value) is $13.63, that's the price, and any number can play. In a closed-end fund, however, anyone who wants to join must purchase a share from someone who is already a shareholder. The price can be more or less than the net asset value of the fund itself, depending on market demand for the shares. As a matter of fact, the shares of closed-end funds rarely sell for their net asset value, and are often quoted at anywhere from 1 to 25 percent more or less. If they sell for more, it's called a premium, if less, a discount. Because of this, and the fixed number of shares, people who have been in the market a long time will tell you that a closed-end fund is just like stock. This is not strictly true, but it acts much like a stock so we will let it pass for the moment. Closed-end funds are listed as their own category in *Barron's*, the *Wall Street Journal*, and the *New York Times*. They can be called up on your computer screen like any other stock or mutual fund, using Telescan, Dow Jones News/Retrieval, Prodigy, CompuServe, America Online, and a number of other services.

In practice, closed-end funds typically sell at a discount to their per-share asset value. In which case you are getting a little something for nothing. Why should that be? Nobody really knows for sure, but there are a couple of explanations that have gained currency over the years. One is that unlike an open mutual fund there will be no new money flowing in for investment; the $10 million you started with is all there's going to be.

note

Actually, a closed-end fund can issue new shares, but they must be offered first to the existing shareholders and are almost always so offered at a discount to true value. The discount might be anywhere from one to ten percent. This is typically referred to as a "rights" offering—as in having the right, but not the obligation, to buy more shares at the stated price. Many shareholders in closed-end funds shrug off such offerings if they're not interested in buying more shares and drop the notification in the wastebasket. This is foolish because these rights have value and can be sold and traded on the open market.

The argument for discounts continues by noting that if the fund simply fulfills its charter and invests in the purpose for which it was created, there is no new money to invest in opportunities that may come up later. The only direct way to get more money is to sell off the existing investments, which must be sold at a loss if the fund made unfortunate choices, and so have less for new investments. If the investments are sold at a profit, the investors are then exposed to a considerable tax liability.

The second and more common argument for shares in closed-end funds selling at a discount is that they are less liquid. In other words, if you want to sell a share in the Magellan Fund or Twentieth Century Fund, which are the more typical open-ended kind of fund, you just call up the fund or your broker and sell. What you get is the "redemption value"—whatever the NAV of the fund is at the close of business that day. Sometimes there may be a fee for leaving the fund—called "back-loaded" in the trade. The argument for these is to create stability in the fund by preventing switchers from jumping in and out whenever the fancy strikes them. In general, you should probably be wary of any fund that has a back-loaded fee for leaving.

If you want to sell a share in a closed-end fund, on the other hand, you have to find a buyer. There is no "redemption value" because the fund is not obligated to buy back your shares. In practice, there are always buyers for shares in closed-end funds, but it is assumed that you will have to offer the shares at a discount to make them more attractive. At least, that's the theory. It's interesting to pay attention to the above arguments, because even though they make perfectly good sense, they seem to have little relation to reality.

The Real and the Ideal, as Plato Used to Say

The shares in some closed-end funds always sell at a premium—sometimes a pretty hefty premium—and have since the day the fund was started. Others always sell at a discount. Still others sometimes sell at a premium and other times sell at a discount.

This is more than a curiosity because many—in fact, most—professional investors and money managers will tell you that it is foolish to pay a premium for shares in a closed-end fund and that it makes sense to buy such shares only when they are selling at a discount. The argument is straightforward enough: why pay up for goods that can be had marked down at another time or place. Buying at a discount gives you a better shot at making a profit, the argument says. This certainly would seem to make sense. And yet I have looked at the premium and discount levels of all the closed-end country funds in America up to this point, and back through all of their history, in an effort to determine what clues these premiums or discounts had to the performance of the fund over the following months, and there was no consistent correlation. In short, the argument that paying a premium is likely to produce a loss, and buying at a discount increases the likelihood of profit, appears to have little going for it.

Since this runs counter to the conventional wisdom on such matters, let's go into it a little further. What it boils down to is that the discount or premium on a fund should be looked at in relation to the historical trend for that fund. In short, some funds always sell at a premium, whether they're doing well or badly. The Korea Fund is a classic in this way, selling at a consistently big premium even while encountering heavy losses. Others always, or nearly always, sell at a discount—ASA (American South African), for example. In between are the funds that swing both ways. In general, if you look at the records of any large number of these funds, the existence of a discounted price—meaning the fund is selling at a discount to its net asset value—does not presage a rise in price for the fund; it's not necessarily a good deal. What does seem to have some predictive value is the size of the discount or premium. When the meter swings too far in either direction, it is usually an indication that something is out of whack. If a fund has typically sold for a 5 percent discount, for example, but now sells for a 20 percent discount, it is likely that people are being too pessimistic about its prospects. The converse is even more likely to be true; any fund that sells for a huge premium over NAV—as the new Germany funds did when they were introduced in 1989 and 1990—simply has too many friends, as they say in the business. The reason this kind of contrary thinking has value is that whenever anything is valued, or devalued, to extreme levels, all the assumptions about further moves have already been made, and anything that disappoints those assumptions is likely to draw an extreme reaction. The trick, of course, is figuring out when the level is extreme.

In general, you will find that nearly all mutual funds do slightly worse than the index of the markets they are invested in—even when they are doing very well. This is true of funds that invest only in the American market as well as the foreign stock funds we're looking at here. There are reasons for this performance drop beyond the obvious inclination to blame the fund's managers. One reason that fund managers like to point out is that the index doesn't pay commissions. In other words, you're going to fall one or two percent short of the performance of the index simply by virtue of the fact that you have to pay commissions to buy and sell the stocks. Another major cause of lower performance is that funds by their nature tend to invest in the largest and most well-established companies; the fact is, they are moving such large amounts of money that they have to buy the larger companies because those are the only ones with enough liquidity to absorb the orders. But the reality of markets is that it is the smaller companies that tend to have the largest moves. After all, add $20 million in sales to BMW and you're not going to do much to the stock. Add $20 million to some tiny company and you've doubled it! Thus, a fund will almost always underperform the stock market it is invested in. On the other hand, it will have much greater safety than by going in and trying to pick the one or two stocks in a market that are going to be the high flyers.

Such subtleties are interesting and worth paying attention to. But they are not the whole ballgame. The real value is in the big picture—the overview of what the world is doing and where the future is heading. To have invested in America in the 1860s would have been a very wise decision, even though the country was engaged in a civil war. To have bought in the 1930s—if you had anything to buy with—would also have been a wise decision, even though the country was in the throes of the worst depression in its history. It would have been very wise to buy shares in Japan at the end of World War II, even though the country was a wreck and its companies made nothing but cheap tin toys. As you look though the funds described in this and the following chapters, remember that what matters most is the prospects of the country or the region, and not the premium or discount on the shares.

The Tour Begins: A Is for Austria

note

The charts for all the closed-end country funds presented in this chapter were pulled from Telescan. They could have been pulled from Meta-Stock or SuperCharts or Windows on Wall Street or any of a dozen other programs, but it was just simpler and easier to use Telescan, which is both software and its own database. Even if you're not interested in the performance of the Austrian market, pay some attention to the explanation at the beginning of this section. I'll discuss some of the basic features of a Telescan chart, which will apply to all the country funds charts shown in this chapter. It will also give you information that you can use for your own online navigations.

The very top line shown in Figure 4-1, "System, Program, Analyzer, Indicators," simply refers to menus that can be pulled down to access additional features of the Telescan program. We'll go into those in more detail when we discuss Telescan in Chapter 15. The next line tells you that this is Graph 1 of 125 in a file that is called "STOCKS." This information is of no particular consequence, but just lets you know that this happens to be part of a file of 125 graphs on closed-end country and sector funds.

Below this information, in the upper left-hand corner of the chart, are the letters "OST." These are the call letters—the ticker symbol—for the Austria Fund, and are what you would type in if you want to follow this fund or call it up from any other database. Whether you use Telescan, the Dow Jones News/Retrieval, CompuServe, or whatever, you will usually need to know the ticker symbol and most database services and

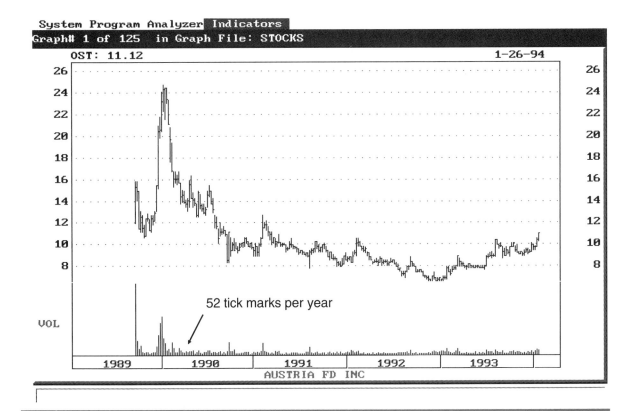

System Program Analyzer Indicators
Graph# 1 of 125 in Graph File: STOCKS

OST: 11.12   1-26-94

52 tick marks per year

AUSTRIA FD INC

Figure 4-1   Chart of the Austria Fund

programs provide a "lookup" or "symbol" function so you can get the call letters for any stock or fund. New funds are being added at the rate of two or three a month. Just to the right of OST is a number that represents the closing price of the shares on the day this chart was pulled. Moving farther to the right on the same line, you will see that it was pulled from the database on 1-26-94 (January 26th, 1994).

The price, by the way, is always shown as a decimal because it is easier for the computer to transmit and use. So 11.12 translates to 11-1/8 rather than $11.12, because even though the number is in decimal form, closed-end funds are quoted in eighths, just like stocks. The main chart itself shows the weekly price ranges (in this case, from 8 to 26) and close. Each vertical bar represents a weekly price range; the close is represented by the tiny horizontal bar jutting out from the bar to the right. The volume is shown in the bottom part of the chart as a series of vertical bars. These values are proportional, not actual volume.

The numbers at the very bottom of the chart, just above the name "AUSTRIA FD INC" (for Austria Fund, Inc.), are the years being shown. The Telescan database carries up to 15 years of data. In every case but one, the charts selected here show the entire history of each fund. The exception is ASA (American South African), which has a history longer than the 15 years covered by the database.

So much for that! Now let's do a little inspection, as the mathematicians like to say. Note the huge price and volume spike around the end of 1989 and beginning of 1990. You will see it on many of the European funds. It represents the breakup of the Soviet Union, the destruction of the Berlin Wall, reunification of Germany, and the wave of optimism this generated throughout the world at the end of 1989. It also shows what can happen when someone buys into a situation of rampant enthusiasm. Because unless the buyer got in and out quickly during that rage, he or she faces a long wait before the Austria fund and most of the others ever come back to the Berlin Wall high. Is there any way to avoid being caught up in a wave of hysterical enthusiasm and stepping into a situation right at the top? No sure way, but it is probably worth recalling at this point the advice of the first Baron Rothschild, who said on these matters: "Buy when the cannons are firing, and sell when the trumpets are blowing." Closer to our own time, the speculator Bernard Baruch explained his extraordinary success in the market by saying: "I buy straw hats in the wintertime."

Austria Bit by Bit

Some services give us the opportunity to look at a fund's portfolio and get the names of individual companies the fund managers have invested in. The independently minded investor may then decide to take some of these stocks individually instead of settling for the fund approach. There are both advantages and disadvantages to doing it this way. The disadvantage is higher risk and more hassle buying and selling the stock; the advantage is a potentially much higher return because one of the things we will notice as we look at this fund and all the others to follow is that virtually none of them do as well as the market they are invested in!

One of the primary sources for this kind of detailed information is the *Morningstar Mutual Funds Newsletter*, based in Chicago. This recently became available on disk and for CD-ROM. Approximately 3,400 mutual funds are on the CD. Much or all of this information is also available through the Dow Jones News/Retrieval and those databases that carry Disclosure, a service that can be called up through most of the major databases. (The Morningstar mutual fund data, covering both closed and open-end funds, became available on America Online as of February 22, 1994.)

Here I used the Morningstar disks to find that the Austria Fund was invested in the following stocks and funds, shown in Table 4-1. Some are obvious from knowing a little tourist German, others would have to be researched through online services or library references. I am printing the whole portfolio here, but will only do so for one other fund because it would simply take up too much space to print them all.

Don't worry if it doesn't add up to 100 percent. We're leaving out the holdings in cash and short-term notes, on the assumption that everyone already knows how to hold cash.

There are a few more things of interest to be learned about the Austria Fund. One is that it sells at a 2 percent discount to net asset value. Furthermore, except for the first few months of its existence, when everybody was wild about Europe, it has always sold at a discount. That discount wouldn't have done you much good, however, because even though the conventional wisdom is that funds selling at a discount are a good deal, the fund declined steadily until this past year. The second thing is that it had a total return of 24.6 percent for the nine months ending September 30, 1993, which was the last official statement period. In fact, that return continued to improve through the rest of the year, as you can see from looking at the chart. Very good! Even so, it was 3.5 percent worse than the Austrian stock market itself.

Emerging Germany Fund

Here again, in Figure 4-2, we see the rush of enthusiasm in early 1990 as Germany was reunified.

The Emerging Germany Fund had a total return of 22.5 percent up to the last report in September, and did even better after that. That was 2.5 percent worse than the German stock market overall.

A list of some of their holdings is shown in Table 4-2. Many of the names will be familiar to the reader, and they can be used as guides for those who prefer to invest in individual foreign stocks rather than funds. (This is easier to do in Germany than in most countries.) As you can see,

STOCK	VALUE $000	% NET ASSETS
OEMV	6,890	10.50
Creditanstalt-Bankverein	6,474	9.86
EA Generali	4,771	7.27
EVN-Energie Versorgung	4,672	7.12
Oesterr Elektrizitaets	4,348	6.62
Oesterr Brau-Beteil	3,923	5.98
Immuno Intl	3,253	4.96
BWT	2,727	4.16
Bank fur Oberoesterr	2,563	3.90
Bau Holdings	2,483	3.78
Viso Data Computer	2,101	3.20
Graboplast Textile	1,875	2.86
Jenbacher Werke	1,743	2.66
Waagner-Biro	1,733	2.64
First Hungary Fund	1,496	2.28
Flughaven Wein	1,366	2.08
Creditanstalt-Bank	1,035	1.58
Austrian Airlines	956	1.46
Brueder-Reininghaus	815	1.24
Zwack Unicum	642	.98
Constantia Industrie	633	.96
E. Europe Dvlpmnt Fund	553	.84
Perlmooser Zement	508	.77
Weinerberger-Baustoff	420	.64
Styl-Ruhagyar	408	.62

Table 4-1 The Austria Fund Portfolio

none of the fund's investments totaled more than 4 percent of assets. The largest holdings were Mercedes-Benz and Daimler-Benz (the truck division), Siemens (electrical and electronic equipment), Hoescht (chemicals), and Deutsche Bank. There were also sizable positions in BMW, Linde (industrial gases), Bayer, and Thyssen (steel).

Interestingly, despite the fund's better than 20 percent return, it sells at a discount of 10 percent to its net asset value (as of the last report). Furthermore, it has always sold at a discount—frequently of more than 15 percent! As I said earlier, there appears to be little relation between whether a fund sells at a discount or a premium and how profitable it is to own that fund.

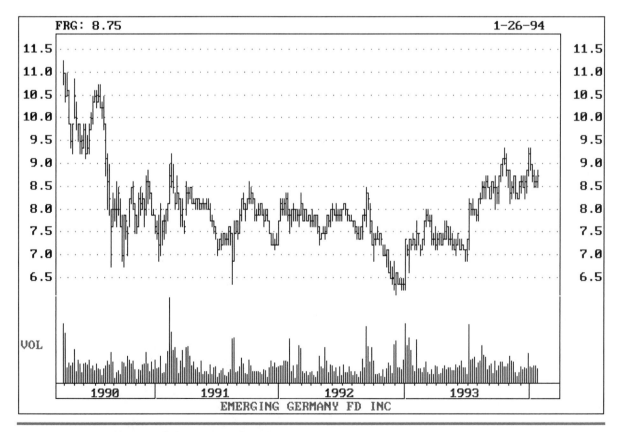

Figure 4-2 The Emerging Germany Fund

STOCK	VALUE $000	% NET ASSETS
Mercedes-Benz	4,311	3.90
Daimler-Benz	4,156	3.76
Siemens	3,934	3.56
Hoescht	3,791	3.43
Deutsche Bank	3,245	2.94
Schering	3,171	2.87
Allianz Holding	3,088	2.79
Man	3,072	2.78
Victoria Holding	2,993	2.71
Berliner Hand-Und Bank	2,965	2.68
BMW	2,908	2.63
Colonia Konzern	2,904	2.63
Degussa	2,828	2.56
Commerzbank	2,809	2.54
Linde	2,775	2.51
Vereins Bank	2,722	2.46
Vereinigte Electric	2,610	2.36
IKB Deutsche Bank	2,556	2.31
Berliner Bank	2,535	2.29
Veba	2,500	2.26
Bayer	2,481	2.24
Douglas Holdings	2,393	2.17
Thyssen	2,389	2.16
Aachen & Munchener	2,360	2.13
BASF	2,252	2.04

Table 4-2 The Emerging Germany Fund Portfolio

European Warrant Fund

What's interesting about the European Warrant Fund, shown in Figure 4-3, is not only its spectacular return of over 100 percent, but the fact that it exists at all. Warrants on common stocks are much more common in Europe than here, where we tend to use options as our primary way of leveraging an investment. Warrants on major Swiss and German companies paid off big as those stocks moved 20 to 30 percent for the year. Warrants have so much leverage that a 20 percent move in the base company can easily translate into a 100 percent move in the warrant.

The European Warrant Fund sold at a premium of 6 percent at the time this chart was pulled, but before then it had almost always sold at a steep discount—sometimes as much as 25 percent less than the per share value. If you examine the chart, you will notice that the price of the fund bumped along a bottom of $6 a share for a year and a half during that discount period, signaling to the sagacious speculator that there was little risk below $6 and much potential above it.

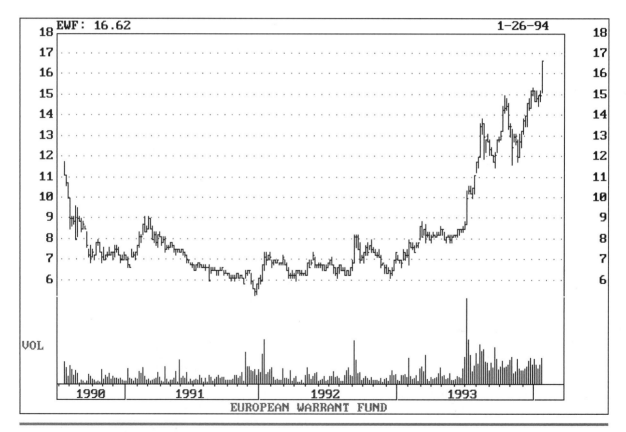

Figure 4-3   The European Warrant Fund

Warrants

For those of you who do not understand what a warrant is, it is the right to buy a stock at a fixed price under certain time limits. The time limit might be just a few months, but often it is two or more years. The warrant might give the holder the right to buy a share of some company at $25, for example. If the stock is presently selling at $20 or less, the warrant is worth very little and might sell for only a dollar or two because, after all, who would turn it in to pay $25 when they could just go buy the stock directly for less. As the stock moves above the price guaranteed by the warrant, however, the warrant itself rises much more swiftly. At a stock price of $29, for example, the warrant would be worth at least $4 and probably sell for more because investors would be willing to pay a premium. (The same kind of leverage works against you on the way down, by the way.)

Europe Fund

More than half the investments of the Europe Fund, shown in Figure 4-4, are in the U.K. (Britain) and Switzerland. Most of the remainder are in Germany and France, all of which tells the observer that the fund is extremely conservative. The total return is 15 percent, which is about one percent less than the total return of a generalized European Fund maintained by the Morgan Stanley investment bank as a benchmark index.

Despite its lackluster performance (one of the worst of the year among closed-end country funds), the Europe Fund sells at a 3 percent premium. For a while during 1993, it sold at more than a 10 percent premium! Go figure, as they say.

There is something worth noting here about what a trader would call the technical action of the Europe Fund. It seems to bottom regularly within a few cents of $10 a share and top out at a bit over $13 a share. One could make a pretty steady gain—and a nice one at that—just by buying at 10 and taking your 30 percent return and waving good-bye. If you look with a critical eye at all the country fund charts presented here, you will see this pattern is by no means an isolated case. Of course, a real trader would make much more than 30 percent because he or she would

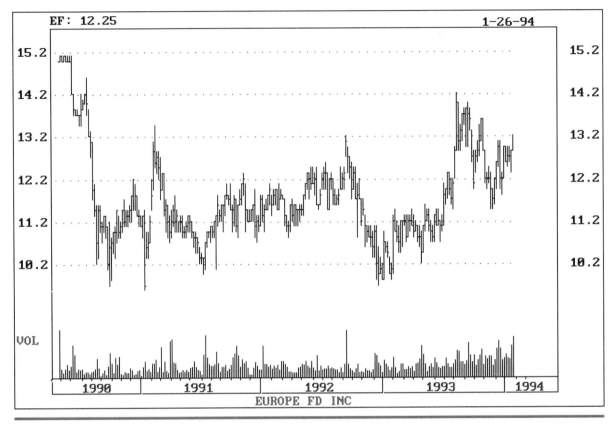

Figure 4-4   The Europe Fund

not only go long at the baseline, as they say, but also turn around and go short at the tops. Not everybody has the nerve for this.

First Iberian Fund

Ah, the name alone is enough to set those castanets clicking and shoes a-tapping. Unfortunately, the performance of the First Iberian Fund (Spain), shown in Figure 4-5, would set your mouth to drooping. Those who bought at 19 during the heady days of the Soviet collapse and the new Europe are still waiting for the flamenco dancers to liven up the party, though things have been looking up a bit of late. The First Iberian

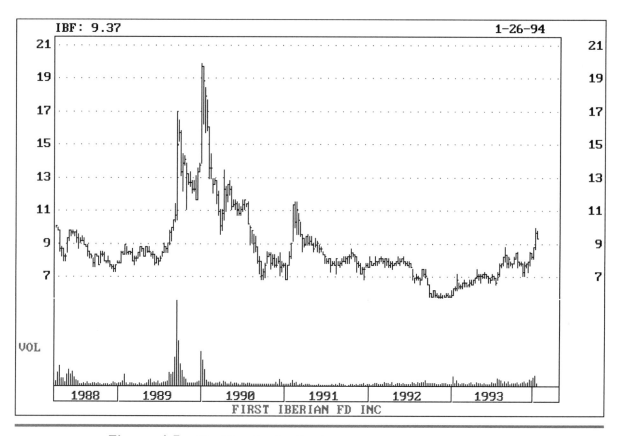

IBF: 9.37   1-26-94

FIRST IBERIAN FD INC

Figure 4-5   The First Iberian Fund

Fund had a total return of 21 percent to the end of September 1993, but an estimated return of about 60 percent through the end of that year. Major holdings included the Banco Popular, Telefonos de Espana, and Empressa Nacional (the electric company). Except for a brief period during the mania of late 1989 and early 1990, the fund has always sold at a discount to net asset value.

France Growth Fund

Total return for the France Growth Fund, shown in Figure 4-6, at the end of the third quarter 1993 was 17 percent, almost exactly the same as the French stock market as a whole. That improved greatly through the

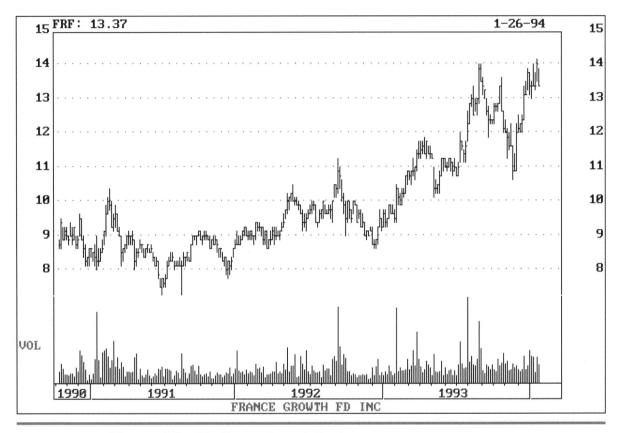

Figure 4-6 The France Growth Fund

rest of that year to finish at about 40 percent. Major holdings included Elf Aquitaine (oil and gas), Moet-Henn Louis Vuitton (an unlikely merging of champagne and luggage), Groupe BSN (supermarkets), L'Oreal, Michelin, and Saint Gobain. In short, all the major French companies. Except for the last part of 1993, the fund has almost always sold at a steep discount of more than 20 percent to net asset value.

Future Germany Fund

This is one of those funds that were started right after German reunification to take advantage of what was a flood of dollars looking to invest in the new Europe—whose future was, of course, limitless. The Future Germany Fund, shown in Figure 4-7, sold at a nearly 20 percent premium back then, and it was all downhill from there. Well, you might say, that proves you should never buy at a premium and always buy at a discount. Maybe, but it has sold at a deep discount ever since and did nothing much until this past year. You will notice the fund has shown a marked (sorry about that) tendency to bottom at around $11 a share, with the occasional quick peek at $10, and then moves up to top out around $14. The fact that it has stayed above that figure for much of 1993 is quite encouraging, and the early investors may someday break even. Major holdings of the fund include the usual suspects (as Claude Rains would say): Siemens, Hoescht, Mercedes-Benz, Bayer, BMW, etc.

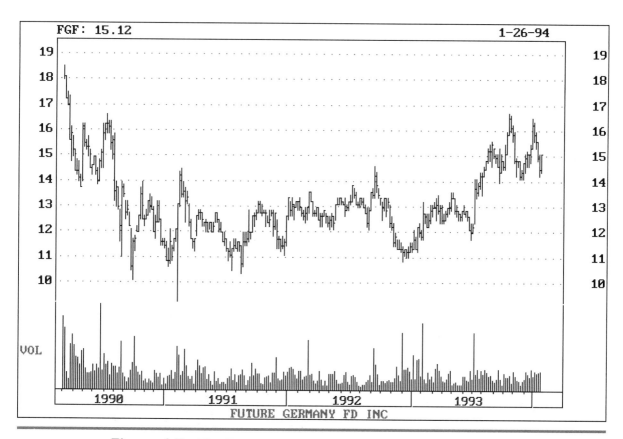

Figure 4-7   The Future Germany Fund

Business Week Guide to Global Investments

Germany Fund

Here, in the Germany Fund, shown in Figure 4-8, we have a long-established fund and can clearly see the spike of German reunification and Soviet collapse. If only you could have sold shares in NATO back then you would have made a mint. Following a top of $25 a share—the last bid coming from somewhere in the Land of Oz—the shares slid precipitously to $11, where they pretty much stayed. In fact, you could have bought at $11 and sold at $13 pretty regularly since then and made yourself a tidy pile of pfennigs along the way. From the look of it, you probably still can. A list of some of the fund's holdings would only bore

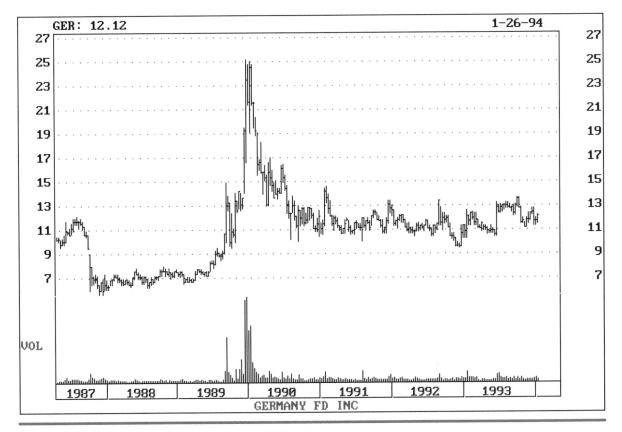

Figure 4-8 The Germany Fund

you; they are the usual giant German companies. The fund sells at almost exactly net asset value.

Growth Fund of Spain

The Growth Fund of Spain, shown in Figure 4-9, bottomed at 7-1/4 in late 1992, just where it had bottomed before. What a coincidence! It also seems to top at about 11, again a remarkable coincidence. Despite the poor performance of the Spanish economy this past year, the gain in the fund and the Spanish market has been a flamenco foot-stomper—about 60 percent. Major holdings include the Banco Bilbao Vizcaya, Hidroelectrica Cantabrico, and Dragados (construction).

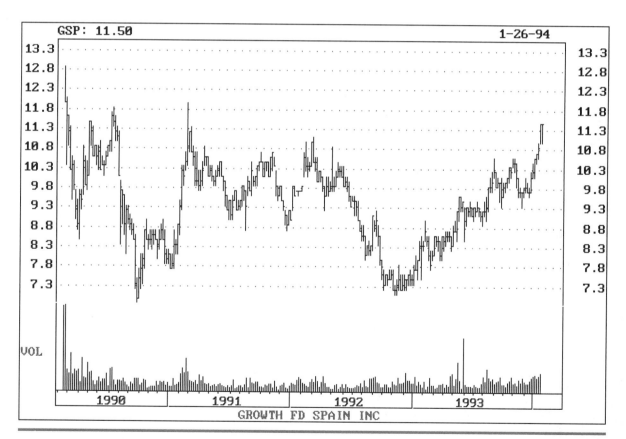

Figure 4-9 The Growth Fund of Spain

G.T. Greater Europe Fund

The G.T. Greater Europe Fund, shown in Figure 4-10, had been a study in total boredom until 1993. Which is probably why it has almost always sold at a deep discount to NAV. An inspection of the chart will show that the fund has bottomed regularly at around $9 a share and topped at $10.50 to $11. The 1993 surge was a hummer, however, carrying the fund up a whopping 70 percent even without currency adjustments.

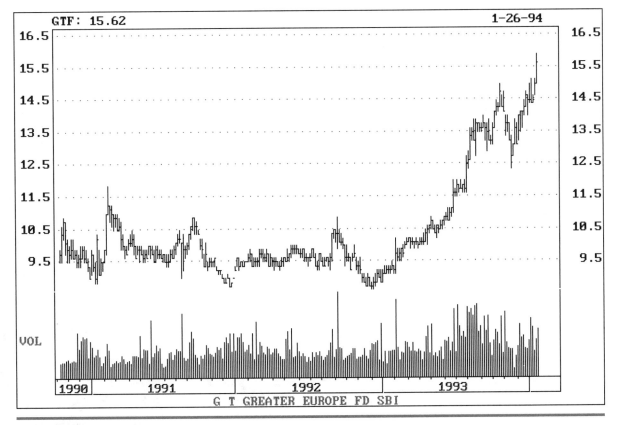

Figure 4-10   The G.T. Greater Europe Fund

Irish Investment Fund

Here again, in the Irish Investment Fund, shown in Figure 4-11, we see a fund bottoming at the same point it had bottomed before. Will it also top where it had topped before? Ah, you can never tell for sure, but if it gets there—only another point—I'd be pretty surprised if there weren't a lot of selling. Through most of its history, the Irish Investment Fund has been a study in frustration, explaining why it has always—and I mean always—sold at a big discount. If you think buying at a deep discount is a sure way to make money, you would have been right last year, but you could have turned to stone waiting for it. The fund is almost 100 percent invested in Ireland, where major holdings include Allied Irish Banks, the Independent Newspapers chain, Irish Life (insurance),

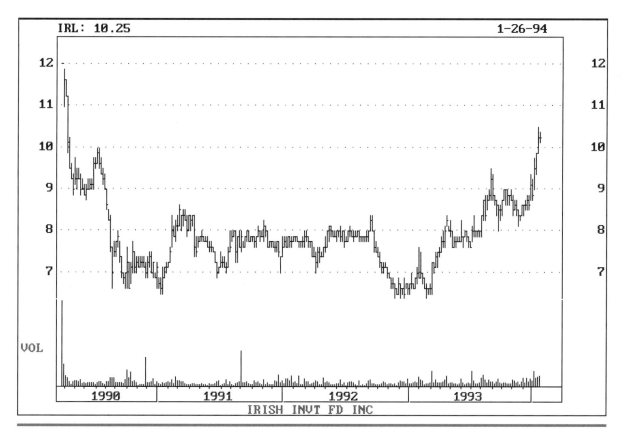

Figure 4-11 The Irish Investment Fund

Irish Wire Products, and Jury's Hotels. The fund manager must have caught a leprechaun last year because there certainly was a small pot of gold for those who held on.

Italy Fund

Mafia murders, bribery, and other scandals rocked the Italian government through much of 1993, causing share prices to appreciate more than 50 percent. Everybody loves a good scandal. The Italy Fund, shown in Figure 4-12, bottomed at $7 at the end of 1992, within a few cents of where it had bottomed before, another of those remarkable coincidences. Will it move back to its old highs as well? Could be; there's a lot more to Italy than pasta and accordions. After all, they invented radio, batteries,

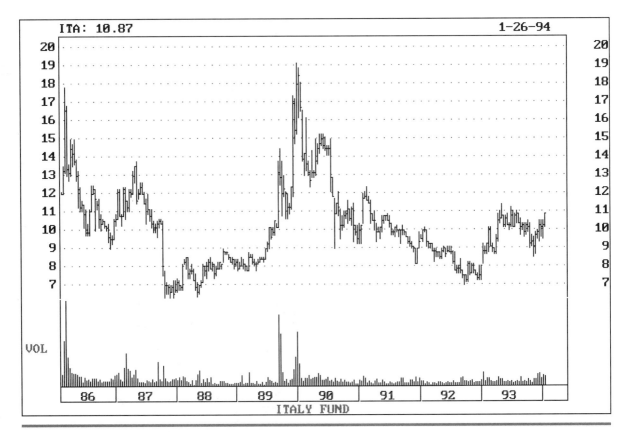

Figure 4-12 The Italy Fund

and nuclear power, and that's just the recent stuff. The fund is 100 percent invested in Italian companies and usually sells at a slight discount. Major holdings include Alleanza (insurance), Mediobanca (banking), Benetton, and Montecatini Edison. The fund was heavily into banks and insurance companies last year.

New Germany Fund

After a moon-rocket start in early 1990, the New Germany Fund, shown in Figure 4-13, bottomed at $9 so often the investors must have thought they were in the Sea of Tranquillity. Another bottom around $9 just before the start of 1993 produced a nice percentage move to a high of 14. You had to be surprised at the nearly 50 percent gain, but not at

Figure 4-13   The New Germany Fund

the potential for a rise anytime you bought around $9. Except for that wild opening, the New Germany Fund has always sold at a discount, and even after the recent healthy move still sold at a 10 percent discount. Major holdings include Siemens, Mannesmann, Munich Reinsurance, Schering, and Hoescht.

Portugal Fund

After three years of decline and doldrums, the Portugal Fund, shown in Figure 4-14, performed handsomely in 1993. From low to high, the gain was about 80 percent. The normal discount of the fund evaporated as the rise continued, and it now sells at a slight premium, though only

Figure 4-14 The Portugal Fund

about 2 percent. Resolving some long-standing political problems and increasing popularity with tourists have provided major benefits to the Portuguese economy, and things haven't looked so good since Vasco da Gama. Some of the fund's major holdings include Modelo (supermarkets), Engil (construction), and Banco Totta.

Scudder New Europe

Scudder New Europe, shown in Figure 4-15, has always sold at a sharp discount to net asset value, but the recent run-up of nearly 40 percent has finally produced a premium on the price of the shares—though only two-tenths of one percent. The fund bottomed around $8 a share several times before making its current move up. Holdings include the Mirror

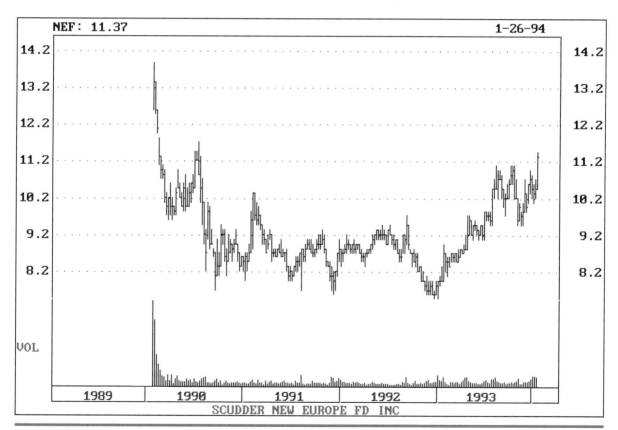

Figure 4-15   The Scudder New Europe Fund

Group (newspapers), Conduril (construction), Generale des Eaux (bottled water), and Ciba-Geigy (pharmaceuticals).

Spain Fund

Here's a pocket rocket. Years of doing nothing much were interrupted by the Spain Fund's scalar climb up the mountain as the new Europe broke out all over the place, following which the fund slid back to doing nothing (see Figure 4-16). Shareholders must have felt like they just came off the weekend part of the century and someone stole the punch bowl in the middle of it. 1993's returns were decent, though, and Spain is likely to still be there next year. Major holdings include Telefonica, Repsol,

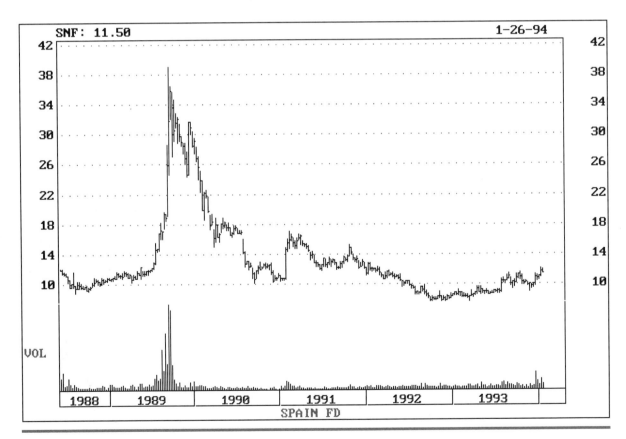

Figure 4-16   The Spain Fund

Banco Bilbao, Banco Santander, Banco Popular, and the Barcelona Water Company.

Swiss Helvetia Fund

Note the misspelling of the fund name at the bottom of the chart (Figure 4-17); you will see these kinds of mistakes often. It is also a mystery why anyone would name a fund Swiss Helvetia, since Helvetia *is* Switzerland. But leaving such grammatical carping aside, the fund has performed as you would expect from the good burghers of that land. The fund had almost always sold at a discount and performed as predictably as a Swiss watch until 1993. At that time, someone poured some joy juice in the mechanism and the fund went up a whopping 80 percent. Holders

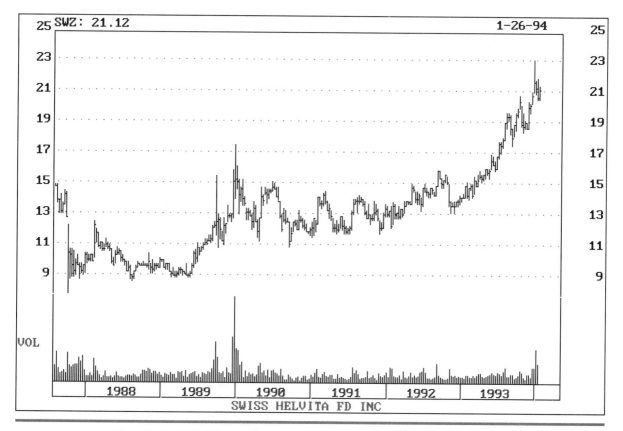

Figure 4-17 The Swiss Helvetia Fund

did even better than that since the Swiss franc went up against the dollar, too. The Swiss franc is one of very few currencies backed by gold, by the way, and has long been the currency of choice among deposed dictators and international criminals; accept no substitutes. Major holdings of the fund include Roche (chemicals and pharmaceuticals), Nestle, Credit Suisse, Ciba-Geigy, Sandoz, Brown Boveri, and the Bank for International Settlements. The fund is 100 percent invested in Switzerland, which any Swiss will tell you is the sensible thing to do. The fund has usually sold at a discount.

Turkish Delight—The Turkish Investment Fund

The Turkish Investment Fund, shown in Figure 4-18, is worth spending some time with. The Turkish stock market was the number one performer in the world in 1993, up some 220 percent! The fund itself didn't do nearly as well as the Turkish stock market overall, but those who bought at the bottom are hardly complaining. A look at that bottom, however, reveals that those who bought earlier have plenty to complain about, because the Turkish Fund has taken years to get back anywhere near its old highs. The marked diminution of the Iraqi military threat and its aggressive posturing, however, along with the likelihood of eventual Turkish entry into the European common market, augur well for continued Turkish prosperity. The streets of Istanbul are thronged with merchants, trucks, shoppers, and all the signs of a boom economy. As the song says: "They don't call it Constantinople anymore." The breakup of the Soviet empire is also a giant plus for Turkey, as it is a lot easier to deal with the fragmented republics—many of which are historically related to the Turks—than dealing with the Russian bear.

Turkish Wet Towels

The Kurds will likely continue their 2,000-year war with the Turks by launching their annual spring offensive. The Turks have always been able to handle it, but it gets expensive. That may be one of the reasons the Turkish lira was devalued by 12 percent on January 26, 1994, the very day this chart was pulled. Inflation is currently running at 65 percent. Meanwhile, back at the Black Sea, the Crimea wants independence from the Ukraine and is supported by Russia. The Ukraine's eastern provinces

Figure 4-18 The Turkish Investment Fund

are largely Russian as well and also want out. If this leads to fighting, it would certainly affect Turkey since all of those places are important markets for them. And then there's Greece, which has been at odds with Turkey since the Trojan War.

One of the odd things about the Turkish Fund is that the shares sold at a marked discount when the fund was doing well and a big premium as it continued to decline steadily. This defies logic, as Mr. Spock would say. Even now—as of the last statement date—the Turkish Fund still sells at a discount to net asset value. Doesn't anybody like a winner? Major holdings of the fund include Goodyear Lartik, Dogan Sirketler (autos and insurance), Finans Bank, Mardin Cimento, and Turk Tubourg.

United Kingdom Fund

Last but not least, we arrive in the U.K., as represented by the United Kingdom Fund, shown in Figure 4-19. The index to pay attention to is the FTSE 100, which stands for Financial Times Stock Exchange top 100 index and is called the "Footsie" in the investment trade. (The Toronto Stock Exchange 100 index for Canadian stocks is called the "Tootsie.")

Alas, the London Stock Exchange is still Europe's biggest, and the British lion still can roar. The United Kingdom Fund has sold at a discount, usually a deep discount, through all of its history. Part of the reason is that British shares are so openly traded and so available through brokers here that there is little need for a fund. In looking at the chart,

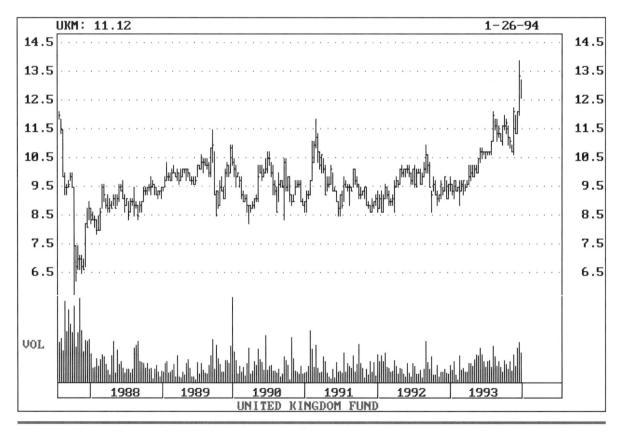

Figure 4-19 The United Kingdom Fund

however, it's worth noting the fund has consistently bottomed around $8.50 for many years and topped around $11. The fact that it has recently gone well above that mark would seem to indicate management has gotten a handle on better performance or simply that the British are doing well. Major holdings include the usual: General Electric of the U.K., Cadbury-Schweppes, BAT (tobacco), Unilever, Glaxo, British Airways, Lucas, etc.

Since we're here in the United Kingdom, let's pick up the Southampton train at Victoria Station and catch the P&O (Pacific and Orient Lines) steamer to the mysterious Orient. Of course they think of us as the mysterious Occident. Remember when you buy your steamer ticket to specify you want "POSH," which has become synonymous with luxury but really is a direction to the chief steward to see that your deck chair is placed on the port side of the ship when outbound (towards Asia), and the starboard side on the way home. That's how you get the best sun.

CHAPTER 5

ACROSS THE PACIFIC

Every investment has risk, but those in foreign lands always generate high anxiety. Just remember what Arnold Schwarzenegger told you: "no pain, no gain." *The Economist* has a country risk rating they publish every few weeks. It ranks the risk of investing in any country based on its political situation, national debt, currency stability, current wars, or no current wars. The ratings go from zero risk to 100 percent. Iraq is 100 percent. Countries like the U.S., England, Germany, and France, by the way, have risks so low they never make it into the top 20. (It's okay—it's not a list you want to be on.)

Iraq has held the number one position for a couple of years, so you might call them the benchmark risk; anything else is practically plain sailing. Well, not quite. The second highest risk, at about 95 percent, is Russia. That's surprising, because every once in a while I read an article or interview that extols the virtues of investing in Russia. No thanks. Then there are the Ivory Coast, Kenya, Brazil, Nigeria, Poland, Venezuela, Argentina, and India. Notice that India is the only Asian country in the top 10 high risks, which is interesting because people here generally think of Asia as just about the riskiest place to put your money.

Most people I know shudder at the thought of investing in Hong Kong or Taiwan, yet the risk of both is placed well below that of investing in mainland China, and far, far below the risk of investing in neighboring Mexico. It must be because you can never get a cab in Hong Kong. A country's risk rating would not determine whether or not I chose to invest there, but it would be a factor to consider. The prudent policy would probably be to have some money in the high risk countries—to pick up the gain if things go well—and some in safer havens.

Table 5-1 presents a rough look at the country risk ratings from *The Economist*. The numbers are only approximate; any attempt to get more precise would be statistically unsound—as when people collect information rounded to the nearest unit or ten and then try to print results that provide decimal positioning. You see this a lot, and it is mathematical nonsense.

Funds spread the risk, of course, and closed-end funds give us the opportunity to pick our countries, and call our shots. As we look at these, keep this in mind, as Count Korzybski used to say: "The map is not the territory; the name of the place is not the place itself." The Count was a semanticist, but his point is well taken. Put into our context, it means that just because something is called the China Fund doesn't necessarily mean that it invests in China. After all, the whole Shanghai stock exchange is something like two dozen stocks, and they don't let foreigners buy anyway. So China funds usually invest in Hong Kong companies, many of which have investments or silent partners in mainland China. You can get a list of the holdings of any fund through online services by looking up their quarterly reports or calling up Disclosure, a service that lists information that must be filed with the SEC (Securities and Exchange Commission).

Remember that an awful lot of money is chasing a small number of shares. Many of these countries don't understand what an American

COUNTRY	RISK RATING	COUNTRY	RISK RATING
Iraq	100	South Africa	50
Russia	95	Israel	40
Brazil	70	Indonesia	40
Nigeria	70	Thailand	30
Poland	60	China	30
Venezuela	60	Chile	30
Argentina	55	Czech Republic	25
Philippines	55	Malaysia	25
Turkey	55	South Korea	22
India	50	Hong Kong	15
Greece	50	Portugal	15
Hungary	50	Taiwan	12

Table 5-1   Country Risk Ratings (*The Economist*)

mutual fund is like or can do. Drop $200 million into some of these markets, which many funds can do, and you don't just own some shares, you own every company on the exchange. With these caveats in mind, let's check out the action, as they say down at the old malt shop.

note

For an explanation of closed-end funds, see the beginning of Chapter 4.

Asia Pacific Fund

The Asia Pacific Fund, shown in Figure 5-1, shows the familiar spike (seen in most of the funds presented in Chapter 4) around the end of 1989 and the beginning of 1990, when the Soviet Union collapsed and the New World Order began. After a while, of course, it looked a lot like the old world order, only with more players and more gunfire. While shares quadrupled from the end of 1987 to the end of 1989, the fund sold

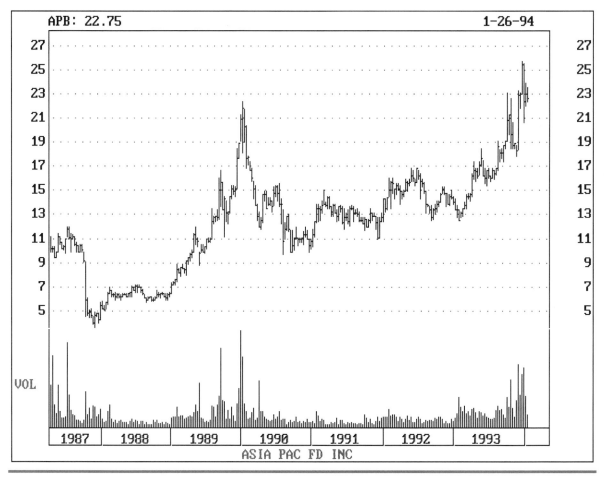

APB: 22.75   1-26-94

ASIA PAC FD INC

Figure 5-1   The Asia Pacific Fund

at a huge discount almost every step of the way. Hard to believe, but nonetheless true. Now the fund sells at a huge premium of nearly 25 percent over net asset value.

The fund is invested in Hong Kong, Malaysia, Singapore, Thailand, and Korea, in that order. Major holdings include Hutchison Whampoa, Thai Farmers Bank, Cheung Kong Holdings, Wharf Holdings, China Light & Power, Swire Pacific, Hong Kong Land, Siam Cement, and Korea Electric Power. If you look at the graph of Asia Pacific, you can see that even though it has hit some air pockets along the way, overall it has been a steady flier. It has an annualized 26 percent rate of return over the past five years and has consistently outperformed the Morgan Stanley benchmark index of Asian stocks. The big premium on the share price must give anyone pause right now. Once again, a premium isn't necessarily anything to worry about until it gets to be very rich; this one is very rich. It might be partially caused by the fact that the fund has filed a registration with the SEC that it intends to make a rights offering. Rights—the right to buy more shares—are a feature of closed-end funds, not regular open-ended mutual funds. Since they typically give shareholders the right to buy more shares at a slight discount to net asset value, they could be viewed as an opportunity to make a quick profit by selling the rights.

China Fund

You gotta admit, a fund named simply "China", shown in Figure 5-2, gets right to the point. Unlike the recent rush of new China funds, this one has been around for a couple of years, and those who bought in early doubled their money. Major holdings include Hutchison Whampoa, China Light & Power, Cheung Kong Holdings, China Travel, Hung Hing Printing, Guangdong Investments, Hong Kong Telecommunications, Bank of East Asia, and Guangzhou Investments. A practiced eye will notice that the investments are almost all in Hong Kong, not China. The names Guangdong Investments and Guangzhou Investments are interesting because those are both the names of the provinces of China closest to Hong Kong and Taiwan, the ones where so much money has been pouring in from investment by the so-called "Overseas Chinese." That doesn't mean those investment companies are in those provinces—in fact, they are in Hong Kong—but it certainly indicates that they want the world to know they have or are obtaining a financial interest in the developments on the mainland.

The China Fund sells at a sharp premium to NAV (net asset value), currently over 10 percent, and yet has under-performed the Morgan Stanley benchmark index by a considerable amount—more than 20 percent. About 30 percent of its portfolio is in cash. That is very high by mutual fund standards, and while it hurts the potential return in a bull market, it provides a cushion against a declining market. One of the

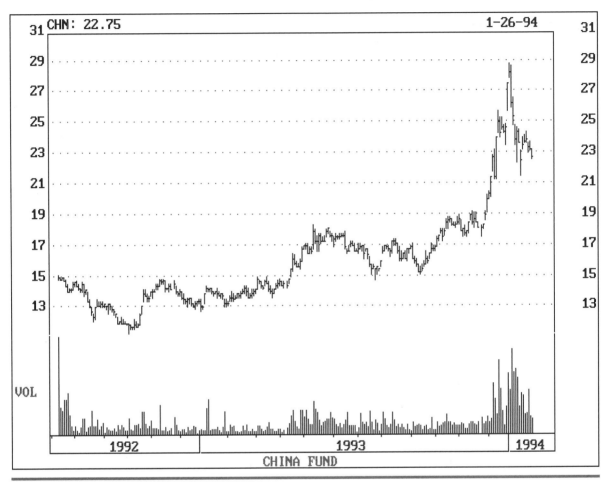

Figure 5-2 The China Fund

advantages of investing in Hong Kong stocks, or funds that do that for you, is the currency risk is minimized. The Hong Kong dollar is pegged to the U.S. dollar at a formula that works out very close to $8 H.K. to $1 U.S. The currencies move in almost complete lock-step, and neither a rise nor a decline in the value of the dollar will affect your investment. Taiwan and Singapore also peg their currencies to the dollar.

First Australia Fund

Yes, I know that Australia is technically not part of Asia and is its own continent, but by gorry, mate, it is close. Except for brief spasms of enthusiasm for all things Aussie—like Vegamite—the First Australian Fund, shown in Figure 5-3, has always sold at a discount, sometimes as much as 30 percent below NAV. If you had sold on the two occasions when the fund went to a premium, you would have been wise, because it was all downhill from there. That situation has arisen again, by the way.

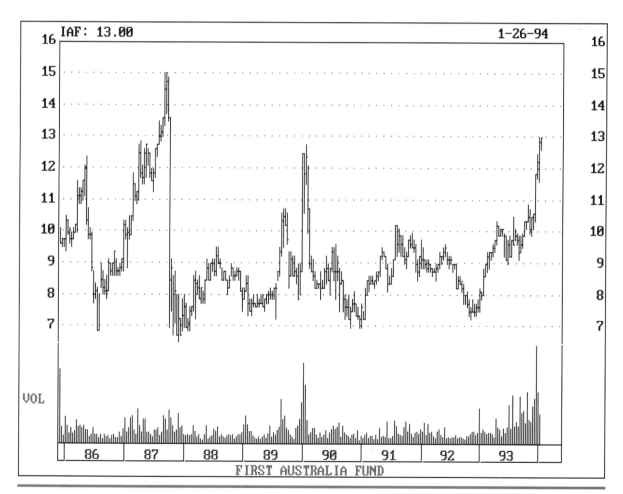

Figure 5-3   The First Australia Fund

The First Australian Fund has a fairly long history for country funds, and if you look closely at the graph of its performance, you will note that it has been as regular as a patient on a laxative program. It has bottomed consistently at $7 a share or a little over and provided handsome profits for investors patient enough to wait a couple of years until the next general election.

The fund is entirely invested in Australia, and its current holdings are mostly in mining and banking. Major investments include Broken Hill Proprietary, National Australia Bank, Western Mining, Salvage Resources, Advance Bank, Pancontinental Mining, St. George Bank, Samantha Gold, Newcrest Mining, etc. A weak Australian dollar is a risk built into the fund.

First Philippine Fund

In the last three years, you could have made 80 times your money in Philippine Long Distance, the phone company, or tripled your money in the First Philippine Fund, shown in Figure 5-4. Your choice. Except for the first few months of its existence, First Philippine has always sold at a discount. That may be changing even as this is written; check your local listings, as they say.

All of the fund's investments are in the Philippines, except for a small cash reserve in U.S. Treasuries. Major holdings include Philippine Long Distance (15 percent of the fund), San Miguel beer (another 15 percent), the Manila Electric Co., Far East Bank & Trust, Republic Flour, and Grand Plaza Hotel. The *Morningstar Mutual Fund* newsletter notes that many Philippine companies have installed their own generators and are thus able to keep operating when the power goes out, which is often.

Greater China Fund

Greater China Fund, shown in Figure 5-5, has produced a double in its two years of existence, very nice but not stunning by Asian market standards. Like all China funds, nearly all of its holdings are in Hong Kong. It also has investments in Korea and the U.S. The portfolio includes the usual suspects: China Light & Power, Hutchison Whampoa, Wharf Holdings, and New World Development. The fund has sold at a premium since the middle of 1993, when its biggest rise began.

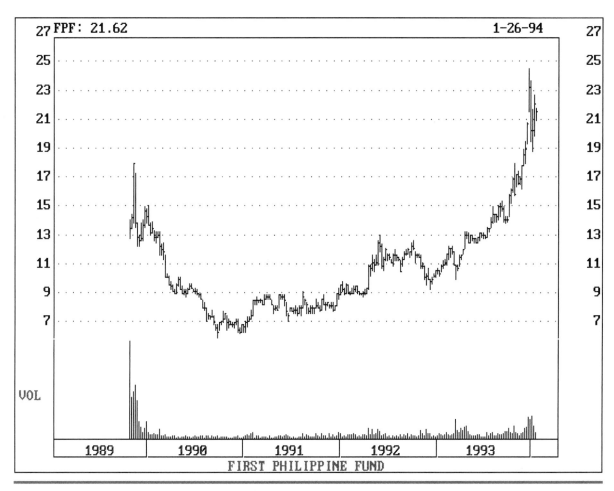

Figure 5-4   The First Philippine Fund

India Growth Fund

The India Growth Fund, shown in Figure 5-6, is entirely invested in India, a gutsy play for an economy with a meager 1.5 percent growth rate. In the U.S. they call that a recession. Government reforms, which have been attempted many times before, are being tried again. Individual foreigners are not allowed to buy stock in Indian companies, and Indians won't buy local new issues unless offered at a discount of 20 percent or

Figure 5-5   The Greater China Fund

more to the market price. The response has been that many Indian companies are offering secondary distributions in London and other European capitals, where investors will not only pay market price, but often will pay a premium to market. Ah, the mysterious Occident.

The price-to-earnings ratio (p/e) on the Indian stock market (the "Sensex") is an average 48-1; stock in some of the larger Indian corpora-

Figure 5-6   The India Growth Fund

tions is selling at more than 100-1. Yum, I can't wait to get in. Despite these numbers, the gain on the India Growth Fund from low to high in 1993 was about 150 percent. A similar run-up occurred from mid-1991 to early 1992. Major holdings include Century Textiles, Colgate Palmolive (of India), Great Eastern Shipping, Tata Tea, Hindustan Lever, and Asian Paints. The fund currently sells at a huge premium to NAV.

Indonesia Fund

Indonesia is the world's fifth largest country by population. Despite the country's size, the Indonesia Fund, shown in Figure 5-7, has languished in the doldrums for most of its existence—and sold at a premium almost all the time. Lift-off finally occurred in mid-1993, and those who got in a lot earlier than that—or went into a coma during the dry years—had a joyride of 150 percent.

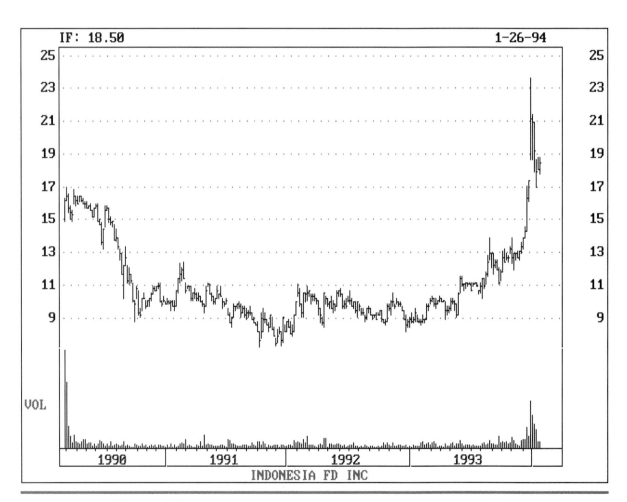

Figure 5-7 The Indonesia Fund

Most of the fund's investments, about 70 percent, are in Indonesia, with other holdings in Turkey, Pakistan, the Philippines, and Thailand. A sizable portion of the fund is held in cash in the U.S. The fund has not been able to perform as well as the Indonesian market as a whole for several quarters. Major holdings include Hadtex Indosyntex, Kalbe Farma, Pakuwon Jati, Neta Telokomunika, and the Pakistan Growth Fund.

Jakarta Growth Fund

If you didn't like it in the Indonesian countryside, maybe you'll like it better in the capital. The Jakarta Growth Fund, shown in Figure 5-8, went nuts in 1990 as it contemplated the New World Order, then slid precipitously. It bumped along a bottom of $6.50 a share for a couple of years before producing a double in 1993. Except for a small cash reserve in the U.S., the fund is invested entirely in Indonesia. It has generally sold at a premium of 10 to 12 percent over NAV and only recently justified that extra charge. The largest holding is HM Sampoerna, the largest local cigarette maker, followed by Kalbe Farma, a large Indonesian pharmaceutical company.

Japan Equity Fund

There are few things quite as exciting as ride on the Nikkei roller coaster. The Japan Equity Fund, shown in Figure 5-9, has always sold at a discount, usually of around 10 percent below NAV. If you were a chartist, you would call the early 1994 topping formation at around $15 a nearly perfect head and shoulders formation. I am not a chartist and so I call it spinach and will await developments.

Except for a small amount of cash in the U.S., the fund is entirely invested in Japanese stocks. Major holdings include Daichi, Nissan Motor, Tokyo Broadcasting, Fujitsu, Noritz, Mineba, and Sumitomo Realty. It's rather amazing that the fund sells at a discount, considering it had about a 60 percent return in 1993.

Japan OTC Equity Fund

The Japan OTC (Over the Counter) Fund, shown in Figure 5-10, has all its assets in Japanese stocks and cash equivalents and a portfolio

Figure 5-8   The Jakarta Growth Fund

that leans toward retailers. The total return in 1993 was better than 50 percent, and the major holdings include Paltac (cosmetics), Nippon Kanzai, Sekiwa Real Estate, Nishio Rent-All, Fuji Software, and Canon Copier Sales.

   Despite its fine performance in early 1994, the fund sells at a discount. The Japan OTC is essentially a bet on the Japanese market; if it does well, the fund will do well. This is the beauty of a closed-end fund: if you like Japan's prospects, it's a simple way to play the country.

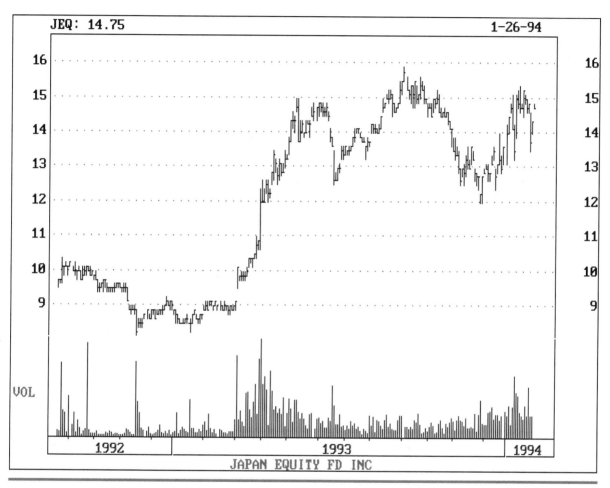

Figure 5-9   The Japan Equity Fund

Jardine Fleming China Fund

The Jardine Fleming China Fund, shown in Figure 5-11, is one of the best of the new China funds, and it has gone steadily upward almost without a hesitation since shortly after it began. One of its advantages is that Jardine Fleming, from whom the fund gets its name, is a leading Hong Kong investment house, and they certainly know the territory. The fund's assets are invested primarily in Hong Kong, with some substantial hold-

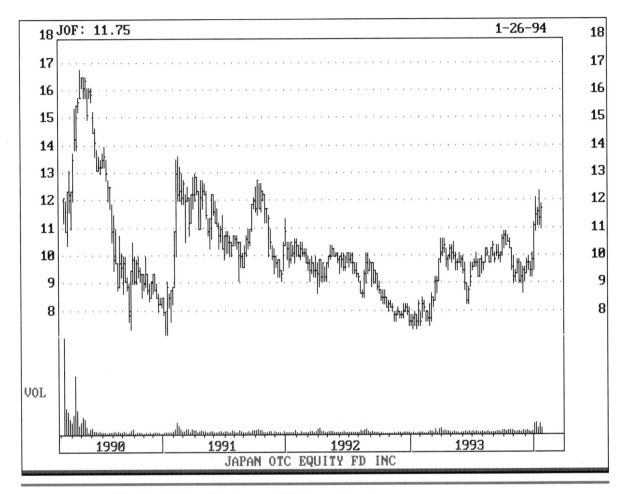

Figure 5-10 The Japan OTC Equity Fund

ings in Korea and Australia and a sizable chunk of cash in the U.S. Its exposure in China proper is minimal.

Major holdings include Television Broadcasts Ltd., Hutchison Whampoa, Dairy Farm International, Champion Technology, and Giordano Holdings. Total return for 1993 was a very satisfying 80 percent. The fund sells for around a 10 percent premium to NAV.

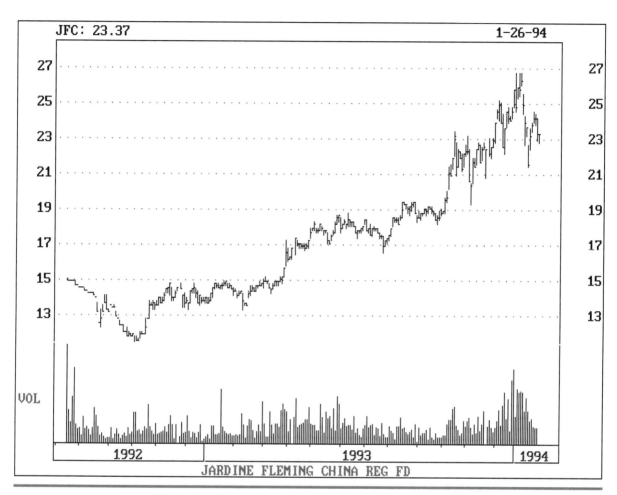

Figure 5-11   The Jardine Fleming China Fund

Korea Fund

The Korea Fund, shown in Figure 5-12, has always sold at a premium. In fact, government officials have let it be known that they would consider it an insult to the nation and its people should the fund fail to sell for a premium. So take that!

From the fund's inception in late 1984 to its high point five years later, the premium was certainly worth it, as you would have made five

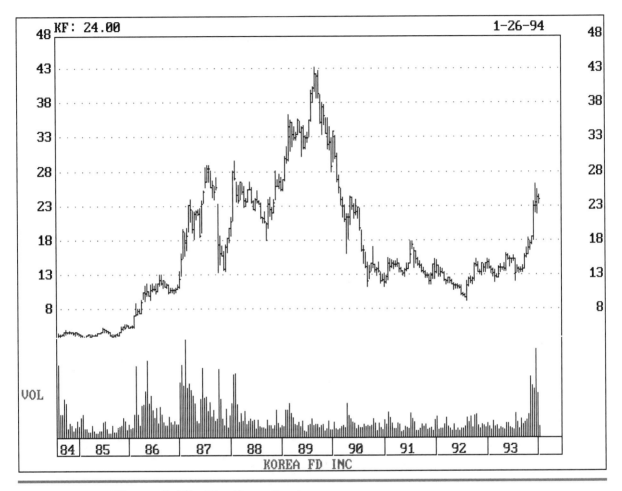

Figure 5-12   The Korea Fund

times your money. Too bad you didn't sell then, because in the following year you would have had a thumping 70 percent loss. Still, the fund sold at a premium all the way down.

All of the fund's assets are invested in Korea, where major holdings include Samsung, Korean Telecom, Korea Credit, Cheil Foods, and Hyundai Motor Services. The fund has had a couple of very lean years and only recently moved up toward the end of 1993. If you like Korea, you'll like this fund.

Malaysia Fund

When you're hot, you're hot, and few places have been hotter than Malaysia the last few years. Despite a fairly steady rise from a low of five to a high of 30, the Malaysia Fund, shown in Figure 5-13, has almost always sold at a discount. The exception was a sudden jump to a high premium during the New World Order—you can see the spike on the chart.

The fund is 100 percent invested in Malaysia. Major holdings include Telekom Malaysia, Genting, Resorts World, Tanjong, Tenaga National,

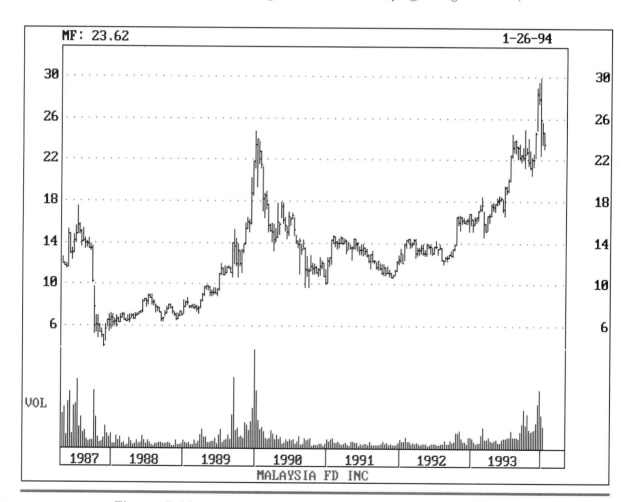

Figure 5-13 The Malaysia Fund

Malay Banking, and Malaysian Shipping. The fund returned close to 100 percent in 1993. The odds of a repeat are slim.

R.O.C. Taiwan Fund

The "R.O.C." stands for Republic of China, which, since there already is a China, and that China has indicated that it is annoyed by other places calling themselves China, tends to downplay its name by using initials. It's been a bumpy ride for the R.O.C. Taiwan Fund, shown in Figure 5-14,

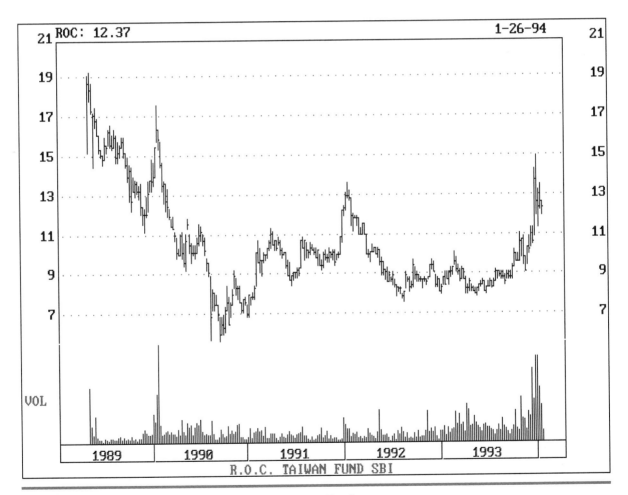

Figure 5-14   The R.O.C. Taiwan Fund

a near 70 percent loss in its first 18 months, a 100 percent gain in the next 18, and a 50 percent loss in the six months after that. Are we having fun yet? The latest rise has been about 80 percent in 1993. Will it continue? Will anyone have enough time to catch their breath to find out?

Major holdings of the fund include Teco Electric, President Enterprises, CMC Magnetics, Asia Cement, Yungtay Engineering, China Motor, and Formosa Plastics. The fund is mostly in cash.

Scudder New Asia Fund

Most of the holders of the Scudder New Asia Fund, shown in Figure 5-15, must have thought they'd gone into cryogenic sleep during the three years before 1993, but at least the fund didn't have any of those heart-stopping drops many other country funds experienced. Eventually virtue, or sheer inertia, was rewarded, and Scudder New Asia had a better than 100 percent return in 1993. That was a happy time, and brought the fund to a premium of NAV; previously it had often sold for a 25-30 percent discount.

Country holdings by order of importance include Japan, Hong Kong, Thailand, Malaysia, Korea, and a bag of cash in the U.S. Major stock holdings include Freeport-McMoRan (copper and gold), Thai Farmers Bank, Sembawang Shipyards, Henderson Land Development, Kalbe Farma, India Fund, and China Light & Power.

Singapore Fund

How can you not like a place where people are ordered where to live depending on their income level? For most of its existence, owning the Singapore Fund, shown in Figure 5-16, was a lot like watching grass grow. If you bought whenever it hit 9-1/8 and sold at 11, you could have made some modest gains. But in early January of 1993, someone came along and injected high octane in their gas buggy. The resulting rubber peel produced a gain of 150 percent if you got out at the top. Of course, no one ever gets out at the top.

As you can see, the fund, which sold at a well-deserved discount for most of its existence, is selling at a premium in early 1994. Assets are invested primarily in Singapore, with about 20 percent in Malaysia. The Singapore government lowered both personal and corporate taxes in

SAF: 25.37   1-26-94

SCUDDER NEW ASIA FD INC

Figure 5-15   The Scudder New Asia Fund

1993, which is almost always good for an economy. That boost could last for a while.

Major holdings include Singapore Press, Natsteel, Singapore Airlines, Sembawang Shipyards, Overseas Union Bank, Overseas Chinese Bank, Singapore Petroleum, and Rothman Industries.

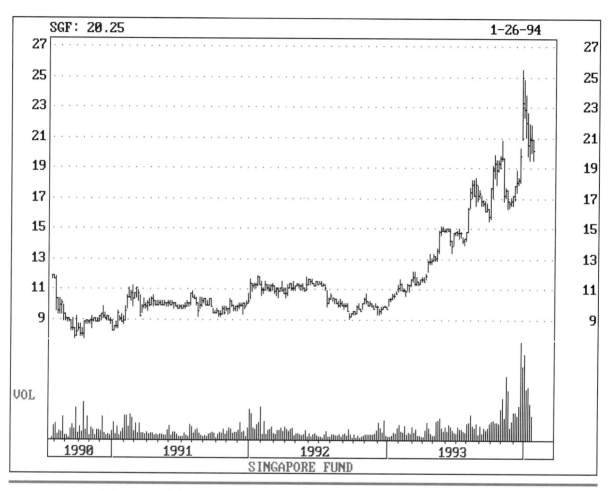

Figure 5-16 The Singapore Fund

Taiwan Fund

After proving for the third time that $17 a share really was the bottom for the Taiwan Fund, shown in Figure 5-17, it began a rise that would have brought you a 100 percent return in 1993 if you caught it just right. The fund has often sold at outrageous premiums—at one time of more than 100 percent over NAV. The premium of around 20 percent at the end of 1993 was low by the historical standards of the fund.

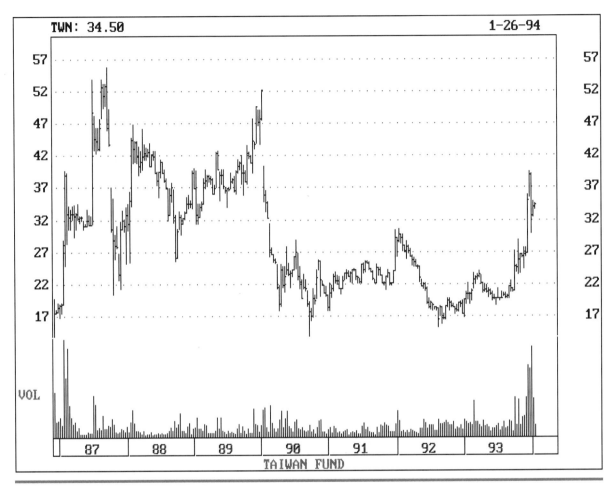

Figure 5-17 The Taiwan Fund

Their major holdings include First Commercial Bank, Chang Hwa Commercial Bank, Hwa Nan Commercial Bank, Teco Electric, and Cheng Shin Rubber.

Thai Fund

The Thai Fund, shown in Figure 5-18, is entirely invested in Thailand, with a small cash holding in the U.S. It bottomed decisively at $14

Figure 5-18 The Thai Fund

in 1992 and began a rise which carried it to a high of $37 a share at the end of 1993. In all, it ranked as one of the best performing funds in the world. The prospects of this continuing are uncertain, but the fact that selling came in at the same high level where the fund had sold in the last mad rush is not encouraging. Management has done very well to date, however. Major holdings are Bangkok Bank, Thai Farmers Bank, Siam Commercial Bank, Siam Cement, International Cosmetics, and Land &

House. At periods of peak enthusiasm and price, the fund has sold at a more than 70 percent premium.

Thai Capital Fund

We finish our Asian tour with a rousing ride on the Thai Capital Fund, shown in Figure 5-19. If you had the nerve to buy at the 1992 low, where the fund had been bottoming for a long time, the subsequent rise was 300 percent over 18 months. The fund has almost always sold at a

Figure 5-19 The Thai Capital Fund

discount and now, in early 1994, sells at a premium much less than would be expected from its recent performance. All its investments are in Thailand, including any cash positions, and major holdings include Bangkok Bank, Thai Farmers Bank, Siam Commercial Bank, Thai Military Bank, Siam Cement, Land & House, and Krung Thai Bank.

At this point we can cash in the return half of our steamer ticket on P&O and buy an airline ticket to Buenos Aires so we can start our Latin American tour. Try and book on Singapore Airlines if you can; they're the best.

CHAPTER 6

SOUTH OF THE BORDER

We'll continue our global tour with Latin America, where the food and rhythms are hot, and likewise, stock markets are volatile.

Things are looking good now. But it's worth remembering that Mexico, Argentina, and Brazil, whose markets represent the vast bulk of investment opportunities in Latin America, all rank very high on *The Economist* magazine's list of risky countries (see Table 5-1 in Chapter 5). Civil strife is an enduring part of the region's history. Medellin, Colombia, for example, is the most dangerous city in the world in terms of risk from violent death or injury—which is the way most people count their dangerous places. In number and frequency of incidents it ranks just ahead of the second most dangerous city. Beirut? Guess again. The second most dangerous city in the world is Washington, D.C.

The promise of Brazil is eternal, and has been that way for roughly the same amount of time. When I was a lad, I would sometimes see articles in the daily and magazine press extolling the future of Brazil, quote, an untapped wilderness, unquote. As the years went by, I saw many more such articles. Still later, in the course of doing research on other topics, I would come across old clippings and articles from the turn of the century, which noted that Brazil was, quote, an untapped wilderness, unquote. It's been a long wait. And it may be a while yet. The *Wall Street Journal* noted in a front page article last year that when the governor of one of the western provinces was accused by a well-known citizen of taking bribes, the governor's response was to walk up to the man in a restaurant and shoot him in the head. The *Journal* noted that what was particularly significant about this action was the response of the nation's newspaper and broadcasting press, which praised the governor's actions as demonstrating his manly sense of honor. As they say in the astronaut trade, "Houston, we may have a problem here."

That said, let us turn first to Argentina, a country that has hardly ever had any internal dissension or trouble with other nations. At least, not for several months.

Argentina Fund

Figure 6-1 is a kind of close-up of the Argentina Fund, showing roughly one year. That's about half the fund's existence and it shows that through the first part of 1993 you might have thought the phone was disconnected or everybody in Argentina had stopped breathing. But round about mid-summer, there were some stirrings, and the rest of the year certainly made somebody's day, so to speak.

The Argentina Fund is about 80 percent invested in Argentina and the rest in the U.S., either in cash or close to it. Except for brief moments here and there, the fund has almost always sold at a huge premium, sometimes 30 percent or more over net asset value. Major holdings include Quilmes Industrial, Nortel Inversora, Baesa, Naviera Perez, Telefonica de Argentina, YPF, Molinos Rio de la Plata, and Banco Frances Rio Plata.

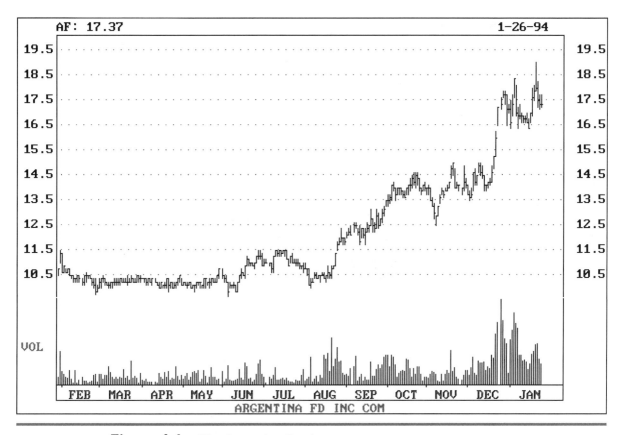

Figure 6-1 The Argentina Fund

YPF is a huge corporation that essentially controls all the country's oil and gas. It was recently listed as an ADR (American Depository Receipt) on the New York Stock Exchange, so you can buy it directly any time the fancy strikes you.

Brazil Fund

The Brazil Fund, shown in Figure 6-2, is totally invested in Brazil. It has historically been a conservative fund, with many long-term holdings. Some of these were long-term through necessity, not choice, since there were almost no buyers. The fund has nearly six years of history, so looking at the chart has some instructive benefits. One is that the fund bottomed twice at just below $8 a share and lifted off nicely from there. Another thing we can notice is that, except for one year, the fund has always hit its low around the turn of the new year and gone up sharply over the next few months. The exception was the beginning of 1990 when it declined.

Despite this regularity and a fairly long track record, the Brazil Fund has almost always sold at a discount. In 1988 and 1989, the discount was close to 50 percent below NAV (net asset value), and if you thought that made the fund an especially good deal, you would have been wrong, because the fund lost about half its value in 1990. Major holdings in 1993 included Telebras, Petrobras, Banco Itau, Souza Cruz Industria, Vale do Rio Doce, Telecom Sao Paulo, White Martins, and Sadia Concordia.

Figure 6-2   The Brazil Fund

Brazilian Equity Fund

The Brazilian Equity Fund, shown in Figure 6-3, is a relatively new entrant dedicated to attracting your money. Despite its youth, it already exhibits the tendency of Brazilian funds—and most Latin American funds, for that matter—to jump sharply at the beginning of the new year. The fund is invested almost entirely in Brazil, with some cash reserves in the U.S. When things were going bad, shortly after its founding until the end of 1992, the fund sold at a big premium. Ever since things started going well—from the beginning of 1993 on—the fund has sold at a big discount, but it moved to a premium early in 1994.

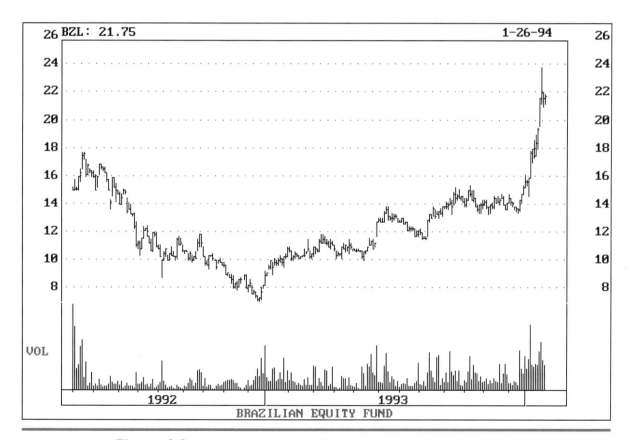

Figure 6-3   The Brazilian Equity Fund

Brazilian Equity is a more aggressive fund than the older Brazil Fund. It moves faster when things are good, and unfortunately it moves faster when things are bad. Currently, things are good. Major holdings include Telebras PN, Bradesco, Telebras ON, Souza Cruz Industria, Usiminas, Lojas Americanas, Bombril, and Cemex. It should be noted that inflation has been a continuing problem for Brazil and so affects dollar investments. "Continuing problem" hardly covers the matter, in fact, as Brazil is annually a world leader in inflation.

Chile Fund

A look at the chart of the Chile Fund, shown in Figure 6-4, shows again the eerie tendency of the Latin American markets to hit their lows at or just before the end of the year and then rise sharply at the beginning of the new year. If you failed to buy in December 1993, you missed out on a big gain again. All in all, the Chile Fund has been a stellar performer, which, despite its nearly four-fold rise in three years, has almost always sold at a discount.

Major holdings of the fund include Telefonos de Chile, Endesa de Chile, Enersis, Copec de Chile, Cartones, Chilectra, and Cervezas. A whopping 54 percent of the fund's investments were in utilities last year, and another quarter in industrial cyclicals—metals, heavy manufacturing, etc.

Emerging Mexico Fund

The Emerging Mexico Fund, shown in Figure 6-5, has never had a down year, and yet it has almost always sold at a discount to NAV. The passage of NAFTA gave a big boost to the Mexican stock market, and betting that Clinton would pull it off and the treaty would pass would have netted you a nifty 100 percent return in six months. Mexico remains high on the *Economist* list of risky countries, and it would surprise many people here that Mexico is ranked as a higher risk investment than South Africa. The fund is heavily weighted in financial stocks, industrial cyclicals, and retailers. Major holdings include Telefonos de Mexico, Cifra, Kimberly Clark de Mexico, Grupo Carso, Cemex, Grupo Financerio Banamex, and Grupo Industrial Bimbo.

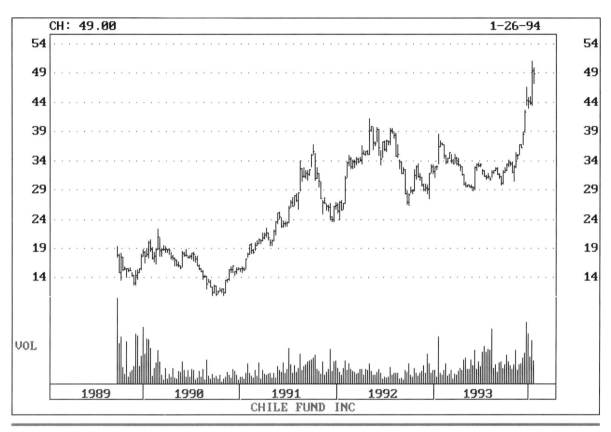

Figure 6-4   The Chile Fund

Latin American Equity Fund

The Latin American Equity Fund, shown in Figure 6-6, invests in Mexico, Brazil, Chile, Argentina, Peru, and the U.S., in that order. The U.S. portion is only cash or equivalents. The fund has always sold at a discount in its short history and had a terrific rise in 1993—more than doubling from low to high. Perceptive investors would have noticed that the fund bottomed just below $13 three times and that seemed to be a baseline. It was mainly invested in cyclicals, utilities, and consumer staples during 1993. Major holdings included Telefonos de Mexico, Telebras PN, Grupo Carso, Cemex, YPF, Masisa, Cifra, and Grupo Televisa.

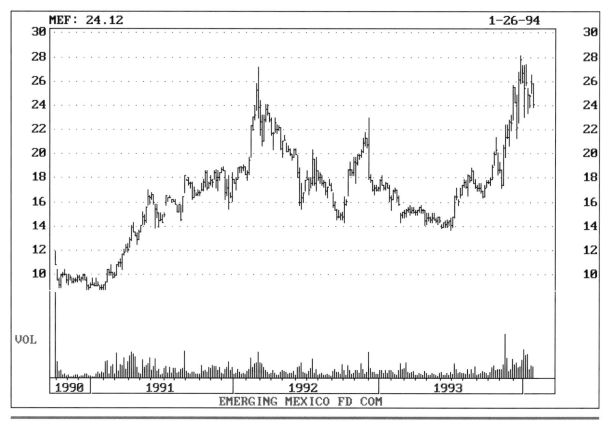

Figure 6-5 The Emerging Mexico Fund

Latin American Discovery Fund

The Latin American Discovery Fund, shown in Figure 6-7, was one of the best performing funds in the world in 1993, and easily tops the Latin American list. It has been a remarkably steady rise, becoming bumpy only at the end of 1993. Despite this absolutely outstanding performance, the fund still sold at a discount at the end of the year. Major holdings included Telebras, Boston Financial Fund, Telefonos de Mexico, Grupo Financerio Bancomer, Sidek, and Cemex.

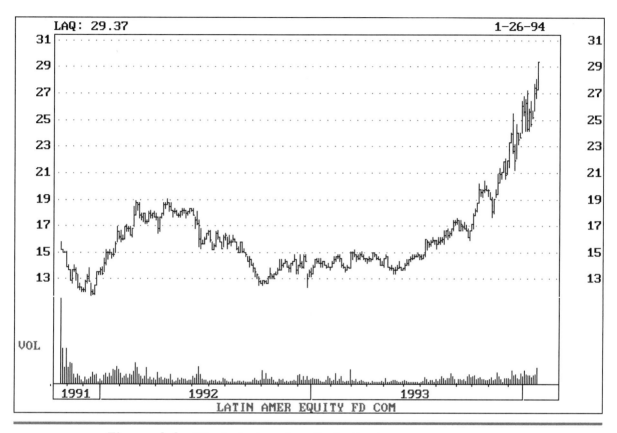

LAQ: 29.37   1-26-94

LATIN AMER EQUITY FD COM

Figure 6-6   The Latin American Equity Fund

Latin American Investment Fund

The Latin American Investment Fund, shown in Figure 6-8, has not been a star performer as these things go, at least not compared to most other Latin funds, but it certainly has been a good performer. Investors who bought early—at $10 a share or less—doubled their money in the next year, then rode flat for a year, and came close to doubling again in 1993. Major holdings include Telebras PN, Grupo Carso, Telefonos de Mexico, YPF, and Cemex. The fund has always sold at a discount—until 1994, that is. The fact that it shifted to selling at a 12 percent premium early in 1994 indicates awfully good prospects ahead or...that the South American equities market is getting a bit overheated.

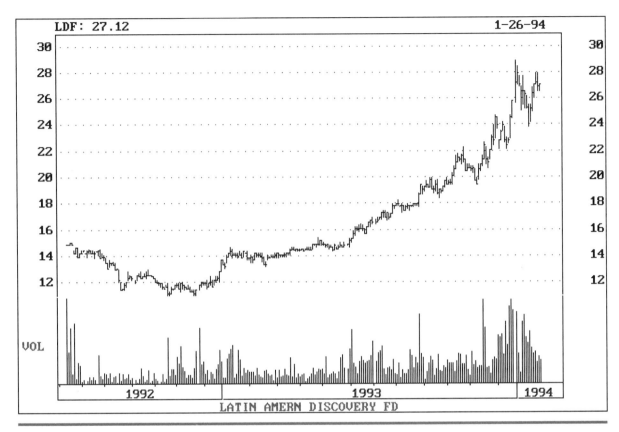

Figure 6-7   The Latin American Discovery Fund

Mexico Fund

The Mexico Fund, shown in Figure 6-9, is one of the oldest international funds and certainly the oldest of the Latin American funds. If you look at the time scale at the very bottom of the figure, you will see the chart extends through most of the 1980s and into the present; it was started in 1982. The Mexico Fund is also one the largest funds, with assets that at current prices stretch well over $1 billion.

Except for 1983 and the last few months of 1982, the fund has always sold at a discount to net asset value. Twice during the 1980s, you could have bought shares for $2. Once you would have been buying at a premium, another time at a discount. It made no difference, because your best strategy at either point would have been to go into a coma and recover on the beach at Cozumel last winter, rich and retired.

The Mexico fund is 100 percent invested in Mexico, and who can argue with that strategy? Many people have, maintaining that the fund management has been too conservative over the years. In fact, the fund has usually under-performed the Morgan Stanley Mexico Index, but most funds under-perform their index. Bursts of buying like we saw in 1993 have usually indicated tops in the fund's price for a while; some people like to time their purchases, some don't. Major holdings at the end of 1993 included Cifra, Cemex, Kimberly-Clark, Telefonos de Mexico, Apasco, Grupo Carso, and Grupo Financerio Banamex. The fund is

Figure 6-8   The Latin American Investment Fund

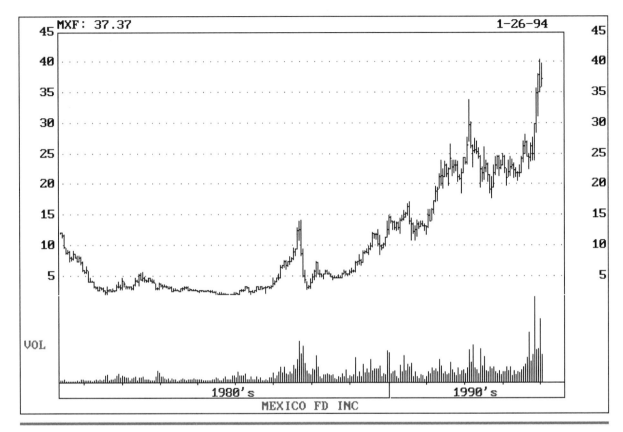

Figure 6-9 The Mexico Fund

overwhelmingly invested in cyclicals and retail stocks. Two more sectors, financials and consumer staples, make up the rest, with less than 2 percent in all other sectors combined.

Mexico Equity and Income Fund

After bottoming twice around $9 a share, the Mexico Equity and Income Fund, shown in Figure 6-10, moved up steadily over the last three years to hit a high of $27 at the end of 1993. It displays a weak pattern of bottoming action sometime in the last couple of months of each year.

Except for a hiccup at the beginning of 1992, the fund has always sold at a discount, often a steep one of 15 or 20 percent below NAV. This changed this year, the fund selling at a premium for the first time ever. Is that a signal or what? Cyclicals and retail stocks represented 85 percent of the stock portfolio at the end of 1993. Major holdings included Cifra, Kimberly-Clark, Telefonos de Mexico, Apasco, Industrias Penoles, Grupo Bimbo, and Cemex.

The Mexico Equity and Income Fund has followed its title and generally used bonds and preferred stock to generate income for its holders. The yield at the end of 1993 was around 4 percent, nothing to write home about but useful to some investors. Like the other Mexico funds, when you buy this you are essentially making a bet on Mexico.

Figure 6-10   The Mexico Equity and Income Fund

Enough of this racing around. Let's leave Mexico City, reputed to have the highest pollution level in the world, and move down to the playa, where we'll lean back on the sand and contemplate the wider world presented in the next chapter.

CHAPTER 7

NEW LANDS AND LOOKS

As with any effort at categorization, there are some things that don't fit. This will be a brief look at other overseas investment opportunities that didn't fit naturally in the previous three chapters.

Even these are by no means the end of ways to approach investing in foreign securities, and perhaps looking at this last group of closed-end funds should also tell you something about the limitations of this book or any book like it. And this is primarily that it is a rapidly changing world. The Israel Fund is here, for example, simply because it does not conveniently fit with funds that concentrate on Europe or Asia.

Yet the funds of the Middle East are not there yet to form their own group. They will be. There will soon be a Jordan Fund and likely an Egypt Fund and likely one devoted to Iran.

In a similar way, we have ASA—American South African—as the only fund for all of Africa. This too will not hold. Zambia has opened a stock market; the country has rich natural resources and a booming economy. We can likely expect greater investment attention to be focused on Zimbabwe and Botswana as well. Someday we will see listings for Kenya, Tanzania, Zaire, Nigeria, and Liberia. Further afield, there is a new fund this year for Sri Lanka (formerly Ceylon), and after that perhaps New Guinea. Anthropologists will no doubt bemoan these advancing waves of investment and capitalization, but the peoples of formerly "primitive" lands have always indicated a preference for a better living standard over having their pictures published in *National Geographic*.

Then too, there are those funds that cannot be conveniently associated with any country. There are funds that just invest in health stocks—medical and pharmaceutical—regardless of country, and others that just invest in environmental stocks. This last is surely a field with long-term potential. Outside of the United States and a few other developed countries, little to no attention is paid to environmental issues. Birds have been known to drop dead out of the sky just flying over Mexico City. Crossing the central square of Cairo, you frequently cannot see the other side, and not because the square is so big. The World Health Organization estimates that two-thirds of the population of Manila suffer from asthma and other respiratory diseases, nearly all caused by air pollution. Large sections of Slovakia, Romania, Poland, and other former Soviet satellites are so polluted that they are uninhabitable. As these countries see their standard of living rise, presuming it does, they will want more effort and money devoted to maintaining a clean and healthy environment. Environmental protection is a leisure activity. It is only after satisfying other requirements that society turns to fields and streams.

Here is a look at some of the more interesting funds available right now.

Alliance Global Environment Fund

Alliance Global Environment, shown in Figure 7-1, is one of the few funds—perhaps the only international fund—to show a loss for 1993. Most of its holdings were in the U.S., most of that in cash. From a high of $17 a share in 1990 when the fund was formed, it has managed to sink

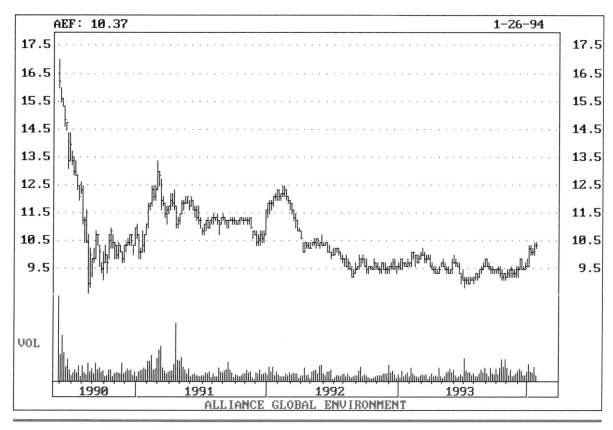

Figure 7-1   The Alliance Global Environment Fund

down to around $10 and stay pretty close to there ever since. Not surprisingly, the fund sells at a big discount of around 12-15 percent less than NAV. Major holdings at the end of 1993 included Generale des Eaux, Allied Colloids, Attwoods, Sealed Air, Wellman, Calgon Carbon, and Nalco Chemical. As its name indicates, the fund tries to invest in stocks with an environmental turn.

American South African (ASA) Fund

As you can tell from the time scale at the bottom of the chart shown in Figure 7-2, ASA has been around a long time. It is primarily a precious

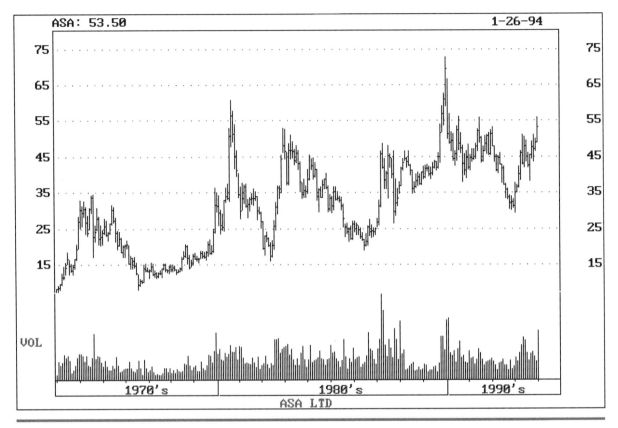

Figure 7-2 The American South African Fund

metals fund, composed of shares in gold, silver, and platinum mines of South Africa, the world's largest gold producer. As you would expect, the shares of the fund fluctuate in response to changes in the price of gold. By the fund's charter and South African law, the major part of earnings must be distributed by the fund as dividends to shareholders, and the fund must be more than 50 percent invested in South African gold mines; 20 percent may be invested in the mines of other countries. The fund has been a steady dividend payer, the amount fluctuating with the price of gold and interest rates. The current rate is about 4 percent, nothing special, but part of a long history of decent returns. The fund has never missed a dividend.

As of early 1994 the fund is entirely invested in precious metals mines and related equipment suppliers. Major holdings include Driefontein Consolidated, Kloof Gold Mining, Vaal Reefs, Southvaal, DeBeers Consolidated, and Rustenberg Platinum. Many of these mining shares are available in the United States for direct purchase as ADRs (American Depository Receipts). The fund has usually sold at a discount—sometimes as much as 40 percent below net asset value—even though it can be considered as one giant gold mine. As you inspect Figure 7-2, you can see that the fund fluctuates considerably, but the general trend has always been up.

America's All Season Fund

The America's All Season Fund, shown in Figure 7-3, has an open charter that allows it to invest in any country or region and to invest in currencies as well. Freedom may be invigorating, but it's not always rewarding, and the fund has had lackluster performance to say the least. After starting at $6 in 1988, the fund declined steadily to $4 and has ranged between $4 and $5 for the past several years. The fund sold at a premium its first year, but quickly moved to a discount after that and now regularly sells for around 20 percent below NAV.

Major holdings of the fund at the end of 1993 included International Nederlander, Gillette, McCaw Cellular, DNA Plant Technology, Amgen, Kimberly-Clark, and WMX Technologies (formerly Waste Management). Eighty-eight percent of the fund's assets were in the United States in 1993, most of that in cash, causing the fund to miss almost all of the rise in other stock markets.

Central Canada Fund

Central Canada, shown in Figure 7-4, is one of the most unusual funds in the world. Despite its title, the fund does not invest in Canadian stocks, but simply holds gold and silver bullion. It buys bars of gold and silver, stores the metal, and rises or falls depending on world prices. The fund has almost always sold at a discount to net assets, even though the assets are pure gold, so to speak. Central Canada Fund is a pure play on the precious metals. If you think they're going to go up, you can buy the fund shares instead of metal.

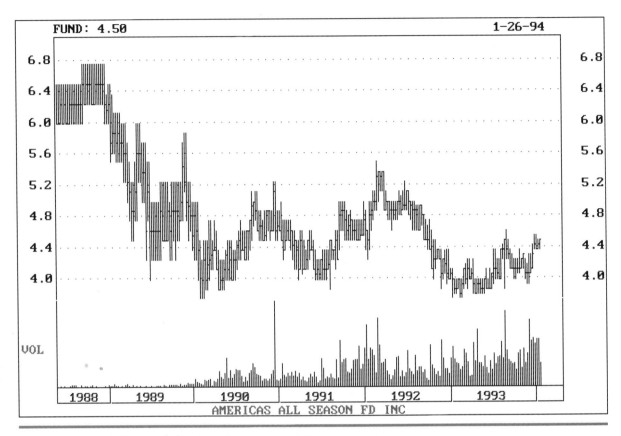

FUND: 4.50   1-26-94

AMERICAS ALL SEASON FD INC

Figure 7-3   The America's All Season Fund

Clemente Global Growth Fund

Clemente Global Growth Fund, shown in Figure 7-5, is a well-established global investment fund and conforms in style and content to the traditional view that people have in such funds. Which is to say, it is not specialized and includes the U.S. in its global view. Most of the fund's exposure is in Japan, with the U.S. next. Korea, Malaysia, and Hong Kong make up the bulk of the remainder. The fund has always sold at a discount, often ranging around 15 percent or more. Despite this supposed advantage for those seeking superior performance, the fund did nothing much from 1990 to the end of 1992, but rewarded the patient with a fine 50

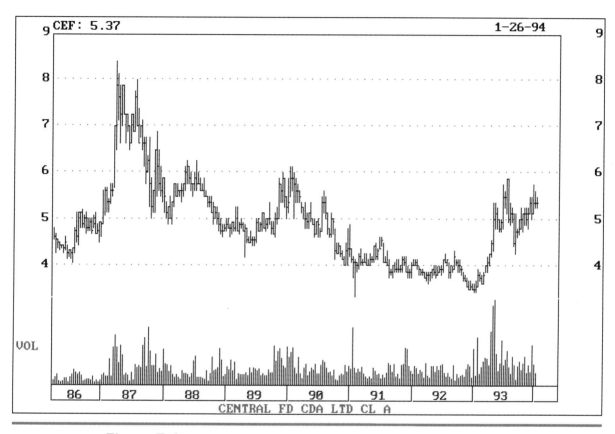

Figure 7-4 The Central Canada Fund

percent rise in 1993. Major holdings include Financier de Valle, Capstead Mortgage, Weru Fenster & Tueren, FKI Babcock, Leader Universal, and Premier Industrial.

Emerging Markets Telecommunications Fund

The Emerging Markets Telecommunications Fund, shown in Figure 7-6, is another new fund and worth some special attention, because it goes right to the heart of the argument concerning the future development of emerging nations. The evidence says that you don't get very far

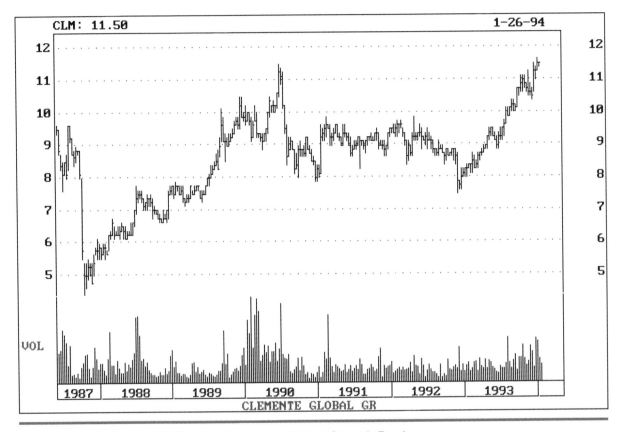

CLM: 11.50   1-26-94

VOL

CLEMENTE GLOBAL GR

Figure 7-5 The Clemente Global Growth Fund

as a developing economy without a good and pervasive communications system. The argument goes that if that is true—and it certainly seems to be true—then it is also too expensive to wire a country for communications in the way that America and other developed countries are wired. The new markets, the argument goes, can only afford to come up to speed by using the new technology of cellular phones and wireless transmission. All of this is probably true. It is not only the central theme of this fund, but much of the reason behind the tremendous surge in American cellular phone company stocks over the past couple of years.

The argument presented above is almost unassailable; you're not going to set up a telephone network in Tajikistan by stringing copper wires

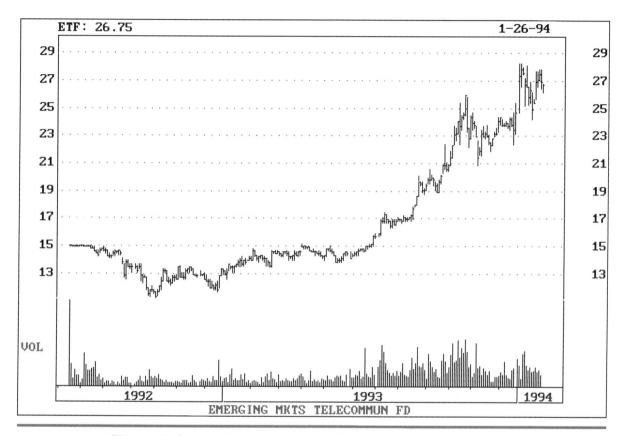

ETF: 26.75   1-26-94

EMERGING MKTS TELECOMMUN FD

Figure 7-6 The Emerging Markets Telecommunications Fund

on poles to everybody's house. The future development of cellular technology and satellite transmission seems assured. For the moment, however, the stocks of traditional phone companies are the way to play it overseas; they have the entry to their markets. On the downside, telecommunications stocks have already had big runs and nobody is sure just when there will be that pause while everybody waits for real earnings to appear. And we don't know how long that wait will be.

The Emerging Markets Telecommunications Fund doubled in 1993, moving from a discount to a premium on NAV (net asset value) in the process. Major holdings include Philippine Long Distance, Telefonos de Chile (ADRs), Telebras PN, Hong Kong Telecommunications, YPF

(ADRs), Telecom Malaysia, Telefonica de Argentina, and Telefonos de Mexico. The fund pays a small dividend.

First Israel Fund

Many investment advisors have argued that Israel is actually a European country that happens to be in the Middle East. Certainly the culture is European and so are the major markets for Israeli goods. That may change if the recent peace treaty between Israel and the PLO and its other neighbors is honored and takes effect. That would open large nearby markets for Israel's industrial capacity as well as buyers for its high technical skills. Israel has emerged as a world-class player in computer technology. On the other hand, a breakdown of the peace agreements would have the opposite effect.

The First Israel Fund, shown in Figure 7-7, has sold at a deep discount since its inception at the end of 1992, but went to a premium of almost 10 percent in late 1993. Overall, the fund had about a 50 percent rise in 1993. Major holdings include Bezeq, Scitex, Tadiran, ECI Telecommunications, Koor Industries, Teva Pharmaceuticals, PEC Israel, Elbit, and Lannet Data.

Global Health Sciences Fund

Global Health Sciences, shown in Figure 7-8, is a two-year-old fund aiming for growth and profits by investing in pharmaceutical and hospital stocks around the world. In practice, about 80 percent of the fund was invested in the U.S. at the end of 1993. The fund sells at a discount of about 10 percent, and if the health-related stocks ever turn around, it figures to turn with them. Major holdings include Amgen, Imperial Chemical, Schering-Plough, Pfizer, Astra, Merck, Mylan Labs, and Smithkline Beecham.

Morgan Stanley Emerging Markets Fund

Morgan Stanley Emerging Markets, shown in Figure 7-9, is a new fund, trying to emulate the success of the Templeton Emerging Markets Fund, and doing very well at it, too. The fund languished through 1992,

Figure 7-7 The First Israel Fund

but participated fully in the global market rush of 1993, nearly doubling. Some of that rise came from an increased premium for the fund's share. They carried no premium at the end of 1992, but a more than 10 percent premium at the end of 1993. Major holdings include Telebras PN, India Magnum Fund, Bangkok Bank, PEC Israel, KOC Yatrim, and Turcas Petrolculuk. The managers of this fund have indicated they intend to invest in eastern Europe in the near future.

Templeton Emerging Markets Fund

Templeton Emerging Markets Fund, shown in Figure 7-10, is one of the most famous foreign stock funds. John Templeton was one of the first

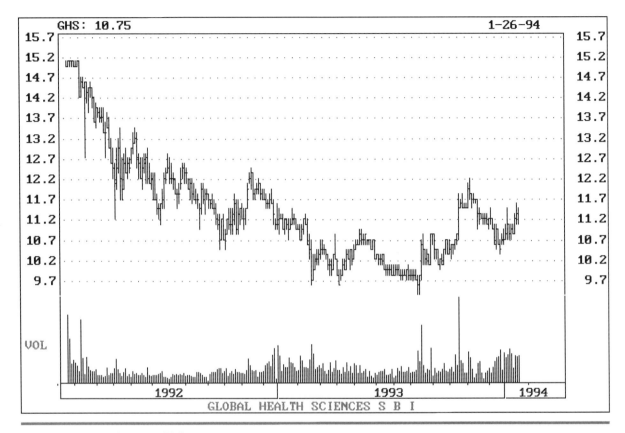

Figure 7-8   The Global Health Sciences Fund

to take a global view and see the whole world as one large stock market. Shares have gone from a low of $5.50 to nearly $30 at the beginning of 1994, and there have been very few dips along the way. During the first half of this rise, the fund sold at a considerable discount and for the second half it has sold at a considerable premium. It keeps rising either way.

There is a companion fund to this—almost a twin, a more traditional open-ended fund called Templeton Developing Markets. That fund has a 5-3/4 percent sales charge up front, while the closed-end fund has none. The closed-end fund was selling at a premium of about 15 percent at the end of 1993, however, effectively creating a 15 percent sales charge. John Templeton made some headlines in the business press at the end of 1993

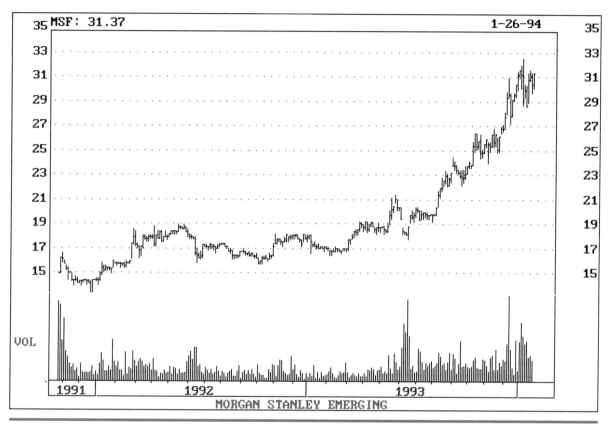

Figure 7-9 The Morgan Stanley Emerging Markets Fund

when he sold his considerable holdings in the closed-end fund and switched to the open fund. It is instructive for the rest of us to have the obvious pointed out: in short, it is worth considering the funds in relation to their respective charges. When one is lower than the other, it is normally the better buy, because the funds are substantially the same.

The Templeton Emerging Markets Fund's two largest positions at the end of 1993 were in Turkey and Brazil, both big winners. Most of the rest of the fund was in the Philippines, Malaysia, and Portugal, showing an independence of mind that has stood it in good stead over time. Major holdings include Philippine Long Distance, Philippine National Bank, Banco Comercial Portuguese, Antofagasta Holdings (Chile), Telefonos

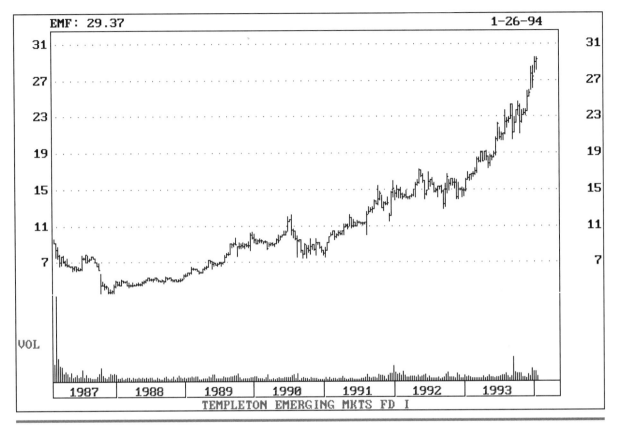

EMF: 29.37   1-26-94

Figure 7-10 Templeton Emerging Markets Fund

de Mexico, Cheung Kong Holdings, Hang Lung Development, Arcelik, and Cukurova Elektrik. The fund pays a small dividend.

Templeton Global Utilities Fund

Anytime you see a utilities fund, you know you're looking at income. Most people invest in utilities for current income and some potential growth. The Templeton Global Utilities Fund, shown in Figure 7-11, has performed beautifully in both regards. The yield is nothing special, 4 percent, but is in line with the returns on many investments in these low inflation and low interest times.

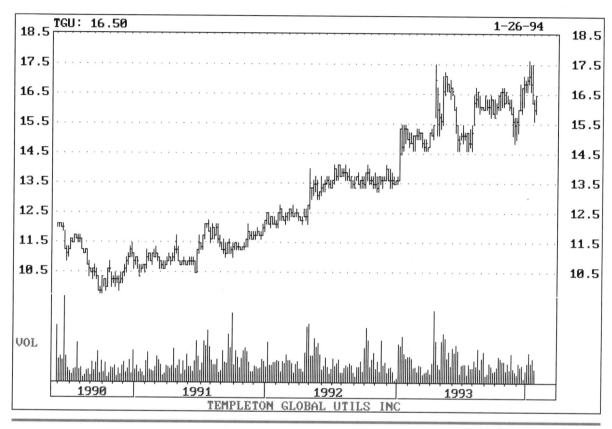

Figure 7-11   The Templeton Global Utilities Fund

The fund's focus is truly global, so it includes the U.S. From a low of $10 shortly after it was formed, the fund has risen fairly steadily to a 70 percent gain by the end of 1993. Unfortunately, its success has attracted a lot of attention, and the fund sells at a considerable premium of 5 to 10 percent. That more than wipes out the yield for the first year or two. Major holdings at the end of 1993 included Hong Kong Electric, American Electric Power, Nipsco Industries, Kansas City Power & Light, Telefonos de Mexico, and MCI.

Worldwide Value Fund

After bottoming twice at $12 in the past three years, the Worldwide Value Fund, shown in Figure 7-12, achieved lift-off in early 1993, rising to nearly $18 at the end of the year, a gain of almost 50 percent. The fund has also topped twice at $19, so watch out.

Except for a brief period of wild enthusiasm when the fund was first launched, it has always sold at a considerable discount of 10 to 20 percent below NAV. The fund has had some stellar years, but also some real clunkers. Overall, those who bought at the outset are just about even today. Major holdings at the end of 1993 included the usual suspects:

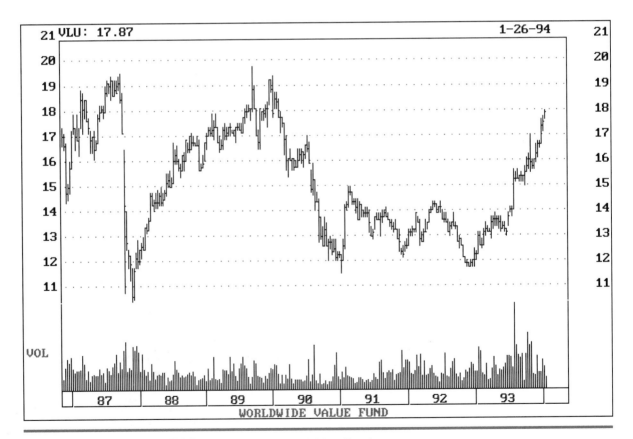

Figure 7-12   The Worldwide Value Fund

Deutsche Bank, Royal Insurance, Hanson, Granada Group, Grand Metropolitan, Banque Suisse, BTR, and Nestle.

Goodbye to All That

The world of investments covers more than just stocks, of course; there are also baseball cards. But most people feel safer in bonds. Bonds pay interest, and what's more, bondholders get paid before anyone else. It's good to be king. So let's turn to the next chapter and look at some funds that invest in foreign bonds.

CHAPTER 8

BOND FUNDS

You've heard of get rich quick? This is get rich slow.

Nobody gets excited about bonds. Too bad, because if you look at the bull market in stocks, which began in August of 1982 with the Dow Jones Industrial Average around 780, to the early part of 1994 with the Dow hitting 4,000, the interesting thing is you would have done about as well holding bonds over that same period as buying stocks. And you would have been a lot safer.

If you look at it in terms of the amount of money involved—the amount of money being moved around—the world stock market is nothing compared to the world bond market. The total bond market is probably 20 to 30 times the size of all stock markets, and that may even be conservative.

Of course, a lot of bonds are by nature conservative. They are designed to get you a steady 6 or 7 percent, or maybe 8 or 9 if you bought a couple years back. They are not designed to get you a double or a triple, the way a hot stock can do. Nobody ever drew a crowd at a party by saying they were into bonds. Bonds are boring. The crowd moves to the guy who tripled his money in WingDing Computers; he's a genius. One of the rules of life, by the way, is that large gains are always the result of intelligence, experience, and good judgment, whereas losses are caused by bad luck.

The good news about international bonds is that they almost always pay higher interest than U.S. bonds. While U.S. long-term Treasuries are hovering around 6.3 percent as of early in 1994, many foreign government bonds pay 10 percent and more. The bad news is they may not pay that in dollars, and sometimes they may not pay it at all.

Here's where currency fluctuations become extremely important—crucial, one might say. If a foreign bond gets you 30 percent more than a domestic (U.S.) bond, but the currency of that country declines by 30 percent relative to the dollar, you are up a well-known creek without a paddle. Your yield (interest paid) might be flat compared to the U.S. bond—meaning, take 30 percent off 10 percent and you get 7 percent, or just about what you would have gotten had you stayed home—but there's much more to the story. You actually lose quite a bit, because the value of the bond you bought also would have declined 30 percent. In other words, drop 30 percent off the value of that foreign currency and the bond you bought for $1,000 is now worth only $700. The drop in the interest rate return—the yield—is trivial compared to the loss of your capital. Fortunately, there are ways to protect against this. Let the tutorial begin.

Stocks Are Equity, Bonds Are Debt

Bonds are counterintuitive. They are confusing to a lot of people. If they aren't confusing to you, go out for a cup of coffee now.

A recent survey by one of the financial magazines found that two-thirds of Americans did not understand that when interest rates rise, bonds fall.

It does seem to defy common sense. After all, when earnings rise, stock prices don't fall—at least not usually. But that's because stocks are equity, bonds are debt. In other words, if people go nuts buying WingDing Widgets to go with their WingDing Computers, the WingDing company makes a lot of money, and you as a shareholder own a piece of the WingDing company and so you make money. But bonds are an obligation to repay a loan, and happy days for WingDing will have no effect on the principal or interest due on that loan, though it might affect the company's credit rating.

What does have an effect on your bonds is the interest paid on similar loans. If your WingDing bond is paying 7 percent, and new bonds with a similar risk rating are issued paying 8 percent, the value of your bond will go down. Why should that be? Well, look at it from the buyer's point of view: why should they pay the full price for your bond when they can buy some other bond just like it and get a better interest rate? The answer is they won't pay full price (or *par,* as it's called), but will offer a discounted price that will take into account the change in prevailing rates. If interest rates fall, the price of your bond will rise; if interest rates rise, your bond will fall.

By the Numbers

The calculation of what a bond is worth when rates change is pretty straightforward and easy to do. A small calculator or pencil and paper will handle it. For example: if you have a bond that is paying 8 percent, and the prevailing interest rate drops to 7 percent, then the price of your bond will be adjusted upward until it too is paying 7 percent. In fact, your $1,000 bond will move up to sell for right around $1,140, other things being equal. In reality, it might sell for more or less than that amount, because the market is not a pure mathematical equation, but is driven by hopes and fears. Fear that interest rates will fall further might cause your old 8 percent bond to move to a premium over its true value; hope that the change in rates was just a momentary blip on the radar screen might cause it to sell at a discount to true value. Such emotional waves are what make the market interesting.

The base equation for calculating the value of your WingDing bond in the face of falling interest rates would run something like this: "8 is to X as 7 is to 100," where "X" is the unknown "new" price of your bond. Multiplied out, it looks like this: $7X = 800$. Divide both sides by 7 to find the value of X and the answer is 1.143, or $1,143. This is all high school algebra, as I'm sure everyone remembers.

If interest rates rise instead of fall, the same equation would apply, except this time the larger interest rate number would go in front of X, the unknown. A rise of 1 percent would reduce the value of the bond in this case by about $125, to a price of $875. This would represent a 12.5 percent loss, though you would, of course, continue to collect the interest payments as before, and if you held the bond to maturity—meaning the full term of the loan—you would get your full $1,000 back.

The above bit of calculation is more than an abstract exercise. The $143 that has been added to the price of your bond by the fall in interest rates represents a return of 14.3 percent all by itself (14.3 percent of $1,000 is $143). If you add that to your 8 percent interest, you are really making more than 22 percent on that bond. This is called *total return*. Other factors affect the total return, like management costs and currency valuations. What you really want to know, then, is the total return. Not just what the interest rate is, but what will be the likely result of all the factors affecting the price of the bond—changes in interest rates in the issuing country or company and changes in the value of the local currency versus the dollar. It is in terms of total return that foreign bonds and bond funds have been particularly rewarding.

Of Human Bond-age

As we look at some international bond funds over the next several pages, here are some points to remember. Most of the funds whose performance charts are pictured and discussed are closed-end funds. The reason is that, just as with stocks, in which we looked at closed-end country and regional funds, closed-end funds are usually a purer play than open-ended mutual funds. (See the beginning of Chapter 4 for an explanation of the difference between closed-end and open-end funds.) They also have no load fees, and more than that, they offer a kicker that even no-load bond funds don't have, and that is the opportunity to buy assets at a discount to true value. We will, however, also show some performance charts on open-ended mutual funds. You will see little difference from the closed-end funds, but there are some non-visible differences, and let's get right to those.

Many studies have shown that funds that carry a *load*—a fee for buying them—provide no better returns than funds that carry no load. This is as true for bonds as it is for stocks. The subject has been sliced, diced, and tossed, and there is no evidence that funds that charge a load perform better than those that do not.

A so-called "load" when buying a fund is simply the amount used to pay the salesperson. It doesn't matter whether the person who sold you the fund works for the bank or brokerage house that runs the fund or is an independent, the bottom line is that the load is a payment to them for selling you the fund. With bond funds, that load is particularly onerous since it bites right into the yield. If the fund yields 6 percent (the interest rate minus management fees and operating costs is typically called the *yield*), which many do, and the load fee is also 6 percent, which it sometimes is, the net return to you is zero. Not only have you wiped out the yield for the year, but you have invested less money than you thought you did. To wit: if the load is 6 percent and you put $10,000 into the fund, you actually put in $9,400, since the load comes right off the top. You would now be making 6 percent on $9,400, which is $564. You would have paid $600 to make $564. What a deal!

Those who charge loads will argue that somebody has to pay for the costs of selling the fund, and that furthermore, their superior management makes the charge a bargain over the long term—though there is no evidence this is so. An even more potent argument for avoiding load funds is the one raised by professional traders and investors, and it has to do with the word "long-term." The load inhibits your freedom of thought and action. In other words, if you have invested your money and paid a fee, which you cannot get back, and the fund you bought in this way declines in value or begins to perform poorly—or you simply want to do something else with the money— you would hesitate about getting out because you would take an immediate loss. The same hesitation applies simply to looking around and seeing something else that is performing better, or looks like a good opportunity; the sales fee in effect locks you in.

The same thing applies to what's called a *back load*, which is a fee charged for leaving a fund rather than entering. Is this legal? You bet. The argument of the fund management is that it keeps out switchers and other investors with short horizons and allows them to have a stable amount of money to work with and thus make better decisions. Whether this is true or not, and I doubt that it is true, it results in the same inhibitory influence on your decision making, since you would be naturally reluctant to leave and absorb an immediate loss. There are enough risk factors to account for without having to add this one. If someone wants a fee for selling you a fund, bond or otherwise, make them show you how well it has outperformed the funds that don't charge a fee.

And Finally: Funny Money

One of the things bond funds do for you—at least that they're supposed to do for you—is manage the currency risk.

Countries with established economies are able to issue bonds in their own currency. These are what my son calls "real" countries, as opposed to those new places which have in the last few years made map-making a growth industry. So if you buy a bond from the United Kingdom, it is issued in pounds sterling, and if you buy a French bond, it is denominated in French francs, and so on. If the currencies of those established countries should rise against the dollar, as the Japanese yen has been doing lately, that is very hunky, and also dory. The holders of those bonds get a double kick—interest rate plus currency rise can mean huge gains.

Recent weakness in the currencies of Spain, Sweden, and Belgium, on the other hand, has meant that the holders of those bonds have taken something of a hit—and we don't mean a home run. Any fund worth its management salt will guard against this sort of thing by dividing its portfolio among the bonds of several countries, some with strong currencies, some with weak. Determining the mixture is something of an art, as the strong currency countries tend to have lower interest rates. To focus exclusively on those would lower the fund's yield and overall return. Some of the high risk stuff has to be in there, or the fund will not perform well. Figuring it all out is why some people get the big bucks and some don't.

Countries with currencies that sound like a new variety of pasta have their own problems raising money—mainly that no one wants to lend them any. This provides an unusual benefit (to us, not to them). These newly rising economies—*emerging markets*, as they are often called—frequently issue their bonds in U.S. dollars to make them more attractive to outside investors. These are called *Yankee bonds* in the trade, for the obvious reasons. It certainly simplifies your life: dollars in, dollars out. The other nice thing about such dollar bonds is that because the countries with newly emerging markets are emerging, as they say, they often pay a higher interest rate to attract buyers. Companies too will sometimes issue Yankee bonds; they want to tap the huge capital pool of the U.S. market, and that is the easiest way to do so.

Whether Yankee or not, the net result is that the interest rates on some foreign bonds are right up there with the yields on so-called *junk bonds* (the high interest bonds of companies with questionable ability to meet the payments), but they are not junk. Until recently, for example, the bonds of Escom, the giant South African utility company, were yielding 17 percent. Even after some publicity, the yield remains around 13-14 percent. South African government bonds were paying 20 percent for several years and still pay a bundle. British bonds pay 11-12 percent. The bonds of Taiwan have paid 13-16 percent interest for years, and their currency is pegged to the dollar.

Remember, the whole world is your market now. Don't dismiss a place just because you saw some hot-breath story on TV; fear is your ally and can provide opportunity if you think your way through the hysteria. (By the way, you want to know the seven countries that have never defaulted on a government bond? Australia, Canada, Finland, Great Britain, New Zealand, South Africa, and the U.S.)

Before we go to looking directly at some bond funds, it's worth mentioning there are other funds that also focus on high yield, and those would be utility and preferred stock funds. In both cases, the object is high present yield, typically for people who want or need income from their assets right now, or those who have put their assets in a tax-deferred plan like a Keogh or an IRA and want the interest to build. The significant difference is that bonds have liquidation preference over stocks. In other words, if the issuing company should fall on hard times, even file for bankruptcy, the bond holders have first call on any assets (after the lawyers, of course). Stockholders, even the holders of preferred stock, do not get anything until the bond holders have been paid.

Bonds Away!

There are literally hundreds of bond funds. The handful presented in this chapter was selected nearly at random and for no other reason than showing a variety of bond investments, mainly foreign but with some domestic ones thrown in. Neither I nor the publisher has any interest in any of these funds. Most all of the funds that follow invest primarily in the bonds of foreign companies and governments, but many of them also invest in U.S. bonds. A few invest only in U.S. corporate bonds. We should keep in mind that U.S. issues—stocks or bonds, are rightfully part of any global portfolio.

The ACM Multi-Market Fund

In a way, the graph of ACM's Multi-Market Fund is misleading (Figure 8-1). And in a way, it isn't. If you were to look at a chart of the fund's return over the period shown (the full life of the fund), it would not show a decline like this one does, but would be a steadily rising line. That's because what's missing from this chart is the yield—the dividend payout—which in this case would be a little over 8 percent a year. Compound that year after year and it adds up pretty nicely. On the other hand, the price decline in the chart reflects the reality of what you can get if you want to sell your shares. And in that sense, the decline is a much truer representation of the fate of your investment. Because if you had

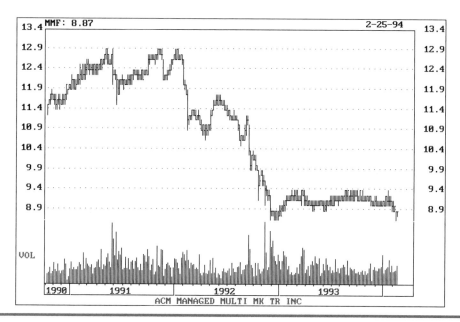

Figure 8-1   The ACM Multi-Market Fund

bought near the high of $13 a share (and some people did) and wanted to sell down here around $9 a share, you would be taking a 30 percent loss. That just about offsets your 8 percent yield over the past three years.

ACM Multi-Market is a closed-end fund. Unlike an open-end fund, where you can turn in your shares for that day's NAV (net asset value), the shares in a closed-end fund must be sold on the open market and will bring whatever the market will pay on that day. Some days that will be more than the NAV, some days less. Some brokers never recommend such funds because, they will point out, if you are forced to sell you may not get the full value (the NAV) for your shares—since sometimes they sell at a premium and sometimes at a discount. Of course, on the other hand, you may get more than the full value. My own feeling is that the reluctance to recommend them may have more to do with the fact that there are no sales commission for buying such funds.

In the first months of 1994, the ACM Multi-Market Fund was yielding nearly 9 percent and selling at a discount of 7 percent to NAV. The total return—yield plus increase in the value of the fund's holdings—was a wimpy 9.74 percent as of the end of 1993.

Aside from these considerations, it is both interesting and instructive to look at some of the holdings in the fund's portfolio. We will do it for the other funds in this chapter because it not only shows you what fund managers buy, but provides you with a view of which bonds pay what and lets you think about what you might be interested in looking at for yourself. If you want to buy foreign bonds singly, the best place to go is an international bank or a branch of a bank of a particular country. It is more difficult for an individual to do this, and the hassle content may be more than it's worth, but some people do it. Many countries have banks with branches in major U.S. cities.

Table 8-1 shows some holdings of the ACM Multi-Market fund. The maturity date is the date the bond comes due; at that point, the bond is redeemed in full at face value. Bonds are typically issued in denomina-

BOND OR SECURITY	INTEREST RATE	MATURITY	% OF NET ASSETS
American Bond Company	6.75%	6/15/94	10.38
Toronto Dominion	10.75%	10/20/94	9.90
Government of Spain	11%	6/15/97	7.74
Offshore Mexican Bond Company	7%	7/20/94	5.19
Peso-linked U.S. dollar	6.65%	7/15/94	5.19
International Bank of Reconstruction & Development	12.5%	7/25/97	5.03
Kingdom of Sweden	11.5%	9/1/95	4.57
Government of Denmark	9%	11/15/95	4.26
Banque National de Paris	8.75%	12/11/95	4.22
Government of Italy	12%	1/1/96	3.70
Kingdom of Sweden	10.75%	1/23/97	3.61
Commonwealth Bank of Australia	13%	9/15/95	2.77
United Kingdom Treasuries	12.75%	11/15/95	2.08
U.S. Treasury Notes	5.375%	5/31/98	2.08
Government of France	8%	5/12/98	2.03
Government of Denmark	9.75%	2/10/95	1.87

Table 8-1 Some of the ACM Multi-Market Fund's holdings

tions of $1,000, but might be issued at $10,000, $100,000, or some other number. As you can see by the maturity dates listed here, the emphasis of this fund is short-term, high interest holdings. In general, the interest rate risk is less in a fund with holdings such as these, as compared to a fund with longer term holdings like the one we'll look at next.

Alliance World Dollar Government Fund

The Alliance World Dollar Government Fund, shown in Figure 8-2, looked like it was going to be a real zoomer. The yield is 7.8 percent, but the total return—yield plus increased value—was a thumping 60 percent near the end of 1993. Not surprisingly, the fund's shares sell at a nearly 17 percent premium to NAV. That is extremely high for a bond fund—or any fund, for that matter! Unfortunately, the fund subsequently crashed and the high premium was a tip-off to its overvaluation. A sampling of the portfolio is shown in Table 8-2.

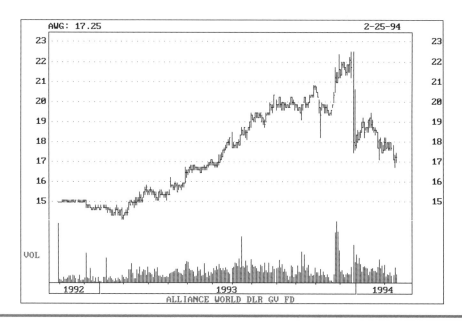

Figure 8-2   The Alliance World Dollar Government Fund

BOND OR SECURITY	INTEREST RATE	MATURITY	% OF NET ASSETS
Republic of Argentina	4%	3/31/23	28
Republic of Venezuela	6.75%	3/31/20	17
United Mexican States	6.25%	12/31/19	14
U.S. Treasury Bonds	0%	5/15/07	9
Government of Brazil	8.75%	1/1/01	7
Central Bank of Nigeria	5.5%	11/15/20	7
U.S. Treasury Bonds	0%	11/15/20	7
Government of Uruguay	6.75%	2/19/21	4

Table 8-2 Some holdings in the Alliance World Dollar Government Fund's portfolio

Some things in this table are worth going over. You will notice that the maturity dates have year numbers lower than the present. It doesn't mean the bond is already dead; it means the date is in the next century.

Next, if you look over the list you will see that most of the bonds are for countries with historically high inflation rates and pay very low interest. And yet the fund had a 60 percent total return. The two go together. Bonds with low interest rates and from risky countries usually sell very cheaply. If interest rates in the rest of the world start to decline, and/or the economy of those countries starts to improve, the price of those bonds will rise. The price rise will be much larger and faster than the interest rate return, which becomes trivial in such a situation; the bond is being bought for price appreciation, not for the interest rate. The same thing is true to an even greater extent in the U.S. Treasury Bonds, listed with 0 percent interest. There are no 0 percent interest rate bonds, so what we have here is a manufactured product, in which the interest rate that the bond will accumulate over the years of its maturity is stripped out and sold to some other party, who will collect that interest. The remaining hulk is called a *zero* in the trade, standing for *zero coupon bond*, because there is no interest payment coupon. Zeroes are sold at a huge discount, often for only $200-$300 on a face value of $1,000. Who would want them anyway, you might ask. Well, if interest rates decline, which they have been doing for the past few years, bonds go up in price. The zeroes go up, too, because even though they pay no interest, they will be redeemed at maturity at their full face value of $1,000 (or whatever the denomination issued). If a regular bond goes up $200, it would represent a 20 percent gain, which is very nice, but the same $200 gain nearly doubles the value of a "zero." Most of the above fund's holdings are in bonds that provide that kind of booster shot in a world of declining interest rates. The return on the other bonds provides some limited protection against rising rates—provided they don't rise too much or too fast.

Blackrock North American Government Fund: Bad Day at Black Rock

As you can see in Figure 8-3, things have not gone well for this fund, which invests heavily in Canadian bonds and includes some U.S. bonds (see Table 8-3). The Canadian dollar has been in a fairly long-run decline. The other major holding of this fund is U.S. mortgage-backed bonds, which have fallen out of favor along with falling interest rates. Here's why: falling interest rates cause many mortgage holders to remortgage at the new lower rates, thus cutting short the payments to the long-term holders of the mortgage notes, who now have to go out and look for

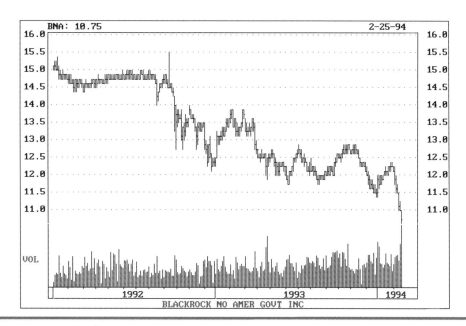

Figure 8-3   The Blackrock North American Government Fund

BOND OR SECURITY	INTEREST RATE	MATURITY	% OF NET ASSETS
Government of Canada	12.25%	9/1/05	12
U.S. Treasury Notes	6.25%	2/15/03	11
Newfoundland Hydroelectric	10.5%	4/15/01	7
Province of Alberta	10.25%	8/22/01	7
Province of British Columbia	9.5%	1/9/12	6
NBC	9%	2/1/97	5
Province of Ontario	8.75%	4/16/97	5
Province of Manitoba	9.25%	5/21/97	3
Province of Saskatchewan	9.6%	12/30/04	3
Province of Nova Scotia	9.6%	1/30/22	3
Province of Quebec	8.5%	4/1/97	3
FNMA CMO REMIC	fluctuates	no maturity date	22
FHLMC	fluctuates	no maturity date	11

Table 8-3   A look at Blackrock North American Government's portfolio

somewhere else to put their money in an environment of falling interest rates. It is a sad tale that can bring tears to the eyes of the rich.

Colonial Intermarket Income Trust Fund

The Colonial Intermarket Income Trust Fund provides us with an example of how a professional manager spreads money among high-yield corporate bonds as well as governments to increase the current rate of return (see Figure 8-4). The yield on the fund is 8.4 percent, and the total return for 1993 was around 16 percent. The shares sell at almost exactly net asset value. The portfolio, shown in Table 8-4, is about evenly split between high-yield corporates and government bonds, both U.S. and foreign. "High-yield corporate bonds" is often a euphemism for "junk bonds," but not all such bonds are junk. Most of the names will be familiar to anyone who reads *BusinessWeek* or a financial paper.

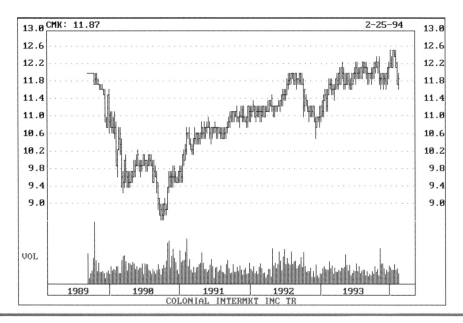

Figure 8-4 The Colonial Intermarket Income Trust

Emerging Markets Income Fund

The Emerging Markets Income Fund (Figure 8-5) has a yield of 7.6 percent and sells at a slight discount of 1.5 percent to NAV. That 7.6 percent doesn't look like much in a fund that calls itself "income," but a look at the total for the first full year of operation shows a gain of nearly 50 percent. There's been a drop-off recently as rising rates in the U.S. have given everybody a bit of a fright. The fund invests in government and corporate debt (see Table 8-5).

First Australia Prime Fund

First Australia (Figure 8-6) has a yield of nearly 9 percent and a total return of about 13 percent for 1993. The fund has been a steady gainer, aided immeasurably by falling interest rates and a rising bond market in Australia. Its shares currently sell at a premium of about 5 percent, but for most of its history they have sold at a discount. All of its holdings are in Australia (see Table 8-6).

BOND OR SECURITY	INTEREST RATE	MATURITY	% OF NET ASSETS
Sea Containers	12.5%	10/15/03	1
Amphenol	12.75%	12/15/02	1
Kaiser Aluminum	12.75%	2/1/03	1
Mesa Capital	13.5%	5/1/99	1
Revlon	11%	2/15/03	1
Auburn Hills Trust	15.375%	5/1/20	1
Ferrell Gas	12%	8/1/96	1
Thermadyne Industries	15%	5/1/96	1
Gaylord Container	11.5%	5/15/01	1
Epic Healthcare	15%	2/1/01	1
Transco Energy	11.25%	7/1/99	1
Embassy Suites	10.875%	4/15/02	1
Inland Steel	12%	12/1/98	1
Magma Copper	12%	12/15/01	1
OPI International	12.875%	7/15/02	1
Riverwood International	11.25%	6/15/02	1

Table 8-4   Some holdings of the Colonial Intermarket Income Trust

First Boston Strategic Income Fund

This fund is composed almost entirely of high-yield corporate bonds, sometimes called junk bonds. The bonds are nearly all American, which might make you think they don't fit with the rest of the funds in this book. But we too are part of global investing, and so it is worth taking a look at what's available here. For the individual investor, junk bonds are almost always bought as funds, the risk of holding single "junks" being too great.

The First Boston Strategic (Figure 8-7) boasted a hefty 10.5 percent yield and had a total return of around 12 percent for 1993. The fund currently sells at a 10 percent discount. The lack of enthusiasm probably reflects the fact that falling interest rates cause conservative bonds to rally strongly (remember, bonds are counter-intuitive), but have less effect on high-yield bonds. Table 8-7 gives a look at part of the portfolio, which provides some interesting ideas for investors with a lot of nerve.

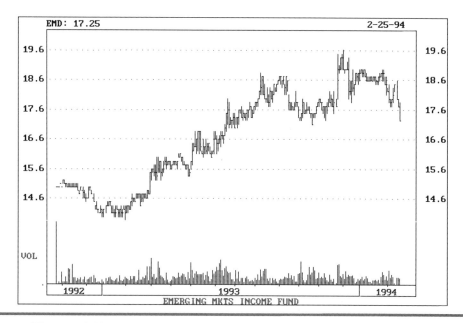

EMD: 17.25   2-25-94

EMERGING MKTS INCOME FUND

Figure 8-5   The Emerging Markets Income Fund

Global Government Plus Fund

The Global Government Plus Fund (Figure 8-8) has a yield of 7.4 percent and sells at a nice 12 percent discount to NAV. The total return for 1993 was around 16 percent. More than a third of the holdings are

BOND OR SECURITY	INTEREST RATE	MATURITY	% OF NET ASSETS
Kingdom of Morocco	4.25%	1/1/09	24
Republic of Brazil	8.75%	1/1/01	10
Cemex	10%	11/5/99	4
Telebras	10%	6/16/97	4
National Bank of Hungary	8.8%	10/1/02	4
Government of Costa Rica	6.25%	5/21/10	4
Petrobras	10%	9/12/96	4

Table 8-5   Some of the bonds held by the Emerging Markets Income Fund

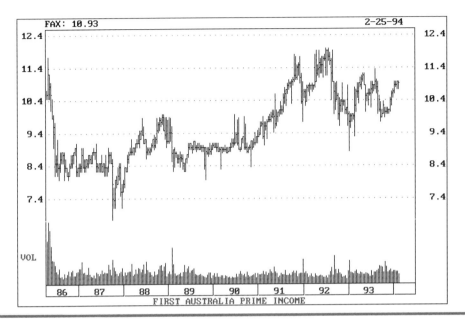

Figure 8-6 The First Australia Prime Fund

U.S. Treasuries of various maturities, averaging less than 7 percent return. The fund buys only in developed countries, and Table 8-8 lists some of the larger and more interesting selections.

BOND OR SECURITY	INTEREST RATE	MATURITY	% OF NET ASSETS
Western Australia Treasuries	12%	8/1/01	5
Australian Overseas Telephone	12.5%	11/15/00	5
Tasmanian Public Finance	12.5%	1/15/01	4
New South Wales Treasuries	12.5%	4/1/97	4
Commonwealth of Australia	13%	7/15/00	3
Northern Territories	12.5%	7/15/01	3
Melbourne Metro Board	12.5%	6/1/97	3
Queensland Treasuries	12%	5/15/97	2

Table 8-6 Holdings of the First Australia Prime Fund

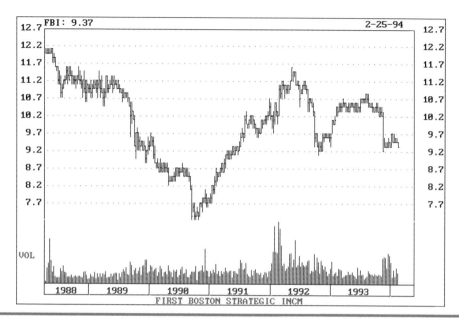

Figure 8-7   The First Boston Strategic Income Fund

BOND OR SECURITY	INTEREST RATE	MATURITY	% OF NET ASSETS
Government of Canada	6.25%	2/1/98	4
Chicago & Northwestern RR	15.5%	10/15/01	1
Container Corp. of America	13.5%	12/1/99	1
Hollywood Casino	14%	4/1/98	1
Kash N' Karry Food Stores	14%	2/1/01	1
Parisian	16.75%	7/1/00	1
Trump Taj Mahal	11.35%	11/15/99	1
Florida Steel	11.5%	12/15/00	1
Maxxam Group	12.75%	11/15/99	1
Evergreen International	13.5%	8/15/02	1
Bankers Life	13.25%	11/1/02	1
Continental Cablevision	11%	6/1/07	1

Table 8-7   Some of the First Boston Strategic Income Fund's holdings

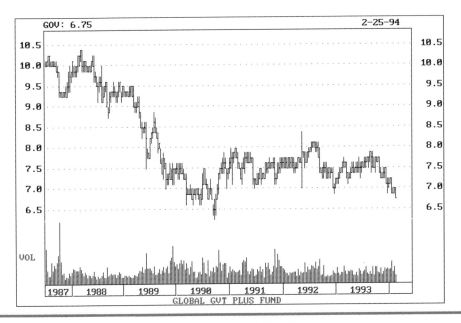

Figure 8-8 The Government Global Plus Fund

Latin American Dollar Fund

Want some high yield? This is the place. Faith in Latin America and the ability of various countries therein to pay off their bonds has provided

BOND OR SECURITY	INTEREST RATE	MATURITY	% OF NET ASSETS
Government of Spain	11.3%	1/15/02	7
Government of Canada	9.5%	6/1/10	5
Government of Japan	5.5%	3/20/02	4
Government of Italy	12%	1/1/02	4
Government of France	6.75%	10/25/03	4
Government of Denmark	9%	11/15/98	3
United Kingdom	9.75%	8/27/02	3
Government of Ireland	8.75%	7/27/97	2
Swedish Mortgage Bonds	12.5%	1/23/97	1

Table 8-8 Some of the holdings of the Global Government Plus Fund

shareholders of the Latin American Dollar Fund, invested primarily in Yankee bonds, with a toothsome 11.2 percent yield (see Figure 8-9). Total return for 1993 was better than 35 percent. The shares were selling for a 5.7 percent premium as of the beginning of March 1994. Table 8-9 shows how the fund looked in close-up.

The oddity here is the Jamaican bond, which says "LIBOR." This means it pays the LIBOR rate, which stands for "London Interbank Offered Rate." This is a rate in Eurodollars and is a European standard for judging interest rates in the dollar market. It fluctuates daily and was around 4-1/4 percent for 12-month notes at the beginning of March 1994, when this chart was pulled.

Strategic Global Income Fund

The names start to sound alike, don't they? There's not a lot of imagination in this business. If you think the names are dull, take a look at the ads run by investment companies. As of this writing, the Strategic Global Income Fund pays an 8.2 percent yield and sells at a 4 percent discount to NAV (see Figure 8-10). The total return for 1993 was around

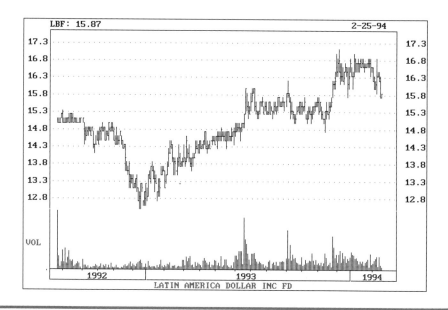

Figure 8-9 The Latin American Dollar Fund

BOND OR SECURITY	INTEREST RATE	MATURITY	% OF NET ASSETS
Sovereign Value	8.25%	12/18/07	14
Republic of Argentina	4%	3/31/23	12
Repubic of Venezuela	6.75%	3/31/20	5
Government of Jamaica	LIBOR	11/15/04	5
Empresas La Moderna	10.25%	11/12/97	4
Republic of Brazil	6%	9/15/13	4
United Mexican States	6.25%	12/31/19	7
Telecom Brasileiras	10%	6/16/97	3

Table 8-9   Latin American Dollar Fund Holdings

18 percent. We've listed so many bonds so far that we'll just list a few in Table 8-10 that don't appear in most other global funds.

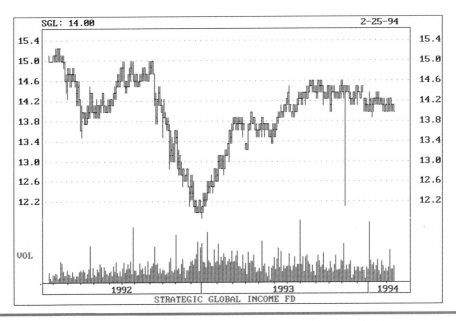

Figure 8-10   The Strategic Global Income Fund

BOND OR SECURITY	INTEREST RATE	MATURITY	% OF NET ASSETS
Republic of Germany	8.75%	8/20/01	5
Finland Housing	10.75%	3/15/02	3
Republic of Ireland	9%	7/15/01	1
Republic of Finland	11%	1/15/99	1

Table 8-10 A selection of heretofore unseen (in this chapter) bonds held by the Strategic Global Income Fund

note

Something worth noting in looking at Figure 8-10 is the very long price bar that appears early in November of 1993. It looks like the price of the fund fluctuated wildly between 12 and 14.5—which is pretty wild for a bond fund—but in fact, it's just an error in the data. In all of the programs we'll be looking at later in the book, you can go into the data and correct such errors, and I could have done it here. But I left it in place so you could see what such mistakes look like. They're startling to the eye, but they have no effect on the prices of other days.

Let's Hit the Road

Where do you find all this information, anyway? Well, you can find a lot of it on remote database services like CompuServe, Dow Jones News/Retrieval, and Prodigy. You can also get price quotes on stocks, funds, and other issues. They are stations on the information highway, which we will tour in the next part of the book.

THE INFORMATION HIGHWAY: ROADSIDE ATTRACTIONS

3

CHAPTER 9

THE BIG ONE: COMPUSERVE

You can get lost in here. CompuServe is like a world—nations, oceans, islands, great cities and bright lights, barren spaces, and high mountains. This is one of the oldest public database services. It is essentially a group of minicomputers in Columbus, Ohio, and is owned by H&R Block, the company that has those tax preparation storefronts next to the laundromat. Once you step past these mundane realities, you are in another universe— the realm of hyperspace—and you can boldly go where no data surfer has gone before. (Well, no more than a million or two.) You can look up movie reviews, buy airline tickets, trade stamps, find your true love, get married (honest), and oh yes...look up some stocks and bonds.

This is a primary source for quotes. The service boasts that it has quotes and market information (like news stories) on 125,000 stocks (U.S. and foreign), bonds, options, mutual funds, commodities, and warrants. Take that with at least a couple grains of salt, because most of those quotes will be for options and other derivative contracts that really pivot around an underlying issue. In fact, whenever you deal with options or other derivatives such as warrants, which are really financial instruments based on some security, that security is known in the trade as the "underlying." There are 12 years of historical data on most of the securities and bonds.

CompuServe has a global membership. If you enter any of the forums, you are almost as likely to get into a conversation with someone overseas as here in the U.S. It is a good way to get other perspectives and a cheap way to do long distance mail.

The First Tollbooth

There are two key things to remember about traveling the land of CompuServe: It is complex and expensive.

The system has excellent resources for researching foreign securities—such as Citibank's Global Report, the Australia/New Zealand Company Library, the German Company Library, the European Company Library, the U.K. Company Library, and U.K. Historical Stock Quotes. All of which will cost you extra.

The CompuServe pricing system is only slightly less complicated than the regulations of the Internal Revenue Service. It is a tribute to the ability of modern man to transcend the limitations of mere language and logic, and brings to mind the observation of science fiction writer Poul Anderson, who once noted: "There is no system, no matter how complex,

which if looked at in just the right way cannot be made more complex."
Here are the highlights:

▶ In addition to the initial startup fee of $25, the basic service
charge is $8.95 a month, which provides unlimited time online
and use of what are called "Basic Services." Unfortunately, the
Basic Services do not include a lot of what we want.

▶ For an extra charge of $4.80 an hour, you get what they call "Ex-
tended Service," which has extensive material of interest to investors and is definitely worth the extra cost. The $4.80 an hour is for
connection at speeds up to 2400 baud. It's $9.60 an hour for speeds be-
yond that, all the way up to 14400 baud—which is very fast indeed.

▶ For an extra $10 a month, plus an extra $15 an hour, you can get
"Executive Service," which provides access to more information
doors and is highly recommended for anyone interested in doing financial research. In fact you must have this even to gain access to
some of the internal databases, like Disclosure, Securities Screening,
and the Institutional Brokers Earnings Estimate System.

▶ Current quotes, which in this case means stock quotes for the
most recent market day, are 1.5 cents apiece. But historical
quotes, which means anything before the most recent market day,
are 5 cents apiece. A little basic arithmetic says that if you want
to download—meaning bring into your desktop system—two
years of daily quotes on 20 stocks, the bill for that will be about
$500. Forty stocks will be $1,000, and so on.

▶ In addition there are various extra charges for some of the services
mentioned above and for other services of particular interest to investors researching foreign stocks. Much information, for example, is
contained in several "Libraries," such as the U.K. Company Library,
the European Company Library, the Asian Library, etc., each of
which can be searched for company credit ratings, financial reports,
news stories in foreign newspapers, reports by overseas analysts, and
so on. A full analysis will run at least $100 a company, though you
can get away for much less if you don't want everything.

▶ A business credit profile report from TRW costs $34, though subsequent reports are only $9.

▶ Sundry other charges range from a few cents to several dollars. Stock market highlights for the previous day, for example, run an extra $15 an hour, though it is doubtful anyone would spend more than a few minutes at this. An options profile costs $1.25, a portfolio evaluation $1, and so on.

All of this does not take into account your telephone line charges, which can range from zero to an astonishing sum. The zero rate is what you pay—or rather don't pay—if you use CompuServe's own network of local access telephone numbers. They maintain these phone numbers in almost all major and many minor cities and there is no line charge for connecting through one of these. They also have an 800 number for modem connections and it carries a charge of $8.50 an hour. If you need to connect through SprintNet or Tymnet it's $11.70 an hour from 8 a.m. to 7 p.m., or $1.70 an hour other times.

When you add all of these charges together it's not at all unheard of for some CompuServe users to get bills of more than $1,000 a month, though $20-$40 is more common. Is it worth it? Yeah, probably. At least there are more than a million people who think so.

CompuServe has 1.5 million members and more than 1,700 categories and special interest groups. Aside from the people you "meet," there are whole storehouses of free programs and valuable commentary from experienced investors. One of the most useful features of any of the public databases we're going to talk about in the next few chapters is e-mail—electronic mail. You can send letters, files, contracts, pictures, etc., and hold conversations in real-time. In fact, the regulars on these systems refer to any communications still done with stamps and envelopes as "snail mail"—useful for sending calendars at the end of the year.

There is a sign-up coupon at the back of this book that will waive the usual $25 startup fee and give you a free hour or so to try out the system. And it's certainly worth taking some time to do so. What have you got to lose? No matter what Milton Friedman says, sometimes there really is a free lunch.

Navigation: Land Ho!

You can sign on to this and any other database service with any kind of computer. CompuServe will provide software for both IBM compatibles and Macs. You can either have this sent to you through the mail or you can download it from the system itself when you connect for your trial exploration. The jewel in their crown is the new WinCIM software, which stands for "Windows CompuServe Information Manager," and will simplify your journey enormously if you use Windows (see Figure 9-1). If you use a Macintosh, you would get MacCIM. There is a $10 charge for the software, but they give you $10 worth of extra time on the service, so it's sort of a wash and certainly worth it.

This is not the only way to navigate, but it's the best way. You can either mouse-click your way through a series of menus and selections or you can use "Go..." commands.

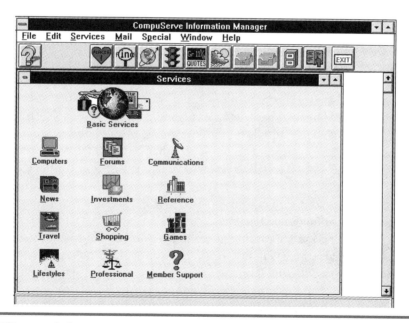

Figure 9-1 The WinCIM main screen

Go for It

At the very top of the WinCIM screen there is a row of icons, each of which can be double-clicked to initiate various activities. (These icons are often called "buttons" in the jargon of Windows users.) One of the icons is a stoplight icon (which glows green on a color monitor) as in "green for go." When you double-click on the stoplight, a dialog box, shown below, appears in the middle of the screen.

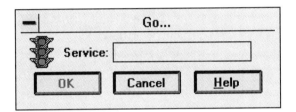

On the blank line, you can type in a "Go..." command, such as QUOTES, which takes you directly to the stock quotes menu. If you type in PORT, you will be taken to the Portfolio Evaluation service, where you can create, monitor, and update the weighted values of all the items in your personal portfolio, of whatever type. (There is a charge for this.) If you can't remember or simply don't know the symbol for a security, Go...LOOKUP. If you want to know who has good payouts these days, Go...DIVIDENDS. If you don't know any commands, Go...HELP. I think you get the picture.

As mentioned earlier, CompuServe can be accessed through local phone numbers in most cities and towns, phone numbers owned by them. That means no long distance charges unless you happen to live in West Pumpkin, Idaho, or its equivalent. If you don't know the number for a particular area, Go...PHONES. For the first-time user, the sign-up feature when you log on for your free trial will provide you with a toll-free number.

Many services are available only on an extra fee basis. The service flashes a notice if you are about to go into an area that has an extra fee. Some of these areas allow some initial free time for new users to roam around. If you don't know what the extra charge is and want to find out before you do any exploring, Go...RATES. If you want to know the status of your current bill, Go...BILLING. If you're not sure about anything, Go...HELP.

note

The CompuServe Customer Service number is 800/848-8990. Their hours are 8 a.m. to midnight, Monday through Friday, and from noon to 10 p.m. weekends, eastern standard time. Representatives in other countries are available during local business hours. At least that's what it says in the fine print. Getting someone to answer that call is another matter. Good luck to you. I once made 42 calls over a period of five days and never got anything but a busy signal. Go...QUESTIONS or Go...FEEDBACK will get you an answer online faster than you're likely to get a call through.

Tick Talk

As you saw in Figure 9-1, the first screen of WinCIM displays some fairly intuitive icons. Right next to the stoplight is another very useful icon, "Quotes." During stock market hours, the quotes are delayed 15 minutes. CompuServe gets its quotes from PC Quote, Inc., in Chicago.

You can't tell the players without a scorecard and if you want a quote you need to know the ticker symbol. You can Go...LOOKUP, but it's easier, faster, and cheaper to make a list of those stocks you usually watch from the symbols shown in the *Wall Street Journal* every day or *Barron's* at the end of the week. Many brokers will also mail you a Standard & Poor's Pocket Guide or something similar, which lists ticker symbols and much other information for stocks on the established exchanges. Some publications and CompuServe itself will also provide a CUSIP number, which stands for the Committee on Uniform Securities Identification Procedures number. Even market indexes and bonds have these identifiers. Using a CUSIP number for calling in quotes eliminates the chance of error. If you look up Borden, for example, and get a symbol, you might be downloading Borden Chemical instead of Borden Foods, or vice versa. There are quite a few companies and funds with the same or very similar names. One symbol comes already preloaded on WinCIM when you first get it, by the way. And what might that symbol be? HRB, of course—for H&R Block.

If you just enter the first few characters in a company or fund name, LOOKUP will offer you a choice of stocks, indexes, currencies, bonds, or options that match it. Pick the one that really does match it. You can also ask for a LOOKUP REPORT, which will give you a list of all the issues for a given company: common, preferred, bonds, convertibles, warrants, etc.

There are about 600 industry indexes, from the universally known Dow Jones Industrial Average to things like the Standard & Poor's Shoe Index—which does not count shoes, but rather measures the activity in the stocks of shoe companies.

There are many foreign indexes, including the most common, such as the Nikkei (Japan), the FTSE (London Financial Times Stock Exchange Index), and the Hang Seng (Hong Kong). You can also call up less-common stock indexes for places such as Germany, France, Italy, Sweden, and many others. There are also symbols for frequently consulted statistical data, such as volume, advances and declines, put and call ratios, etc. To find any of these, Go...INDICATORS. Commodity prices require a special access symbol because, unlike stocks or bonds, they are contract based and the contracts have a time limit. These symbols are found under CSYMBOL.

Basic Services: The Investments Menu

The material from here on is arranged in the same order as the CompuServe menus appear as you move through the system. If you go to the main screen of WinCIM (Figure 9-1), for example, you will see an icon of money and a chart, labeled "Investments." Just double-click the button and you're on your way.

The next screen, shown in Figure 9-2, reads CIS:MONEY. It displays the Money Matters/Markets menu and one of the items is "Basic Quotes." This is a quick way to enter a ticker symbol or CUSIP number for a security and get a quote, one stock at a time. You can enter a short list of ticker symbols for occasional quote monitoring by clicking the "Quotes" icon button at the top of the screen. Enter a symbol or CUSIP number and you'll get the volume, high, low, and the most-recent trade.

Up to 20 quotes can be retrieved in a single session under Basic Service. Extended Service and Executive Service allow you to pull more,

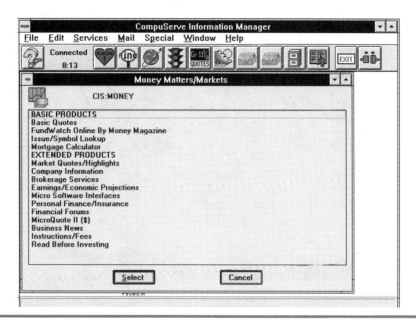

Figure 9-2 WinCIM's Money Matters/Markets menu

but there is an extra monthly charge. MetaStock users can sign up for unlimited quote use at a preferred customer rate. For more information, Go...EQUIS. You can also Go...FINHELP, which is in the same menu area as quotes and will provide answers on session and product surcharges, update times, and the chance to offer suggestions.

Fund-Watching for Fun and Profit

The best of the four items in the Basic Products menu of the CIS:MONEY screen is probably *Money Magazine*'s FundWatch Online (see Figure 9-3), where you get to create your own screens to sift through more than 1,900 mutual funds. That's about all there are, because even though you will often read or hear the usual investment gurus tell you there are more mutual funds than there are stocks on the New York Stock Exchange, the truth is that over half of those are merely "money market" funds and have no significance for an investor. Most people don't realize it, but money market accounts are mutual funds. By choosing "Screen

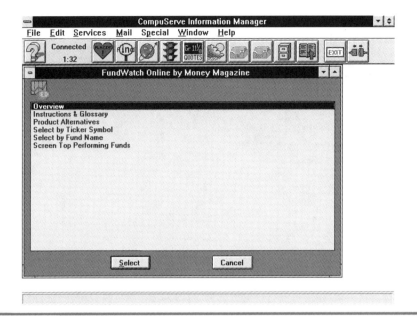

Figure 9-3   Money Magazine's FundWatch top-level menu

Top Performing Funds" from the menu shown in Figure 9-3, you'll be taken to the menu (Figure 9-4) where you can select your search criteria.

FundWatch currently offers information on 142 international funds and is updated monthly. The reports are fairly detailed and can also be screened according to your own criteria. All you need to know is the ticker symbol or the first few letters of the fund's name. (Figure 9-5 shows a report on a Latin American fund.) This service provides a glossary of terms that sometimes confuse people, such as "beta," a measure of volatility.

You can download this or any other material and read it later when you're off-line, saving yourself some charges. To save anything for later reading, just click the button at the bottom of the screen that says "File It." The item is then filed in your Filing Cabinet, which you can see as a filing cabinet icon up on the main menu bar. Anytime you want to look at what's filed there, just double-click on the button.

FundWatch reports are detailed, but are not the last word. They contain information on a fund's assets, yields, annual expenses (in percentages), maximum load fee, net asset value per share, redemption

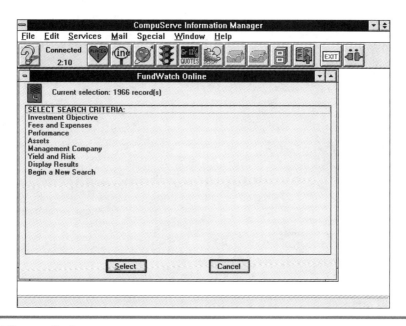

Figure 9-4   With FundWatch Online, you can select search criteria for mutual funds

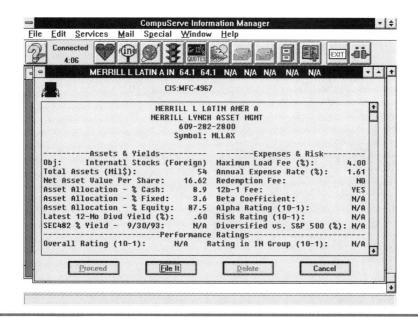

Figure 9-5   Sample FundWatch display for a Latin American fund

Screening for Gems

Screening funds is a simple matter with the FundWatch service. You can screen with the following factors, each with its own characteristics:

▶ **Investment Objective:** You can ask for an initial screen that would just look at aggressive growth, income, international, or precious metals funds.

▶ **Fees and Expenses:** Load fee, redemption fee, annual expense rate.

▶ **Performance**: Fund return by time period, rating by investment objective, overall ranking among all funds for the period.

▶ **Asset Allocation**: Among cash, stocks (by industry sector), and fixed income (bonds by sector).

▶ **Management Company:** Enter the management company you prefer, if any. Fidelity, for example, or Putnam, or Vanguard.

▶ **Yield and Risks**: Volatility, risk rating, risk adjusted return.

You don't have to use all the variables; you can choose only one, if you prefer. Once you've done that, you'll be able to get a ranking of the funds of interest to you by their return over the current year-to-date, the last full year, three years, five years, ten years, or how it performed during the latest bull market and the latest bear market. Pretty impressive.

fee, if any, asset allocation (percentage in cash, fixed income, equities), beta, alpha, and risk ratings.

Extended Financial Services

Extended Financial Services, like the mutual fund screening described earlier, carry extra charges. If you see a "$" sign alongside the menu or an item, it means this is a "Premium Service" and there will be a surcharge beyond the usual hourly rate. If you see a "$E," this means it's an "Executive Service," which carries the regular hourly rate plus a surcharge, plus an Executive Service membership fee ($10 a month).

If you just want a quick look at the NYSE, Dow Jones Industrials, Standard & Poor's 500 Option index, NASDAQ, London Gold Fix, and a peek at the yen, pound, and Deutsche mark, there is a feature of the

Extended Services called Current Market Snapshot (see Figure 9-6). If you want to go there immediately when you first log on to the system, just Go...SNAPSHOT.

That's okay for the current day. If you want to see a historical view, you would go into CompuServe's MicroQuote II database (Go...SECURITIES), stocked with 12 years of historical data covering more than 125,000 exchange-traded equity, debt, option, mutual fund, unit, and warrant issues. It is updated by 7:00 a.m. (eastern standard time) following the previous day's close. This database includes Canadian and OTC (Over-the-Counter) market securities. It also includes foreign exchange prices for major currencies. It does not, however, include prices for foreign securities.

You can call up a graph of any stock you're interested in with Go...TREND, as shown with the chart of the Standard & Poor's 500 Option index in Figure 9-7. The chart can be daily, weekly, or monthly. The range can be as short as 15 days or as long as 70 months—nearly six years. Different charts have different information. Bonds and foreign exchange charts do not include volume, for example.

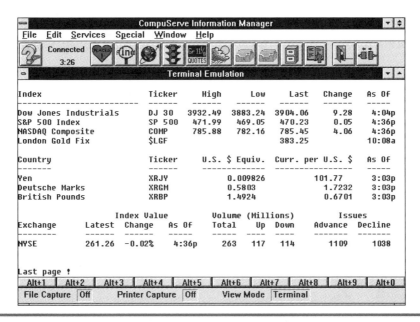

Figure 9-6 The Executive "Snapshot" service provides a quick market summary

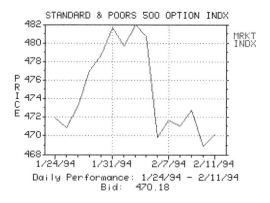

Figure 9-7   Graph of the Standard & Poor's 500 Option Index

tip

Here's a tip from the house: In specifying intervals to create a chart, experiment first with H&R Block (symbol: HRB), since CompuServe doesn't charge for information on their parent company. That way, if you suddenly realize that the time span you're downloading includes not 25 different prices but 2,500, you won't have to pay a huge quote charge to see the mistake.

Go...PRISTATS offers a way to compare the prices for a security over time and looks at their standard deviation from the mean. Statistically, this lets you see whether some unusual price or volume action is really unusual or just a fluctuation within previous bounds for this issue. In short, it doesn't matter much if a stock's volume swings up to twice its daily average if that sort of swing happens fairly often.

Go...OPRICE lets you look at all the options trading on any given stock or index (see Figure 9-8). The updating on this is continuous throught the day.

Go...UKPRICE lets you look at historical quotes on more than 5,000 British equity issues and some 350 market indexes. If you need to find a symbol for one of these stocks, you have to go to a different place from the U.S. LOOKUP file. It's called SEDOL and the command to get there is Go...SEDOL, which will produce a number to go with the stock name you type in. The SEDOL number acts the same as the CUSIP number we talked about earlier.

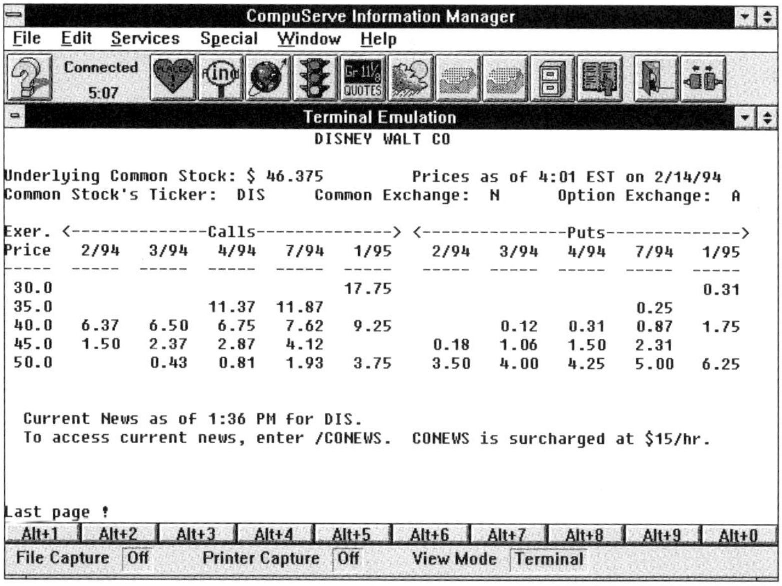

```
 ┌─────────────────────────────────────────────────────────┐ ▼▲
 │               CompuServe Information Manager              │
 │ File   Edit   Services   Special   Window   Help          │
 │ ┌──┐ Connected  ┌─┐ ┌─┐ ┌─┐ ┌─┐ ┌─┐ ┌─┐ ┌─┐ ┌─┐ ┌─┐ ┌─┐ ┌─┐│
 │ ?    5:07        ♥  find ◉  ☰  QUOTES                      │
 ├─────────────────────────────────────────────────────────┤
 │                   Terminal Emulation                     │ ▼▲
 │                      DISNEY WALT CO                       │
 │                                                           │
 │ Underlying Common Stock: $ 46.375      Prices as of 4:01 EST on 2/14/94 │
 │ Common Stock's Ticker:  DIS     Common Exchange:  N     Option Exchange:  A │
 │                                                           │
 │ Exer. <--------------Calls-------------> <--------------Puts-------------> │
 │ Price  2/94   3/94   4/94   7/94   1/95    2/94   3/94   4/94   7/94   1/95 │
 │ -----  -----  -----  -----  -----  -----   -----  -----  -----  -----  ----- │
 │  30.0                              17.75                                0.31 │
 │  35.0                11.37  11.87                               0.25       │
 │  40.0   6.37   6.50   6.75   7.62   9.25           0.12   0.31   0.87   1.75 │
 │  45.0   1.50   2.37   2.87   4.12           0.18   1.06   1.50   2.31       │
 │  50.0          0.43   0.81   1.93   3.75   3.50   4.00   4.25   5.00   6.25 │
 │                                                           │
 │                                                           │
 │   Current News as of 1:36 PM for DIS.                     │
 │   To access current news, enter /CONEWS.  CONEWS is surcharged at $15/hr. │
 │                                                           │
 │                                                           │
 │                                                           │
 │ Last page !                                               │
 ├──────┬──────┬──────┬──────┬──────┬──────┬──────┬──────┬──────┬──────┤
 │ Alt+1│ Alt+2│ Alt+3│ Alt+4│ Alt+5│ Alt+6│ Alt+7│ Alt+8│ Alt+9│ Alt+0│
 ├──────┴──────┴──────┴──────┴──────┴──────┴──────┴──────┴──────┴──────┤
 │ File Capture │Off    Printer Capture │Off    View Mode │Terminal   │
 └─────────────────────────────────────────────────────────┘
```

Figure 9-8   Option pricing

Go...MARKET gets you the highlights of the previous day's market action (see Figure 9-9). This is a good way to start out the trading day, recapping the previous day's activity before starting the new one. You can get such reports on the NYSE, the Amex, the OTC, and 15 other markets.

Go...CPRICE lets you check on commodity prices, one contract at a time, by day, week, or month. The program displays open, high, low, and settling prices, with volume and open interest. Cash market prices are also available. There is a commodity symbol lookup feature which can be reached with Go...CSYMBOL.

Screen Test

Go...ANALYSIS has a feature that lets you do screens, as in *filters*. This feature has a 25 cent a minute surcharge. To go there directly from any screen or menu, type Go...COSCREEN. You can do a screen of the Disclosure II database of 10,000 companies (see Figure 9-10). Selection criteria include a variety of rates of growth and financial ratios, along with

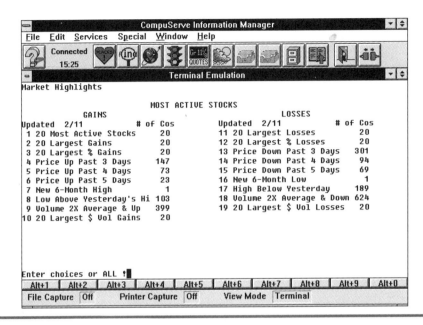

Figure 9-9 The Market Highlights screen (Go...MARKET)

industry codes, home state, total assets, book value, market value, annual sales, net income, cash flow, latest price, etc.

One of the preset filters contained in this section is the well-known CANSLIM screen from William J. O'Neil, author of *How to Make Money in Stocks* (McGraw-Hill, NY: 1990) and publisher of *Investor's Daily*. For those of you unfamiliar with this screen, the letters of the mnemonic CANSLIM describe the following:

C   =   Current quarterly earnings per share

A   =   Annual earnings increase

N   =   New product, new management, new highs

S   =   Shares of common stock outstanding

L   =   Leader or laggard in its industry

I   =   Industry sponsorship (usually the underwriter if a new offering)

M   =   Market direction

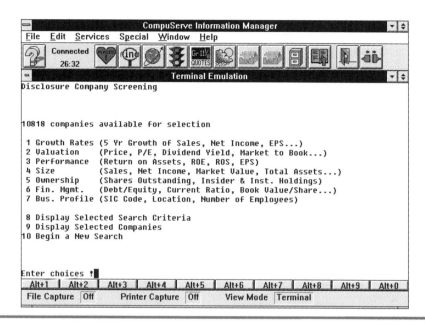

Figure 9-10 Screening potential holdings for particular criteria using the Disclosure II database

Ten Days in a Quandary, and Other Travelers' Tales

It's starting to get complex. Why, any reasonable person might ask, doesn't somebody just create a function that would give me a quick list of all the databases that contain information on any company I'm interested in? Even better, why couldn't it construct a menu that would also allow me to retrieve charts and graphs, pricing statistics, a detailed issue examination, and current news on that company? Good idea! It's called Go...ANALYZER. And Figure 9-11 shows an example of what it looks like when you give it a company name to compile.

Go...ANALYZER is fast and, as usual, there is an extra charge. On the other hand, it can save a lot of online time. You can get a rough idea of the kind of reports you'll find by taking a look at the H&R Block sample

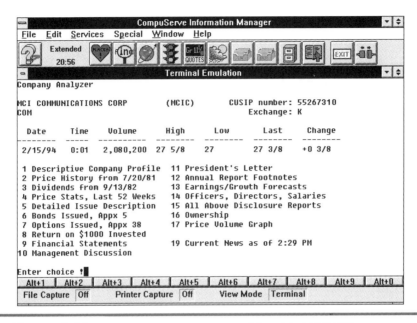

Figure 9-11   The ANALYZER screen (Go...ANALYZER)

report, for which you are charged only at the flat Basic Services rate. (Anywhere there's H&R Block sample information on CompuServe, they won't charge you beyond the flat rate for that information.)

Go...BUSDB provides the full text from five years' worth of 500 industry newsletters and one year's backlog of 550 newsletters. Take your choice. A similar product is Business Dateline: Go...BUSDATE. This consists of full-text articles from more than 115 regional business publications in the U.S. and Canada (see Figure 9-12, which you'll notice has a news item on L.L. Bean's operations in Japan). The emphasis here is on local economic conditions, retailing, real estate, management, financial institutions, transportation, and electronics. The files go from 1985 to the present.

One of the more useful services within this giant database is InvesTEXT. You can reach it with Go...INVTEXT. It is a compilation of full-text reports from over 50 brokerage houses and investment research firms. The report shown in Figure 9-13 is from the brokerage and investment banking house of S.G. Warburg Securities, London, and concerns BP—British Petroleum. Not only can you pull company profiles

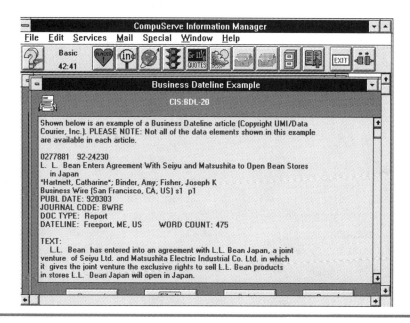

Figure 9-12 Example Business Dateline Screen (Go...BUSDATE)

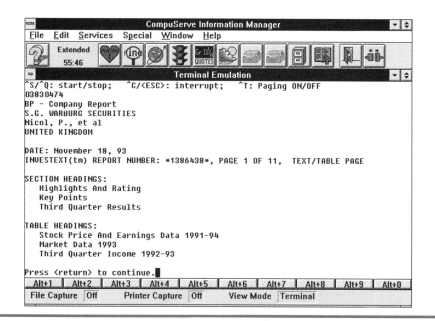

Figure 9-13 A sample company report (Go...INVTEXT)

with the usual financial statistics, but you can also get the analysis and recommendations from the brokerage or research house, plus forecasts of future performance. There are reports on 8,200 U.S. public companies and 2,300 publicly held foreign companies. Also available are reports on more than 50 industry groups, plus new technology and product development, and competition and market share estimates.

Go Global!

Go...COINTL places you smack dab in the middle of International Company Information, the area that comprises databases of U.S., Canadian, European, German, U.K., and Pacific Rim companies. From the menu choices, shown below, you can select a number of international areas and pick your stock from there.

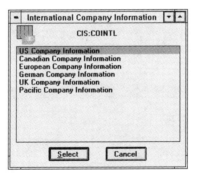

Europe

Go...EUROLIB takes you to the information set on European companies, which contains Citibank's Global Report (see Figure 9-14), Business Database Plus, and InvesText. The only unfamiliar product in this collection is the European Company Library. The library contains selected financial information on more than 2 million European companies. It's a ridiculous number, but most of them are private and not suitable grist for the investment mill.

Report sources include

▶ **ABC Europe:** Directory information on European companies and products, especially in Germany. Updated quarterly.

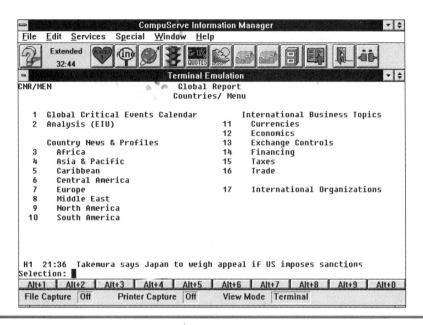

Figure 9-14 The Citibank Global Report menu

▶ **D&B-European Dun's Market Identifiers:** Updated quarterly.

▶ **Financial Times Analysis Reports - Europe:** Updated weekly.

▶ **Financial Times Mergers & Acquisitions International:** Summarizes mergers, acquisitions, buyouts, and pre-bid speculative announcements in all key non-U.S. companies. Updated daily.

▶ **Hoppenstedt, Austria:** Directory of leading Austrian businesses. Updated semi-annually.

▶ **Hoppenstedt, Benelux:** Directory of companies in Belgium, the Netherlands, and Luxembourg. Updated quarterly.

▶ **Kompass Europe:** Directory of companies and products in selected European countries. Updated annually.

▶ **Telefirm Directory of French Companies:** Directory of over 90 percent of the companies registered in France. Updated monthly.

Germany

International Company Information has a section for German and U.K. companies, and has better coverage of the latter. Of the four databases under German Company Information, only the German Company Library has not yet been discussed, the others being Global Report, Business Database Plus, and InvesText. Go...GERLIB will gain you access to five databases:

▶ **BDI Germany Industry**: A directory of "export-oriented" manufacturing companies in Germany. Updated annually.

▶ **CREDITREFORM**: Profiles German companies of all sizes, with a summary of products and services. Quarterly updates.

▶ **D&B-German Dun's Market Identifiers**: Data taken from the D&B-European Dun's Market Identifiers database.

▶ **Hoppenstedt Germany**: Directory of German companies with more than 20 employees. Updated quarterly.

▶ **Kompass Germany**: Directory of German companies and products. Updated annually.

United Kingdom

Go...COUK stands not for eccentric behavior, but for the U.K. Company Information. The menu shows Citibank's Global Report, InvesText, and Business Database Plus. You'll also see U.K. Historical Stock Pricing, which covers over 5,000 U.K. equity issues and about 350 market indexes. The updates are usually daily—that is, 9:00 p.m. EST for individual issues and 12:00 a.m. EST for the market indexes. You'll need to look up the SEDOL (their CUSIP) number before obtaining a price for a U.K. security. Remember, this is one of the largest stock markets in the world, so there is a lot of information.

Go...UKLIB takes you to the U.K. Company Library, a combination of directories and financial information.

▶ **D&B-European Dun's Market Identifiers - U.K. Countries:**
Summary descriptions of over 1.2 million public and private companies in the U.K. Updated quarterly.

▶ **ICC British Company Directory:** Directory of every company registered at the Companies Registration Office of the U.K. Updated weekly.

▶ **Jordans Registered Companies:** Directory of all companies registered within the U.K. Updated weekly.

▶ **Kompass U.K.:** Product information, number of employees, and names of managers. Updated quarterly.

▶ **Extel Cards:** Detailed financial information on over 4,000 British companies. Updated annually.

▶ **Financial Times Analysis Reports:** Business summary, profit and loss statement, geographical analysis, five-year balance sheet, capital structure, and directors' names. Updated weekly.

▶ **ICC British Company Financial Datasheets:** Financial results for leading U.K. companies. Updated weekly.

▶ **Infocheck U.K. Company Financial Datasheets**: Financial details, news, and industry sector comparisons for over 400,000 companies in the U.K. Updated weekly.

Online Brokerage

Some investors enjoy personal interaction with their broker, but if you're going to do your own research anyway, you can save money by using discount brokers online—Go...BROKERAGE—shown in Figure 9-15. You'll also find a range of other financial services available through these brokers—IRA accounts, Keoghs, etc.—and even a stock market trading game that pays the monthly winner $50.

The online broker with service stations here and elsewhere on the electronic highway is E*Trade, based in Palo Alto, California. E*Trade is cheap. A 200-share lot at $35/share costs $77 with Quick & Reilly, $100 with Charles Schwab, $162 with Merrill Lynch, but just $35 with E*Trade. In fact, every trade costs $35 with E*Trade until you get past 2,500 shares. After that, it's any number, any price, at 1.5 cents per share. The E*Trade discount on options is similarly deep.

There is no connect time surcharge for E*Trade. You can open an account, manage a portfolio, get news alerts, place orders, and receive

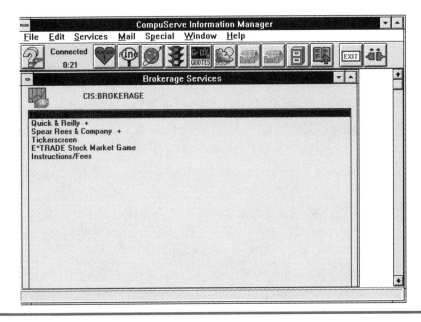

Figure 9-15 CompuServe's Brokerage Services menu (Go...BROKERAGE)

automatic confirmations—all online. E*Trade is a member of the Securities Industry Protection Corporation, which "protects securities in an account up to $500,000, cash up to $100,000. Additional insurance for $2,000,000 is in force through Lloyd's of London, for $2,500,000 total protection."

You can set up margin accounts, option accounts, and a choice of five money market accounts with automatic cash sweeps. E*Trade will also allow you to set up as many as 75 portfolios, each automatically updated when you trade. An existing brokerage account can be transferred to E*Trade (and vice versa) using the industry standard brokerage account transfer form.

You can also reach Quick & Reilly through CompuServe. This company started in 1974 and was the first member of the NYSE to offer discount brokerage to the public. It now has 700,000 customers and 90 branch offices. Q&R puts its own brokers on the trading floors, rather than using an automated order entry method. You may be able to get a better price execution this way. Q&R has a no-fee cash management service, with daily sweeps and free check writing. They have the usual range of account options, such as IRAs, Keoghs, pension, profit-sharing, custodial plans, trust, estate, corporate, partnership, and investment club accounts. The minimum account size is $10,000.

E*Trade Games: At Play in the Fields of the Bourse

E*Trade also lets you choose from two online games. One game is for stocks only, the other for stocks and options. The high profit maker each month wins a $50 prize. Go...ETGAME to mouse-click for dollars. You can play as many times as you like, using different "handles" (playing names). Since it's only a mind game, the losers only lose their minds. You start with $100,000 of game money and can trade as frequently as you like. You may also have a real account with E*Trade; there is no connection or mingling of records between the game and real accounts.

The Fine Art of Guessing

The I/B/E/S Earnings Estimates database stands for Institutional Broker's Estimate System and represents a kind of consensus of annual and long-term forecasts from more than 2,500 analysts at 130 brokerage and institutional research firms. The database covers over 4,500 U.S. companies and reports the most optimistic and pessimistic EPS (earnings per share) estimates, as well as median, mean and variation, and current share price, earnings per share, and price to earnings ratio (see Figure 9-16). I/B/E/S is updated every Sunday and market values updated daily.

Go...MMS takes you to the MMS International Financial Reports, a service used by money managers worldwide as a primary analytical source of economic and financial information. It compiles analysis from more than 50 economists in 12 financial centers to form a 24-hour network of market-watchers. MMS provides economic and technical analysis of the debt, currency, and equity markets to some 20,000 market participants worldwide. Highlights include

▶ **The Global Critical Events Calendar**: Major speeches and other events likely to affect market activity. There is no surcharge and the service is available weekly at 8:00 p.m. EST.

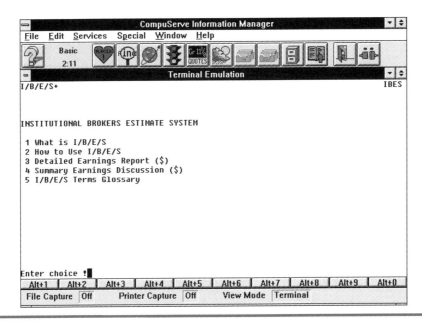

Figure 9-16 The International Broker's Estimate System screen

▶ **The Daily Equity Market Report:** This is where you find the MMS Recommended Portfolio of 20 specified stocks, each with buy/sell prices. There is a charge of $5 per report.

▶ **The Daily Currency Market Report:** Factors influencing spot and future prices for foreign exchange. Long-term forecasts for the five major currencies are provided. $5 per report.

▶ **The Daily Debt Market Commentary:** Analysis of interest rate trends, relevant to all financial markets.

▶ **FEDWATCH:** A newsletter written by senior MMS analysts and released each Friday afternoon. It focuses on Fed policy and key interest rates.

▶ **MMS Weekly Economic Survey:** A snapshot of the expectations forecast by 200 of the nation's top dealers, traders, and economists.

Meet the People

The Financial Forums offer the first direct contact with other humans on CompuServe.

The Forums are the club meeting rooms of CompuServe, but there's more than just gossip and brainstorming with fellow enthusiasts available here. Each Forum has its own list of current downloadable messages and replies on a variety of subjects, as well as a searchable library of older lists (see Figure 9-17). The two Financial Forums of interest to us are the Investors Forum and the NAIC (National Association of Investors Corporation) Forum.

Go...INVFORUM and get ready for a good time, because this takes you to the Investors Forum. Their library of files includes a Global Investing category (see Figure 9-18), within which at any one time are perhaps 20-30 messages from Forum members on all kinds of related subjects—commission fees, the risks of Indian mutual funds, how to invest in Poland, etc. (Under a general heading like Mutual Funds, there were 56 messages at last log-in.)

Welcome To The Investors+ Forum

Welcome to the Investor's Forum (GO INVFORUM)!

This forum is devoted to all aspects of investing -- stocks, commodities, mutual funds, options, real estate, bonds, financial planning, and software designed to aid you in investing and trading. If you are just getting started in investing, we invite you to explore our NOVICE INVESTOR Message Section and Library. Users of MetaStock Professional and Other EQUIS International software products now have an area in the forum of their own: EQUIS/MetaStock. Of course, any questions concerning CompuServe's Financial, Business, and News services are welcomed.

To join us here, all you need to do is select the "JOIN" button. No other

Name: ▮▮▮▮▮▮   [Join]   [Leave]
Interests: [Visit]
[Help]

Figure 9-17   The Investors Forum Welcome screen (Go...INVFORUM)

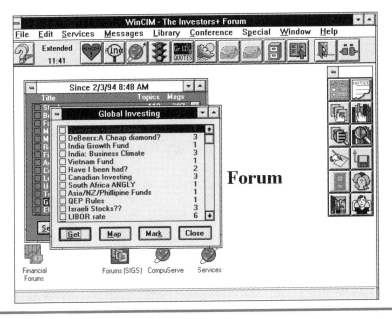

Figure 9-18   The Global Investing message base in the Investor's Forum

There's a section called the Novice Investor that is probably worth browsing through if you're new to the game. You can leave a message here on just about any question and get back a mix of replies, some sharp, some dull. The Town Square is the general, catchall message board for the Investors Forum, where you'll find such questions as, "How do you like E*Trade?" or "What can I do with $500?"

It's News to Me

Business News is the last major database under our Extended Financial Services offerings on CompuServe. We've got four products to choose from here, beginning with the Executive News Service.

Go...ENS and you get access to an electronic clipping service that monitors the Associated Press, *Washington Post*, United Press International, Reuters, and the OTC News Alert. What the computers search for is the name of any company or companies you specify—or the name of an industry, a market, or even just a phrase. This Premium Service even puts your clipped stories into special folders for you to review at your convenience. If you really want to stay up with breaking news about both your business and personal interests in a thorough fashion, this is one way to go. For business, U.S., and world news, Go...NEWSGRID (see Figure 9-19) gets you world headline news. The headlines change as the news changes. You can also do a keyword search for stories appearing in the last seven days.

A Word Before We Go...

This is by far the largest database service we will look at in this section. The only larger one would be the Internet which, despite all the recent attention it has been receiving, is largely a service for information interchange between academics and researchers. Let's turn our attention now to Prodigy.

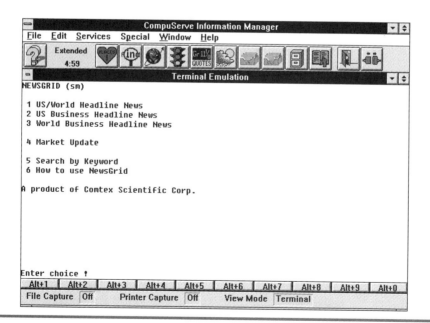

Figure 9-19   The NEWSGRID menu (Go...NEWSGRID)

CHAPTER 10

PRODIGY

The two great strengths of Prodigy are its ease of use and graphical look. Its greatest weakness is that it is slow, at times unbelievably slow.

CompuServe, when operated through the new WinCIM program for Windows or MacCIM for the Macintosh, is much easier to navigate now than even a few months ago. But Prodigy was designed from the start to be a family-oriented general purpose news and entertainment service, and it is truly easy to use. You cannot get lost in Prodigy because subject areas are color-coded. All Business/Finance menus are green; News/Weather is dark blue; Sports, red; Reference, brown; Shopping, gray, and so on.

Small directional triangles at the bottom left of the screen move you ahead a page or back a page with the click of a mouse button. At the far left, a single button, looking like a miniature version of the main Prodigy screen, immediately takes you back to the main menu, no matter where you are at the moment. Clicking on a button with the letter "M" takes you back to your previous menu.

What this kind of navigational simplicity means for our purposes is that if you are a Prodigy member, or want to become a member, this is the fastest and easiest way to get a pretty good market snapshot at any time during the day. (There's a coupon for a free Prodigy membership at the back of this book.) The information is not deep compared to what's available on CompuServe or Dow Jones News/Retrieval, but the water is clear and free of turbulence. There's not a huge amount of financial information on Prodigy, but there is a good amount of material here and it's easy to get to. Instead of just talking about it, let's step through it—just as if we were logging on to the system.

Raising a Child Prodigy

Figure 10-1 shows the Prodigy opening screen. The left-hand side provides news headlines and a couple of items on the bottom that relate to using the Prodigy service itself. The right-hand side is a column of menu bars that take you to the various sections and departments. The bars are different colors, and that color coding continues as you go through the database, so you have a ready visual guide to what section you are roaming. The menu bars start with News/Weather at the top, then Business/Finance, Sports, Communications, Entertainment, etc.

The top menu bar (on some versions the menu bar is on the bottom) provides options on how to save a file, print it, set up mail for automatic sending, and so on. The third item from the left—labeled "Jump"—provides the same function as the "Go..." commands in CompuServe. Once you know your way around the system, you no longer have to work through the layers of menus. You can simply "jump" to the key word that defines your target section—as in "jump" to "quotes."

As mentioned earlier, the menu bar on the bottom shows a small icon of the Prodigy screen at the left, then two triangles for paging forward or

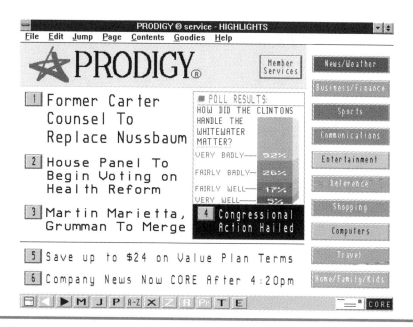

Figure 10-1   The Prodigy opening screen. The shaded bars along the right-hand side are different colors. As you move through the system each subject area will retain its color

backward. You can see that the right-pointing triangle is dark, indicating there's more if you want to turn the page. The left-pointing triangle is white, which indicates you are already at the first page and there is nothing to be seen by turning back a page. The meaning of the other letters at the bottom will become apparent as you use the system. They simply provide shortcuts for various functions; "Pr," for example, prints the screen. Near the bottom right of the screen, there is a picture of an envelope with a stamp. This indicates that there's mail waiting for you on the system. Often, it will just turn out to be pitches to buy stuff—you can get junk mail on Prodigy. In fact, one of the things that annoys some people about Prodigy is that there are ads running along the bottom of the screen. The ads change as you move along, and often they change even if you stay in one place. As I say, this annoys some people, but it doesn't bother me in the least. Some of the ads are even interesting, though I have never bought anything they offer.

And Now, A Word from Our Sponsor

This seems like an appropriate moment to talk about shopping on database services. Prodigy has "Shopping" as one of its main menu selections; CompuServe has its "Mall." One of the dreams of all the companies that run database services is that these will become the equivalent of electronic shopping malls, or at least mail-order catalogs, and that millions of people will do much of their shopping from their computer screens. Sure, and someday people will live under the oceans, but don't hold your breath till it happens. A natural question most users would have is, "Do you get good deals shopping through database services?" My general observation has been that you don't. It's amazing when you consider that these companies' cost of sales is virtually zero— no store, no rent, no salespeople, etc. But instead of passing that savings on to you, the shopper, they apparently want to keep the extra profit, because the prices on almost all goods are no better than you can get at your local discount store, and often they're worse.

Back to Business

Skipping over the "News/Weather" menu button, let's go right to the heart of the matter and click on "Business/Finance." What we get is shown in Figure 10-2—more on the Grumman-Marietta merger. After the first three items, we start to get Prodigy house ads. The menu selections on the right have now changed to More News, Quotes, Markets, Research, Online Trading, Online Banking, Home Office, Financial BBs, and Products. These are the main headings under Business/Finance, and they too have their sub-menus which will appear as you go deeper. You can tell where you are at any time by looking at both the left-hand edge and the top line of the screen. This says "Business/Finance" now, the main menu for the Business/Finance catagory. In order to get back to the previous menu—the one you used to get to this point—simply click on the button with the letter "M" at the bottom of the screen. That always takes you back one menu.

Starting at the top of Business/Finance, we select the first button, "More News," which brings up a list of items. If we choose "Economy News," from the list, we get a screen that looks like Figure 10-3. Now we're getting to some actual information. Everything up to this point has

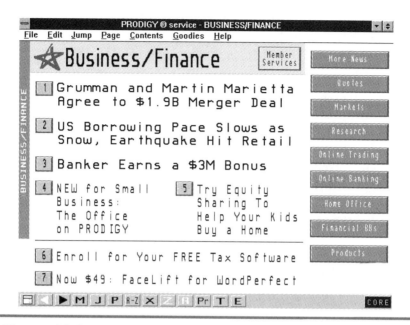

Figure 10-2   The Business/Finance menu. This is the second choice from the top on the main menu (Figure 10-1)

been mostly dancing, but now we can select stories on consumer credit, what Hosokawa is going to do about American pressure to ease trade restrictions between the U.S. and Japan, criticism of the Fed, news about Poland, etc. At the bottom, of course, there's an ad. At the right, there's a new set of menu buttons, this group taking us to major features of the Prodigy financial services. The first button is Business News, and right after that we get International Business, Company News, Market Update, Market Close, Quote Track 1, Quote Track 2, etc.

Most of these button titles are self-explanatory, but Quote Track 1 and 2 probably are not. These are where you can create your portfolio or track lists of stocks, indexes, and commodities that you want to follow on a regular basis. Instead of having to enter those items over and over, you just do it once, save the list, and whenever you log on again you can simply click on your "track" and everything you have there will be updated. This kind of simple, auto-pilot navigation shows off Prodigy at its best.

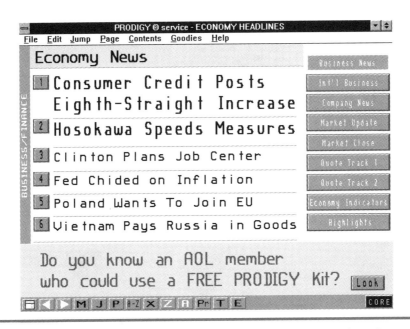

Figure 10-3   The Economy News menu. More news and market updates fill the other choices on the right-hand side

The Brotherhood of Nations and Other Fantasies

Selecting the second menu button in Figure 10-3, "Int'l Business," gets us to the screen shown in Figure 10-4. Now the information is more focused, and we see stories on BMW's marketing strategy, how Germany is working to squelch the Saudi deal to buy billions of dollars' worth of planes from Boeing, and how the European Commission is trying to kill General Electric's purchase of an Italian electronics company so G.E. can funnel its products into the European Common Market. If you get the impression from these headlines that the Europeans don't want us competing in their markets, or anywhere else for that matter, you would be right.

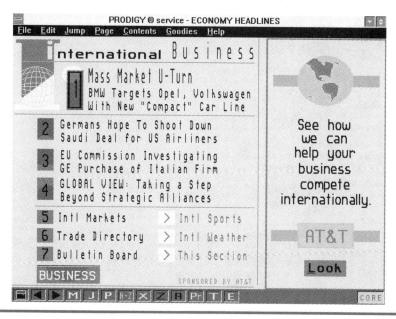

Figure 10-4   The International Business menu brings up a screen which offers still more menu choices. But here they are almost all related to foreign company news

Up with Ordinaries

The third button on the menu shown in Figure 10-3 is "Company News." You can select "Company News" to get stories on any company you're interested in, and later on we'll show you an example. For now, we'll skip this and select the fourth button, "Market Update." This takes us to the menu shown in Figure 10-5, which is what most people would want to see first. The Market Update gives you a snapshot of financial market activity all over the world. It is one of the quickest, clearest screens you get from any database service. Go down the list along the left of the screen. You can see it starts with the Australian market, followed by the Nikkei index from Japan, the Hang Seng index from Hong Kong, as well as market information from Singapore, Frankfurt, Paris, Zurich, etc.—a quick look at the whole world. The Dow Jones Industrials is the second index from the bottom. The index description "All Ordinaries," shown

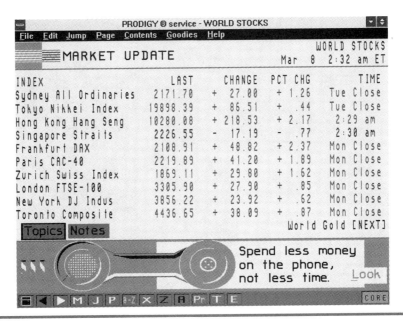

Figure 10-5 The Market Update screen is one of the best features of Prodigy for investors interested in overseas markets. All the major markets come up at once, providing a quick overview. At the right near the bottom you can see a note indicating that reports on the world gold market are coming up on the next page

at the top for the Sydney exchange, may be an expression that is unfamiliar to most American readers—it is what Australians mean by common stock. Ordinaries are common stock, as opposed to preferred shares, which are not ordinary.

There are a few other things worth noting about the screen shown in Figure 10-5. One is that the European and North American markets show a Monday close along the right-hand side of the screen, but the Sydney and Tokyo exchanges show a Tuesday close. That is because they are on the other side of the International Dateline and one day ahead of us on the world clock. The Hong Kong and Singapore markets show no "close," but simply show a time. That's because this screen was pulled at 2:30 in the morning, U.S. eastern time, and since Hong Kong and Singapore are almost exactly on the other side of the world, 12 hours away, their markets were still open. The other item of interest is near the bottom right, just above the usual ad, and it tells you what's coming up if you turn the page to the next screen of the Market Update—the World Gold Market report.

So let's turn the page (by clicking on the black right-pointing arrow at the bottom of the screen). This brings up the last bid prices on gold in Hong Kong, Zurich, London, and New York (see Figure 10-6). Once again the bottom right of the screen tells us the next page is the World Dollar, which would mean currency prices in relation to the dollar. We bite, turn, and get to the screen shown in Figure 10-7, the yen, pound sterling, and German mark in relation to the dollar.

The Actives: Who's Hot and Who's Not

Since we're in Market Update, let's keep going. The next page, shown in Figure 10-8, gives us the most active stocks on the New York Stock Exchange for the previous day. Note that the third most active was a foreign stock, Telefonos de Mexico. The line at the bottom right of the

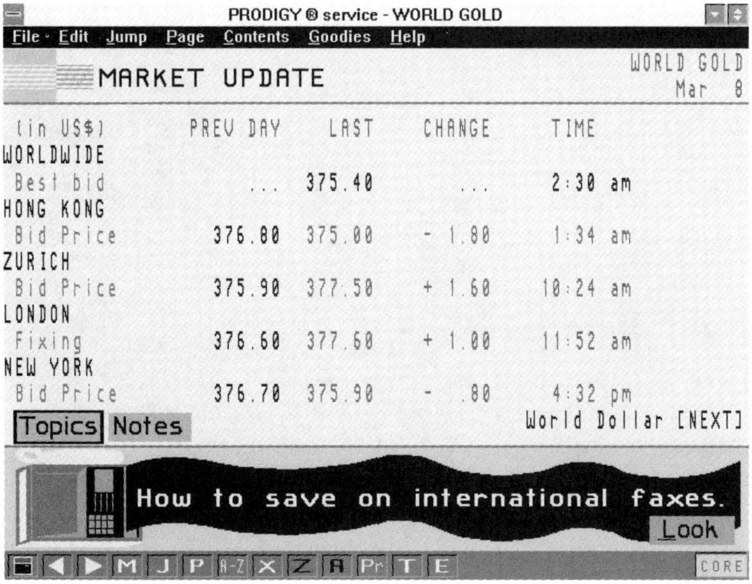

Figure 10-6   This is the next page of the Market Update screen. You can follow gold quotes with the rising and setting of the sun

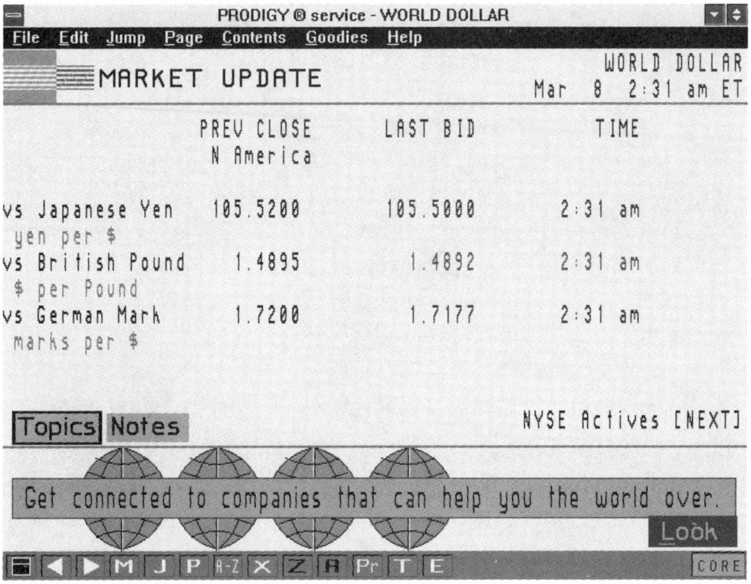

Figure 10-7   The Market Update screen showing the dollar against major currencies

screen tells us that if we want to continue, the next page will provide a list of most active stocks on the NASDAQ. But we'll stop here and go back to the last menu (Figure 10-3) where we can select the next button in the list: "Market Close."

It's History Now

The "Markets at the Close" screen, shown in Figure 10-9, provides a quick, easy-to-grasp update of the market in one glance: stocks, bonds, and the dollar were up, gold down. And at the very bottom we're enticed to buy a Pontiac, and asked to consider whether "safety and horsepower are mutually exclusive." I have to admit, it is a question I have pondered long and hard over the years, but have yet to reach a satisfactory conclusion.

Turning the page on "Markets at the Close," we get a report on the close of major and minor U.S. market indexes and a nice snapshot graph

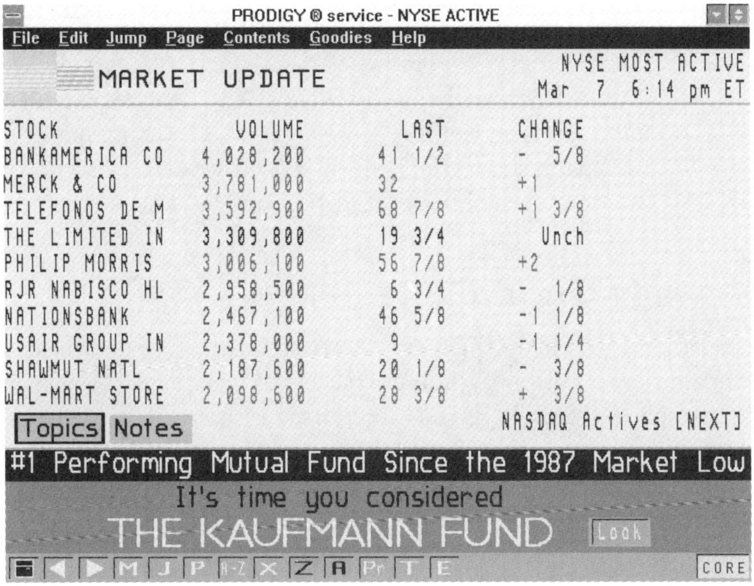

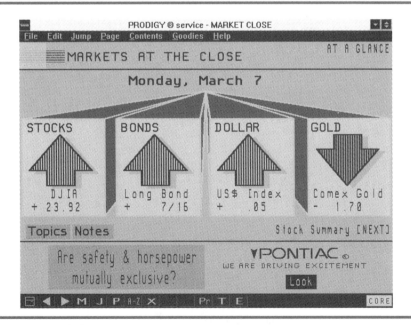

Figure 10-8 The New York Stock Exchange "most active" list

Figure 10-9 A quick look at the four major financial indicators. Prodigy excels at this kind of flash view of the markets

of the Dow for the last 30 days (see Figure 10-10). Turn the next page, and we get a more detailed breakdown of market action that includes up and down volume, block trades, and advances and declines (see Figure 10-11). A lot of reports leave these items out, but they're important and useful. The next page, shown in Figure 10-12, provides us with the same kind of information for the NASDAQ (the over-the-counter market).

More News Is Good News

Now we'll go back to the menu shown in Figure 10-3 and select the "Company News" button. A prompt asks you to type the name or symbol of the company. I selected Exxon, simply because it's the largest company in the world. The story that comes up, shown in Figure 10-13, talks about new oil reserves and some drilling successes for the company. A point worth noting is the short line right below "Company News," which tells us this is "story 1 of 18." A lot of stories to go.

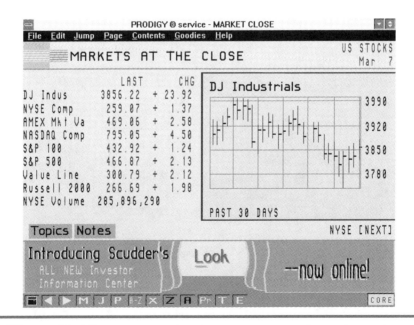

Figure 10-10 Calling up the close on major market indexes also produces a one month chart of the Dow

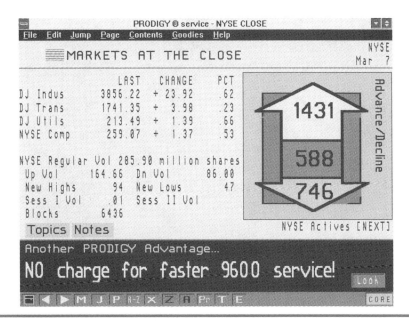

Figure 10-11   The Advance/Decline indicator. If the market keeps going up but the Advance/Decline ratio deteriorates, it usually means trouble

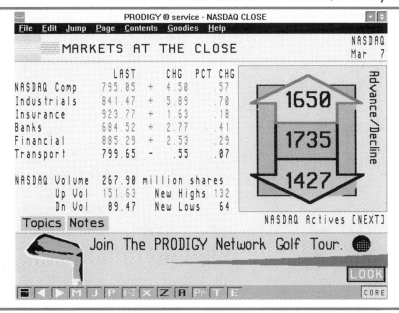

Figure 10-12   Here is a screen similar to Figure 10-11 but this one is focused on the Over-the-Counter market

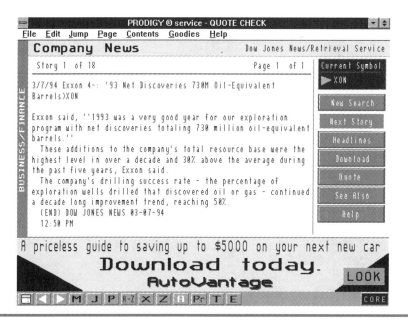

Figure 10-13   Company News, one of the selection bars on the Business/Finance
menu, lets you see recent news stories on any stock

Famous Quotes

The "Quote Track" menu items shown in Figure 10-3 let you set up
the list of stocks you want to track, but they are not conveniently set up
to take a single quote you're simply curious about for the day. For that,
you're better off selecting "Quotes" from the Business/Finance menu
(Figure 10-2). It's best if you know the symbol, but it will also accept
names and can find most of them. I typed in Volvo (for the Volvo ADR)
and got the report shown in Figure 10-14.

All quotes are delayed 15 minutes when the market is open. This is
a regulation of the stock exchanges, not Prodigy. You can get to quotes
directly by using Prodigy's "Jump" feature, which is a menu selection along
the top of the screen. Select "Jump" and a box comes up for you to enter
the location you want to jump to. Type Quotes and off you go!

If there is recent news on any company you look up, Prodigy flags
that with a little mark. You can then turn to "Company News," which is
a button on the same page as the stock quote. If you don't know the

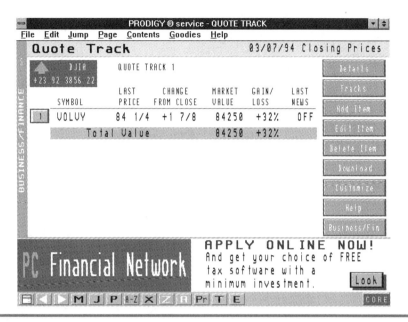

Figure 10-14   Quote Track, shown here, lets you look at a set list of stocks you follow. It can also be used to maintain a portfolio, updating it each day

symbol for a stock, you can use "Find Symbol," another button on the same page. In all, moving through the features of Prodigy is remarkably simple.

Stalking the Wild Growth Stock

Another button we can choose from the Business/Finance menu is "Research." A new menu pops up in the middle of the screen, as shown in Figure 10-15. There are some newsletters and a bunch of other items listed in this pop-up menu, but the one we're going to turn to first is "Strategic Investor." And the important part of this is Stock Hunter (Figure 10-16). If you can read the text in this duplicated screen shot you'll see that it's a screening system, which lets you select stocks according to criteria of your choice—price-to-earnings ratios, earnings growth, price-to-sales ratios, etc.—as well as what we might call "guru Guides" (actually referred to as "Featured Models" in the screen). These are screens recommended by famous stock pickers: Graham & Dodd, the value guys; CANSLIM, from William O'Neil; and the methodology

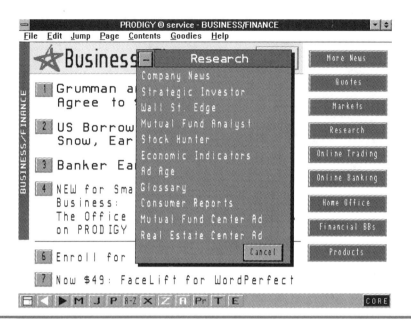

Figure 10-15 The Research menu offers several useful services, such as Strategic Investor and Stock Hunter

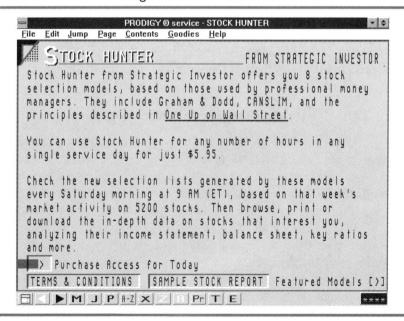

Figure 10-16 Stock Hunter does automatic screens at the end of the week which can be collected each Saturday morning

described in the book *One Up on Wall Street*, by Peter Lynch. If you want one of those screens, you don't even have to do them yourself; they're done automatically every Friday night. Plug in Saturday morning and get the results. The use of Strategic Investor carries an extra charge of $15 a month. Various reports can cost another $5 each. It's not the most expensive research service among the databases, but you can run up quite a bill here.

On-line and Off the Wall

Now let's round up a few other selections of interest from the Business/Finance menu (Figure 10-2). One of these is Online Trading. Where CompuServe has E*Trade for their tourist class ride into broker land, Prodigy has PCFN—the PC Financial Network, shown in Figure 10-17. Is this a better deal? Only if you're brain-dead. There are a number of options on this screen. Figure 10-18 shows the commission schedule. It's more expensive than CompuServe's discount broker system—for that matter, it's more expensive than my own broker.

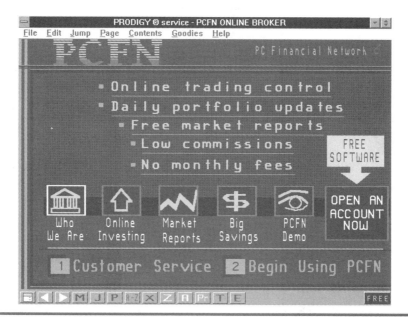

Figure 10-17   PCFN is one of several online brokerage services. The fees, however, are relatively high (see Figure 10-18)

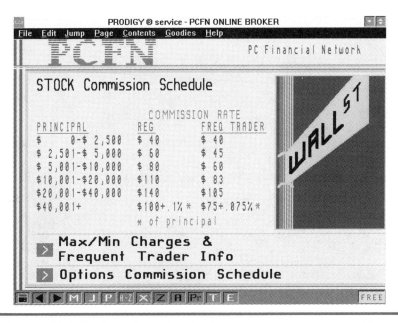

Figure 10-18 Fees for online brokerage services using PCFN on Prodigy

Moving right along, if you want to go to "Online Banking," you can click on one of the menu buttons on the Business/Finance main menu. Or you can pull down the "Jump" command menu from the top of the Prodigy screen and simply type Banking in the box that appears. Online Banking is an opportunity to pay your bills online through a bank in your area that offers such services (Figure 10-19). You can also set up such a service through the accounting software from Quicken. There is no apparent advantage to paying your bills online. In fact, it costs more to do it that way since they charge a $10-15 monthly fee. (Why should there be a fee for paying your bills more promptly is utterly beyond me, but it does show there are people who will pay to be on the technological edge of anything. I'm thinking of charging a monthly fee for reading this book.)

Bulletin Boards

Finally, one of the last items from the Business/Finance menu is "Financial BBs." These are bulletin boards, and they're fairly interesting. To get to "Financial BBs" simply click on that button from the Business/Finance main menu. Remember that when you have a green main heading

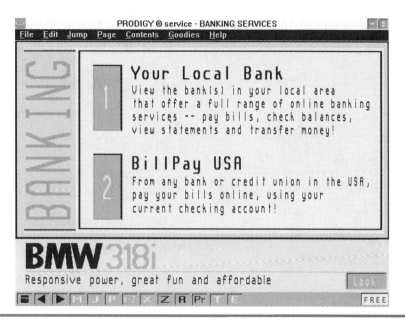

Figure 10-19   You can also do online banking through Prodigy, paying your bills via your computer. There is a $10 a month fee for this and it seems to offer no benefit except to the bank

or green menu choices you are in the Business/Finance group. If your menu choices are not green, there's no use struggling to find a choice that isn't there. When that happens—when you have wandered afield somewhere—you can get back to this group by simply pulling down the "Jump" command from the top of the screen and typing Business. You can also type Bulletins to take you to a list of bulletin boards.

The main bulletin board for financial topics is called "Money Talk," and it in itself contains numerous bulletin boards. When you first call up the Money Talk bulletin board it will have a date box in the upper right-hand corner. The box is there simply to ask you how far back you want to go when viewing bulletin board messages. Some of the bulletin boards contain hundreds of messages going back six months or more. You may not be up to that, so you can type in a cut-off date, such as two months ago. The box will already contain a default date, which will be the date you are calling it up. But even selecting that doesn't mean you are limited to that day's messages; it will also give you replies going back several weeks.

Here is a partial list of the subject areas contained within the larger Money Talk bulletin board:

- Stocks
- Options
- Bonds
- Futures
- Mutual Funds
- Clubs and Groups
- Investment Theory
- Technical Analysis
- Brokerage
- Insurance
- Financial Planning
- Banking and Credit

Each of these constitutes its own bulletin board, since you would not expect to find comments on insurance under "Technical Analysis." But that doesn't mean you are restricted in any way; you can wander in and out of any bulletin board that interests you. What you will see is a collection of messages, often containing commentary on a running theme and sometimes containing quite interesting and unusual information. These related commentaries are called "threads" in the bulletin board world.

One other Prodigy bulletin board you might find interesting (which is not part of the Money Talk BBs) is the International Business BB (see Figure 10-20). This BB has its own sub-menu which breaks down by region: Pacific Rim, South America, Africa, etc. The discussions go on for pages, far too many to repeat here. The most interesting one seemed to be on South Africa and the possibility of civil war or widespread violence following the first multi-racial elections. Respondents who had actually been to South Africa or lived there weren't worried; respondents who knew little or nothing about South Africa were hysterical.

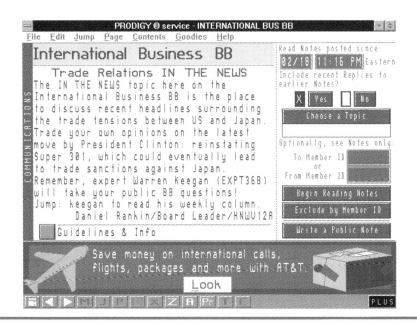

Figure 10-20   The opening screen of the International Business BB

CHAPTER 11

AMERICA ONLINE

The name of the service is grandiose, but the feeling is laid back. If CompuServe betrays its techie origins—"We understand this stuff, and you don't"—and Prodigy has somewhat the air of a carnival barker—"Step right up! See the tattooed lady!"—then America Online is "How ya doin?" At first I thought it was Midwestern friendliness, because the initial screen comes up with an activity button showing the Chicago skyline, which I recognized right away because I'm from Chicago. I thought maybe it was a personal touch: if you were from New York, there would be a button showing New York, and another for San

Francisco, and so on. But reality, as it so often does, turned out to be much more mundane. America Online cut a deal with the *Chicago Tribune* and the *San Jose Mercury-News*, which makes those papers available for reading online. So there's lots of Chicago news, a toddling town. Okay, you may not care about who's playing at the local blues clubs. From San Jose there's news about computer companies; after all, it is in Silicon Valley. Meanwhile...on to our kind of news.

Every database service has strengths and weaknesses. There are half a million members of America Online (known by its friends as AOL), and they must be interested in other things, because the financial information here is not at all up to what you get from CompuServe or Prodigy, and naturally enough, nothing is up to what you get from Dow Jones. You can't download historical data, because there is none. If you want to see how Glaxo or Goodyear performed over the past couple of years, you won't find it here.

And yet...this is a really nice database. As I said, every service has its strengths and weaknesses, and one of AOL's big strengths is that you get Morningstar, the Chicago-based mutual fund reporting service. It's very good and definitely worth the trip, despite the fact that America Online doesn't offer you all of it. After all, that would be a cheap way to subscribe to a service that costs considerably more than AOL. But you do get quite a bit of the Morningstar service, and you will see this as we move through the screens of a visit to the AOL financial world.

A big strength here is the forums, where the users share information. Another strength is the fact that the news stories on AOL are provided by the Knight-Ridder/Tribune service and Reuters. Reuters is the British-based news service and is probably the best in the world for foreign news, especially foreign business news. In talking with writers from some of the computer magazines, I have found that many of them prefer this service over all the others, and with all its shortcomings, I'm inclined to agree. It appears to be the fastest growing service and is a public company; the stock has tripled in price in the past two years.

Let us begin the magical mystery tour.

The Navigator

Figure 11-1 shows the opening screen for logging on to America Online, and since this is the opening, it brings up our first point—it's all fixed price, no unpleasant surprises in the bill. The charge for AOL is $9.95 a month—call it ten bucks—and there are no extra-charge services. Roam where you will, it's all the same price. That $10 monthly fee provides five free hours of roaming, after that it's $3.50 an hour. The connect speed is only 2400 baud if you use a Macintosh, but it is now up to 9600 baud for any other equipment and will move to that speed soon for the Mac as well.

Figure 11-2 shows the screen that appears once you've signed on, and here we see part of the Chicago skyline near the top right. The icon bar which spreads all the way across the top of the screen provides pictorial recognition, some of it intuitive, some not, for various services. The icon with the zig-zag arrow rising against a background of graph paper takes you right to stock quotes; the icon with a newspaper front page gets you news; the one with a front page and a globe gets you world news. The

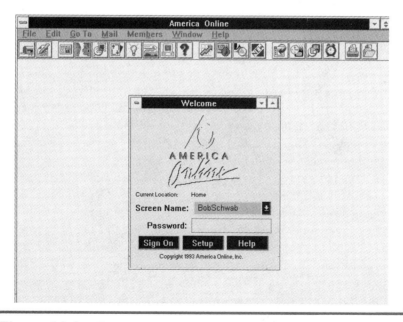

Figure 11-1   The sign-on screen for America Online

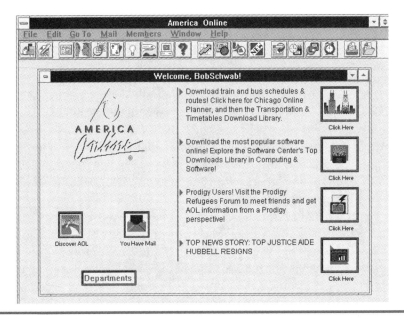

Figure 11-2   The first online screen. This will not always look the same since AOL changes the information listed on the right

mailbox is obviously for mail, the pen and letter for writing, and so on. But what on earth is the purpose of the clock near the right-hand end of the menu bar? If you click on that, it tells you how long you've been plugged into the database, so you can have an idea of what it's costing you. CompuServe has a running time log that is always visible on its menu bar, and I find that far preferable to this procedure.

For readers interested in business news, the best way to start moving through AOL is by clicking on the button that says "Departments" (seen in Figure 11-2). From here you can select the menu choice "News & Finance," which in turn gives you a menu choice called "Personal Finance." One of the selections in the "Personal Finance" menu is the "Morningstar" mutual fund reports. Another is "Business News," which will take you to "Companies," "Commodities," and a selection called "World Business News." From "World Business News" you can select "Europe," "Japan," "Asia," etc. It is a nested system. I don't particularly like it, but it's universal in large bulletin board systems like this.

note

AOL is still under construction. Which is as it should be. Times change, information sources change, and all of the database services will make changes to accommodate this. Among the changes we've already noticed is that the "Business & Finance" menu and its "Stocklink" button now only appear if you're calling up AOL with a Macintosh. If you're using an IBM compatible, the main menu for business and stock market news is called "Personal Finance" and is a selection button from the first menu that comes up when you select "Departments" from the opening screen. Even this could change by the time you log on. AOL does not have the advantage of color-coding that you get in Prodigy, so you have to mill around a bit to get to where you want to go. One way out is the "Go To" pull-down menu at the very top of the screen. It lets you type in a keyword, like "Stocks." Another way is to choose "Directory Services" from the same pull-down menu. This will let you scroll through all the services AOL has, even if they've moved them around.

In Windows, by the way, each one of these menus is piled on top of the other. You can still see the headings for the menus you left behind. If you want to go back to one of those, you can either close the ones on top until you get back there, or you can click on that heading and you will be back there immediately. It is wise to remember, however, that another characteristic of Windows is that those other menu screens will remain open, even if you are no longer looking at them. If you leave enough menus open your computer will eventually begin to have memory problems—it will not be able to handle all the windows that are supposed to be open. So a little house-keeping—closing open windows—will keep things running smoothly.

After you've moved around for a while and know where you want to go, you can get there right away by using the pull-down menu called "Go To," found in the menu bar (Figure 11-2) just above the icons. (The icon for this feature is the button that shows a broad arrow curving inwards toward what looks vaguely like a television screen.) This is the equivalent of CompuServe's "GO" commands. Here the system is called "keywords," and the keyword will usually be understood even if it is misspelled or not exactly the right word for where you want to go. Typing in "music," for example, produces "Music Forum," all right, but also brings up "Rock Link," which has no "music" in its title but is nonetheless about music, not geology.

Looking at the menu icons stacked vertically along the right-hand side of the screen in Figure 11-2, you'll see that the third one down invites you to visit the "Prodigy Refugees Forum." (You may or may not see that when you log onto America Online; they change this stack from time to time. In any case, you can also get to the Prodigy Refugees Forum with the keyword "Prodigy.") That's kind of an amusing way to look at it and of course implies that a lot of people have flooded into AOL because they can't stand Prodigy anymore. I doubt that this is true, and it bring up a point worth mentioning: all of the members quoted for database services do not belong exclusively to AOL. It is common for people to sign up for more than one service. And so, if we go to the Prodigy Refugees Forum, we find a lot of messages from people complaining about things on Prodigy, but a lot of them are complaining about things on AOL, too.

The Morning and the Evening Star

Clicking on the "NEW" button found in the icon bar brings up the menu seen in Figure 11-3. If you can make out the words, you'll be able

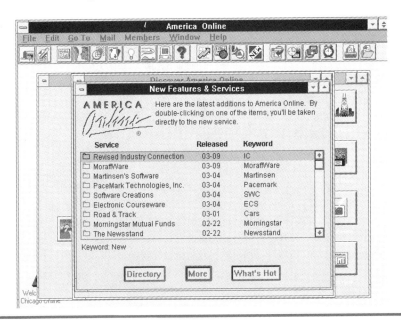

Figure 11-3   AOL's "New Features & Services" screen. Most database services have a something similar to this

to see that near the bottom of the list it shows "Morningstar Mutual Funds" as one of the new services. In fact, it came online February 22, 1994.

Totally entranced, we double-click on that line and up pops the Morningstar menu, shown in Figure 11-4. It has its own menu list of topics, and the first one is "Top 25 Overall Mutual Funds." Other selections give you the opportunity to look at "Aggressive Growth" funds, "Equity-Income" funds, "Europe Stock" funds, etc.

One thing worth noting about this screen before we move on: it offers a service—a keyword search for funds—that isn't found on any of the other databases. Selecting the magnifying glass icon labeled "Fund Search" at the top right of the screen lets you type in key search words. At least, that's the theory. Sadly, however, this tool doesn't live up to our expectations. For instance, typing "Ireland," to see what funds to invest in Ireland, produces no information at all on that front, but does provide a couple of funds with officers named "Ireland." A little more experimentation eventually produced some nice results, but all in all, it has to be rated as poor. It's in its early days yet, and maybe the folks at AOL will get around to making it really useful soon.

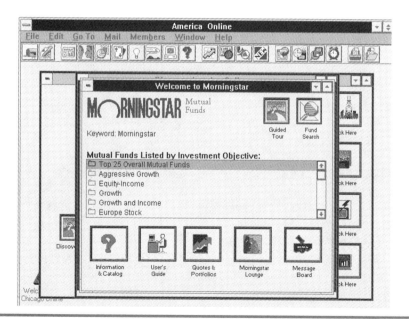

Figure 11-4   The Morningstar menu (when it was a "New Feature," see Figure 11-3). Morningstar is a very popular mutual fund rating service

"Conventional Wisdom"

A few comments on researching funds based on their most recent performance: I've been hearing the conventional wisdom on this issue all my life, and like most conventional wisdom, it's wrong. The wisdom says that a fund's short-term performance is not a good guide to use in selecting it for investment, that what really matters is how the fund has performed over a long period—at least five years. The truth is that a recent study by Dalbar Financial Services in Boston has found that the chance of picking a fund that will out-perform the market averages is exactly the same whether you go by a fund's three-month record, one-year, three-year, or any number you care to choose. In short, it makes no difference. The chance of any fund outperforming the market averages, by the way, is quite low. This should anger a sufficient number of fund managers to keep the mailbox full.

Double-clicking the first menu item ("Top 25 Overall Mutual Funds") produces another menu, shown in Figure 11-5, that lets you look at the top funds by their most recent three-month performance, one-year, three-year, etc. This is the standard way of researching funds but it makes no sense to me. Morningstar also ranks funds that invest in foreign stocks; in Figure 11-6 we see a screen of the top 25 funds that invest in Europe. You could also see screens on Asia and South America.

All the News That's Fit to Digitize

News in AOL is conveniently divided into categories: general, business, sports, etc., and if we select "Top Business News," we get a lot of stories on overseas business (Figure 11-7). This is probably because of the Reuters connection. "Top Business News" is a category that is just one selection from a much larger menu called "Business & Finance," shown in Figure 11-8. If you can read the menu lines here, you will see news on Japan, Europe, and Asia among your choices. Further down the menu list there is a heading called "Market News & Indicators," which includes USA Today's Moneyline section. You can also branch off to other maga-

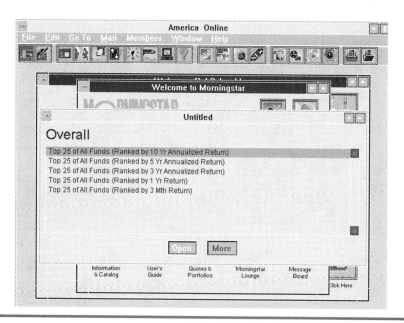

Figure 11-5   With Morningstar, you can select funds with top performance for the last few months or take a long-range view of 10 years

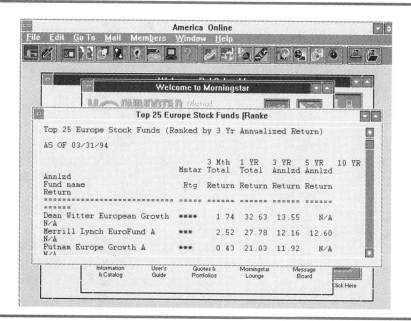

Figure 11-6   An example of Morningstar's ranking of funds investing in foreign stocks

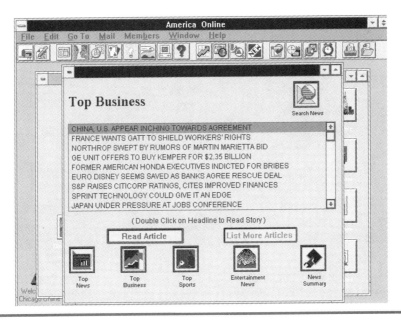

Figure 11-7   The stories and topics covered in "Top News" and "Top Business News" are extensive

zines and newspapers, like *Time*, *Worth Magazine*, columns from the *Seattle Post*, etc. Icons on the right-hand side let us select stocks, company profiles, personal finance, and a few other items we won't bother about right now.

From the main "Business & Finance" menu, we can select Asia (under the heading "Business News") and get some fairly interesting news, shown in Figure 11-9, about Japan, Korea, Singapore, and points thereabouts. (There is some overlap; for example, there is also a section for Japan, which will further subdivide the Asia stories.) If we choose "Latin America" and decide to go one layer deeper than just headline titles, we get a news story about General Motors' plans to re-open an assembly line in Argentina after a lull of 15 years (Figure 11-10). As the story continues, we can see that General Motors clearly thinks the Latin American turnaround is for real and is willing to back that opinion with big bucks. Another feature of Business News is a quick digest—a one-sentence summary—of top stories having to do with foreign companies or foreign

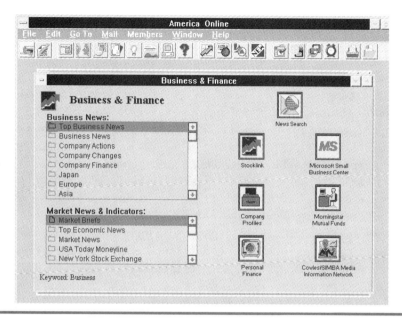

Figure 11-8   From "Business & Finance," you can call up stock quotes, get company news/profiles, and begin to explore all of AOL's business features

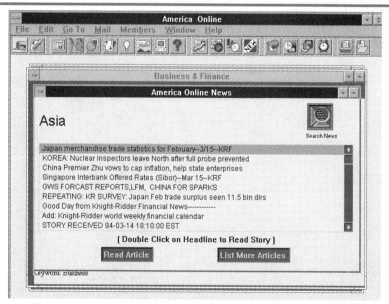

Figure 11-9   The "News" menus subdivide by region; shown here are the stories on just Asian business

trade, as shown in Figure 11-11. There are hundreds of them. Reading these stories, or even just looking at the headlines, can give you a good perspective on what's going on around the world. U.S. newspapers and television generally give little attention to world events unless there is fighting going on. "Market News" (under "Market News & Indicators") from the "Business & Finance" menu is an eclectic collection of news, columns, commodity flashes, tax information, and more, as shown in Figure 11-12. Notice that you can read the "Stock Talk" column of the *Seattle Times* here. This is a regularly featured column that appears by special arrangement between the *Times* and America Online.

Selecting the "Stocklink" icon from the "Business & Finance" main menu (refer back to Figure 11-8) brings a prompt asking for a name or a symbol, and typing IBM, for example, yields a lot of numbers about IBM's market activity for that day but not much else (see Figure 11-13). Remember, there are no historical quotes in this system, so you only get the most current quote. But you can set up a portfolio here and have it updated automatically on the day you call it in.

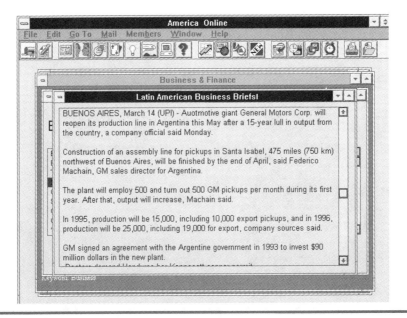

Figure 11-10 Latin America Business Briefs is another subset of "Business News"

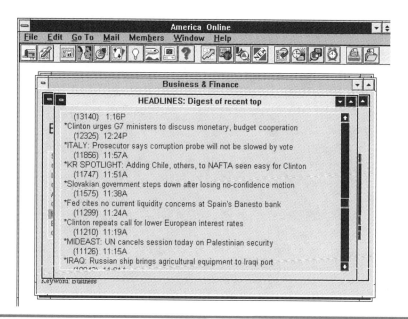

Figure 11-11   "Business News" also gives you a digest of top stories involving foreign companies or trade

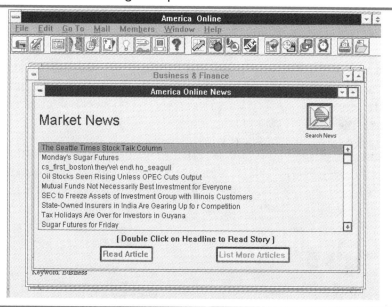

Figure 11-12   A sample of what's offered in "Market News"

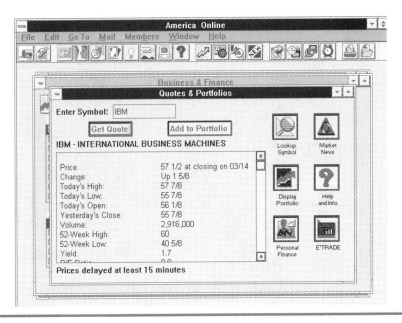

Figure 11-13   Calling up stock quotes on AOL only gets you the most recent day

Selecting the "Company Profiles" icon from the "Business & Finance" main menu gives us a huge alphabetical list (Figure 11-14) that includes at least a couple hundred foreign companies. (The companies shown in the list in Figure 11-14 act as a guide to the alphabet, much like the entries on the spines of encyclopedias.) Here you can find quick summaries of a company's business, performance data, etc. That's the good news. The bad news is that the profiles are for the most part hopelessly out of date. Many of them show no sales or earnings figures later than 1991! The reports look exhaustive because they include a lot of historical material, like who got the first telephone contracts in Mexico (Figure 11-15). It's interesting, but practically useless.

Can We Talk?

Much more useful are the numerous investors' forums on AOL. You can get to the forums area from a menu dealing with your area of interest, or you can enter the keyword "Forums," after selecting either the "Go To"

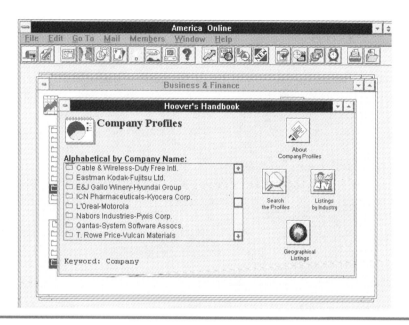

Figure 11-14   Hoover's Handbook, AOL's company profile service. The icons on the right help you specify your searches

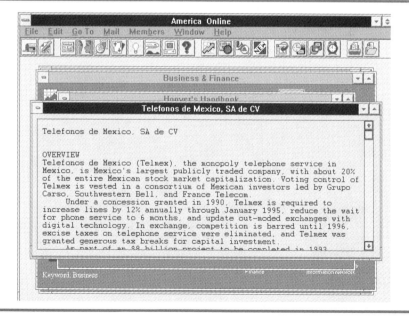

Figure 11-15   An example Hoover's Handbook entry, for Telefonos de Mexico

icon or pull-down menu. Here are hundreds of notes offering tips, suggestions, commentary on users' investing experiences, etc. It's fascinating. I find myself spending more time reading the notes than all other travel through the database combined. In the "Foreign Investing Forum" (Latin American division), shown in Figure 11-16, we see a note from one of the members pointing out that Investor's Business Daily lists 30 major Mexican stocks and eight to ten Argentine stocks several times a week. Such stocks are also listed in the *Wall Street Journal* and *Barron's*, but he doesn't mention that.

In the forums under the "Morningstar Mutual Funds" menu, shown in Figure 11-17, you can see a quick summary of current postings. There, are 57 messages on closed-end funds, 163 on the problem of when to hold a fund and when to dump, 72 about a "great stock," etc. One of these, for example notes how much the writer loves closed-end funds as a great

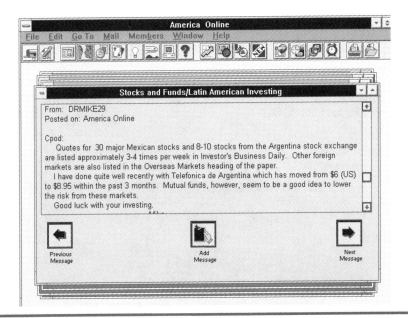

Figure 11-16 An example AOL forum screen. This one offers advice on finding Argentine and Mexican stocks

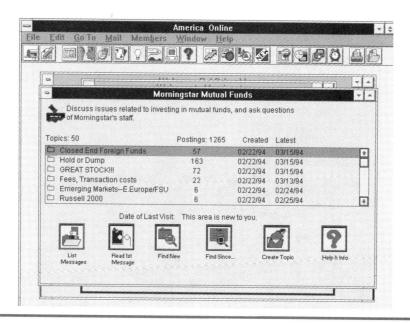

Figure 11-17   The menu for the Morningstar Mutual Fund Ratings forum

vehicle for investing in other countries. He then gives some very useful tips on how to avoid getting stung on transaction costs and taking hits when the fund falls to a discount from a premium. In another example, a forum writer notes that ASA (American South African fund, essentially the largest gold mine fund in the world) is selling at an 8 percent discount and has a very low expense ratio (management fees). He thinks it may be too early to buy, but is watching the situation closely. He forgot to mention the 4.4 percent dividend on top of the discount.

As we said, the forums are useful places for browsing and picking up tips. Nearly all of what they have to say you will have already learned from reading this book, but there's always some chance of picking up a nugget or two, so to speak. As Yogi Berra once remarked: "You can observe a lot just by watching."

CHAPTER 12

DOW JONES NEWS/RETRIEVAL— THE MOTHER LODE

f CompuServe is like a giant suburban mall, with hundreds if not thousands of shops, Dow Jones News/Retrieval (DJN/R) is a walk in and out of every office in every building on Wall Street. The service is enormous; the user's guide alone is the size of a small-city telephone book.

DJN/R is not all business. You can go shopping, read movie reviews, buy airline tickets, and other trivial pursuits, but I doubt that anyone signs up for Dow Jones News/Retrieval so they can go shopping. This is stock-quote land! A major drawback for some users is that you can only download one year's worth of daily data. Over one year, it automatically switches to weekly data. Some care, some don't. Many other services, like Telescan, CompuServe, Dial Data, etc., may offer more years worth of data on some issues than Dow Jones, for those of you who like to see the long view. For the global investor—or any kind of investor—however, this is the mother lode. Here are some of its most important features:

▶ **Proprietary news services:** This is the only place you can access present and past electronic editions of the *Wall Street Journal* and the *Asian Wall Street Journal*. You can, in fact, read the *Wall Street Journal* before it's printed. News stories are made available on Dow Jones News/Retrieval as soon as they have cleared the final editing desk—which is hours before the paper comes out.

▶ *Barron's Financial Weekly*, from January 1987 to the present. For anyone interested in overseas investments, this weekly newspaper is more important than the *Wall Street Journal* itself. *Barron's* carries a complete list of closed-end funds every week. These include bond funds and the popular country and sector funds, which allow an investor to spread risk when buying in a foreign market. Each fund is listed with its current price, yield (dividend), and—very important—the premium or discount to net asset value. The same is true for open-ended funds. *Barron's* International Markets section also lists weekly and annual performance to date of stock markets in more than two dozen countries.

▶ **Dow Jones News Wires,** including International News and the Capital Markets Reports, from June 1979 to the present.

▶ **WorldScope:** A database from Wright Investor's Service, with wide coverage of non-U.S. corporations. The database contains reports on 6,600 corporations in 32 countries, including corporate profiles, operating summaries, balance sheets, income statements, financial ratios, stock data, etc.

▶ **Tradeline:** Quotes and statistics on U.S. and foreign securities. The Tradeline database contains up to 15 years of historical information on foreign stocks, bonds, mutual funds, indexes, exchange rates, and other international issue information, including a list of well over a thousand currently traded ADRs. As we've mentioned elsewhere in this book, ADRs are "American Depository Receipts" and are a legally valid instrument that stands for a set number of shares of stock in a foreign corporation. The ratio is usually one-to-one: one ADR equals one share of stock, but it doesn't have to be. Each ADR in Telefonos de Mexico, for example, represents 20 shares of stock.

World Without End

You can read articles from the *Washington Post*, *New York Times*, *Los Angeles Times*, *BusinessWeek*, the *China Daily*, *Eastern European Energy Report*, *UK Venture Capital Journal*, *Toshiba Weekly*, the *Latin American Telecom Report*, to name just a few. You can search for and read articles from an astonishing collection of more than 1,400 newspapers, magazines, and professional journals. You can read the *Baton Rouge Morning Advocate* (Louisiana), the *Ottawa Sentinel* (Canada), *Billboard* for show business, or *Optical Materials and Engineering News* for the latest developments at the cutting edge of laser technology. Just printing the titles would occupy nearly a quarter of this book. Figure 12-1 shows you the opening screen for this enormous database.

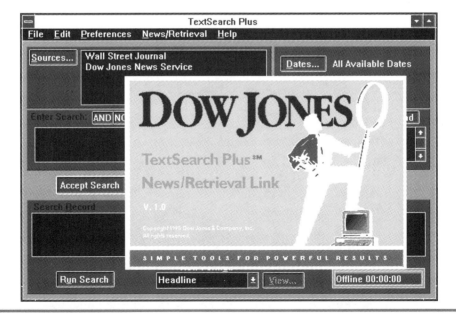

Figure 12-1   The snappy Dow Jones News/Retrieval title screen

Getting with the Program

The initial sign-up charge is $29.95, with an $19.95 annual fee on top of that. Several financial software packages carry special coupons that waive those fees, however, and there is one of these coupons at the back of this book. Use it to get a copy of Dow Jones' TextSearch or E-Z Online software, which comes free when you sign up. These packages simplify the job of automatically logging you on to the system.

They also allow you to store your online sessions so that you can print, view, and edit them offline, when you're not being billed for time. The DJN/R is expensive. In fact, it is the most expensive database service available except for a few services aimed at lawyers, like Lexis and Nexis. The online charge goes as high as $1.95 a minute during business hours, which they call "prime time" and count as 6:00 a.m. to 8:00 p.m. And they measure that zone by your local time, not New York time, Monday through Friday. In the off-hours, the charge drops as low as 15 cents a minute—which is still $9 an hour.

In addition (and the addition adds up pretty fast here), there are extra charges for various services and what are called "information units." An information unit is charged for every 1,000 characters transmitted by the service, including spaces and carriage returns. That represents about one-half of a single-spaced typed page. Those costs add anywhere from 76 cents to $1.14 to the line charges during prime time, 30 cents a unit in off-hours. Here are some examples of extra service charges beyond the per minute and information unit costs: using Disclosure or WorldScope costs $9 per document in prime time, $3 each in off-hours. Doing a screen (a filter looking for certain kinds of stocks) on Tradeline, which is where most of the foreign stock data resides, costs a minimum of $5 for each screen plus 25 cents for each stock in the resulting list. Dun and Bradstreet reports cost $25 to $84 apiece. If you're not careful, you can easily run up $1,000 during prime time. For users willing to work mostly during off-hours, costs can be more manageable.

Become a Member of the Club

Dow Jones News/Retrieval offers some membership packages with limited and full service. "Market Monitor" service is the cheapest way to go: a flat-fee, "after-hours" charge of $30 a month for unlimited usage outside of prime time hours. You don't get all the services, though. What you do get is:

- News from five Dow Jones news wires.
- "Plain English" searching of articles from the *Wall Street Journal* and 500 other publications important to investors.
- A year's worth of daily quotes.
- Security snapshots, including earnings per share, p/e ratio, yield, etc.
- Daily and weekly stock quotes, going back two years.
- International news.
- Abstracts of research reports from the analysts.

You get all the online time you want, so long as you confine that to the hours of 8:00 p.m. through 6:00 a.m., Monday through Friday, your local time, plus weekends and major holidays. You also get a 50% discount on the suggested retail price of Dow Jones software programs (technical analysis and portfolio management packages).

The two basic membership plans for full service are "Standard Membership" and "Corporate Membership." Here's how they differ:

- **Standard Membership** has the same $29.95 start-up fee per account and provides three free hours online (for U.S. and Canadian accounts only). The $18 annual service fee is waived for the first year. Standard per-minute and information unit charges apply. (Remember, one unit = 1,000 characters, including spaces and return keys, in Dow Jones arithmetic.) The Standard Membership is limited to new subscribers on a one-time only basis.

- **Corporate Membership** is what the DJN/R recommends if you're going to use more than three hours a month of prime time. The charge is $75 a month per account per location. In other words, if you are dialing in from two different phone lines, that's two locations and two monthly fees. The annual service fee is waived, and there is a 33-1/3 percent discount on prime time and information unit charges. You get 10 free hours before those charges kick in.

For help with questions on these levels of service (or any other service matters), call DJN/R's Customer Service at 609/452-1511, from 8:00 a.m. to midnight weekdays (ET), and 9 a.m. to 6 p.m. Saturdays. Unlike many other database services, they actually answer their phone. You can also enter the command //GUIDE on the system to view a reference menu that is continuously updated and free of charge.

Navigation

When you load Dow Jones' software, you will see two icons in a desktop folder. One is for the News/Retrieval Link, which logs you directly onto the main system. The other is TextSearch Plus, which loads a program that lets you construct automated searches offline. It can take 15 or 20 minutes to put together a set of search commands when you're dealing with a service as large as Dow Jones, so you want to do as much of that offline as you can. Everything will proceed automatically once you log on, but you are not stuck there irretrievably; you can move out of auto-pilot and back to manual control simply by pulling down a menu bar and making a choice.

Slashing Your Way Through the Underbrush

This is not a warm, fuzzy service. There will be no colorful menus and icons like you see on CompuServe, Prodigy, and America Online. Every system betrays its origins, and this one shows its mainframe bones through the old IBM Job Control Language—called JCL in the trade.

It's a lot better than it used to be. There are pull-down menus now, or you can enter various code names for database destinations after one or two forward slashes, which is the equivalent of CompuServe's "Go..." command on DJN/R: /W, for example, takes you to the Welcome menu; //QUOTES takes you to the quote section. The slash commands are entered at the bottom of the screen in the box reading "Enter Command:" If you want a quick snapshot of the main facts about any company—any company at all—type //SNAP. When the menu for that command comes up, type in the symbol of the company you want. If you don't know the symbol, type //SYMBOL before you use //SNAP. The system is not case-sensitive; it makes no difference whether the letters following a slash command are in upper or lower case. If you don't know a command you can type /HELP or //GUIDE, which will tell you how to find the command you need. //GUIDE gives you lists of two-letter source codes for major Dow Jones services; IN, for example, takes you to International News. Commands can also be strung together; //WIRES IBM, for example, gets you all the references for stories on IBM. You get a booklet with a list of all commands when you sign up for the service. After a while you'll develop a routine for the services you regularly search.

Figure 12-2 is the first menu you see any time you fire up the DJN/R. It shows highlights: a prominent news headline is always there, along with a selection for *Wall Street Week*, which has a transcript available here weekly. Like all DJN/R menu screens, it shows a list of numbered choices. The strong, assertive guy in shirtsleeves in Figure 12-1 is gone forever. Take a minute to read over the lines on this screen and get a feel for your

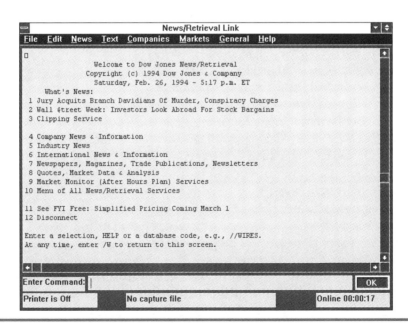

Figure 12-2   DJN/R's opening menu. Items 4, 5, and 6 are particularly important for our purposes. Item 10 provides a map of the territory

Navigation: The Basics

The Dow Jones News/Retrieval database is so large that it can get confusing, and it's easy to feel lost and unsure of just how to get back to where you were. Once again, bad as it is, it's nothing like the way it used to be, which was downright user-hostile. The two most useful commands to keep in mind or jot down somewhere near the machine are /R, which takes you back to the previous page, and /M, which takes you to the previous menu. If you want to go back to the main menu within a section, you type / T. The "T" is for "top," as in "top menu." When you want to get off the trolley, you type disc—for disconnect. Should you forget to properly disconnect, the system will log you off automatically after a certain period of inactivity, usually five minutes.

options. If you select a number, you can go to that option. Selecting item 6, for example, takes you immediately to the "International News & Information" section.

You can open a file in your word processing program at this point and capture the entire online session for offline reading and printing later. It's the smart way to do it; files can get very large and printing while you are still online is slow and burns expensive time. If you don't want to capture every step of your journey through News/Retrieval Link—and frankly, it's pretty boring stuff—you can wait to turn on the "Capture" feature until you reach a place that means something. The center box at the bottom of your screen toggles the text Capture feature on and off. You can also activate the Capture feature either by pulling down the File menu and selecting "Capture," or by pressing the F9 key. In either case, a normal Windows box will appear asking you to select a filename and location for the captured file to be stored. The typical answer is to create a file in your word processing program and have your online session stored there.

There's a timer in the lower right-hand corner of each screen where you can read your elapsed time online. If you want to know how many specific information units you've used, type //USAGE and a screen will appear with your current totals broken out by categories. You can capture that screen like any other, and so you will have a record of what you or someone else spent time on.

There is a Dow Jones News/Retrieval customer newsletter, called *FYI*, which is free and contains news on new products and pricing. You can check it out anytime by typing //FYI.

The Next Tour Starts in One Minute

If you don't have the log-on software from Dow Jones you can sign on to the system with any communications software. In that case, once you get the connect signal you can get to the same screen as shown in Figure 12-2 by typing the command /W for Welcome. The software is free, however, so you might as well get it. Let's look again at Figure 12-2 and see if the engines on our little yellow submarine will fire up. Yep, they will. We're off!

Item 1 will take you to the news of the day, item 2 to *Wall Street Week*, but just to be perverse, we'll start with item 10, which takes you to a menu of all DJN/R services (see Figure 12-3). Read this list, and each one that

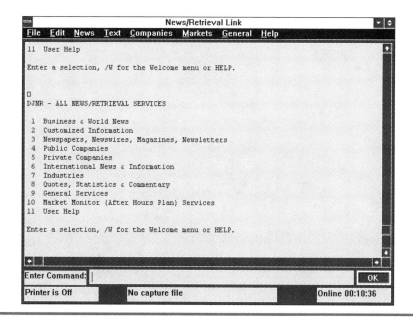

Figure 12-3   The All News/Retrieval Services menu (item 10 shown in Figure 12-2). Item 3, for example, contains more than 1,400 selections

follows, because the lists themselves constitute the tour. This is, remember, a text database.

Selecting item 6 from this new menu brings up "International News & Information," shown in Figure 12-4, with its menu of wire service news reports from the Pacific Rim, Japan, United Kingdom, Germany, Canada, etc. Selecting item 1 "Business & World News" instead brings up the "Business and Finance Report," shown in Figure 12-5, which is itself a menu. (You can also get there by with the command //BUSINESS.) Using /T, we can go back to the top menu for this section (Figure 12-4), and select the last item, which is the User's Guide, shown in Figure 12-6. You can get to the User's Guide anytime by typing //GUIDE. Item 9 in this User's Guide menu provides an alphabetical index to all the subjects in Dow Jones News/Retrieval. Remember, if you get really lost—and you will—you can always come back here with the //GUIDE command and go through the alphabetical list to find your way home.

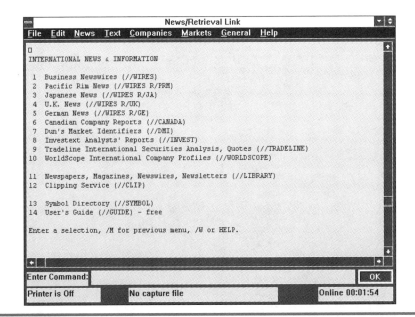

Figure 12-4   This menu is the source for news and financial information on foreign companies. The stories are updated almost every minute

note

You might recall that you saw the option for "International News & Information" in the screen shown in Figure 12-2. Selecting this option from there or from the screen shown in Figure 12-6 will take you to the same place. As with most databases, the same option often appears on more than one menu.

Now, go back to the International News & Information Screen shown in Figure 12-4. Item 12 on this menu is a feature called Clipping Service. If you enter the command //CLIP, the system will prompt you through the steps of setting up a file for automatic data collection. What this means is that while you're walking the dog or doing push-ups, the online system can automatically scan the Dow Jones news wires and the

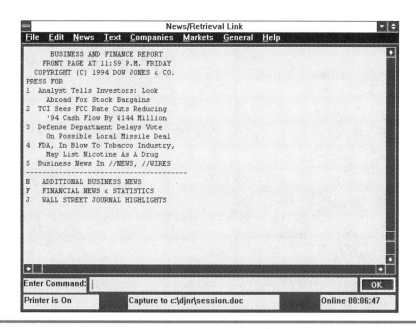

Figure 12-5   The Business and Finance Report menu provides one-sentence summaries of late-breaking stories

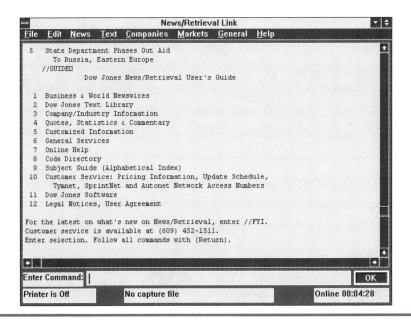

Figure 12-6   The User's Guide screen (//GUIDE). Item 9 is especially helpful

Text Library, //TEXT, and collect all the stories relevant to the stocks or companies you're currently following. They will be retrieved and deposited in a folder for later collection. Or, if you wish, the whole file will be sent to a fax machine, your AT&T Mail, SprintMail, MCI Mail, or EasyLink mailbox. You can have up to ten //CLIP folders operating at once, each tracking a different company, market, piece of legislation, technology, executive's name, etc. An alternative search method is //TRACK, which tracks both news and current quotes on the stocks you're following. This is a better way to go if you're in the office and the market is open.

Returning to the Dow Jones News/Retrieval User's Guide screen (Figure 12-6), you'll find a topic near and dear to our hearts: "Quotes, Statistics & Commentary," item 4. A tap on the keyboard here brings up Figure 12-7, with current and historical quotes on just about every-thing—stocks, bonds, indexes, futures, mutual funds, etc. This menu also tells us that if we want historical quotes from Tradeline, where the foreign stocks live, we should type //TRADELINE. Let's go there now.

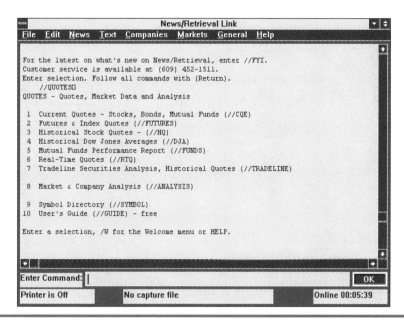

Figure 12-7 Here you can get quotes on stocks, bonds, futures, commodities, and options. Daily quotes on stock go back only one year

Welcome to the World—Tradeline

Figure 12-8 is the Tradeline menu—with, as it says up top, "Information on 142,459 Stocks, Bonds, Options, Mutual Funds & Indexes." Item number 9, "International Issues," carries the info squib, "Pricing and more for over 30,000 equity issues." About 25,000 of those are actively traded. There is no more exhaustive source for foreign issues.

The Tradeline service is almost certainly the one you would use the most for investing in foreign stocks or bonds, so spend some time looking over the menu items. The first one, "Screening Reports," is interesting, allowing you to screen for a virtually limitless number of selection criteria—earnings, growth, industry, etc. Going to Tradeline International (item 9) gives us the menu shown in Figure 12-9 that starts again with "Screening Reports," but this time the screening will be for foreign stocks.

Tradeline International has historical securities information on more than 25,000 international stocks more or less actively traded on approxi-

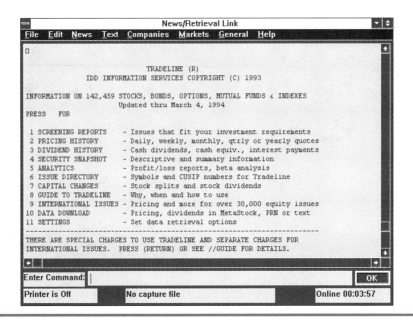

```
                              News/Retrieval Link                        ▼ ▲
 File   Edit   News   Text   Companies   Markets   General   Help
 □                                                                         ▲

                              TRADELINE (R)
                IDD INFORMATION SERVICES COPYRIGHT (C) 1993

         INFORMATION ON 142,459 STOCKS, BONDS, OPTIONS, MUTUAL FUNDS & INDEXES
                           Updated thru March 4, 1994
         PRESS   FOR

           1 SCREENING REPORTS    - Issues that fit your investment requirements
           2 PRICING HISTORY      - Daily, weekly, monthly, qtrly or yearly quotes
           3 DIVIDEND HISTORY     - Cash dividends, cash equiv., interest payments
           4 SECURITY SNAPSHOT    - Descriptive and summary information
           5 ANALYTICS            - Profit/loss reports, beta analysis
           6 ISSUE DIRECTORY      - Symbols and CUSIP numbers for Tradeline
           7 CAPITAL CHANGES      - Stock splits and stock dividends
           8 GUIDE TO TRADELINE   - Why, when and how to use
           9 INTERNATIONAL ISSUES - Pricing and more for over 30,000 equity issues
          10 DATA DOWNLOAD        - Pricing, dividends in MetaStock, PRN or text
          11 SETTINGS             - Set data retrieval options
         ----------------------------------------------------------------
         THERE ARE SPECIAL CHARGES TO USE TRADELINE AND SEPARATE CHARGES FOR
         INTERNATIONAL ISSUES.  PRESS (RETURN) OR SEE //GUIDE FOR DETAILS.     ▼
 ◄                                                                          ►

 Enter Command: |                                                    |   OK
 Printer is Off       No capture file                        Online 00:03:57
```

Figure 12-8   The Tradeline screen is the entrance to detailed information on 142,000 issues

---

mately 90 exchanges in 35 countries. From its opening menu of 11 options, you should start with the last, the International Guide, which will provide an overview and summary of commands for the system, as well as an explanation of the other 10 options on the menu.

The securities in this database are displayed in the currency of the country where they trade. If you select item 9, "Settings," however, you can request that the prices of any of the more than 150 currencies used by Tradeline be converted into any other currency you like. Presumably you would want that conversion to be into dollars, but any currency may be chosen. It would be wise to choose this conversion setting before exercising any of the screening functions, so that you get a uniform basis of comparison all along the search line.

The screening functions are many and complex. You can review them online, but it makes more sense to go over this area in the manual you get from Dow Jones. Make a note of all the codes you'll need when you log onto the system and start doing screens. Do it carefully, because there

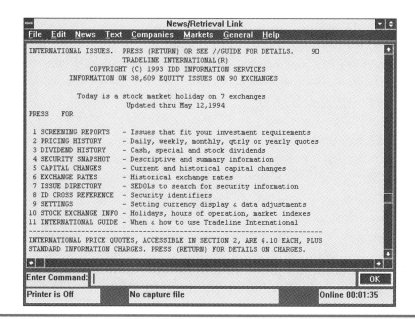

```
 ═                        News/Retrieval Link                      ▼ ▲
 File  Edit  News  Text  Companies  Markets  General  Help
┌──────────────────────────────────────────────────────────────────┐▲
│ INTERNATIONAL ISSUES.  PRESS (RETURN) OR SEE //GUIDE FOR DETAILS.  90│
│                      TRADELINE INTERNATIONAL(R)                    │
│               COPYRIGHT (C) 1993 IDD INFORMATION SERVICES          │
│          INFORMATION ON 38,609 EQUITY ISSUES ON 90 EXCHANGES       │
│                                                                    │
│                 Today is a stock market holiday on 7 exchanges     │
│                      Updated thru May 12,1994                      │
│ PRESS   FOR                                                        │
│                                                                    │
│  1 SCREENING REPORTS   - Issues that fit your investment requirements│
│  2 PRICING HISTORY     - Daily, weekly, monthly, qtrly or yearly quotes│
│  3 DIVIDEND HISTORY    - Cash, special and stock dividends         │
│  4 SECURITY SNAPSHOT   - Descriptive and summary information       │
│  5 CAPITAL CHANGES     - Current and historical capital changes    │
│  6 EXCHANGE RATES      - Historical exchange rates                 │
│  7 ISSUE DIRECTORY     - SEDOLs to search for security information  │
│  8 ID CROSS REFERENCE  - Security identifiers                      │
│  9 SETTINGS            - Setting currency display & data adjustments│
│ 10 STOCK EXCHANGE INFO - Holidays, hours of operation, market indexes│
│ 11 INTERNATIONAL GUIDE - When & how to use Tradeline International  │
│ ------------------------------------------------------------------ │
│ INTERNATIONAL PRICE QUOTES, ACCESSIBLE IN SECTION 2, ARE ¢.10 EACH, PLUS│
│ STANDARD INFORMATION CHARGES. PRESS (RETURN) FOR DETAILS ON CHARGES.│▼
│◄ ▒▒▒▒▒▒▒▒▒▒▒▒▒▒▒▒▒▒▒▒▒▒▒▒▒▒▒▒▒▒▒▒▒▒▒▒▒▒▒▒▒▒▒▒▒▒▒▒▒▒▒▒▒▒▒▒▒▒▒▒   ► │
├──────────────────────────────────────────────────────────────────┤
│ Enter Command: |                                          │  OK  │
├──────────────────────────────────────────────────────────────────┤
│ Printer is Off    │     No capture file          │ Online 00:01:35│
└──────────────────────────────────────────────────────────────────┘
```

Figure 12-9   Tradeline International should interest us the most. It covers 38,000 issues on 90 domestic and foreign stock exhanges

will be no friendly menus and hand-holding to guide you through it. Again, this is not like the other databases.

News of the World

Let's go back to the "International News & Information" menu (Figure 12-4) for a minute (//NEWS). Behind this group of menus, we'll find most of the worthwhile international investing information on DJN/R.

The first item, Business Newswires (//WIRES), is a 90-day collection of global news gleaned from the following services:

▶ The **Dow Jones News Service** offers real-time news on U.S. and Canadian companies, industries, U.S. government agencies, financial markets, the stock market, and the economy from the Dow Jones Broadtape. Updated continuously between 7:30 a.m. and 7 p.m. (ET) each business day.

▶ The **Dow Jones International News Services** offers the same type of coverage worldwide, including foreign exchange coverage, country-by-country financial market roundups, and selected stories from the *Wall Street Journal Europe* and *Asian Wall Street Journal*. Updated continuously from 6 p.m. on Sunday to 11 a.m. (ET) on Saturday.

▶ **Professional Investor Report** offers news, trading alerts, and statistical reports on active stocks, plus coverage of overall market activity at NYSE, Amex, NASDAQ, and OTC.

▶ **Dow Jones Capital Markets Report** provides real-time coverage of all major sectors of the international fixed-income and financial futures markets, especially Federal Reserve matters, and central bank activity worldwide, including Eurobonds. Updated continuously from 6:30 a.m. to 8 p.m. (ET) each business day, stories kept for at least 48 hours.

▶ **Federal Filings** offers real-time notification of filings with the Securities and Exchange Commission, with detailed analysis of those of greatest significance, as well as comprehensive coverage of all merger and acquisition-related documents, etc. Updated continuously from 7:30 a.m. to 7:30 p.m. (ET) each business day.

▶ **PR Newswire**, **Business Wire**, and **Canada NewsWire** offer unedited business, financial, and general press releases from over 15,000 publicly traded U.S. and Canadian companies, government agencies (including economic releases), industry associations, labor unions, stock exchanges, etc. Updated continuously from 7 a.m. to 7 p.m. (ET) each business day.

What follows on the menu, items 2 through 5, are really sub-groups of item 1, Business Newswires. In other words, if you want news from the Pacific Rim, the command would be //WIRES R/PRM. This code merely tells the main computer to search all the wire news and retrieve any items that relate to the Pacific Rim. The result, a list of the latest news stories from that region, is shown in Figure 12-10. The list goes on for pages, and the screen printed here is just the first page. It's almost overwhelming, but after you've done it a few times, you'll find that you can skim through the list in a couple of minutes and tell just from the summary line what's of interest and what isn't.

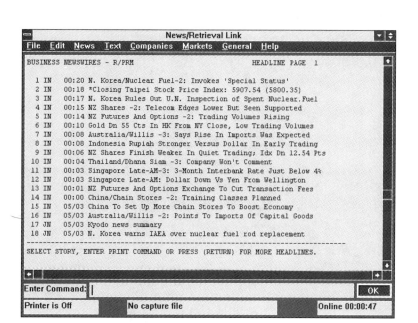

```
═                        News/Retrieval Link                   ▼ ▲
 File  Edit  News  Text  Companies  Markets  General  Help

BUSINESS NEWSWIRES - R/PRM                      HEADLINE PAGE  1            ▲

   1 IN    00:20 N. Korea/Nuclear Fuel-2: Invokes 'Special Status'
   2 IN    00:18 *Closing Taipei Stock Price Index: 5907.54 (5800.35)
   3 IN    00:17 N. Korea Rules Out U.N. Inspection of Spent Nuclear.Fuel
   4 IN    00:15 NZ Shares -2: Telecom Edges Lower But Seen Supported
   5 IN    00:14 NZ Futures And Options -2: Trading Volumes Rising
   6 IN    00:10 Gold Dn 55 Cts In HK From NY Close, Low Trading Volumes
   7 IN    00:08 Australia/Willis -3: Says Rise In Imports Was Expected
   8 IN    00:08 Indonesia Rupiah Stronger Versus Dollar In Early Trading
   9 IN    00:06 NZ Shares Finish Weaker In Quiet Trading; Idx Dn 12.54 Pts
  10 IN    00:04 Thailand/Dhana Siam -3: Company Won't Comment
  11 IN    00:03 Singapore Late-AM-3: 3-Month Interbank Rate Just Below 4%
  12 IN    00:03 Singapore Late-AM: Dollar Down Vs Yen From Wellington
  13 IN    00:01 NZ Futures And Options Exchange To Cut Transaction Fees
  14 IN    00:00 China/Chain Stores -2: Training Classes Planned
  15 IN    05/03 China To Set Up More Chain Stores To Boost Economy
  16 IN    05/03 Australia/Willis -2: Points To Imports Of Capital Goods
  17 JN    05/03 Kyodo news summary
  18 JN    05/03 N. Korea warns IAEA over nuclear fuel rod replacement
----------------------------------------------------------------------
SELECT STORY, ENTER PRINT COMMAND OR PRESS (RETURN) FOR MORE HEADLINES.
                                                                          ▲
 ◄                                                                  ►

Enter Command: |                                                      OK

 Printer is Off        │ No capture file             │ Online 00:00:47
```

Figure 12-10   You can request stories from Business Newswires on a specific subject, such as the Pacific Rim

If you're following a stock which you suspect is likely to be affected by some news item, you can enter a quick search of these eight news wires by typing //WIRES followed by the stock symbol. If you don't know the symbol, you can get it by typing //SYMBOL, which carries symbols for both domestic and international stocks. You can also select various subsets of the news wires (to search only Dow Jones news wires, for example). Your search request can have up to three stock symbols, three different //WIRES codes (for the different news wires), or a combination of both.

Item 6 in Figure 12-4 is "Canadian Company Reports" and covers Canadian financial markets, public, private, and Crown (government-owned) companies. Articles from the *Globe and Mail,* one of Canada's leading newspapers, are retrievable here.

Item 10 is "WorldScope International Company Profiles," which for $9 a pop will give you a fairly complete financial report on any of 6,500 foreign corporations. Figure 12-11 shows you what the WorldScope lead

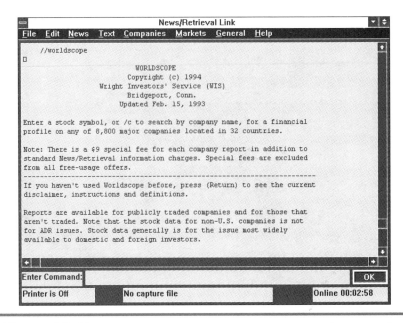

Figure 12-11   The WorldScope service is expensive, but provides financial profiles on 8,800 foreign companies

screen looks like. From here you would enter a stock symbol or a company name and proceed to generate your report.

You can get a simpler and usually quite adequate report from the regular DJN/R service by typing //COMPANY in the command line at the bottom of any screen. These reports are logically divided into Public Companies and Private Companies. Inside the Public Companies menu you'll find databases with international company information.

Sometimes the most useful information is breaking news. A solid company in Thailand is of no consequence if the political situation turns bad. To find out what's happening, you can type //NEWS and get the World Report, shown in Figure 12-12. World Report has three menu-driven sections: the top menu, featuring the most important news stories; the national news menu, signified by the letter "N" near the bottom of the screen; and the "Additional Foreign News" menu, at the very bottom, designated by the letter "F." Selecting that choice brings up the screen shown in Figure 12-13. There are the usual problems in South Africa, the former Yugoslavia, the Ukraine, and Haiti. Are these the right places to

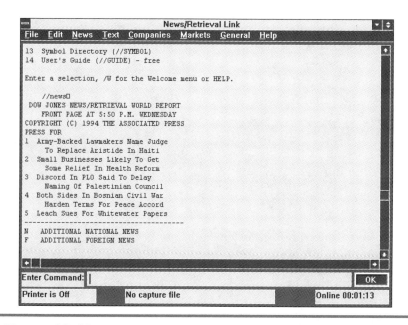

Figure 12-12   Headline summaries of news highlights (//NEWS)

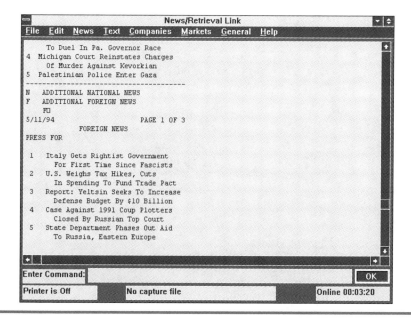

Figure 12-13   Selecting "F" from the menu in Figure 12-12 brings up foreign news

invest now, when everyone else shies away? Who knows? Remember the advice I quoted earlier from Baron Rothschild: buy with the cannons, sell with the trumpets.

CHAPTER 13

THE LAST OF THE BIG TIME BBS: GENIE AND DELPHI

In this chapter, we're going to discuss two well-known bulletin boards that are of little use, and in the next chapter, move on to two little-known names that are very useful.

Bulletin boards? You didn't know we were talking about bulletin boards? Well, yes. We were. Because while almost everyone has heard of CompuServe, Prodigy, America Online, and Dow Jones News/Retrieval, and thinks of them as these enormous storehouses of electronic information, the truth is they are just bulletin boards. They are, in essence, no different than the sixteen-year-old kid who plugs a phone line into his computer and decides to be a hub for talking about Star Trek. The commercial bulletin boards are just much larger. The size and the number of departments, groups, and services they provide depends entirely on how big the computer is and how many lines are attached to it. In practice, the very large databases can't fit on a single computer and are usually operated as a gang of linked machines, each taking care of certain subject matter and/or a certain number of callers.

The reason I go into all this is because what the boards carry is determined not just by size but by the aims and whims of the "sysop." A sysop is the "system operator," and can be an individual or a corporate committee. Sysops rule the online world. If a sysop decided, for some reason or another, not to include certain useful data or helpful features, there would be little or no recourse for the system's users but to go elsewhere. The sysop's interests may not coincide with yours, and often they don't. Thus, it's possible to have an enormous remote database (bulletin board), like America Online, that doesn't allow people to download historical stock quotes. By historical quotes, by the way, we don't mean what happened during the Civil War, but where the stock closed three days ago, or last month. On Dow Jones, we can't get a chart of the stock's motion or even daily data for more than a year ago. It's not because they're all stupid (at least I hope not), it's because of how they see their market. For the same reason, prices are all over the lot. Some services charge 1.5 cents for a stock quote; others, like GEnie, which we're going to look at in a moment, charge 6 cents.

Think about that for a moment: you can pay four times as much for information from one service to another, and it's exactly the same information! I've met people who have found themselves staring at $1,000 and even higher phone bills from well-known database services when they could have had the same information, or very nearly the same, for $10 somewhere else. Pay attention to what these services charge. That said, let's turn to the most outrageously expensive database service we've been able to find for investors. Poof! It's GEnie!—a cute name derived from the logo of its owner, General Electric.

Rub the Magic Lamp

Figure 13-1 shows the opening screen of GEnie. It's not jazzy, and despite the fact that they have about 200,000 members, many of whom are kids, there are none of the pictures or colorful icons you get with

```
                         GEnie PC Aladdin 1.71
   Esc Menu    F6 RTC   F7 Echo    F8 Blanks    F9 8th bit    F10 Look back
   11. Power Mac and the Power PC, talk about it Sunday in.........IBMPC
   12. HURRY - grab these commercial games before it's too late....SOFTCLUB
   13. Fantasy Sports Leagues RoundTable - GRAND OPENING...........FSL
   14. The Programmers' Cafe is OPEN tonight in..................PROGRAMMING
   15. Register for Spring Courses.............................CALC

   Enter #, <H>elp, or <CR> to continue?

   GEnie                          TOP                        Page    1
                        GE Information Services

    1.   About GEnie                  2.   New Members' Information
    3.   Communications (GE Mail & Chat)   4.   Computing Services
    5.   Travel Services              6.   Finance & Investing Services
    7.   Online Shopping Services     8.   News, Sports & Features
    9.   GEnie Games                 10.   Career/Professional Services
   11.   Business Services           12.   Leisure Pursuits & Hobbies
   13.   Education Services          14.   Entertainment Services
   15.   Symposiums on Global Issues  16.   Research & Reference Services
   17.   Leave GEnie (Logoff)

   Enter #, <H>elp?
   On  RDY 7bit ECHO        Blanks OK  Capture OFF        Terminal mode
```

Figure 13-1   The opening screen of GEnie, which has the plain text appearance of most bulletin board systems

CompuServe, Prodigy, and America Online. This is a text-based service, and you can connect to it with any communications software or their own package called "Aladdin." GEnie—Aladdin. Get it? I thought you would. After you get over the attack of the cutes, take the Aladdin package and drop it in the trash; it may not be the worst program I've ever seen, but it's certainly a contender. It works, but it is user-hostile. Nonetheless, it was used for the GEnie screens you will see here. It only took seven attempts and three calls to technical support. New software, and perhaps a new look, is supposed to appear this summer. Keep rubbing that lamp.

Part of the reason the software is so hard to use and the system so unfriendly, by the way, is that, like all services, this one betrays its origins, and many of its subscribers are "techies." The Computer Press Association makes its home here, for example, as do numerous programmers. None of this has any particular significance for our purposes, however, so if we look at the main menu more carefully, we see that item 6 covers "Finance & Investing Services." We'll go there now.

Take a look at Figure 13-2. Item 2 says "Dow Jones News/Retrieval" (DJN/R), and you might look at this and say to yourself "Oh boy (or something similar depending on your background and educational level), I can sign up for GEnie and use it to log on to the DJN/R." Yes, you can. However, you will pay all DNJR charges, including their numerous "extra fee" charges and pay GEnie online time on top of that. Oh boy. Several of the other services listed here also have charges in addition to the regular GEnie charges, and let's look at that right now.

Normal GEnie rates are $8.95 a month, plus $3 an hour in off-hours. The first four hours of non-prime time are free. If you call in prime time (8 a.m. to 6 p.m. your local time), there is a surcharge of $9.50 an hour. That's in addition to the $3 regular connect time charge, so you're paying $12.50 an hour. There's another $6 an hour charge for using 9600 baud instead of 2400 baud. This one is a pretty serious surcharge since almost everybody is going to the higher baud rate now.

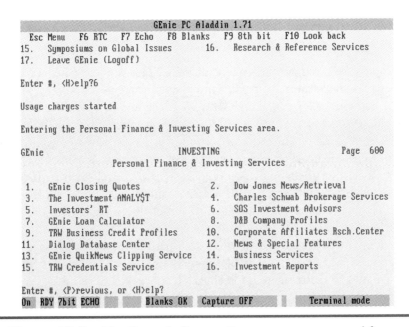

Figure 13-2   The "Investing" menu lists numerous personal finance and investing services, most of them available only at an extra charge

Please Pay the Genie After Every Wish

Figure 13-3 shows us a menu of rates for financial services. If we select item 2, "Investment ANALY$T Rates," we get Figure 13-4, a screen which says right at the top: "Significant charges in addition to GEnie's hourly connect rates apply..." Take that message to heart; it's going to get a lot worse. This screen tells us right off the bat that it will cost about $20 to look up the basic facts about a company.

Back to Figure 13-3. Other charges worth noting here are

Charles Schwab & Co. is the resident discount broker, and you can connect to Schwab through GEnie and get quotes and other information online for $1.45 a minute. The point of this completely eludes me, since I could call Schwab directly by telephone for the price of a local call and get quotes for just a few cents a minute. Even if I lived in a town that did not have a Schwab office (are there any such towns?) and had to call long distance, the

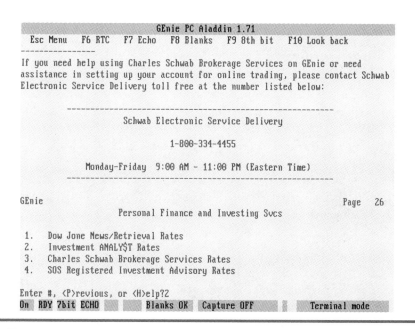

Figure 13-3 The menu of rates for GEnie's personal finance and investing services

```
                    GEnie PC Aladdin 1.71
   Esc Menu    F6 RTC    F7 Echo    F8 Blanks    F9 8th bit    F10 Look back
   =========================

   Significant charges in addition to GEnie's hourly connect rates apply to search
   and retrieval in Investment Reports. The following charges apply to your
   searches:

   Charges for Investment Reports are directly related to the searches you perform
   and the information you retrieve. Each step of your search and retrieval falls
   into different classifications. Here are the rates for each part of your search
   in Investment Reports effective December 1, 1992:


   Initial Search            $7.50 (each set of up to 10 report titles)
   List of Report Pages   No charge
   Full Company Record       $12.00
   No-Hit Search             $1.25


   The first step searches through more than 320,000 analyst report titles in the
   Investment Reports database on Dialog to find each record which matches your
   search. You can display report titles which match in groups of up to ten. The
   first ten matches will automatically be displayed. Each additiona
   On   RDY 7bit ECHO          Blanks OK   Capture 9651            Terminal mode
```

Figure 13-4   Here we see some examples of GEnie charges for analysts' reports

call would only cost me 20 cents a minute. Why would I want to contact Schwab through GEnie?

► You can get Zacks Earnings Estimates for $6 a company. Zacks is a well-known service that compiles corporate earnings by analysts from many brokerage houses. If you want a full report on analysts' commentaries for the company, they're $39 each. Ouch.

► Investment ANALY$T Services, which we mentioned briefly earlier, charges 6 cents a quote—current or historical. Then they really get you:

$6 for each news story about a company.
$6 for a volume chart on any company.
$6 for a chart with moving averages.
$6 for a chart with on-balance volume.
$6 for a chart showing stock price and insider trading.
$6 for a chart with MACD (moving average of accumulation and distribution—which we'll talk about in Part 4, in the chapters on

using MetaStock and other programs).
$6 for a relative strength chart.
$6 for a chart with stochastics.
$6 for what they call an "over and under"—which usually refers to a histogram of an oscillator or crossing averages.
$6 for a company fact sheet—number of shares outstanding, book value, earnings, etc.

If we add it all up, it comes to a stunning $48 for each stock you're interested in. Want to find out about 10 stocks? That'll be almost $500. What makes it so stunning is that you can get everything here, except current news stories, from Telescan for about 10 cents. In fact, when we read the fine print on the ANALY$T service, we find that the information and charts *come* from Telescan! Skip the middleman. Just sign up for Telescan and save yourself a bundle. Their connect software is much better, too.

We could go on at some length about the charges here, and some would say we already have. But as your mother told you: "If you can't say anything nice, don't say anything at all." Since it's much too late for that, let's say a word or two about GEnie's strong suit.

GEnie prides itself on its research services. A look at Figure 13-5 shows a menu of their "Research & Reference Services," (item 16 on GEnie's opening menu shown in Figure 13-1) and if you read down the list it's pretty impressive. Here we see some of the choices that we saw earlier in the "Investing" menu (Figure 13-2), such as Dow Jones News/Retrieval and Investment ANALY$T. We've mentioned the extra charges you build up in those research areas, so it should come as no surprise that most of the items listed in this menu also carry stiff extra charges. Most of them are also found in other large database services.

At this point, we will leave GEnie with some final observations. There are a lot of useful research sources but the prices are high. If you are interested in the service, it would probably be worth checking the rates again because prices here and elsewhere in the database world change often. For those of us interested in stocks and investing, other services provide the same information or more at a lower cost. There may be something here that is not in one of the others, like CompuServe, but if there is, I could not find it. Still, one of the uses of any of these services is signing onto forums and talking with other people who may know

```
                    GEnie PC Aladdin 1.71
  Esc Menu    F6 RTC    F7 Echo    F8 Blanks    F9 8th bit    F10 Look back
PC Magazine states "GEnie excels at research tasks". See Dialog (#9).
GEnie                         RESEARCH                     Page   302
                  GEnie Research & Reference Services

   1.   About Research & Ref. Services    2.   Bibliographic Citations Center
   3.   GEnie BookShelf                    4.   Canadian Business Center
   5.   Commerce Business Daily            6.   Computer & Electronics Center
   7.   Consumer Medicine                  8.   Corporate Affiliates Center
   9.   Dialog Database Center            10.   Dow Jones News/Retrieval
  11.   Dun & Bradstreet (D&B) Databases  12.   Educator's Center
  13.   Grolier's Encyclopedia            14.   Investment ANALYST
  15.   Investment Reports                16.   Law Center
  17.   Medical Professional's Center     18.   GEnie NewsStand
  19.   Worldwide Patent Center           20.   Public Opinion Online
  21.   GEnie Reference Center            22.   Quotations Online
  23.   TRW Business Credit Profiles      24.   Thomas Register
  25.   Trademark Center                  26.   Tradenames Database

  27.   U.S. Federal Center               28.   Business Resource Directory
  29.   Genealogy KB                      30.   Microsoft KB

Item #, or <RETURN> for more?
On  RDY 7bit ECHO          Blanks OK   Capture 13143          Terminal mode
```

Figure 13-5　The GEnie menu for research services, one of the strong suits of this database. There is an extra charge for nearly everything shown here

things you don't. In that regard, the people who participate in GEnie forums tend to be very knowledgeable about computer technology and the computer industry.

Delphi: Consulting the Oracle

There are a lot of services, clubs, groups, etc., on Delphi, but the system is probably best known for providing direct access to the Internet. The Internet is the buzzword of the moment, and while several database services provide the ability to send messages, for now, Delphi is the only big online service that provides full Internet access. Delphi makes its Internet connection through the New England Research Council—NERC. (If they had had their wits about them, they really should have called themselves the New England Research and Development Society.)

There's an extra charge of $3 a month for the Internet service, which is not much, and we'd really like to get all excited about it, but there is little value here for investors. You could raise the issue that since the Internet is international you can talk to people all over the world and ask about stocks and other local invstments. But you can do that on CompuServe and Prodigy and America Online, too. Nonetheless, we'll give you some Internet information in a minute; first let's turn to the financial services on Delphi itself.

Charges on Delphi are simple. They have two plans: the 10-4 Plan, which costs $10 a month and provides four free hours and $4 an hour beyond that, and the 20-20 Plan which costs $20 a month and provides 20 free hours. (See Delphi's coupon at the back of this book offering a free five-hour trial.) Certain services, like Donoghue's Money Letter, carry an extra charge, which will be shown on the screen.

Figure 13-6 shows the Delphi main screen. They don't provide any software, so you connect through any communications package you have lying around. This connection was made just using the Terminal program that comes with Windows. The opening message tells us the Delphi T-shirt is in and available for just $9.95 plus $2 shipping. This may or may not make your heart beat faster. It also tells us that starting April 1 there

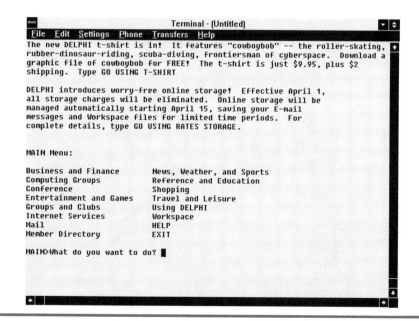

Figure 13-6   The first menu to come up when you connect to Delphi

will be no storage charges for e-mail messages and some other files. That's nice, but CompuServe has had that for years.

You can navigate through Delphi with the tab and arrow keys, or by entering the selection you want at the prompt. Let's go now to item 1, "Business and Finance." What we see is Figure 13-7. Just for the fun of it, we'll select the "MarketPulse" Report, shown in Figure 13-8, which carries an extra charge of 50 cents. We get the usual report on the averages plus the big gainers and losers. You get this faster, better-looking, and for free on Prodigy. So even though it's only 50 cents, and we had a good day at the track and so can afford this, it is not in any way a deal.

Let's pause here and give another look to the market report in Figure 13-8 that we just paid 50 cents for, because it has problems of the kind that come up all too often. What caught my eye and stopped me cold as I glanced over the display was the section on NYSE (New York Stock Exchange) Percent Gainers on the left-hand side of the screen. It shows some stock with the symbol DQE as selling for 32, up a whopping 28-1/4 points, and then AN selling for 54-7/8, up 27-3/8. Those would be unusual moves on any day for any stock, and to see two of them is totally

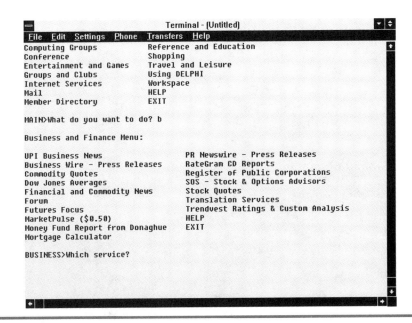

Figure 13-7 Delphi's "Business and Finance" menu

```
┌─────────────────────────────────────────────────────────────┐
│ ─                  Terminal - (Untitled)                ▼ ▲ │
├─────────────────────────────────────────────────────────────┤
│ File  Edit  Settings  Phone  Transfers  Help               │
│ MARKETPULSE  24-MAR at 12:33 Eastern Time                ▲ │
│                                                              │
│ Dow Jones Indus: 3820.22 dn 49.24  Market Composite Indices:│
│ NYSE Advances  : 397             NYSE   N/A                  │
│      Declines  : 1684            AMEX   N/A                  │
│      Unchanged : N/A             OTC    783.52              │
│                                                              │
│ NYSE Most Active (Current Price, Movement, Volume in 00's): │
│ RAD    18 7/8  dn    1/4  ******  SSC    2 3/8  up    1/8  20154│
│ TMX    60 5/8  dn  3 1/8  73661   SCH   30 1/8  dn  1 1/8  20095│
│ C      56      dn  2 1/8  24452   F     60 5/8  dn  2 3/4  19687│
│ MRK    30 3/8  up    1/4  24338   LTD   21 3/8  up    3/4  17201│
│ GM     58 1/8  dn  2 3/8  21315   PDG   25 1/2  up    7/8  12857│
│                                                              │
│ NYSE Percent Gainers:            NYSE Percent Losers:       │
│ DQE    32      up 28 1/4    130   IPC   21 1/8  dn  8 1/8   321│
│ AN     54 7/8  up 27 3/8   2175   ZOS    1      dn    3/8   558│
│ CO     32 3/4  up 12         63   HTT    7      dn  2       419│
│ LTC    13 3/4  up  4 3/8    236   PLT   13      dn  3 5/8    13│
│ NGX     1 1/4  up    1/4   1951   CRC    0 1/2  dn    1/8  1601│
│                                                              │
│ NYSE Point Gainers:              NYSE Point Losers:         │
│ DQE    32      up 28 1/4    130   CCB   703      dn 15 3/4   224│
│ More?█                                                       │
│                                                              │
│ ◄ ■■■                                                    ► │
└─────────────────────────────────────────────────────────────┘
```

Figure 13-8 For a 50-cent charge on Delphi you can call up a stock market summary through MarketPulse

out of normal activity. A couple seconds later I realized that "AN" was the symbol for Amoco, one of the largest oil companies in the world, and the only way Amoco was going to move 27 points in a day was if some oil sheik made a takeover offer. I shut down Delphi and went immediately to Telescan to call up these stocks and see what was happening.

1. DQE turned out to be an electric utility, the former DuQuesne Electric Company, and it was indeed selling for $32 a share, but was down 3/4, not up 28-1/4.

2. AN (Amoco) was selling for 54-1/2, down 1/4.

3. CO turned out to be the symbol for Corrpro CO., an engineering firm, and turned out to be selling for 21-3/4, not 32-3/4, and was up 1/2, not 12.

4. LTC was a real estate company selling for 13-3/4, just as the MarketPulse report said, but was actually down 1/4, not up 4-3/8.

5. And finally, NGX, a wildcat oil exploration company, was in fact selling for 1-1/4, and was up 1/4, just as the screen said. The next day it was down 1/4.

So four out of the five stocks shown as big gainers on the New York Stock Exchange were not only completely wrong, but three of them were down, not up. There's little point in jumping up and down at Delphi about this or the provider of the MarketPulse service Delphi carries, because I have seen this sort of grossly erroneous information many times and from several places. What it points out is there is a lot of dirty data around. It may be a small amount on a percentage basis when you consider the huge volume of quote information that goes by each day, but it is nonetheless pretty important if it happens to be one of the stocks you're following.

The moral of the story is check your data if it looks wrong to you. Data is more important than people seem to realize. A study published in *Futures Magazine* at the end of 1993 found a number of trading systems that produced losses with data from most sources, produced profits when

Dirty Data-ing

The problem of dirty data seems to be getting worse rather than better. Consider the reality of the situation: most people assume that quotes are all recorded electronically, by some vast computer somewhere that is keeping track of every trade taking place on every exchange in the world—certainly every exchange in the U.S. Few things could be farther from the truth. Data is typically entered manually—someone typing on the keyboard—and the people hired to do this are clerical staff, sometimes just high school students, some very competent, some not. But frequently I have noticed that they will type in a price like "6" for a stock that is selling for around 60, and what really baffles me thereafter is that they look at the incredible price spike created by this jump in the sequence and it will look all right to them. What on earth are they thinking? Or rather not thinking. It reminds me of a cartoon I saw a couple years ago in the *New Yorker* that shows a guy sitting in a big chair listening to the radio, his hair standing on end. The radio announcer is saying, "The Dow Jones Industrial Average was down 700 points in early trading, recovered to move to plus 400 during the afternoon, and finished unchanged for the day."

the data was from other sources, most notably Tick Data Corp. (mentioned in Chapter 2). These are systems that would be triggered by a technical indicator, say, something like the crossover of moving averages or the relative strength indicator or the stochastic, which we are going to talk about in the last section of this book. Using exactly the same indicators for buy and sell signals, the systems were unprofitable with data from large suppliers like Dial Data, but profitable from Tick Data. Unfortunately for our side, Tick Data does not do stock quotes, but confines itself to futures and commodities.

Figure 13-9 shows a sample screen of Delphi business news. It goes on and on, and if you can read the summary lines here you'll see there's a lot of stuff.

Wrapping it up: Delphi is kind of a fringe service for our purposes unless you want to spend a lot of time on the Internet. Delphi was recently purchased by Rupert Murdoch, however, always referred to in the media as a "press lord." I'm not sure what a press lord is, but it sounds exciting, and things are likely to get more lively.

```
—                          Terminal - [Untitled]                    ▾ ▴
File  Edit  Settings  Phone  Transfers  Help
                                                                    ▴
   1   24-MAR 12:35   Daxor makes announcement
   2   24-MAR 12:32   Infinity Broadcasting joins Business Week 1000 ranking of
                      America's Most Valuable Companies
   3   24-MAR 12:31   Philip Morris Companies Inc. sues ABC for libel
   4   24-MAR 12:30   Sequoia Systems Names Former NYNEX Executive to Board of
                      Directors
   5   24-MAR 12:28   0232 BC-BW-MIDWEST-RECAP
   6   24-MAR 12:28   The Standish Care Company offers to exchange 2.4 shares of
                      common stock for each outstanding share
   7   24-MAR 12:28   U.S. Gold announces new CEO for Gold Capital
   8   24-MAR 12:17   American Red Cross & earthquake victims to benefit from
                      building Character
   9   24-MAR 12:17   0215 BC-BW-RECAP-4
  10   24-MAR 12:12   Advanced Magnetics announces Japanese filing for
                      manufacturing approval of its liver contrast agent
  11   24-MAR 11:57   SEQUA REPORTS FOURTH QUARTER/FULL YEAR 1993 RESULTS
  12   24-MAR 11:52   ADVISORY/IIN broadcasts CeBIT '94: Tandem, Symantec,
                      Siemens-Nixdorf & Unisys
  13   24-MAR 11:50   ADVISORY/Free disaster relief seminar for accountants,
                      businesses and individuals to be sponsored by the Institut

Enter Item Number, MORE, or EXIT: ▮
                                                                    ▾
◂ ▮                                                              ▮ ▸
```

Figure 13-9   This screen shows a few of the literally hundreds of news stories available on Delphi

CHAPTER 14

SMALL BBS, BIG BANGS

We're going to look at some small bulletin boards here—small, that is, only by the standards of CompuServe or Prodigy. They are specialized services, and, frankly, this is where the pros go when they want to collect quotes to feed their analytical software. These services are cheap and they're fast.

Pisces: **Nothing Fishy About This**

This is a Chicago bulletin board that provides four years of daily quotes on all listed stocks. This bulletin board is aimed primarily at MetaStock users and is home to one of the largest MetaStock user groups. They have lots of other stuff, too, but MetaStock is Topic A. The annual membership fee is $80 a year and for that you get unlimited downloading of current and historical quotes. You also get access to all the discussion forums and quite a bit of free or low-cost software of the freeware/shareware variety. Some of it is very good. Figure 14-1 shows you the Pisces title screen. There are no graphics here, no nifty pictures; it's all text and mostly all business.

Pisces can handle 14.4k transmission, which is modem talk for 14400 bits per second, and that's a lot of action, as they say down in the grain pits. It can even handle 28.8k, but hardly anyone has that. If you do, you can download a stock a second. (Maybe next year.)

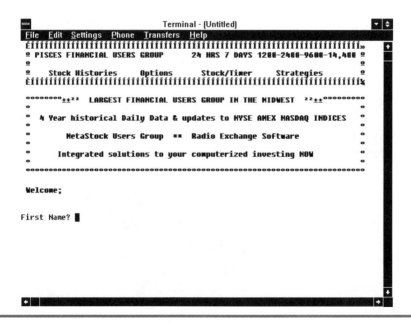

Figure 14-1   The opening Pisces screen presents a series of questions designed to identify you as a potential customer

Since Pisces is run by the Midwest's largest MetaStock dealer, all that data can be downloaded automatically in MetaStock format and even slugged directly into MetaStock by Pisces' own programs. If you don't use MetaStock, don't worry; most programs in the technical analysis field can read MetaStock data.

People who are very serious about their stock market data can pre-load a list of all the stocks they want, dial up at 14.4k and inhale a couple hundred. Downloading takes about two seconds a quote. If you do a hundred, you're in and out in three or four minutes. Figure 14-2 shows the Pisces screen that lists all the rates. It's very straightforward. This rate screen also cautions you that it is not feasible to download more than 1,000 stocks at a time. Seems reasonable. If you want to keep track of more than 1,000 stocks, you probably should have a long, quiet talk with somebody, but you can just start a second batch. Remember: a little over 2,000 stocks and you're looking at the entire New York Stock Exchange.

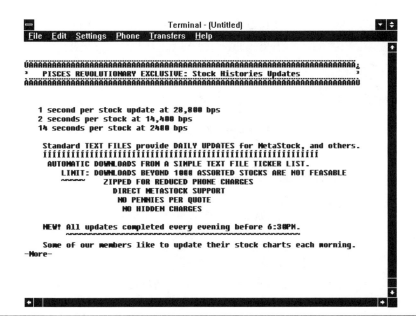

Figure 14-2   Service is fast: a stock a second at 28800 baud, or every two
seconds at 14400 baud

One of the best features of this bulletin board—and one that you seldom get with other services—is that you do not have to update every day. If you're away for a couple of weeks and want to update your list, just dial in. The Pisces software knows how many days you're missing and will automatically backfill and bring all lists up to the present. Pisces will handle this fill-er-up for as much as three months of missing data. Longer than that, you have to ask for specific dates. You can also do this with QuoteLink from Telescan (on the disk included with this book) and from almost any database that has stock quotes provided you have the Downloader for MetaStock. This is a separate program from Equis that costs $49 and I highly recommend it. I have used it for years.

The next screen warns you that some of "the legal stuff" is coming up, and the usual disclaimers file by before you sign up. Figure 14-3 shows you the main menu screen. You can see immediately the difference

Chicago, Zipped

One of the things that might give you pause is that when you call Pisces you're calling a Chicago phone number. And if you happen to be from out of town, that's a long distance call. But such is the nature of long distance calling these days that it only costs 20 cents a minute during business hours anywhere in the continental U.S. with most calling plans, no matter what the distance. During evening hours, it's typically 10 cents a minute—once again, no matter where you're calling from. So it's hard to work up more than a 50-cent bill here, unless you decide to stay and chat on some of the investment forums. Even then you can't go over $6 an hour in the evening.

Pisces tries to keep everybody's phone bill down by transmitting most files *zipped*. This is computer jargon for files that have been compressed, using the program PKZip. There are other programs that do file compression as well, but the expression "zipped" has become generic for all of them. Compression usually cuts the file size in half and sometimes it cuts it to a fifth or sixth of its previous size.

Of course, the file then must be decompressed to be useful again.

You should have a copy of PKZip on your own computer for compressing and decompressing files. PKZip is shareware, and it is so widely used that you can download a copy from Pisces or almost any other bulletin board you ever connect to. That includes CompuServe, Prodigy, America Online, etc. There is a $10 or $15 charge to register your copy of PKZip and receive technical support and information on how to use some of its more advanced features. Some people do the registration procedure and some don't; it's all voluntary— that's what shareware is about.

```
┌─────────────────────── Terminal - [Untitled] ─────────────────▼│▲│
│ File  Edit  Settings  Phone  Transfers  Help                      │
│ÜÄÄÄÄÄÄÄÄÄÄÄÄÄÄÄÄÄÄÄÄÄÄÄÄÄÄÄÄÄÄÄÄÄÄÄÄÄÄÄÄÄÄÄÄÄÄÄÄÄÄÄÄÄÄÄÄÄÄÄÄÄÄÄÄÄÄ¿│ ▲
│ ³    PISCES FINANCIAL BB$         MAIN GALLERY       US Robotics 14,400 Dual ³°│
│ÄÄÄÄÄÄÄÄÄÄÄÄÄÄÄÄÄÄÄÄÄÄÄÄÄÄÄÄÄÄÄÄÄÄÄÄÄÄÄÄÄÄÄÄÄÄÄÄÄÄÄÄÄÄÄÄÄÄÄÄÄÄÄÄÄ³°│
│ ³ PISCES SOFTWARE SALES  ³      FREE          ³           MESSAGE      ³°│
│ ³  & MEMBERSHIP AREAS     ³  PUBLIC FILE AREAS ³            AREAS       ³°│
│ÄÄÄÄÄÄÄÄÄÄÄÄÄÄÄÄÄÄÄÄÄÄÄÄÄÄÄ³ÄÄÄÄÄÄÄÄÄÄÄÄÄÄÄÄÄÄÄÄ³ÄÄÄÄÄÄÄÄÄÄÄÄÄÄÄÄÄÄÄÄ³°│
│ ³ (1) Software Catalog   ³ (F) File Downloads  ³ (A)dvantages of Pisces ³°│
│ ³ (2) Ordering Info      ³ (7) File Uploads    ³      Membership        ³°│
│ ³ (3) Software Upgrades  ³ (8) Top 40 Downloads³ (N)ew User Tips        ³°│
│ ³ (4) Product Support    ³ (D) Data Bases      ³ (S)pecial $$ Bulletins ³°│
│ ³ (5) Membership Files   ³ (9) Special Services³ (C)onferences, Email,  ³°│
│ ³                        ³                     ³      & Messages        ³°│
│ ³                        ³                     ³ (Q)wk Offline Express  ³°│
│ ³                        ³                     ³                        ³°│
│ÄÄÄÄÄÄÄÄÄÄÄÄÄÄÄÄÄÄÄÄÄÄÄÄÄÄÄÄÄÄÄÄÄÄÄÄÄÄÄÄÄÄÄÄÄÄÄÄÄÄÄÄÄÄÄÄÄÄÄÄÄÄÄÄÄ³°│
│ ³                                                                    ³°│
│ ³ (G)oodbye    (U)tilities      (T)ime on system    (M)essage to Sysop ³°│
│ÄÄÄÄÄÄÄÄÄÄÄÄÄÄÄÄÄÄÄÄÄÄÄÄÄÄÄÄÄÄÄÄÄÄÄÄÄÄÄÄÄÄÄÄÄÄÄÄÄÄÄÄÄÄÄÄÄÄÄÄÄÄÄÄÄÄÄÄÄÄÄÄÄÄÄÜ°│
│ °°°°°°°°°°°°°°°°°°°°°°°°°°°°°°°°°°°°°°°°°°°°°°°°°°°°°°°°°°°°°°°°°°°°°°°°°°°°°°│
│                                                                          │
│                                                                          │
│ Command:                                                                 │
│                                                                        ▼ │
├──┬───────────────────────────────────────────────────────────────────┬──┤
│◄ │                                                                     │ ►│
└──┴───────────────────────────────────────────────────────────────────┴──┘
```

Figure 14-3   The main menu of Pisces

between this and a large commercial database. There are no listings for world news, UPI, *New York Times*, Reuters, etc. Other than that, however, it looks pretty much like any database, even though, remember, this is just a bulletin board. Item 8 on the menu is "Top 40 Downloads." This refers to shareware and freeware programs. Like many bulletin boards, Pisces has a great deal of shareware and freeware—programs you can download and use for little or no cost. Many of these are programs for analyzing stocks and bonds or portfolio management. Pisces also offers discounts on commercial investment programs.

Pisces has numerous forums online to discuss market conditions, investment ideas, etc. And since this is an investment bulletin board and located in a city that houses the major options and commodities markets, the talk is very knowledgeable.

If you want to sign up for Pisces, you can call 312/281-2916. Or you can call with your modem to 312/281-6046 and sign up online, using your favorite credit card.

The Free Financial Network

The Free Financial Network, based in New York, is the Big Apple's answer to Pisces, if anybody ever asked the question. The name is misleading; it's free to sign up and use some of the forums and services, but if you want to download unlimited quotes (and also have e-mail), the price structure is almost the same as Pisces: $80 a year or $50 for six months. As befits the heart of the financial world, the service here is blazingly fast.

Let's look at Figure 14-4 for an idea of what's going down, as they say. This is one of the best available services for low-cost, high-speed loading of stock quotes. The bottom portion of the screen shows that you can download 10,000 daily quotes in less than 60 seconds. You would need very fast hardware for that and not many people have the equipment to try it. That's okay; it's plenty fast without going to that level.

That's for current quotes. The charge for historical quotes is one penny for every 30 days worth, but they throw in 30,000 days worth for nothing first. That's right, 30,000 days worth of quotes on the house. Practically speaking, that would be a little more than a year's worth of quotes for 100 stocks. That ought to keep you busy for a while. As with Pisces and most other bulletin board systems, you can use the Free Financial Network for electronic mail, meetings and investment forums, and a large library of shareware and freeware (Figure 14-5). One of the items on this screen makes a point of bragging that they have 30,000 files in their library on CD-ROM. Most of these would be programs—shareware and freeware. And while it may seem incredible that anyplace can offer 30,000 programs to be downloaded into your computer, I assure you it is not. I have disks for my own use that contain 1,500 to 3,000 programs on each disk. You can buy them from magazine ads or at trade shows for as little as $15-$20 apiece.

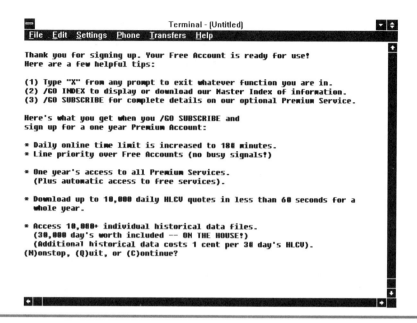

Figure 14-4   One of the opening information screens for the Free Financial Network

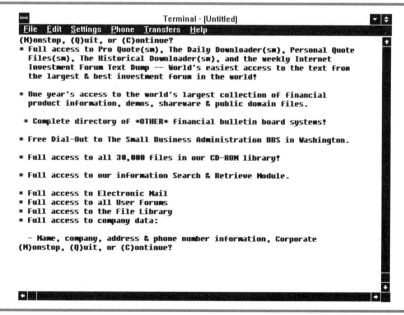

Figure 14-5   A list of the services available with Free Financial Network's 1-year membership

Figure 14-6 shows a screen of rates for the Free Financial Network. You can see that you can buy blocks of quotes if you prefer that and don't want to sign up for six months or a year's membership. It's cheaper, but the savings hardly seem worth it since the full membership charge is so close. The full menu is shown in Figure 14-7. Look this over carefully. You'll notice that selections B and C provide "Technical Analysis & Charting by Equis International" and "Options Analysis & Trading by OptionVue Systems International." These are the leading software makers for the technical analysis of stocks and market indices for the first, options for the second. The modem number for the Free Financial Network is 212/752-8660.

There are other bulletin boards that might be worth your attention, certainly none more generally helpful than AAII.

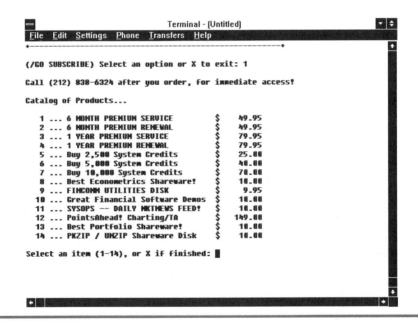

Figure 14-6   A list of prices for the services and software offered by Free Financial Network

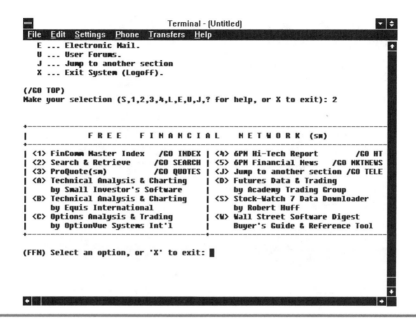

```
━  Terminal - (Untitled)                                            ▾ ▴
File  Edit  Settings  Phone  Transfers  Help
    E ... Electronic Mail.                                             ▲
    U ... User Forums.
    J ... Jump to another section
    X ... Exit System (Logoff).

(/GO TOP)
Make your selection (S,1,2,3,4,L,E,U,J,? for help, or X to exit): 2


  +----------------------------------------------------------------------+
  |            F R E E   F I N A N C I A L   N E T W O R K  (sm)          |
  +----------------------------------------------------------------------+
  | <1> FinComm Master Index   /GO INDEX | <4> 6PM Hi-Tech Report    /GO HT
  | <2> Search & Retrieve     /GO SEARCH | <5> 6PM Financial News  /GO MKTNEWS
  | <3> ProQuote(sm)          /GO QUOTES | <J> Jump to another section /GO TELE
  | <A> Technical Analysis & Charting    | <D> Futures Data & Trading
  |     by Small Investor's Software     |     by Academy Trading Group
  | <B> Technical Analysis & Charting    | <S> Stock-Watch 7 Data Downloader
  |     by Equis International           |     by Robert Huff
  | <C> Options Analysis & Trading       | <W> Wall Street Software Digest
  |     by OptionVue Systems Int'l       |     Buyer's Guide & Reference Tool
  +----------------------------------------------------------------------+


(FFN) Select an option, or 'X' to exit: █
                                                                       ▼
◄                                                                   ►
```

Figure 14-7   In the menu shown here Item B, "Technical Analysis and Charting," provides a daily view of stocks and the market using MetaStock or The Technician

The AAII

The bulletin board of the American Association of Individual Investors (AAII) is called "Computerized Investing" and is in Chicago. The AAII is a huge and highly regarded non-profit association that does research on investment strategies and costs. They provide software discounts and research reports, and their bulletin board numbers are 312/280-8565, 280-8764, 280-9043, and 280-9623. Their regular phone number is 312/280-0170. They also maintain a list of bulletin boards of particular interest to investors. There are about 60 such boards right now.

Other Roadside Attractions

A few other bulletin boards are worth noting, even though they are not financial boards. Here you will meet people who can tell you what's hot and what's not in this ever-shifting world.

The WELL, in Sausalito, California, is the granddaddy of them all. Although not the first bulletin board, many people believe it was because it was the first to attain national prominence. The membership is large and composed mostly of people in the computer industry, including many chief executives of computer corporations. There are more than 100 conferences going on every day. Membership costs $10 a month, plus $2 an hour. The modem number is 415/332-7190.

Exec-PC is in Wisconsin and is the largest bulletin board in the country outside of the big commercial boards like Prodigy and CompuServe. It averages 4,000 to 5,000 callers a day. It holds 650,000 files on a vast variety of subjects and has one of the fastest search programs ever written; it can scan 10,000 files a second for a particular piece of information. The system is used largely for games and business conferences. Many companies use this and other private boards for meetings, rather than the giant public ones, because the service is responsive and personal and the set-up is arranged for no waiting. The modem number is 414/789-4210.

Final Thoughts

There may be as many as 10,000 open bulletin boards. Beyond these are the boards maintained by software companies for technical support, businesses for communicating with their employees, universities, government agencies, and other institutions—perhaps as many as 80,000. There is no master list. You learn as you go.

Now that we know the ground, let's call in the heavy artillery. The section coming up deals with those programs that endeavor to forecast or at least identify the likely direction of stocks and markets. Four programs will be discussed; three of which are on the disks included with this book. The tools they bring to bear are powerful and you should enjoy discovering what they can do for you.

GENTLEMEN, CHOOSE YOUR WEAPONS

4

CHAPTER 15

TELESCAN

This is the good part. I've been waiting all through the book to get here. This is the section with the power tools, and we're going to start off with a combination power tool and database: Telescan.

The basic Telescan program is included on a disk at the back of this book, and was specially prepared by them for inclusion only with this book. While it does not come with all possible modules that you can buy and add to Telescan, it is a full working program, not a demo, and does come with a couple of extras that would otherwise have cost you around $150 more. The core program is so powerful it was used to write this chapter. In other words, all of the screens you see here were done with the same program packaged with this book.

The real strength of Telescan is in its database. It contains daily data going back 20 years and covering 8,000 stocks (the number continues to increase), 1,800 mutual funds (U.S., ADRs, and Direct Listings), 35,000 options, 197 industry groups, and 560 market indices. And this data is available immediately. If you want to take a look at the performance of some company that has caught your attention, you do not have to download several years of data; the touch of a key or a mouse button will bring up all 20 years at once—or any period you want: five years, six months, ten days, etc. No matter what time period you request, it will literally come up on the screen within a few seconds.

If you don't know the stock or index symbol, you can simply type in the name and Telescan will display a chart that includes the symbol. Sometimes it will give you a stock or index you did not want. For instance, if you type "Dow Jones" because you wanted the Dow Jones Industrial Average, it doesn't know that and so will give you a graph of Dow Jones, the publishing company. Typing Borden got me Borden Chemical instead of Borden Foods. At that point, you can turn to a "lookup" option and get a list of symbols that might be close to your request. Even with these oddities, my experience has been that typing in the company name will get you the right chart nine times out of ten. Otherwise, any day's copy of the *Wall Street Journal* lists the symbols for all listed stocks after their name. They do not, however, list the symbols for all foreign stocks.

Once you get your company or fund on screen, the program has tools for both technical and fundamental analysis. You can call up a screen of basic facts, for example, and get sales, earnings, book value, relative strength, number of shares outstanding, institutional ownership, etc. Touch another key or select from the pull-down menus, and you can get information on insider trading or have the stock price adjusted for inflation. There is no extra charge for these features, though there are extra charges for some others, which we'll get to later in the chapter. But since we're on the subject of charges, here are some of the fees for the Telescan service.

Costs

The basic service costs $45 a month for unlimited time in non-peak hours. There is a coupon in this book for one month's free service and a discount on signing up for more. On top of this, there is a $50 annual fee billed at the end of your first year. It's not cheap, but you get a lot. I've often felt that if one were a member of an investment club, or simply got together with a couple of friends, it would be worth it to share the cost of many of these services. Makes sense to me. Here's a general rundown on Telescan software costs:

▶ Telescan Analyzer (included with disk in this book), plus ProSearch and MacroWorld: $295

▶ Mutual Fund Search: $100

▶ Profit Tester and Optimizer (included with disk in this book): $100

▶ QuoteLink (included with disk in this book): $30

If you don't want to pay a monthly fee, you can just pay by the minute. Line charges are 94 cents a minute in prime time (7 a.m. to 6 p.m., your local time), depending on the speed of your modem. Outside of prime time, the rate is 41 cents a minute. There is an additional charge of 10 cents a graph (these are what you were being asked to pay $6 for on GEnie). If you pay a $99 monthly fee instead of the minimum, you get unlimited prime time use plus line charges of $9.60 per hour. This is a big discount for prime time users, who would otherwise pay line charges of more than $50 an hour.

There are a few additional charges for services from outside providers, which you may or may not want:

▶ $2 for a Zacks Earnings Report or $15 a month unlimited use ($39 for one report on GEnie).

▶ $17 a month if you want S&P MarketScope; $27 a month in prime time.

▶ $2 for Morningstar mutual fund reports or $25 a month unlimited use.

As with any program or service, charges change, features are added, and things in general move along. For the latest information on any of this, you can simply call them up at 800/324-8246. But enough of this money talk; let's get on with the show.

Just Type Install

To start the Telescan program that comes with this book, insert the disk in your disk drive, type the letter of that drive (usually A or B) and then type **install**. The program is self-installing. When it is finished you will see a "C" prompt on your screen and right after it you should see "TELE30," which means everything has gone smoothly. If you now simply press the letter T, for "Telescan," the program will start, and the main screen will come up.

note

The installation procedure for Telescan is standard, but if you have trouble with it, or have any technical support questions, please call Telescan Inc. at 800/324-4692. For more information on how to contact Telescan Inc, please refer to the coupon for Telescan at the back of the book.

If you click on the first menu with your mouse, or use the ALT key, you will see that one of the choices is System Setup. You have to take care of this first. Call Telescan and get a password and the phone number to use for dialing the database and enter those in the System Setup screen. Once you've done that, you can select Log On from the same menu, and the program will automatically dial Telescan and, well, log on.

When the program has connected, you will usually get a beep from the computer and a screen will come on that gives information on new Telescan services or other news that might be of interest to the user. To leave this screen, go up to the Analyzer menu and click on Analyzer. Select how many charts you want on the screen at any one time—you can have one, two, or four. I usually choose one.

What now, you might ask. You can simply type the name or symbol of a stock, and Telescan will go get it. When you type something, by the way, look at the bottom left-hand side of the screen and you will see the letters you type. If you made a typing mistake and don't like what you see there, press the ESCAPE key to clear it and type something else.

Riding the Tiger

The nice thing about Telescan is that it allows you to make a quick survey of many issues, whereas with any other program you would have to take the time and expense of downloading a large amount of data. Two or three years worth of data on any issue would cost you $25-$30 on CompuServe and take several minutes to bring in. A dozen issues would cost a considerable amount and might take half an hour.

One of the first things we might type in Telescan is **TKF**. This brings up the Turkish Investment Fund. Remember the Turkish stock market that was up 221 percent in 1993? Well, a quick look here will show you that it was down 50 percent in the first three months of 1994.

It was a tough quarter all around. In other Asian markets, China (the Shanghai Exchange) was down 38 percent, Thailand down 26 percent, Malaysia down 25 percent, Hong Kong down 24 percent, Indonesia down 16 percent, Singapore down 15 percent, and Taiwan down 14 percent.

Over in Europe, London was down 10 percent, Paris down 8 percent, Frankfurt down 6 percent, and Zurich down 5.5 percent. Latin America in general was down 25 to 30 percent, and in Africa you couldn't tell what the drop was because most of what you can buy wasn't trading anyway.

Things weren't all bad. Tokyo was up 10 percent in the first three months of 1994. Milan and Helsinki were up 12 percent.

Are we having fun yet? Volatility is built into most global markets. If the Dow Jones Industrial Average dropped 50 percent like Turkey's, it would be selling at 2,000 and there would be congressional investigations and pressure on the Fed to drop interest rates through the floor. In other places, it's just a tough couple of months.

Does this make anybody nervous? Probably, but I think it's great. Back around the turn of the century a reporter was interviewing J.P. Morgan and had the temerity to ask him what the stock market was going to do. "The market," said J.P. with what I'm sure were portentous tones, "will fluctuate."

And that was the good news! Because the truth is, if a stock or a fund never moved, why would anybody buy it? The only reason would be to eventually own the company or for the dividend, and most stocks don't even pay a dividend. No, it is precisely because of volatility that people are willing to buy and sell stocks at all. Therefore, it behooves us to take a look at volatility from both sides of the swing, trying to duck or push at the appropriate moment, or simply get out of the way and out of the playground. That's what this section, and maybe investing in general, is about.

Let the Tour Begin

Figure 15-1 shows the Telescan main screen with one of its menus pulled down. You'll notice there are only two menus here: System and Program. System is where you set up the program by telling it about your modem, your password, program identification number, and the phone number to dial to log in.

The other pull-down menu, Program, is shown in the following illustration. It shows the main program, Analyzer, plus some other expensive features that are being thrown in free for readers of this book. One of the most valuable of these is QuoteLink, which lets you download data on any stock, fund, index, or option Telescan has in its database. This is going to be very useful indeed, because this data can be read by other programs.

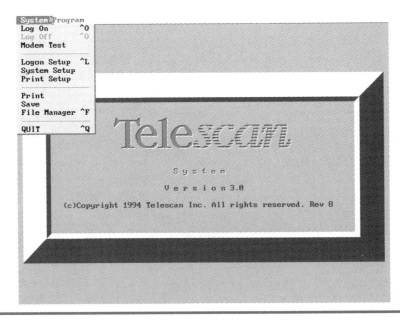

Figure 15-1 The Telescan main screen showing the systems menu

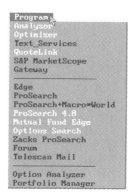

Let's Log On and Get Started

If you haven't logged on yet, select Log On and if all the information you gave the program in the setup phase is correct, the program will dial the Telescan database and you'll be in. The first screen you'll see is one like Figure 15-2. Notice how much this screen looks like one of the bulletin boards we talked about in the last chapter. That's because it is a

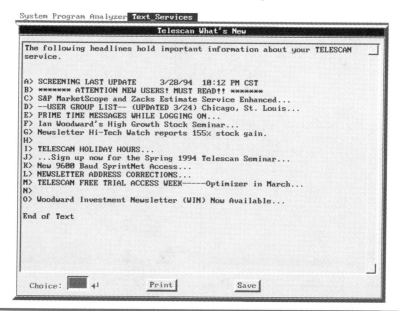

Figure 15-2   The first screen that comes up once you log onto Telescan Text Services. It contains new announcements and all items can be viewed cost free

bulletin board. Just as we said before, all the database services, whether the screen is plain or fancy, are really large bulletin boards. The items on this first screen contain information about the service itself and notes about additions, like newsletters. If you want to look at any of these announcements, like the Woodward Investment Newsletter mentioned on this screen, just type the letter in front of it. Telescan carries several newsletters, and you can usually see a couple of issues and decide if you want to subscribe.

If you now move your cursor up to the top of the screen where it says Analyzer, and click on that, you can go right to the database itself and type in a stock.

Analyzer gives you a choice of viewing a one-, two-, or four-graph screen. Figure 15-3 shows a four-graph screen. To use it, you simply click on any one of the four squares and type in a stock symbol or name. Here I've started with the symbol EMF, which stands for the Templeton Emerging Markets Fund. The other divisions contain graphs of the Swiss Helvetia Fund, Emerging Markets Telecommunications Fund, and the

Figure 15-3 Telescan Analyser displaying four stocks or issues at once—its maximum number

GT Greater Europe Fund. Figure 15-4 shows the Analyzer with two stocks to a screen; the size of the screens cannot be changed, so there is a slight distortion in the aspect ratio which minimizes the effect of vertical movement. Figure 15-5 shows the Analyzer with just one stock filling the whole screen, which is the way I normally use it. There's also something different at the bottom of this screen—an indicator. Yes, we've started our tricks, and let's look at some of what Telescan can do here.

If you look at the top of the screen on Figure 15-5, you will see that new menus have appeared and one of these is called Indicators. Figure 15-6 shows what this menu looks like when it's pulled down. It happens to be pulled down over a graph of the Japanese stock Canon, but it looks the same no matter where you pull it down. It is worth going down the list and reading this menu, because there is a lot of potential action available here.

Notice that we can perform various technical analysis functions, including the currently popular Japanese tool called Candlestick. There is also a line that says Fundamental Menu, and clicking on this would

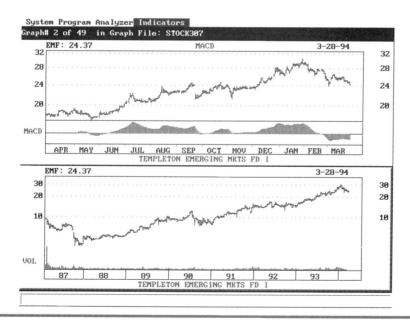

Figure 15-4   The Analyser with two issues displayed. The slight distortion in the aspect ratio minimizes the effect of vertical movement

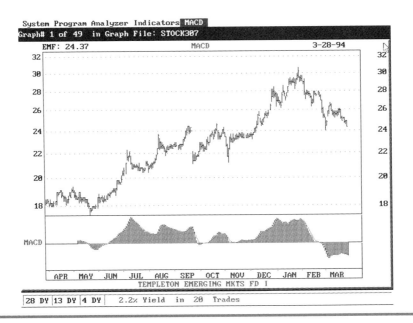

Figure 15-5   The Analyser with only one displayed. This is the clearest way to view any selection

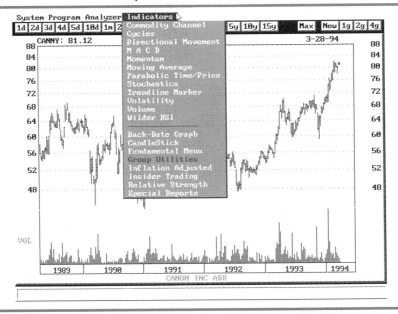

Figure 15-6   The Indicators menu. This is the menu that shows the primary technical analysis tools available to the user

Technical Indicators

Although they could be the subject of an entire book alone, here's a quick summary, which should be sufficient for our purposes, describing the basis of six commonly used technical indicators.

A Simple Moving Average

This is surprisingly effective. A 200-day moving average overlaid on the market averages, such as the Dow Jones or the S&P 500, has proved to be a more effective indicator of bull and bear markets than almost anything else. Selling when the market index moves below the 200-day moving average and buying when it moves above it, has

produced about a 20 percent return over the past several years.

Crossing Averages

Two moving averages of different lengths are selected; for example, a 30-day average and a 10-day average. When the short-term average falls below the long-term average, it's a sell signal; when it rises above, it's a buy signal.

The Advance/Decline Line

This is started at any point and is simply the cumulative sum of advancing stocks minus declining stocks. As long as the line trends upward the market is all right, when it turns downward the market nearly always declines.

New Highs Minus New Lows

Similar to the Advance/Decline Line: if the market is making new highs but the number of stocks participating is declining, it does not bode well for a continued advance. Conversely, bottoms are

typically marked by fewer stocks making new lows each day—sign of selling exhaustion.

Wilder Relative Strength

An indictor developed by J. Welles Wilder Jr. for the examination of movement in commodities. It measures an issue's relative strength against itself. In other words, it calculates the latest price against an average of prices over a previous number of days, the time period to be selected by the user.

MACD

This stands for Moving Average Convergence and Divergence and is an indicator that was developed by market analyst Gerald Appel. It is essentially the difference between two exponential moving averages—usually the 12 and 26-day averages. The result is an oscillating curve.

add still more menu items to the top of the screen, allowing us to get earnings, book value, sales, price-to-sales ratios, etc. You can go nuts here, and by now you should be beginning to see that each line of a menu brings up new possibilities. Some are just questions asking you what kind of analysis you want to perform, and others open whole new menus and let you delve ever deeper.

Selecting the last line item, Special Reports, for example, brings up a new menu as shown in the following:

```
Special_Reports
Comtex Newswire
Reuters Newswire
Zacks Earnings Est
Zacks Earnings Est II
Technical Data
Valuation Data
Option Quotes
MarketScope Report
Quarterly Earnings
Macro*World Report
Insider Text
Fact Sheet
MarketGuide Investor Service
```

This menu shows us we can call up the Comtex Newswire, Reuters, Zacks Earnings Estimates, Valuation Data, Quarterly Earnings, Insider Text, etc. Insider Text, by the way, means we can not only see whether corporate insiders were buying or selling their company's stock, but just who was buying or selling and how much and when. Calling up Zacks Earnings Estimates for Canon gives us Figure 15-7, which tells us that Canon is currently earning 90 cents a share and is expected to earn $1.10 a share next year. Since the price of the stock is in the 80s (more than

```
System Program Analyzer  Special_Reports
                    Zacks Earnings Est
                  Zacks Earnings Estimates
              CANON INC ADR              3/19/94
           WALL STREET ESTIMATES

                 MEAN     HIGH    LOW   NUMBER MEAN CHG
                                          EST  LAST MNTH
                                                 ($)
 FISC YR END 9312  0.90    0.90    0.90     1    0.00

 FISC YR END 9412  1.10    1.10    1.10     1    0.00

 QUARTER END 9312  N/A     N/A     N/A      0    N/A

 QUARTER END 9403  N/A     N/A     N/A      0    N/A

 NEXT 5 YR GRTH (%) 8.50   15.00   2.00     2    0.00



                  CANON INC ADR            3/19/94
                COMPANY VS INDUSTRY

            --------- EPS GROWTH RATES ---------
                  (CUR FY=9312)
            LAST 5 YRS  CUR/LAST  NXT/CUR  NXT 5   P/E ON
            ACTUAL (%)    (%)       (%)   YRS(%)  CUR YR
                                                  EPS
                  Print                 Save
```

Figure 15-7   A Zacks Earnings Estimates Report for the Japanese stock, Canon. Zacks is the leading service for earnings reports

$80 a share) that gives us a price-to-earnings ratio of about 80-1—very scary for an American stock, but about normal for Japan.

Targeting

If you press the letter T from just about anywhere in Telescan, or go to Trendline Marker in the Indicators menu, you get crosshairs showing on the screen (see Figure 15-8), called the T-Marker. A new menu heading also appears at the top of the screen, T-Marker.

You can move the crosshairs around with your mouse or the arrow keys on the keyboard. Clicking on what seem to be significant points on the chart lets you draw trendlines. Here I just happened to call up the stock chart of KLM, Royal Dutch Airlines, for no particular reason other than I like Holland. I put the crosshairs up on the screen as a guide to looking at the stock's movement.

Notice first that KLM has been traded here for a long time and the chart goes all the way back to the early 1970s. The stock took a ragged

Figure 15-8   A chart of the stock of KLM Royal Dutch Airlines for 20 years, with the T-Marker

but generally upward trend to around $27 a share during the market high of 1987, and placing the horizontal bar of the crosshair at that high shows us at a glance that the stock has made at least two other attempts—maybe two and a half attempts—to break through that price. The most recent attempt was right about when this chart was pulled, March 28th, 1994 (you can read the date in the upper right-hand corner of the screen). Without doing any more analysis at all, the stock's present price should give us pause. It might sail through $27 with no resistance at all, but that's not what the record shows, and caution would dictate that any reasonable investor hold back at this point and see if it happens. Otherwise, chances are fairly decent that you would be buying at the high.

A simple horizontal line told us something here, largely because we were able to so easily see many years of data. Let's move on to more sophisticated views. One of the most interesting is shown in Figure 15-9. This particular indicator is a favorite of the president of Telescan and I learned about it from him. Here's an explanation of what you're looking at.

Figure 15-9 A chart of several years of the Templeton Emerging Markets Fund with a "Least Squares" line drawn through the center

Once again we're looking at a chart of the Templeton Emerging Markets Fund. It was selected because it invests in overseas markets, has been running for several years, and has a generally rising trend and so can be assumed to be well-managed. That's not an endorsement, by the way, but an observation. In a bit of an aside here, it reminds me of all the serious advice I have heard over the years from brokers and bank officers about how you have to know about a fund's management before you invest, and it's hard for someone outside the business to know who's good or not. Nonsense! If I want to know how good the management is, I just call up a chart of their fund or their company; the report card is there on the screen.

Putting the Sights on Target

Three things were done to the chart in Figure 15-9. The first was moving the crosshairs to the low point of the chart—down where you can just barely make out the number 1—and clicking the mouse button. Alternatively, you can press the F1 key on your keyboard. The sight was then moved to the high point on the chart and the button clicked again. Or you could press F2. You can now go up to the T-Marker menu and select Trendline from one the menu choices, which will draw a trendline connecting the two points you made on the chart (or you can just press F4). This produces a line that looks fairly useless initially, but will end up being very interesting. Maestro, a little background music, please.

Whenever you select T to activate the crosshairs, the T-Marker menu pops onto the screen. One of the selections on this menu is a study called Least Squares. This is a common tool used by statisticians to measure what is called "regression to the mean." This is a characteristic observed in almost all aspects of life and fundamental to the laws of physics, and that is that events tend to center around a trend or some similar moving point of equilibrium. They may swing to extremes in either direction, but over the long term they tend to return to the mean, which is the trend. You see it in seasons, temperatures, emotions, fortunes, colors, flavors, and fragrances. It is, in short, a universal. The middle sloping line in Figure 15-9 is the result of taking the line we drew connecting the lowest and highest points and regressing it to the mean. It is obviously the trend.

We then move the crosshairs to the high point again and select Parallel Line from the T-Marker menu. Move down to the low point and again draw a line parallel to the mean. The result is Figure 15-9 as you see it. What is interesting about this simple study is that whenever the price of the fund deviated enough to cross or touch the bottom parallel line, it started up again because it tended to move back to the mean, which was a rising trend. It could also be said that whenever it hit the top line, that was a sell point, because it started down toward the mean. That last observation is also true but of problematical value, because the mean is a rising line. Will this go on forever? Probably not. But it has gone on a long time here and with many other funds and stocks, and it would be hard for anyone to say just when it would end.

What we just did made use of a technical indicator, but Telescan can also construct fundamental indicators. An example is shown in Figure 15-10. Here the computer has constructed a channel comprised of the high and low annual readings of a composite of the dividends, book value, cash flow, capital spending, and sales of Glaxo Holdings, a British pharmaceutical company. You can construct channels of these and other fundamental indicators either separately or as new composites.

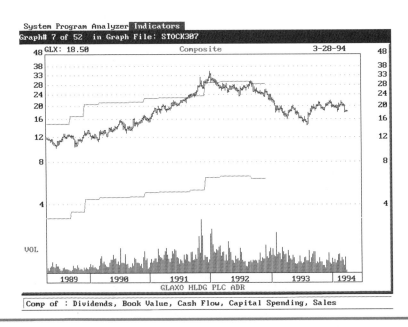

Figure 15-10   Telescan can construct a composite channel of earnings, book value, dividends, and other fundamental facts about a stock

You will notice that when the price of Glaxo exceeds the top boundary of this fundamental channel, the stock is overpriced and tends to come back into the channel—which is rising. Similarly, when this or any other stock falls below the bottom boundary of its fundamental channel, it tends to move up again. All these things, while generally true, are also relative and should be used as part of the information assembled to make a judgment. Glaxo broke out of its proper fundamental range at $24, for example, but continued rising to $34, a meaningful gain that would have been completely missed by religiously following the fundamentals.

The Trend Is Your Friend, Until the End

Let's travel back to Turkey for a moment and use some of the basic tools we just discussed to examine what used to be called "the Turkish problem."

Could we have used these tools to tell us when to get out of the Turkish Investment Fund before its collapse? The answer, like so many things in investments, is yes and no. Some people would have gotten out in plenty of time, scared off by the tremendous increase in price and volume in a very short period. When trends go asymptotic they almost never hold. Let's look at these trends and you can see what happens when a fund does not return to the mean.

The rise that began at the start of 1993 follows the upward sloping channel of Figure 15-11, and everything looks smooth enough until the break downward and out of the channel in late January and early February. At that point, you could have said either it's just another flick downwards in a rising trend or it means trouble. In general, anytime the movement of a stock or fund touches the edge of its corridor, it's time to pay particularly close attention because it may mean trouble.

Some people got out at the very top, obviously, probably because it is their conviction that you should get out and look around for a minute or two anytime a price chart reaches the top of its directional channel. It's a cautious view of the world and basically follows the maxim of an old Swiss banker I once interviewed who said, "Fear is a sign of good health." If you're not afraid of price spikes, he added, you just don't understand the situation. One other thing that would have made the cautious investor certainly heed his advice was that the top of the price spike was accompanied by an enormous increase in volume, which can be seen in

System Program Analyzer Indicators **T-Marker**

TKF: 7.75   TRENDLINE-MARKER   3-28-94

TURKISH INVT FD INC

Date: 4/22/94   PRICE: $ 7.00   [ESC] to Exit

Figure 15-11   The Turkish Investment Fund, 1993's big winner among closed-end funds. The lines drawn show the rising trend channel and when it was broken, with a horizontal line indicating a possible support level on the way down. Note the huge increase in volume (vertical bars at the bottom of the chart) when the fund price topped out

the vertical bars at the bottom of the chart in Figure 15-11. It's what a professional trader would consider an excessive and perhaps unwarranted display of enthusiasm. Experienced traders call this a "blow-off top." Or to put it more simply: bye-bye time.

Does that mean the end of the Turkish Investment Fund? Certainly not. And by the way, I am not focusing on Turkey here for any reason other than it was the biggest winner in 1993, and attracted a lot of attention because of that. The observations made about this fund would apply equally well to all of them and to individual stocks as well.

Is there a likely stopping point in the fall of the fund? Sure. I have drawn a horizontal line on the chart in Figure 15-11 to indicate what most active traders would consider a likely stopping or turning point. That is simply because for much of 1992 and part of 1993 there was a lot of churning—inconclusive price action—around the $6 to $7 level. This is called a support level in the trade, rather perversely but nonetheless rationally because it was previously a price resistance level. As Will Rogers once said, it's stupid to make predictions, especially about the future, but I would guess the share price would go no lower than between $6 and $7 a share. It may stop above or well below that range—there's never any guarantee—I am simply pointing out the way many professionals would look at it.

More Tricks with Simple Chemicals Found in Your Kitchen

Telescan has a substantial list of indicators that can be played with, but the next program we'll be talking about, MetaStock, has even more. So it makes greater sense for us to use the space here to pay attention to things Telescan can do that are not found in other programs. One of the most eye-opening of these is the ability to adjust any stock or fund for inflation. I would say, in fact, it's more than eye-opening—it's mind-opening, and will teach you as much about investing as the "How I Made a Million Bucks In..." books.

Before we look at the next set of tricks, I'd like to pause, because I detect a nagging fear in many hearts and minds that all of the stuff we've been doing so far will run up a line-time bill the size of the national debt. Fear not. Everything we did up till now, except for the initial downloading of the stock or fund data itself—which takes only a few seconds—can be done offline. We wouldn't draw all these trendlines and do regressions to the mean or add further indicators like relative strength or stochastic (more on these in next chapter) while we're online. What are we, crazy? That costs money! Download the stock and get offline; the indicators are built into the program, not the database.

Getting Slick with Burmah Oil

Figure 15-12 shows a chart of about 20 years of the British oil company Burmah Castrol. You see their ads on television all the time. They make motor oil, among other things, and you can find it in

Time Is Money

We've already told you how to log on to the system, but not how to log off. Fortunately, when you logged on you probably noticed that one of the other choices on the same menu was Log-Off. It means just what you think it means, so the only problem that remains is *when* to log off. You should log off the system as soon as you have collected the stocks you want to look at or as soon as you no longer want to use their computer to calculate an indicator. We'll talk more about making that choice in a minute.

Remember, you're paying for line charges and you want to keep those to a minimum. One way is to set up all the stocks you want to see as an "autorun." One of the items on the Analyzer pull-down menu is called Autorun. If you select that while you're offline, it will bring up a screen that lets you type in a whole bunch of stock symbols. Later, when you log on to Telescan and go to the Analyzer menu to start looking at stocks, you can simply select "Autorun" and the program will start calling up those stocks a lot faster than you can do it by typing. From the Analyzer menu, select "Edit Autorun." A screen will come up that prompts you to enter as many symbols you want, specify how much time you want to download, and what technical or fundamental indicator you

want to pull with it. You can also click on a button that sets the Autorun to automatically disconnect from Telescan when it is finished, or you can remain online and look at something new that wasn't included in your autorun.

The reason for logging off after collecting the stocks is that most of the technical indicators contained in Telescan are built into the program you have on disk. You don't need the computer back in Houston to provide relative strength, draw trendlines, or make a least squares analysis. Your own computer can do that, so why stay online? But some analyses can only be done by the base computer back in Houston. Read on for some examples.

supermarkets and drugstores. I've used it myself for more than 20 years. My purchases apparently had little effect on the stock, however.

Looking at the chart we see that Burmah Castrol sank like a rock in the market swoon of the early 70s, but then gradually worked its way back up to new all-time highs in March of 1994. Or so it appears to the naked eye. But watch very closely, folks; my fingers will never leave my hands.

We go up to the Indicators menu (Figure 15-6) and select Inflation Adjusted from the bottom portion of the menu. You must be online with Telescan to do this. The computer in Houston will then adjust Burmah

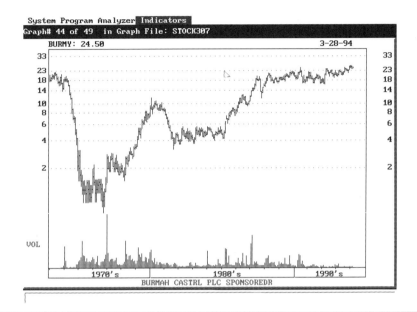

Figure 15-12 A price chart of 20 years of Burmah Castrol, which finally went to new highs in 1993

Castrol's stock price for inflation over the past 20 years and transmit the result, which is seen in Figure 15-13.

At first glance it may look the same as Figure 15-12, but believe me, it's not. In Figure 15-13 we see that once all prices are adjusted for inflation, far from reaching a new all-time high of $25 a share in March of 1994, Castrol is selling for around $7. To repeat: those are inflation adjusted dollars. But they mean that the reality of the situation is that the purchaser who bought Castrol at $21 back in 1973 now has $7—a loss of two-thirds on the original investment even while the stock is hitting new highs. This is not something we're making up, this is a very real display of the loss of purchasing power and the constant decline in value of an investment that is allowed to simply sit.

Closer to Home

You think we were just picking on old Burmah Castrol? Well, let's go to something as American as apple pie, and maybe even Mom.

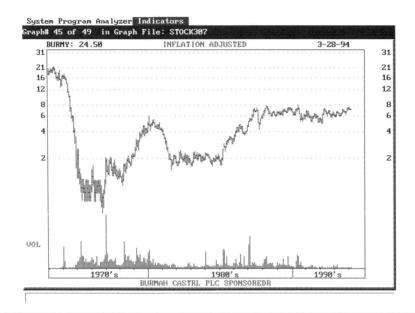

Figure 15-13   The same chart shown in Figure 15-12, but with the prices adjusted for inflation. You can see that there was no new high in the stock price

Figure 15-14 shows the stock of General Motors, adjusted for all splits. There have been some rocky times all right, but we see that after many trials and tribulations the stock of the world's largest auto manufacturer finally broke out in 1993 and moved to new all-time highs. Or did it?

Figure 15-15 shows exactly the same chart as in Figure 15-14, adjusted for inflation. Now we see the sad news. Not only has GM not hit new all-time highs, but the purchaser who paid $40 a share back in 1973 and patriotically held on all through the next 20 years would now be sitting with a stock worth about $18. Adjusted into dollars of constant value, the buyer has a more than 50 percent loss. And this is while the stock market has multiplied 10 times!

It is almost impossible to convince people of the reality of this kind of deterioration in their wealth and purchasing power. In fact, I know someone who has owned General Motors stock through that whole period. She remains convinced that it was a good buy

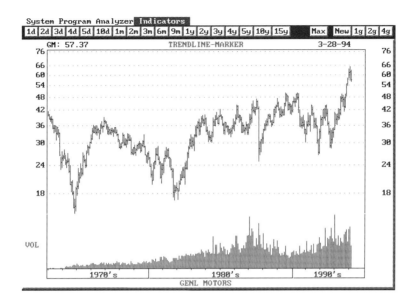

Figure 15-14 A simple price chart of 20 years of General Motors stock, which hit new highs in 1993

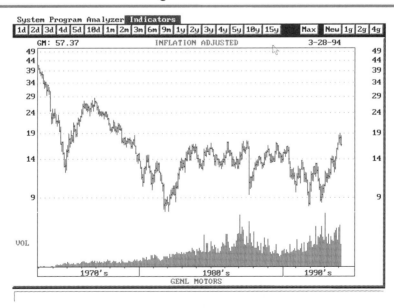

Figure 15-15 The same chart as shown Figure 15-14 but here the price of GM stock has been adjusted for inflation. It now tells quite a different tale

and that she has a profit, and adds that she will never sell, that she bought it intending to hold it for her lifetime. The company must love shareholders like her. Dividends gave her a huge profit, she says. Believe me, they didn't.

Figures 15-16 and 15-17 show the course of the Standard & Poors 500 Index (more representative than the Dow Jones Industrial Average) as a nominal price chart (Figure 15-16) and inflation adjusted (Figure 15-17). As you can see in comparing the two, the American stock market has hit new highs in the late 1980s and early 1990s, but nothing to get excited about.

For Our Next Trick...

One of the other items on the Indicators menu is labeled Insider Trading. Telescan maintains a database of insider trading reports, which by law must be filed with the SEC (Securities and Exchange Commission). These are not the golden treasure many investment advisors like

Figure 15-16   The S&P 500 Index for 20 years. Professional investors pay attention to this index rather than the Dow Jones Industrials

System Program Analyzer Indicators
1d 2d 3d 4d 5d 10d 1m 2m 3m 6m 9m 1y 2y 3y 4y 5y 10y 15y   Max New 1g 2g 4g

SPX: 460.00   INFLATION ADJUSTED   3-28-94

Figure 15-17 When adjusted to show constant dollars, the S&P 500 Index has a gain of only about 15 percent after 20 years

to tell you they are, but they do have their uses. Once again, you must be online to use the Insider Trading function, since your computer does not have that information in its own memory banks.

Figure 15-18 shows a graph of IBM for the last six years, showing insider trading as a set of wide bars at the bottom of the screen. The stock chart itself looks like a train wreck, but in some ways the insider trading shown at the bottom looks even worse.

A lot of people lost a lot of money in IBM over the past few years, but not many of them were insiders. The bars going below the center line in the bottom portion of the chart indicate selling, the bars above the line, buying. The wider and longer they are the more the buying or selling. You can see that IBM insiders sold heavily in late 1990 and early 1991, just as the long decline was beginning, then bought heavily through 1993 and early 1994, when the stock was bottoming. In fact, the heaviest buying came right at the lows of around $42 a share. Does this show any probability of inside information? Are you kidding?

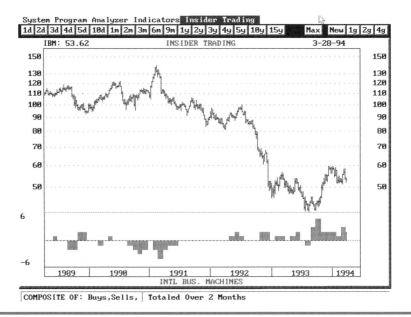

System Program Analyzer Indicators▐Insider Trading▐

|1d|2d|3d|4d|5d|10d|1m|2m|3m|6m|9m|1y|2y|3y|4y|5y|10y|15y| |Max|New|1y|2y|4y|

IBM: 53.62   INSIDER TRADING   3-28-94

INTL BUS. MACHINES

COMPOSITE OF: Buys,Sells, | Totaled Over 2 Months

Figure 15-18   Telescan can show insider trading in most stocks and funds. This chart shows the last five years' price action of IBM. The bars at the bottom of the chart pointing upwards indicate insider buying, the bars pointing down, insider selling. Note the heavy insider selling before IBM's huge decline in 1991 and 1992, then heavy insider buying in 1993 before the stock started up again

The insider trades shown here have been averaged over two months. You can set the time span to whatever you want. The picture the trades paint is actually more insidious than it looks, since insider trades do not have to be reported to the SEC for 30 days after they take place. In practice, they're usually later than that, accompanied by some kind of note saying, "Gee, I'm sorry—just slipped my mind." Since the SEC never does anything about this late reporting, it has become standard practice. Then there is a delay in the actual publishing of the reports, which are already late, so as a practical matter you can mentally shift all those insider trading bars a couple of months to the left. That would be when the trades actually took place. I hope none of those people forgot to call you up and tell you they thought it was a good idea to get out of the stock, or when to get back in. Maybe you weren't home and your answering machine was turned off.

Screens

Telescan has an extra function called ProSearch, which does stock screens (see Figure 15-19). These are filters which screen out stocks according to certain criteria: earnings, sales, momentum, volume, etc. A lot of people like to do them. I haven't done any here because that function costs a lot and is not activated on your disk unless you pay Telescan an extra fee, though that is only $15 a month. I have another reason as well, which I'll get to in a moment.

First, I have selected some screen shots (different from doing stock screens) to show you what kinds of things you can do if you elect to extend your usage to ProSearch. The reason I have not done any actual screens and printed them here is because I think they are very dangerous unless you take the time to really figure out what you're doing. Practically everybody likes to do them—my son can spend hours at it—but very few people understand what they're looking at when they get the results. Read on.

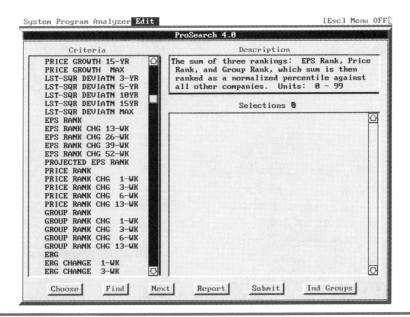

Figure 15-19 A portion of the "ProSearch" menu, Telescan's stock screening feature. The entire database of 9,000 stocks can be screened for earnings, relative strength, volume changes, and 200 other factors

The most common screens people will do are for low price-to-earnings (p/e) ratios and high dividend yield. Everybody wants a stock selling at a p/e of less than 10 to 1 and paying a 10 percent dividend or better. If I were to do a screen using such criteria now, or almost any time, it will come up with at least a dozen stocks. If I drop the dividend requirement down to 5 or 6 percent, the screen will probably come up with a hundred stocks. That doesn't mean they're good buys.

Try to remember that literally thousands of people are doing these screens and you will not be the first or the only one to discover hidden treasure. The other thing to realize is that whole groups of stocks, like autos and deep cyclicals like steel and aluminum, tend to have their lowest p/e numbers when they are near the top of their price cycle, not the bottom. That is because they have heavy investment in fixed plants and equipment. So when business is terrible, they have high p/e ratios, because they have no "e" (earnings) to go with their "p," which is a high fixed cost. And they have a low p/e when they are at the top of their earnings cycles, because the costs don't go up nearly as fast as the earnings do when a capital-intensive business starts generating sales. The classic case in this kind of situation has always been Chrysler, which can be near bankruptcy putting out a million cars a year (or whatever their break-even number is), and making pure profit on everything over that. So what's a low p/e and what isn't depends on the kind of business and the historical relationship of that stock to that number. Telescan will show you that historical relationship, by the way, but it is often difficult to read and interpret and always runs months behind current prices.

The second popular screen, dividends, has its own pitfalls. My son started screening for dividends one day and kept raising the ante higher and higher. At 20 percent, there were still a dozen companies paying that much. At 50 percent, he finally got it down to just one, a gold mine paying a 50 percent annual dividend. No, I'm not going to list it here, and in a minute you'll see why.

Sub Sighted. Sank Same

"Look at this, Dad," my son yelled one day, "I found a stock that pays a 50 percent dividend!" And indeed he had. In doing some checking into the company—calling up news reports, annual reports, etc.—I found that it was literally a gold mine, a going-out-of-business gold mine. It had sent out notices to the shareholders that it was going out of business and would pay out all assets. For some obscure tax reason at the time, it was better for the assets to be paid out as dividends over the course of the next two years. Thus you would get a 50 percent dividend this year (50 percent of the value of the stock) and an equal payment next year, and that would be the end of it. Since the stock price was exactly twice the dividend, you were in effect paying $10 to get back $10, an exercise in futility.

You might say you would catch those kinds of mistakes now that you understand them, but what about a company paying 12 percent? Would you understand the reasons? It might not be possible for an outsider to understand what's going on there. Companies will frequently pay dividends that are greater than their earnings, a condition that obviously cannot continue for very long but is nevertheless done for reasons of pride—or to artificially support the price of the stock so insiders can unload, or because an imminent turn-around is expected, or a buy-out offer, or heaven knows what.

One of the things Telescan has done to help you avoid those traps is provide ready-made screens. They provide 10 screens that have already been screened, so to speak. One of these is the popular CANSLIM screen developed by William O'Neil, the publisher of *Investor's Daily*.

Figures 15-19 and 15-20 show some of the criteria that can be used to make searches. Read down the list of items on the left-hand side and you can see things like growth projections for many time periods, least square deviations, which we looked at earlier in this chapter, changes in ranking for their industry group, changes within that group, relative strength within the group within the overall market, and on into the night. There are nearly 200 of these criteria, and they can be combined in any way you want. I'm not saying they're not useful—they're very useful. I'm saying be careful.

Figures 15-21 and 15-22 show you can do the same kind of screening with mutual funds instead of stocks. Figure 15-23 shows an additional kind of program screen we haven't seen before but which comes up for screening either stocks or funds. It lets you give a weighting to the various factors used in your screening categories. You can have high weight to recent momentum, for example, and low weight to earnings, and do this with several criteria. You can even have some of the criteria not included in the selection of a stock but merely show on the computer screen, as something you just want to see for a quick visual check on whether you're headed in the right direction or not.

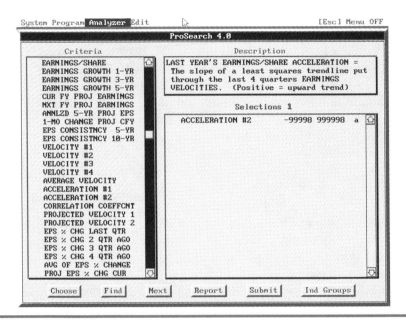

Figure 15-20 This is similar to Figure 15-19; the left-hand side shows some of the additional search factors that can be brought into play

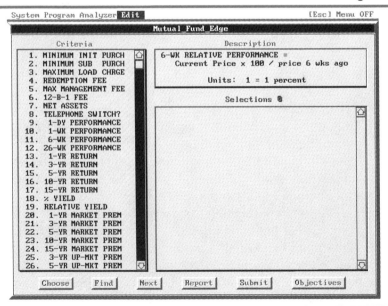

Figure 15-21 This looks like Figures 15-19 and 15-20, but the heading at the top shows that this is for selecting mutual funds rather than stocks

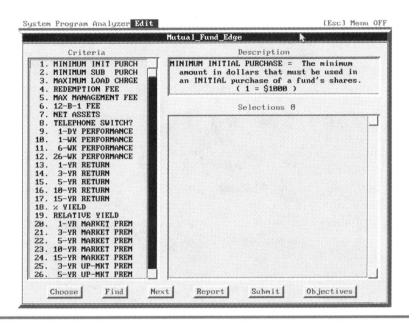

Figure 15-22   More criteria for selecting mutual funds is shown at left, with a box at right providing a brief explanation of each selection item

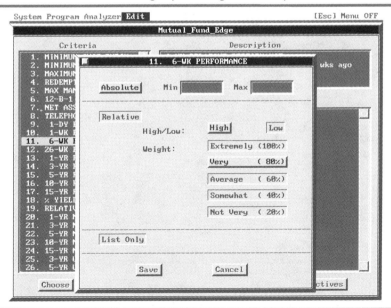

Figure 15-23   A further refinement—screening elements can be given different weights, so some selection points can be emphasized

ProSearch screening costs about $15 a month if you're willing to confine your hunting to off-peak hours. That doesn't seem like a stringent requirement.

Can We Quote You on That?

Finally, we'll close with a screen shot of something very nice you get with the disk in this book: It's QuoteLink (see Figure 15-24). You can get to QuoteLink from the Analyzer menu; it's one of the menu choices. Notice at the top of the QuoteLink screen that you can collect current and historical quotes and even news stories. Simply enter the symbol, the dates you want to collect, and the file you want them to be dumped into, and click on OK.

The data can be collected in any of several formats listed near the bottom of the screen: Telescan format, ASCII-5, ASCII-7, etc. Just what

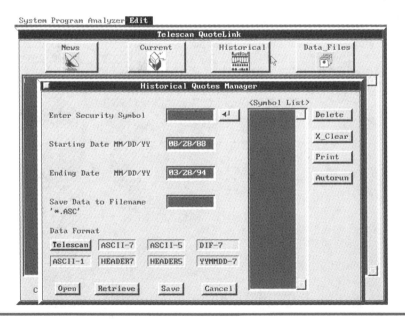

Figure 15-24   The Telescan "QuoteLink" screen, a feature that lets you download daily and historical quotes on any stock or fund contained in the Telescan database. These quotes can be used by other programs

those letters and numbers mean is of no particular significance for you right now. ASCII-7 is similar to MetaStock format.

You don't have to do this a stock at a time, and it's recommended that you don't do it that way. Type a whole list of symbols you want to call up from Telescan and give that list a file name—"Hot List" or whatever strikes your fancy. You can have as many lists as you want, which is handy, because you can then have a list for fund symbols, another for stock symbols, another for indices, or you can break the lists into regional or industry groups. Just as with Autorun, a screen comes up that will take a large number of symbols that you can type in. Do that while you are offline; there's no sense spending money just to type up a list. When you are finished, then you can log on.

Leaving the Country

Despite the length and scope of this chapter, it covers only a fraction of what you can do with Telescan.

One of the things we have not even touched upon, but which is included with your free disk, is the Profit Tester and Optimizer. This is a program that will examine various technical and/or fundamental indicators you select and determine whether or not it would have been profitable to trade the stock according to buy and sell signals generated by those indicators. It will even tell you how much profit you would have made and how many trades you would have done to make it. This is a book-length discussion in itself. It will be your pleasure and adventure to examine the profit tester on your own. There is no charge for experimentation and no risk of loss.

Like the chapters on CompuServe or Dow Jones, there is just too much going on here. Telescan, technical indicators, and stock screens are book-length subjects in their own right. Consider then, my trepidation as we begin the next chapter: a journey into MetaStock, the leading and in my opinion the most powerful program for stock and market analysis. Fortunately for our side, it is also the smoothest one.

CHAPTER 16

METASTOCK: THE POWER

This is the king of the hill, the best program in technical analysis and the number one seller in computer stock market software. There is a special custom edition of it in the back of your book. The features are not exactly the same as the full $350 copy you buy in a store, but they are very nearly the same.

To start the program, insert the disk in one of your drives, change to that drive, and type **install**. The program will come up on your screen as MSSE. The first two letters are for "MetaStock," the last two for "Special Edition." To start it, just type **MS**.

note

The installation procedure for MetaStock is standard, but if you have trouble with it or have any other technical support questions, please call Equis International at 800/882-3040, ext. SE. For more information on how to reach Equis International, please refer to the MetaStock coupon at the back of the book.

This special edition comes preloaded with more than 300 days of data on 17 country funds and three stock indexes. Space has been left clear for ten more stocks, bonds, or whatever you like. You can also remove the items already on the disk and replace them with others you'd rather follow. Uploading will be a problem right now. Pressure to get it in the book in time for distribution has left the MSSE disk with no convenient method of adding new data except by hand. Equis International, maker of MetaStock and other programs, will try to solve that for you when you call in and get a free bundle of material from them. The number and other information are on their coupon page at the back of the book. The easiest solution is to get a subsidiary program called The Downloader. It sells for $49 and I have used it for the past several years.

A dozen years ago at a small trade show in New York, MetaStock was the smallest exhibit of all—a programmer, his wife, and a card table at the back of the room. Today, most of the financial programs at that show aren't even around, and MetaStock is the market leader. MetaStock sets the pace in technical analysis and has for many years; the program is as smooth and clear of flaws as any I've seen, and I've seen hundreds. The best way to begin would be to just dive into these clear waters.

Figure 16-1 is the title screen, which you saw earlier in Chapter 3. Right after this screen disappears, you'll see the Load Security dialog box shown in Figure 16-2. This dialog box includes a list of stocks, indexes, or whatever you want, ready to go. In this case, the list will show about 300 days of data on 17 closed-end country funds and three market indexes—the Dow, the Nikkei, and the London Financial Times Index, often called the "Footsie" in the trade, because of its symbol: "FTSE." You

Figure 16-1   MetaStock title screen

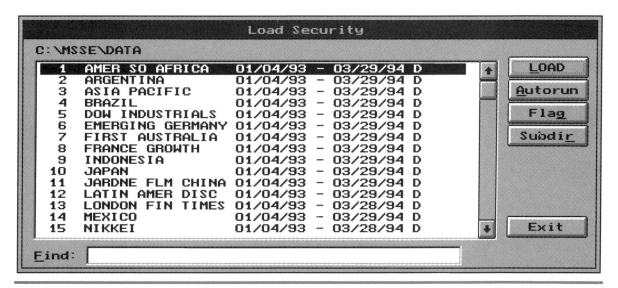

Figure 16-2   MetaStock "load" file showing the list of securities, commodities, etc. currently available for analysis

can add up to ten more or dump any of these and replace them with your own choices; either way, the limit is 30 issues. If you follow more stocks than that and you want to use MetaStock, you should upgrade to the full version of the program, which allows an unlimited number of issues to be stored.

Now Loading

Any time you want to get to your stock list, no matter where you are in the program, you simply type **L**, for "load," and a list similar to what you see in Figure 16-2 will come up. Any time you want a pointer on the screen—so you can draw trend lines, zoom in on a section of the graph, etc.—you simply click on the left mouse button. Even though this is a DOS program, not Windows, it is mouse driven. If you don't like using a mouse, it can also be driven entirely from keyboard commands, or a combination of both. I find the operation of MetaStock to be straightforward and intuitive. Anyone can run it, and you should feel free to just dive in and paddle around. The very worst that can happen is that you end up someplace that confuses you or seems to be a dead end. You can always start over. To back out of almost any screen or command, simply hit the ESC key. To quit and start over, type **Q**, for "Quit." A brief tutorial comes with the program, and you can start with that or go through it whenever you want. Now let's go back to the Load Security menu that comes up when you first start the program.

After selecting anything on the list, you get a box that looks like the one shown below. Let's spend some time with this seemingly boring little box, because it tells us a lot about what we're working with.

In this case, it says "Date Range" at the top and "Security: NIKKEI" right under that, to indicate we have elected to display the Nikkei index. It's worth noting here that you can name the security anything you want. We could have called the Nikkei Index "Tokyo" or "Japan." If you follow IBM, for example, you might prefer to call it "Big Blue." The other lines in the box tell us that there are 300 records—usually indicating 300 days of data, but it could mean 300 weeks if you were collecting weekly data. Under that, it says "Maximum Records: 400." This looks like you're limited to 400 days or weeks of data, but that's not so. You can set that limit to whatever number you like—5,000, if you wish—it just comes preset to 400. The lines immediately underneath that give dates for the "First Record" and "Last Record." This means you can select any period within those dates simply by entering the starting and ending date. But most people want to look at the most recent data or just view the entire run. So instead of typing dates, you can start faster and easier by hitting the ENTER key if you want to display the entire run of available data. If you want to look at just the last 90 days, the quick way is to type **–90.** for "minus 90" in the box that asks for first record to load. That tells the program you want to load the most recent 90 days. Either way, the screen will go dark for a second or two and the security will come up.

Agua Caliente—Hot Water

I've selected the Mexico Fund here, as shown in Figure 16-3, from the list of available stocks for no particular reason other than it's one of the largest funds and has a lot of public interest now because of NAFTA. Let's look first at the menus and button bar at the top of the MetaStock screen. The button bar is much like the ones you see in Windows programs, and most of the icons have obvious functions: the picture of an open manila folder is clicked if you want to open files, the picture of a printer clicked if you want to print. You will learn to use these over time, and there is nothing particularly important that has to be said about them right now. Some of the icons open into complex features; the booklet available from Equis will explain them.

Figure 16-3 Screen showing one year's worth of daily closing prices on the Mexico Fund. This and other closed-end funds come preloaded on the MetaStock program disk included with this book

The Charting Menu

The first pull-down menu is the Charting menu shown here:

Charting	
Blank Screen	**Alt+B**
Chart Colors/Styles	C
Chart Selection	Alt+C
Redraw Charts	R
Transparent Chart	Alt+T
Layouts	Ctrl+L
Load Security	L
Templates	Ctrl+T
Edit Smart Charts	E

You activate it by moving the mouse pointer to the word "Charting" in the upper left-hand corner and clicking the left mouse button. If you don't use a mouse, simply hold down the ALT key while you type the underlined letter in "Charting," the letter **r**. This same procedure will bring down the other menus as well—the ALT key plus the first letter of the menu name. Most things work faster and easier with the mouse, so if you have one, get used to it.

As you look at this and other menus, it is hard to realize how much is contained in them. As with many programs, each menu opens up a realm of choices which often produce still other menus, some of which in turn produce still more menus to choose from, and so on. I can't go through them all here, because it would take up too much space and I think it would probably bore you out of your mind. You will navigate through these menus as time goes on and you learn the program. Some of them you will never use, simply because you're not interested in those tools or topics. Going back to the first menu, this is where we select our style for displaying charts. The second choice, you'll notice, is "Chart Colors/Styles."

If you select Colors/Styles you get another menu (not pictured) which shows a wide range of color choices for just about everything you see on the screen. You can pick colors for the stock chart itself, other colors for the boundaries of the screen, others for the menus, and so on. Have fun, pick whatever you want. You're going to be looking at these screens for a long time. You can also select whether or not to have horizontal and vertical dotted lines, throwing a grid over the screen. I have elected to do this because I like a ready reference grid for looking at a stock and perhaps because I'm used to it from studying mathematics. Some people like a clear screen.

Notice that one of the choices on this menu says "Transparent Chart." This lets you make whatever chart you're looking at "transparent," allowing you to see an overlay of the chart on the previous chart you selected. In this way you can get a quick look at how a stock has performed compared to the overall market, or to another stock in the same industry. You would start with the Dow Jones Industrial Average, for example, then move on to a stock or fund index, and if you make that "transparent" it will be shown as an overlay against the Dow. It's a neat thing to do, and will entertain many people.

The Files Menu

The next pull-down menu is the Files/Data menu.

```
Files/Data
 Data Maintenance      D
 File Maintenance      F
 Subdirectories      F10
```

This is where you enter the names and symbols of new securities you want to follow, delete the ones you're no longer interested in, change the number of allowable days, etc. We might call this menu Housekeeping. Notice that the bottom choice is sub-directories. In the full version of MetaStock you can have an unlimited number of sub-directories—one for foreign closed-end funds, one for individual stocks, one for bond funds, one for indexes, etc. I usually just mix everything into one directory, but if you're one of those super-organized types, or you plan to follow hundreds of issues, you'll want to be able to use several directories.

The Indicators Menu

Now let's look at the Indicators menu shown here:

```
Indicators
 Custom Formulas          O
 Indicator Help       Alt+F1
 Indicators               I
 Moving Averages          M
 Option Indicators    Ctrl+O
 Option Worksheet     Ctrl+W

 Bar Chart                B
 Japanese Candlesticks    J
 Point & Figure      Shift+F8

 Indicator Buffer     Ctrl+B
 Pointer Mode On          P
```

This is the big one. MetaStock is, after all, a program for technical analysis, and this is where the technical indicators live. There are tons of them, some extremely useful, others merely curiosities. It behooves you to go through these yourself and in considerable detail. While many people think technical analysis is nonsense, still others think it is a rigorous set of indicators that tell you exactly when to buy or sell. It is neither. A great deal of judgment goes into the interpretation of technical indicators, and the result of that judgment always has a large subjective component. That means that people find certain technical indicators that speak to them louder than others. There tend to be some indicators that have wide popularity, but many others that only appeal to certain users. You're going to have to decide which ones make the most sense to you.

The first item on this menu, "Custom Formulas," is not active in this special edition for the book. This would allow you to write your own formulas and create your own, well ..."custom indicators"—like the "Figby Indicator for creeping volume." I never use it, but some people like it. If you fancy doing that, you will have to get the full version. The next line, "Indicator Help," contains a brief description of what the indicators signify. This is useful information since some of the indicators are slightly more obscure than the Dead Sea Scrolls.

The next line simply says "Indicators," and this is the heart of MetaStock. Later you'll see the expanded menu that comes up when you select "Indicators." You can see the beginning of the list, which goes on to include about 50 technical indicators. Even that understates the case, since some of those indicators expand to have their own sub-menus. Get to know this section well, as you will spend most of your time working with the Indicators menu.

As you go down the items on the Indicators menu, you see lines that other programs consider full indicators in their own right, but which here are merely doors to still more indicators. "Moving Averages," for example, lets you draw either a simple or exponential moving average, but among its other choices it also allows you to elect "Bollinger Bands." Many people consider these to be important indicators, but there is so much here that they are just thrown in as an added feature for moving averages. Bollinger Bands, by the way, draw a moving corridor of parallel lines that center around a moving average of an issue's closing prices. The width of the corridor is adjustable, and the point of it all is that stock prices tend to move within a restricted range around their main trend. In this sense, it is much like the notion of deviation from the "least squares" line discussed in the Telescan chapter. But whereas that is linear, this is dynamic, or curvilinear. It will be clearer to you in the doing than the explaining.

Other indicator groups listed in this menu include options, bar charts, point and figure charting, and Japanese Candlesticks. Many hours, even days, will be spent going through all these things. When you're done, you will dismiss some of it as useless for your own purposes and find some of it crucial to what you want to do. That's what big programs are all about.

The Scaling Menu

Now let's visit the Scaling Menu shown here:

```
┌─────────────────────────────────────┐
│ Scaling                             │
├─────────────────────────────────────┤
│ Chart Size          Alt+U           │
│ Date Compression    Alt+D           │
│ Grids                   G           │
│ Inner Windows           W           │
│ Reset ALL Defaults  Alt+F2          │
│ Scaling                 U           │
│ Statistics             F2           │
│ Volume Scaling      Alt+V           │
│ Zoom Scaling        Ctrl+Z          │
└─────────────────────────────────────┘
```

The more astute among you will notice that I skipped over a menu completely—the Printing menu. It seems fairly self-evident what the Printing menu does. The Scaling menu, however, is a different matter. This allows you to change the size of charts, their parameters, show relevant statistics at a glance, zoom in on a particular part, etc.

MetaStock can show many charts at once, for example—just like Windows programs such as Windows On WallStreet (discussed in Chapter 18). You do not need Microsoft Windows to be able to have "windows" on a screen. MetaStock has been able to do this in DOS for many years. You can change the size and number of windows displayed on your screen using this menu in combination with selections made from the Charting menu. I do not show that here, but you will probably want to experiment with it.

The Other Menu

This might be called the "end of the menus menu," where you go to configure your systems, get help on other topics, or quit. The Other menu is shown in the following illustration.

```
┌─────────────────────────────────┐
│ Other                           │
├─────────────────────────────────┤
│ Configuration              Y    │
│ Help Index                F1    │
│ Macros               Shift+F1   │
├─────────────────────────────────┤
│ The Explorer          Alt+F10   │
│ System Tester        Ctrl+F10   │
├─────────────────────────────────┤
│ Quit to DOS                Q    │
└─────────────────────────────────┘
```

It's also where you go to record macros. Macros are simply records of commands. Let's say you want to look at every one of your stocks and funds in turn, each with the same technical indicators and for the same time period. In fact, this is a common way of using the program. You could select each stock individually from the Load menu, select the proper indicators for it, and then go through the same routine over again for the stock in the list. Or you can do a macro that records all those steps and goes through the list automatically. You can also select macros from the button bar; the icons at the right-hand side that look like tape cassettes are numbered one, two, and three, and clicking on one starts or records a macro. Once triggered, it records every keystroke you do thereafter until you click on the cassette again. To replay the sequence, double click on the cassette.

Two other items on this menu are not active in the SE version of MetaStock included with the book. These are "The Explorer" and the "System Tester." If you want them, you must upgrade to the full version of MetaStock. Here's what they do.

The Explorer is a program within a program that will look at a number of different indicators, examine their correlation with the motion of the stock, commodity, or index, and recommend which ones seem to offer the best insight into the movements of those stocks, commodities, or indicators. (Yes, MetaStock will examine commodities as easily as stocks.) This exploration is complex and can take anywhere from several minutes to an hour or more. It seems like a useful feature to have, and yet, while I have it, I never use it. The Explorer doesn't suit my style, though it may be just the cup of tea for other people. My objection to the mechanical examination of indicators boils down to this: times change. In other words, options may trade correctly in a Black-Scholes valuation model for many weeks, being correctly identified as either "over-valued" or "under-valued" with great consistency. Until that time comes when the model says the options are over-valued, and you sell and they continue to rise. What the market is saying at that point—and the indicators are not—is that the options (or stock or commodity or whatever it is) are over-valued for good reason: they're going up. Most indicators tend to reach over-valued or under-valued positions, and stay there, in strongly trending markets. They provide the greatest accuracy in sideways, or trendless, markets. Thus a high over-valued condition not only doesn't necessarily mean it's time to sell, it may well mean it's time to buy and stay with the long position. It is because of problems like this that technical analysis gets a muddied reputation; people expect it to be mechanical, and it's not mechanical. Judgment must be applied.

As I just mentioned, the "System Tester" indicated in this menu also comes only with the full version of MetaStock. What it does is try out various trading approaches and tell you which ones would be the most profitable or which ones would produce varying probabilities of profit. My objection to this kind of testing is exactly the same as the objections outlined in the previous paragraph. Times change, markets shift, and the machine doesn't know what's going on out there in the real world. It only knows what's going on inside its own data files. That knowledge is useful, but it's not everything.

Buena Vista, Baby

Let's go back to the chart of the Mexico Fund, shown in Figure 16-3, because it shows again what Yogi Berra used to say: that you can observe a lot just by looking. Even without applying any indicators or any other of MetaStock's tools we can see that the Mexico Fund bottomed pretty decisively around $20 a share from March through June of 1993 and then began a rise which led to a double in the price of the fund in the next six months. The rise went nearly vertical in early November after NAFTA passed Congress, and then went into a bit of a stall at around $37 to $40 a share, and dropped back to between $30 and $31 a share at the end of March. Could we have foreseen that drop? If so, its foreshadowing lay in the inconclusive motion at the top. It's that area of congestion, so to speak, that we're going to look at next.

First we use the Zoom function from the Scaling menu to draw a rectangular box around the area of congestion at the peak of the Mexico

Figure 16-4   Rectangle marking the area to be enlarged for closer viewing. This area represents the top of the fund's price action in early 1994

Fund's movement (as shown in Figure 16-4). We're going to blow up that area to take a closer look. Click on Zoom. A tiny square appears. Move that square to the upper-left corner of the area you want to blow up and hold down the mouse button to draw a box around whatever you want to magnify. When you let go of the mouse button the area will be magnified.

The zoomed view can be seen in Figure 16-5. Something else has been added: we've used one of MetaStock's technical indicators, the Welles Wilder Relative Strength Indicator, and added that to the top of the chart. This is an indicator developed by J. Welles Wilder and first made public in *Futures* magazine in June 1978. It was originally intended just for use in analyzing commodity prices, but it proved to be so useful that it has become a standard indicator for stocks as well. To add it to the chart, click on "Relative Strength" from the list of indicators. A box will appear asking you to enter a time period. Type in a number and press the ENTER key.

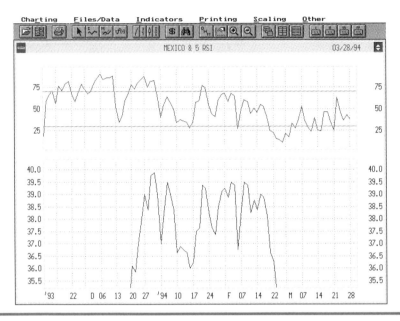

Figure 16-5   Zoomed view, with five-day Welles Wilder Relative Strength
indicator above

At this point, there should be a brief pause to explain what is meant
by Relative Strength, because the more common and older use of the
term meant a stock or commodity's relative strength compared to the
movement of the whole market. In other words, if a stock was rising faster
than the market as a whole, it had a positive relative strength. If it was
falling faster, it had a lower relative strength. The same was true if you
compared the issue in question to others in its group—if Bethlehem Steel
was rising faster than steel companies taken as a whole, for example.

The Relative Strength of Relative Strength

Welles Wilder did not mean any of that at all. What his indicator
does is measure a stock or commodity's relative strength compared to
itself. In other words, is the issue moving better or worse that it has been
moving in the recent past? The phrase "recent past" is relative. We can

look at how the stock is doing compared to how it's been doing over the past six months, past six weeks, or just a few days. The shorter the time period, the more sensitive the indicator. It may seem good to make the indicator automatically as sensitive as possible, but in fact this would not serve the purpose for most uses. A very sensitive indicator would suggest trades that attempt to take advantage of changes over a brief period, a pointless activity for someone who bought the issue to hold it for several months or years. Welles Wilder himself recommended using 14 days, so many programs use that number as the default for calculating relative strength. In Figure 16-5, I have elected to use five days. You will see at the top of the chart the words "Mexico & 5 RSI"—the Mexico Fund and a five-day Relative Strength Indicator.

What we now see is that while the Mexico Fund was topping several times at almost exactly $39.50 a share, the five-day RSI (the indicator above the stock chart) was declining over the same period. This is not a good sign. And in fact it presaged a 20 percent drop in the Mexico Fund over the next few weeks. A declining Welles Wilder RSI does not always indicate an imminent drop in the underlying security, but I have checked it out with the profitability tester in this and other programs and found that it's right about 85 percent of the time. Similarly, a rising Welles Wilder RSI in the face of a declining stock price indicates an imminent rise in the stock price about 85 percent of the time. It's nice to rub your hands in glee at the prospect of such strong technical indicators, but it's also prudent to recognize the 15 percent when it will be wrong—because you can get absolutely creamed in that 15 percent. Fortunately, we have other tools.

Figure 16-6 shows a chart of Apple Computer and a 14-day RSI. You can see that Apple stock bottomed in October, but the Relative Strength Indicator bottomed two months earlier and was already rising. The Relative Strength Indicator tends to begin rising or falling before the stock itself does.

Burgers as a Commodity

If we pull down the Indicators menu and select "Indicators," or if we simply press the I key on the keyboard, we get the list of indicators shown in the following dialog box:

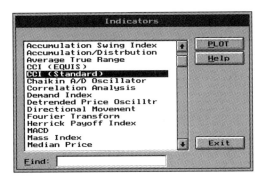

You see only the beginning of the list here. I've selected the indicator CCI (standard) and will apply it to a chart of McDonalds, in Figure 16-7. CCI stands for Commodity Channel Index, and like the Welles Wilder indicator was originally meant for commodities and found to be useful for stocks. It also has a selectable time period, and I have selected 21 days here. If you look closely at the chart of the stock and its indicator, you'll notice the uncanny ability of the CCI to call bottoms in the price of

Figure 16-6 One-year chart of Apple Computer, with 14-day Relative Strength indicator above

Figure 16-7 One-year MetaStock chart of McDonalds, using a 21-day CCI indicator

McDonalds. Whenever the CCI bottoms below its lower horizontal bar, so does McDonalds. It's not as good at calling tops, but it's not bad either. Accuracy here is about 85 percent, like Welles Wilder RSI.

Andrews' Pitchfork

This odd indicator gets its name from its developer and its shape—somewhat like the three tines of a pitchfork. A long-term example of it is shown in Figure 16-8, along with a CCI indicator and a look at six years of the Dow Jones Industrial Average. Notice again the ability of the CCI to call bottoms in the Dow as well as individual stocks. But pay attention to the pitchfork. This comes from the "Studies" menu that pops up when you select "pointer mode" in MetaStock, shown in the following:

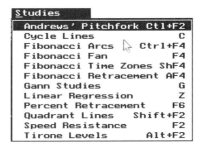

```
Studies
Andrews' Pitchfork Ctl+F2
Cycle Lines              C
Fibonacci Arcs      Ctrl+F4
Fibonacci Fan           F4
Fibonacci Time Zones ShF4
Fibonacci Retracement AF4
Gann Studies             G
Linear Regression        Z
Percent Retracement     F6
Quadrant Lines    Shift+F2
Speed Resistance        F2
Tirone Levels      Alt+F2
```

You can go into pointer mode any time you want by just clicking the left mouse button. Selecting Andrews' Pitchfork from the Studies menu, you go to a low or high point at the beginning of the chart. (If it's a rising chart, you would click on a low point; for a falling chart you would click on a high point.) Next, click on one high point and one low point further along on the chart, and the program draws a set of three parallel lines, somewhat reminiscent of our least squares example in Telescan. Notice that in 1990 the Dow topped out at a point very close to the upper tine

Figure 16-8   Six years of weekly data on the Dow Jones Industrial Average; movement of the average is overlaid with Andrews' Pitchfork

of Andrews' Pitchfork. The lower tine has not been reached for several years, though it was approached closely near the end of 1992 and 1993. Its present extension shows that any market drop now would bottom a little above 3,500, around 3,550.

note

Just a few days after the chart in Figure 16-8 was pulled, the stock market began a sharp decline of nearly 300 points over the next several days. I saw and heard expressions of fear and dread from market gurus in the press and on TV. The decline seemed relentless, but for some reason stopped at around 3,550, right at the edge of Andrews' Pitchfork. Does this mean that's the end of the decline? No one ever knows for sure, but the indicator says that's a good bet. It turned out to be a very good time to step in and buy. If the decline later moves below the pitchfork, it's time to re-evaluate the whole situation. In fact, it is inevitable that at some time the market will move below the pitchfork's boundaries. Until then, I continue to be amazed at the power of technical indicators.

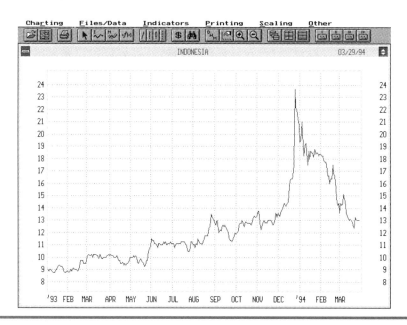

Figure 16-9 Indonesia Fund showing the pronounced price spike experienced by many country funds in late 1993 and early 1994

Yogi Berra Is Right

I'm going to finish with a chart of the Indonesia Fund (see Figure 16-9, previous page), which dropped like a stone following its late 1993 peak. It interests me because it illustrates that, despite our wonderful technical indicators, a lot can still be observed just by looking. The enormous decline of the Indonesia Fund seems, for the moment at least, to have stopped around $13 a share. Since it bounced around there for quite a while before beginning its meteoric rise, that constitutes what a trader would call a "support area." It certainly looks like support.

Will the Indonesia Fund go lower? I don't know. I only know that there seems to be support here. If events later prove otherwise, you can readjust your thinking about the issue. The market is a moving target. In the next chapter, let's look at "The Technician," a program that looks at the market as a whole, not individual stocks.

CHAPTER 17

THE TECHNICIAN

This is the only chapter in this section that does not come with a disk packaged with the book. It is here because it is a personal favorite and because it illustrates a different kind of program. The Technician does not analyze stocks, it looks at the overall market—the Dow, the S&P, Value Line, etc. Other programs have their own specialties; we might have chosen OptionVue, for example, which is aimed solely at evaluating options. In short, The Technician is here to show you other views and other possibilities. Because we haven't included a disk, we won't provide you with the step-by-step instructions that we've given you with the other chapters in this part. Our goal here is to show you how a program like this works.

The Technician is made by Equis, the same company that makes MetaStock. There is no particular significance to that, other than it gets its data directly from Equis. They charge $10 a month for that service, a price that has not changed in a decade. Alternatively, you can enter the required data manually. You would typically find the required data—advances and declines, up volume and down volume, etc.—in the next day's *Wall Street Journal* or *Investor's Daily,* or *Barron's,* which comes out at the beginning of each week. This may seem like an incredible nuisance, but actually there are quite a few people, including professional traders, who prefer to enter their data manually, because it lets them get a feel for the changes taking place in the market.

The opinion has been voiced that there's little point in paying attention to the overall market, because "It's a market of stocks, not a stock market." Like many aphorisms that sum up conventional wisdom, this one borders on the moronic. While it seems to contain some great truth buried within its apposite phrasing, in fact there is none. Ninety percent of all stocks move with the trend of the market as a whole. If you do happen to have one of those stocks that continues to rise while the market falls, you are very fortunate indeed. The vessel of your fortune, however, is in the position of bucking a powerful current every day.

Just Follow the Little Girl with the Ruby Slippers

Let's dig in and see what The Technician has told us in the past about market movements and what it might be likely to tell us in the future. Figure 17-1 shows the opening menu, a very plain and straightforward list of choices.

> **Graphic Charting** takes us directly to the main program.

> **Custom Indicators** opens an area that lets you write your own formulas for technical analysis—restricted to using that used by the program for its own indicators.

Data Maintenance either opens to the automatic dialing and communications program which calls the company computer in Utah to fill in the data, or lets you do this manually.

Utilities include system setup and the ability to go into any part of the data and repair errors.

Quit is self explanatory. Type Q from wherever you are to exit the program. Similarly, hitting the ESC key will negate almost any command.

When you select "Graphic Charting" to open the program, a screen comes up that tells you how many days of data you have and asks how many units you want to load. This may seem too simple to mention, but it's worth a little explanation. All of the data in The Technician is daily. But you might want to look at the market's action on a weekly or monthly basis. For this reason, the Load Data box asks you for a compression factor.

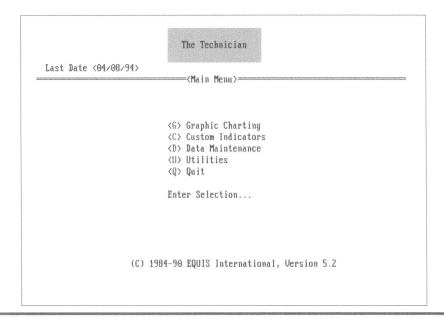

Figure 17-1   The Technician's opening screen, letting you move directly to charts or to loading data

If you just want to load daily data, you hit ENTER and skip it. But if you want a weekly view, type **5** to tell the program you want to load five units at a time, which translates to five market days—one week. If you want a monthly view, you would select 22 units—because there are 22 working or market days in a month, not 30. This is important because many programs would accept 30 as the measure of a month, and this would generate a false view.

That settled, what I've drawn up for an example in Figure 17-2 is a chart of weekly data for the NYSE index going all the way back to 1979. What we're looking at here is the whole bull market. The NYSE is an index composed of the 2,000 stocks trading on the New York Stock Exchange. It is one of the largest indexes and hence one of the most conservative, meaning most resistant to sudden shifts. The top portion of this screen is occupied by one of the indicators put together by Equis to go with The Technician. It is a composite of several of the individual technical indicators used in the program. This one is called the Medium

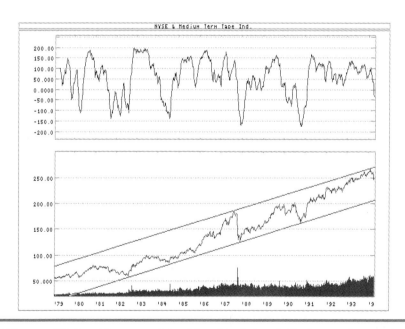

Figure 17-2   15 years of the New York Stock Exchange (bottom); the rising corridor is occupied. The top portion contains a composite indicator that comes with the program

Term Tape Indicator—dips in this indicator have always been good times to buy. You can keep it, dump it, and/or create your own.

Stay on the Road

I've also taken the liberty of drawing a trend channel for the entire bull market of the last 12 years. To show a trend, here or anywhere else, draw a line connecting the lows, then draw another one parallel that touches one of the highs. When the market touches that line again, it is likely that it is topping out. If it were a declining market, you would connect the tops first and try to define the bottom of the channel with a parallel line.

Most observers would agree that the current uptrend began in August of 1982 and continues to this day—at least to April 1994, when this chapter is being written. The channel was created simply by starting at that low point in August 1982, and connecting that point with the other major lows up to the present. To most people's surprise, including my own, the straight line touches all the major lows. That line represents the bottom, or what traders would call the "support" for the bull market. A parallel line was drawn simply by selecting the first significant high point—the market top in August 1987. It was from here that the market dropped a thousand points, culminating in the disastrous 500-point fall of Monday, October 19, 1987. This channel represents the equivalent of the market's own "Yellow Brick Road." A casual observation of the road indicates that the broad-based NYSE index recently hit the top boundary for the first time since 1987, and started down immediately. When the index leaves the road by dropping through the bottom boundary, the most long-lived bull market of this century will be dead.

Most technical indicators are arranged so that their low points indicate areas where the market is over-sold and their high points indicate where the market is over-bought. Most indicators are much better at picking bottoms than tops, and no indicator is perfect at either kind of call, so judgment is always required. In Figure 17-2, the Medium Term Tape Indicator was quite good at calling market bottoms, but not so hot at calling tops. In Figure 17-3, I have thrown a chart of the same stretch of the market with an indicator I consider pretty good at calling both bottoms and tops—a moving line of new highs minus new lows. It forms

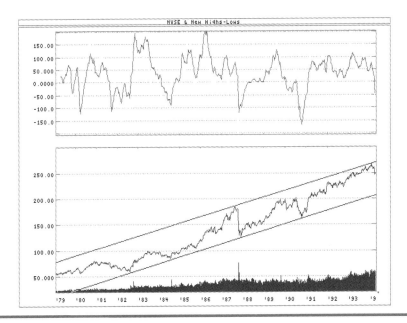

Figure 17-3   The NYSE is at the bottom; the top portion shows new highs minus new lows

the top graph of Figure 17-3. Whenever the new highs minus new lows has gone down to minus 100, the market has been a good buy.

Feeling Low

It can be seen that the bottom points of this indicator coincide nicely with bottoms in the stock market itself, but the tops in the indicator also warn of coming tops in the market. Several weeks before the market tops out, the number of new highs exceeding the number of new lows begins to shrink. At the top, in 1987, it began to shrink severely.

This indicator is created by taking all the new highs on any given day and subtracting all the new lows, and it comes very close to the boundary line of another sort, which is the continuing argument against technical analysis—and the question, "What is technical analysis anyway?" It is a gray area. Here we can see that the *technical* indicator—new highs minus new lows—is made up of data that is not technical but *fundamental*, namely, the number of new highs and new lows. Surely nothing is more fundamental to the stock market than whether a stock goes up or down, and in this case the program is simply charting how many go up and down over time. In Figure 17-4, I have drawn vertical lines at the beginning of each year to make it easier for the eye to correlate the upper graph (the indicator) with the lower graph (the stock market).

New Roads to the Emerald City

We are not restricted to looking at the NYSE index. Figure 17-5 shows The Technician's available selection. Looking it over, you see the choices include the Dow, the Shearson Lehman Bond Index, and the NYFE—New York Futures Exchange index, called "the knife" in the trade.

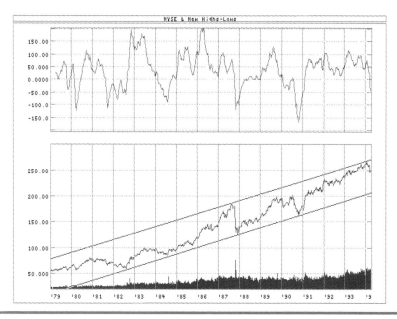

Figure 17-4   The Technician allows you to overlay vertical lines, simply by pushing the V key

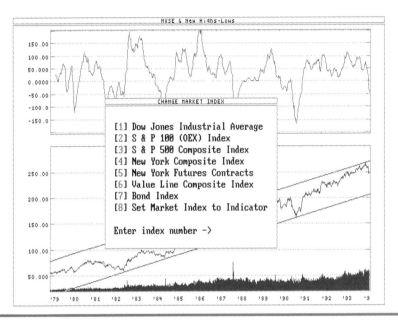

Figure 17-5   Indexes that can be used to follow market trends. Not all are stock
indexes; item 5 covers future's contracts, item 7 covers the bond index

In Figure 17-6, I have selected the Dow Jones Industrial Average
instead of the NYSE as the market index, and I have drawn the same
upward-sloping channel. Notice that the channel, which was already
clearly defined in 1984 and 1985, became an impenetrable wall after the
crash of 1987. At the time of the crash, I remember hearing cries of fear
and predictions of doom from practically every so-called "market expert"
in the world. It was going down another thousand points from here, was
the uniform view. Even market guru Elaine Garzarelli, who correctly
predicted the 500-point decline of Black Monday, predicted a second
500-point decline within the next few days. It never happened. In fact,
the market stopped dropping right there, as soon as it hit the boundary
of its rising channel. More recently, it has hit and gone through the upper
boundary of that channel in March 1994, the first time it has hit the upper
boundary since August 1987. The fact that it went through is of no
particular significance except that it shows why professionals in the
market pay less attention to the Dow than the NYSE or the S&P 500.

Figure 17-6 In this chart, we've substituted the New York Stock Exchange with the Dow Jones Industrial Average. The top portion shows the Advance/Decline line

The DJIA is, after all, composed of only 30 stocks, and subject to more erratic movements than larger indexes.

The upper part of this chart, by the way, shows the "Advance/Decline line," one of the most closely followed indicators. It is created by taking the number of advances each day and subtracting the number of declines. The argument behind it is simple enough: a market cannot long continue to rise if more stocks are going down than going up.

Figure 17-7 shows the same rising channel graph, this time using the S&P 500 index instead of the NYSE or the DJIA. Once again, with this larger index (based on the 500 largest corporations), the index remains steady within its channel. The upper chart now shows the stochastics indicator, a statistical technique that compares the proximity of closes of a recent period to the closes of a longer period. It is frequently used by active traders to examine market swings over short periods. Some active traders use almost nothing else.

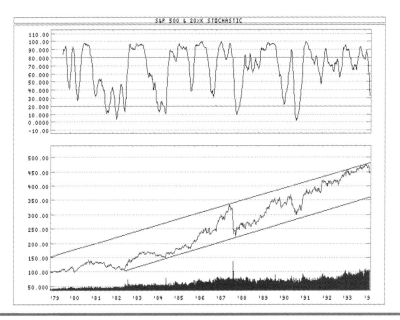

Figure 17-7   The S&P 500 index which still holds within the same channel as the NYSE. The upper portion of this chart shows the stochastic, which many traders follow for buy and sell decisions

The Technician tracks a few markets that do not involve stocks. One is the gold market. Figure 17-8 shows a chart of the S&P 500 index at the bottom and the price of gold over the same period of many years. We might well be interested in the gold market itself, and The Technician lets us change the "indicator" portion of its display—which in this case is the price of gold—into the market or lower portion of the display. This is done by selecting item 8, "Set Market Index to Indicator," from the menu shown in Figure 17-5. Doing this produces the results shown in Figure 17-9. If you look this over you will see that the market portion is now the price of gold going back to 1979. Putting it down here enables us to use some of the same technical indicators created for the analysis of stock markets to make an analysis of the gold market.

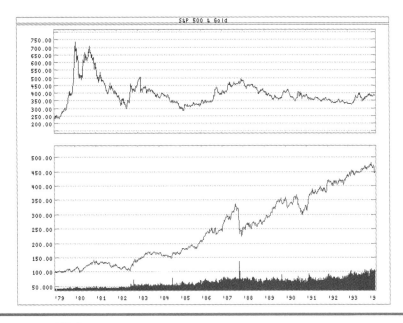

Figure 17-8 The S&P 500 (bottom) and gold (top)

A Truly Yellow Brick Road

One of the first and simplest analytical tools is the definition of a range where the price of any stock or commodity appears to meet resistance from buyers, and another price level where buyers seem willing to step forward and make enough purchases to halt a decline. It seems fairly clear after topping out near $750 an ounce in early 1980 (I believe the price went over $800 an ounce momentarily in what is called "intra-day" trading), gold began a long and steep decline to slightly under $300 an ounce. That price would be used to mark the beginning of support—a place where buyers were willing to step up in sufficient quantity to halt the slide. Similar points along the price chart are noted, and two horizontal lines have been drawn to indicate what appears to be the range of gold prices since the collapse of 1980 and 1981.

What we see in the lower half of Figure 17-9 is that when gold again got down to around $290 an ounce it again found support (buyers) and started up. Resistance was met and met again at around $500 an ounce. Now, despite the recent rapid rise in the price of gold and even faster rise

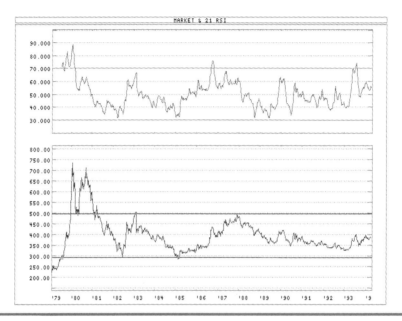

Figure 17-9   Here the market index (S&P 500) has been set to the indicator (price of gold). Horizontal lines have been drawn to indicate the top and bottom of the range for gold prices for the last 12 years

in the shares of gold mining companies, a trader would say that support and resistance have yet to be broken. Should gold continue to rise, almost any trader would likely begin to sell as it neared $500.

The indicator we have called upon for the top half of the display is the Welles Wilder Relative Strength. Its motion has for the most part accurately reflected and forecast the price movements of gold thus far. For instance, the RSI (Relative Strength Indicator) failed to recover when gold prices surged upward again in 1980 and then later had already reversed and started upward again even when gold hit a low of less than $300 in 1982.

None of this is to say that you can now play the gold market with impunity by simply watching the RSI. There is always a percentage of the time when indicators fail to accurately reflect the underlying market. Unfortunately, you never know when that time will be, so risk always remains. But indicators are certainly a valuable tool.

Frankly Speaking

The Technician also tracks the Swiss franc and the Japanese yen. While these have only a peripheral effect on the U.S. stock market, they provide a useful view of the U.S. dollar and how it is being valued overseas. The Swiss franc is backed by gold, making it one of the hardest of the world's hard currencies. So a rise in the Swiss franc can, and should, also be viewed as a fall in the dollar. The same can be said for the price of gold. In a very real sense, gold and currencies backed by gold hardly fluctuate at all; it is the dollar that is fluctuating.

This becomes especially apparent with the price of gold, since its price is denominated in dollars. If you take a truly long view this is easy to demonstrate. In an interview I listened to recently on the BBC (British Broadcasting Company), an elderly English writer recalled that when he was very young, early in the century, his father would sometimes take him into London for the weekend, where they would have tea and dinner at the Savoy and stay for two nights. The cost was two gold crowns—two ounces of gold, he noted. Well, the Savoy exists to this day, and the same weekend for two would cost about $750 today—just about two ounces of gold. Looking further back, a fine carriage in 18th century France, suitable for a wealthy merchant or minor nobility, cost 100 ounces of gold—just about what a luxury car costs today. During the 16th century, in the Italian Renaissance, ancient Greek vases sold in Florence for 100 to 150 gold florins, about what they cost today.

Now let's turn back to the franc. Figure 17-10 shows a chart of the Swiss franc compared to the NYSE. Some market analysts believe the collapse of the U.S. stock market in late 1987 was caused as much by a decline in the value of the dollar as a rise in interest rates. Indeed, the two are related. A glance at the chart shows that the Swiss franc had been rising steadily for nearly two years, indicating an equally steady deterioration in the dollar.

Whether this shift did indeed precipitate the sharp sell-off in U.S. equities is the stuff for academics and learned papers, but it reflects exactly the same conditions that influence—or should influence—your decision whether or not to invest in foreign stocks. If the Spanish peseta is declining, you do not want to be in Spanish stocks or bonds, because you will get back fewer dollars for the same number of pesetas. You will probably lose money even if the stocks do well. Well, the truth is, you should view your own market in the same way. The investors of other

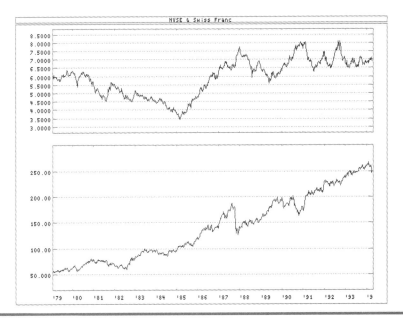

Figure 17-10   The NYSE (bottom) and the Swiss franc (top). A rise in the franc means a fall in the dollar. Some think this has significance for the American market

countries will view it that way. If the dollar is declining—and you can tell this easily enough by watching the price of gold and/or the Swiss franc— then you will be paid back for your investment in a cheaper currency. Better to go elsewhere, a foreigner would say, and so should you.

Getting Technical

Figure 17-11 shows the NYSE (lower chart) and a 30-week moving average of up volume minus down volume. You simply take the volume in rising stocks on any day and subtract from that the volume in falling stocks. The result is sometimes a negative number. Unless you are in a raging bear market, it turns out that whenever the 30-week moving average of this indicator falls below zero the market is at or near a bottom. Look at Figure 17-11 again and you will see that in fact such points have

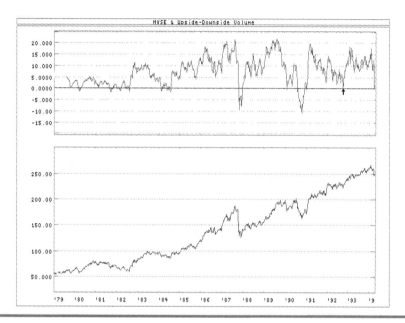

Figure 17-11   The indicator above shows upside minus downside volume. This has almost always been a good indicator for market action

almost always been favorable times to buy. Curiously, we are very close to such a point on this chart.

The reason we elected to take a 30-week moving average of up volume minus down volume is that many indicators when viewed as they come out of the box, so to speak, don't look like much. They are obscured by what statisticians call "noise." That is the chattering of day-to-day data as the market goes up and down that often obscures the general trend.

Figure 17-12 illustrates this perfectly. The chart at the bottom is our by now familiar NYSE index over a period of 14 years, but the chart at the top is a weekly graph of advances minus declines. This can be viewed as both technical and fundamental. In short, it is self-evident that a market cannot continue to rise unless more stocks are advancing than declining. At least not a market as large as the New York Stock Exchange. The Dow could continue to rise while the rest of the market declined because the Dow contains only 30 stocks, and those 30 might be doing very well. So we turn to the number of advancing issues minus the number

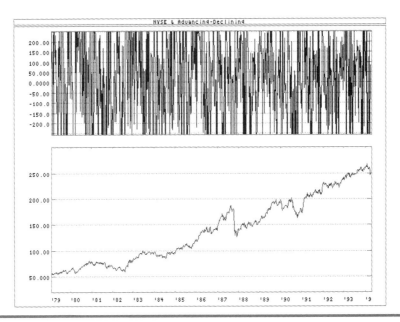

Figure 17-12   The NYSE with Advances minus Declines at the top. Looks like garbage, doesn't it? Well, we're going to take care of that problem

of declining issues in the same way and for the same reason that we looked at the volume ratios.

But what we get looks like nothing but noise. No one would look at the top part of Figure 17-12 and say that this tells us anything at all about the market. But it will. Figure 17-13 shows exactly the same data viewed in the form of its 30-week moving average. It points out major market bottoms with startling clarity and is even fairly decent on tops. The noise of weekly and daily activity often has to be filtered in some way to make it readable. The simplest filter is to simply take a moving average. This is exactly the same argument behind monthly investment plans—that steady buying will filter out the noise of up and down prices over time and provide an attractive average price. The purpose of filtering technical indicators is to let you buy at the best price, not the average.

We're going to finish up with a new look. Figure 17-14 shows not the familiar NYSE index, but one that's even bigger: the Value Line. The VLCI (Value Line Composite Index) is made up of 6,000 stocks. Most of

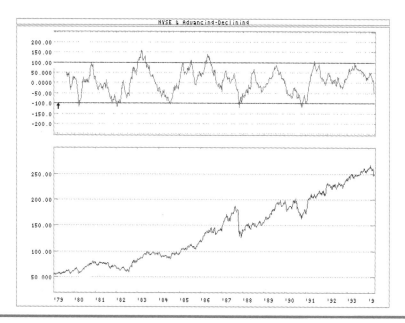

Figure 17-13 The "noise" of weekly Advances minus Declines from Figure 17-12 has been smoothed by a 20-week moving average; now it shows a very significant correlation with market movements

these are small over-the-counter stocks, and their predominance accounts for the wide swings you see. It also accounts for the difficulty, perhaps impossibility, of finding the same kind of smooth channel that characterizes the movements of the Dow, the NYSE, and S&P 500 indexes. The size of their individual components carries a certain inertial quality that inhibits their movements to extremes.

You may not think it's the end of everything when your big New York Stock Exchange listed stock is down 20 percent, but when the big stocks are down 20 and 30 percent, the little ones will be down 50 and 60 percent; some much more. So it is sometimes easier to see the big picture with the Value Line Index than with the slower and more conservative indexes.

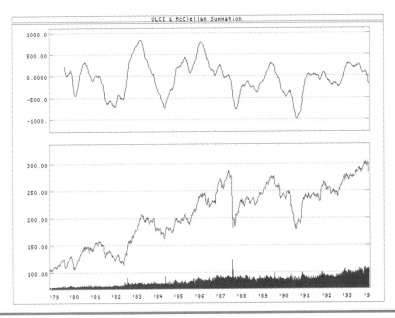

Figure 17-14 A new market index, the Value Line (bottom). The McClellan Summation indicator (top) correlates beautifully with the wide swings of the Value Line

McClellan Summation

The indicator used at the top of Figure 17-14 is the McClellan Summation, not found in most programs. It is based on another indicator called the McClellan Oscillator, much used by active traders, and its calculation is something you never want to do. It's one of the reasons we are all so glad we now have computers to do this work for us. The McClellan Oscillator is the difference between 19-day and 39-day exponential moving averages of advancing minus declining issues. The McClellan Summation is a cumulative total of those values. It is not a difficult calculation to make, but it would be very time consuming to make it by hand. As you can see from the chart, it's a fairly good indicator.

And Away We Go

The next chapter, the last in this series, takes a look at Windows On WallStreet, or WOW, as they call it for short. All of the programs discussed thus far have been DOS programs, mostly because Windows wasn't around when they were written, and another reason being that almost all the brokers and money managers who used such programs didn't use Windows even when it did come out. Since virtually every new IBM compatible now sold comes with Windows already installed, a shift to Windows is certain to take place. So this may be the future—and maybe not. You do not need Windows to analyze stocks; we've demonstrated that pretty conclusively thus far. But it does provide a different look. Let's go see in Chapter 18.

WOW! IT'S THE NEW LOOK

In the stock market of the Great Depression, windows were for jumping, but here they're for looking. The main advantages to using Windows for investment analysis is that you can display multiple stocks and indexes, each in its own window. These windows can then be dragged around with the mouse pointer, brought forward and enlarged or shrunk and moved back—like browsing the shelves of an electronic library. In a few years we will be so used to it that we will begin to wonder that it was ever done any other way.

Windows On WallStreet (WOW) has a colorful look, which unfortunately you won't be able to see in these pages, and while most people would take a stern Calvinist view and say "so what," I find it's easier on the eyes. Windows has become the de facto standard in PC compatible displays. Not only do new computers come with it, but they come with those arcane control files—autoexec.bat and config.sys—already altered to make Windows come up on the screen when the machine is first turned on. There are loads of people today who think this is the way the PC is *supposed* to look. This is certainly the way things are going. Sometime soon, MetaStock is also supposed to be out in a Windows version, and eventually everything will be that way, but for now WOW has the lead.

Speaking of MetaStock...except for this difference in DOS and Windows display, WOW and MetaStock are nearly identical in their features. You may or may not notice this as we go along, but if you don't, take my word for it: they do almost exactly the same things. Some differences will be immediately apparent, however, in the versions that come with this book.

As with the chapters on Telescan and MetaStock, this chapter on Windows On WallStreet was written using exactly the same version of the program that is packaged at the back of the book. That is not a demo program, but a working version; limited in a few ways that some users may want, but probably satisfactory to most.

What's In and What's Out

The primary limitations:

▶ The program will only track 20 issues, no matter what those are. It comes already preloaded with data on 15 stocks and indexes, and you can either continue to track those or erase them and substitute something that interests you more. Five spaces are left blank for your own choices.

▶ The Personal Investment Assistant has been disabled. This is a feature that accepts a "script" for automating a set of actions. It can be set to dial up and collect data at certain times, search your list of stocks for buy and sell trigger points, and print out a report that will be waiting in the morning. MetaStock does this with their little "tape cassette" icons on the right-hand side of their top bar.

▶ Import/Export features have been disabled. These would allow you to read the data from other programs or send WOW data to those programs. It has no effect on WOW's ability to take in new data from an outside service, like Dial Data (which I'll describe later). A free sign-up and one month's free service are being provided with Dial Data at the back of the book and these should be used to add data to WOW. Data can also be entered manually.

▶ Online Research has been disabled. This is another "script" which searches for pertinent news stories on flagged stocks when you call up one of the major database services like CompuServe or Prodigy. Those services also have their own online search scripts that can focus on a specific stock or country, so there's really no loss here.

The onboard features:

▶ All technical and fundamental indicators are active. There is no difference in these or the full program.

▶ Free Dial Data hookup. If you bought the full version of WOW, you would have to pay another $70-75 to connect with Dial Data so you could update your stock list. Here it costs nothing. See the Dial Data promotional page at the back of the book for the number to call.

▶ The manual and a set of beginner's instructions are all included on disk as a Windows Help file. When you call on help from the main program, you can get full information on the feature you're working with.

What it boils down to is this program is fully operational for our purposes. So let's start.

Everyone Please Be Seated

To install the program, you should start Windows (if it is not already started). Double-click on the File Manager or use its pull-down menu to start. Insert your WOW disk into a floppy drive and click on that drive letter in the File Manager. If the disk is in the A drive, for example, click on the little drive picture labeled "a" in the File Manager. In a few seconds, a list of the files on the WOW disk will appear on the right-hand side of the File Manager display. Double-click on the one that says "Install." This will start the installation procedure. Follow the prompts onscreen.

One of the advantages of Windows is that all programs tend to work in much the same way. To make anything active you move the mouse so the pointer arrow is on it and then click the left-hand mouse button. To make that feature open up, instead of merely being active, you double-click; that is, click twice rapidly.

If you double-click on the group titled MarketArts, the maker of Windows On WallStreet, you'll get a small picture titled "WOW." Double-click on that picture and the program will start.

note

The installation procedure for Windows On WallStreet is routine, but if you have trouble with it or have any other technical support questions, please call MarketArts at 800/998-8439. This applies to Dial Data connection as well—you can reach them at 800/275-5544. For more information on how to reach MarketArts or Dial Data, please refer to the Windows On WallStreet coupon at the back of the book.

Figure 18-1 shows you the WOW startup screen. The icon buttons on the left-hand side activate its features. For example, clicking on the top button, "Securities," brings up another set of menu icons: Download, Maintenance, Import, Export, and Composites. This is called "nested menus" in the computer business, for the obvious reason that menus are nested within other menus. You've noticed by now that the same approach is used in other programs. If you click the mouse on the "Download" icon for instance, that brings up a list of your stocks and several option buttons, one of which is again labeled "Download." Clicking on

Figure 18-1 The Windows On WallStreet startup screen

this one will bring up a screen in which you enter your new password and ID number, as well as the phone number for connecting to Dial Data. It comes up because when you clicked on the "Download" icon the first time, the program had no downloading information and didn't know what to do. Once you've entered the new data, clicking on the "Download" icon next time will start the automatic downloading procedure.

Clicking on "Charts" brings up the most important set of menus, shown here, for our purposes, the charting features. This sub-menu will open the analysis functions of WOW. The top button, "New Chart," would start charting a new security; the next one would open a saved chart, the one after that a group of charts. The fourth button down this menu group is for a feature not found in the version of WOW packaged with the book. In fact, it's not found with the full regular version of WOW either. It's found only in the "professional" version. What it does, if you ever want to get it, is go through the data and look for situations that would trigger buys or sells. You would set these triggers yourself—rising bottoms on the relative strength indicator or the stochastic, for example.

Two of the other main menu buttons, "Research" and "Assistant," are inactive in this version. If you want them you will have to upgrade to the full version of WOW. The Help menu button, however, is fully active, and clicking on it brings up useful information, like that shown in Figure 18-2. Take a careful look at this screen, because this is a tutorial on how to use Windows On WallStreet. It will not only tell you how to use the various indicators, but also what the indicators mean.

Let's click on the "Securities" button now. One of its sub-menus is "Maintenance," and clicking on it brings up the Security Maintenance dialog box—a list of the securities that are already on this disk, shown at the top of the next page. You will see that all the items are foreign stock or foreign stock indexes. This is deliberate, of course. All these were pre-loaded because, after all, this is a book about global investing. They can be kept or stripped out and replaced at your pleasure.

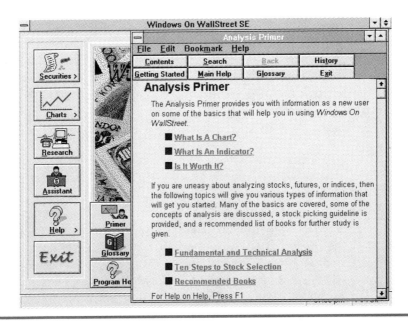

Figure 18-2   This shows you the Help screen that will take you through the basic steps of Windows On WallStreet. It is a self-contained tutorial

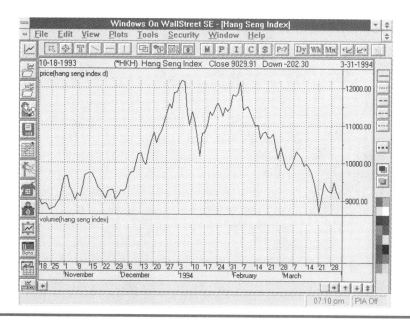

Hang Seng and Hang On

Click on the "Charts" button and select "New Chart." A list of what's available for charting will come up on the screen. We selected the Hang Seng Index, which will also be on your disk. To load it and generate your first chart, simply double-click on the line that says "Hang Seng." What you get is Figure 18-3. This is our first look at a chart from Windows On

Figure 18-3 Hanging loose with the Hang Seng. A classic double top. Leads to a 3,000-point slide in February and March 1994

WallStreet, so let's spend some time going over what's here—and there's a lot going on.

Most obvious, of course, is the chart of the Hang Seng Index, which occupies the center of our screen. This is the index for the Hong Kong stock market, and I love the way it came back to its previous high in early February and then backed off like it had seen the edge of the world. Notice that the previous time it had gone above 12,000, at the beginning of the year, it lingered there for a couple of days, enjoying the view. The next time, it stayed no more than a few minutes, and then dropped like a stone—more than 3,000 points, over one-fourth of its value—in six weeks. The equivalent in the U.S. market would have been a loss of more than 1,000 points on the Dow.

The Hang Seng is the most volatile stock market in the world, and it has been for more than 20 years. Almost all foreign markets are more volatile than the U.S. Does this scare you? It shouldn't. Because while the Hang Seng has been the most volatile market in the world for decades, it has also been the most profitable.

Going back to Figure 18-3 now, let's look at the icons that rim the chart of the Hang Seng Index. Clicking on each of these starts an action or makes a change. The meaning of some of them is obvious—like the telephone on

A Tale of Two Markets

The average return in the S&P 500 stock index over the past 10 years of a strong bull market has been around 15 percent. That includes dividends. The average return on Hong Kong stocks over that same period has been around 40 percent. In fact, if you go back over the past 20 years, which would cover the period starting at the bottom of the worst bear market since World War II, up to the present, the total return in the U.S. stock market has been 18 percent—which is terrific, much higher than the average for the century. But the average return in the Hong Kong market for those 20 years has been over 45 percent. The difference in these returns is much larger and more significant than it first appears. Because if you had been a long-term investor who started with $10,000 in U.S. securities and held on through that whole period, you would have ended up with $320,000, not counting taxes. That's a great return. But the same $10,000 invested in the Hong Kong market over the same period would have become more than $10 million. That is what different growth rates can do for you, and to you.

the left-hand side, or the color chart on the lower right-hand side. The meaning of all the others will be just as easy to decipher, because one of the characteristics of working in Windows is that as you move the mouse pointer to any of these icons, a brief description of what it does appears at the bottom of the screen. Try it: let your fingers do the walking and your mouse do the talking. The third button from the bottom on the left-hand side lets you resize the chart windows and move them around.

An Indication of What to Do

The icon you'll probably use the most is the one at the top just to the right of center, with the capital "I" on it, looking sort of like the letter on a college jacket—if you went to Indiana, Illinois, or Iowa, that is. This brings up the Indicators dialog box, which lists a bunch of indicators. This dialog and the some of the indicators are shown here:

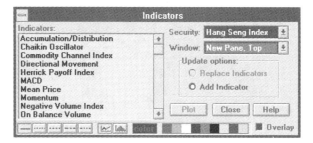

If you look closely at that box at the bottom right of the screen, you'll see that in addition to letting you choose which indicator to display it lets you select the line style—straight, dots, dashes, whatever. You can also choose line color and whether or not you want the indicator overlaid onto the security or displayed separately above or below. I always display it separately. Click on the MACD indicator to bring up a screen like the one shown in Figure 18-4.

Figure 18-4 shows a chart of Telefonos de Mexico with the MACD indicator on top. The letters stand for "Moving Average of Convergence and Divergence." It is calculated by subtracting the value of a 12-day exponential moving average from a 26-day exponential moving average of the stock under examination. While measuring the difference of moving

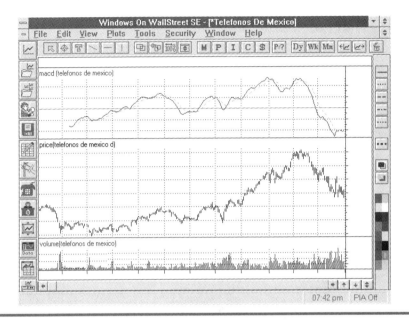

Figure 18-4   One of the most popular common stocks, Telefonos de Mexico is
actively traded on the NYSE. You make the call

averages is a standard analytical tool, this one carries it a step further by
measuring the difference in the rate of change of those averages.

Like most indicators, the interpretation of MACD is that you buy
when it hits a bottom and starts up again, and you sell when it tops and
starts down. This works best in level or slowly trending markets. In very
strong bull or bear moves, this and almost all indicators will move to
extreme levels and stay there for a while.

Two from Menu A, and One from Menu B

Not everything in WOW is done by clicking on icon buttons. The
pull-down menus contain those and still more functions, and are perhaps
easier to understand because they're in English. Figure 18-5 shows what the
View menu looks like. While the number of choices seems bewildering, in
practice the user tends to settle on one or two and leave it that way.

Figure 18-6, the Tools menu, gets into features you've seen in some
of the other programs we've talked about and whose uses are not

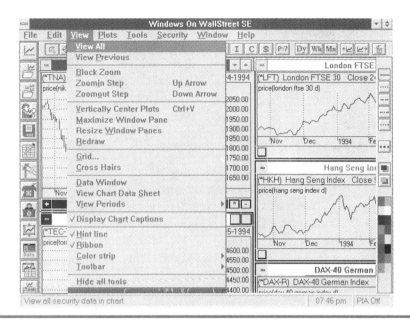

Figure 18-5   The pull-down View menu gives you all the controls for sizing and moving windows around the screen. It also controls the look of those windows

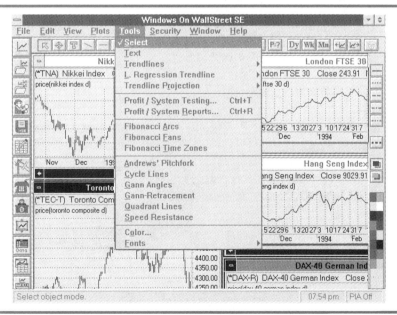

Figure 18-6   The Tools menu provides quick access to trendline features and some of the more complex technical indicators.

immediately apparent. They too are indicators, very sophisticated, used by some traders, dismissed by others. This book is not meant to be a primer on technical analysis; it would take another book, almost as long, to examine all the indicators available and talk about their uses. Maybe later. For now, you can learn a lot simply by experimenting.

The Wide-Angle View

Figure 18-7 shows the easy ability of a Windows program to display multiple charts at once. You can display multiple charts with Telescan and MetaStock, too, but Windows was designed as a graphical interface, and one can overlap, shrink, enlarge, and move windows about with ease. Here we see the Japanese Nikkei Index as the primary display, and scattered around it are windows showing the major stock market indexes for the U.K., Canada, Hong Kong, and Germany. The third button from the bottom on the left will let you size windows to your heart's content. From the very top of the WOW screen you can use the pull-down menus

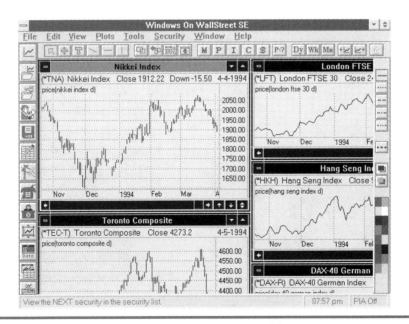

Figure 18-7   Here we see the ability of WOW to display multiple charts in almost any order

labeled "View" and "Plots," which contain many more commands for creating and sizing new windows.

Why would anybody want to do this? Well, historically, markets tend to move together. You don't have a bear market in one without a bear market in all. But that's increasingly a view of the past. As the economy becomes global, and less and less dependent on the U.S., markets have more of a tendency to go their own way. This kind of display is a good way to take in the world at a glance. You look for divergences; see who's bucking the trend.

On the face of it, Figure 18-8 is the same as Figure 18-7, but there is a significant difference, and that's why we stuck it here. The window with the Nikkei Index now has some numbers on the left-hand side and a vertical bar in its center. You can do this by selecting "Data Window" from the View menu and then clicking anywhere you want with the mouse. What you then get is the open, high, low, and close of the index for that

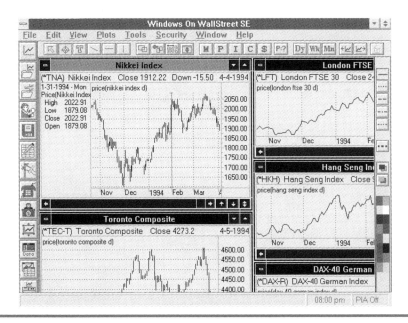

Figure 18-8   This looks a lot like Figure 18-7. The Nikkei Index, however, now displays data figures for any point on the graph

day. If you click on the window bar instead of a specific day, you get the range for the whole graph.

Figure 18-9 shows a WOW display of the London Financial Times Index (the "Footsie") with three British stocks. A 30-day moving average has been overlaid on the stock screens. The 30-day moving average is a popular indicator in itself and it's supposed to tell you it's time to sell when the stock crosses below it and time to buy when the stock crosses above. It never said a thing to me, but I put it in here because you read about it fairly often. To add a moving average to any chart, click on the button labeled "M" at the top of the screen.

Rolling Along in Your Mercedes

We'll finish up with Figure 18-10, a look at Daimler-Benz with some indicators I like. The chart of the stock itself has been overlaid with a 20-day moving average and a five-point envelope. Plotting an envelope is one of a number of choices you have when you click on the "M" button

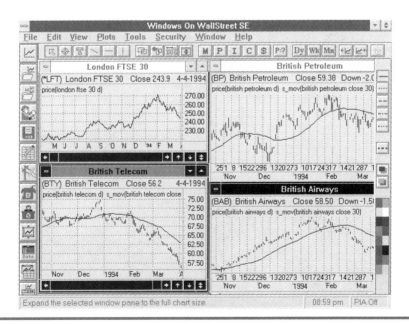

Figure 18-9   WOW can display groups of related graphs. This is the British group, showing the "Footsie" with three British stocks

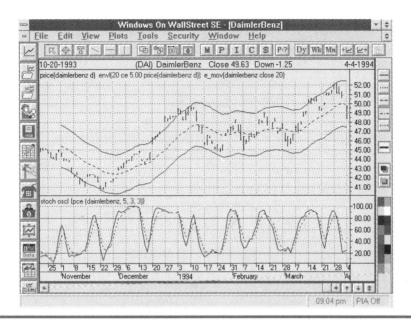

Figure 18-10   Here German automaker Daimler-Benz travels the open road of a 5 percent price band. The dotted line through the middle of the band is not a yellow lane marker, but a 20-day moving average

to select a moving average. It can be a simple line, an envelope, or an envelope or line that is displaced by a certain percentage from the stock's highs and lows. Experiment with these. Some moves will turn out to be useless, and some will give a new perspective on the stock.

Using an envelope here is useful. A staid, conservative stock like Daimler-Benz doesn't move around all that much, but it does move. Nearly all those moves, however, will be contained within a 5-point band that centers around its 20-day moving average. When the stock penetrates or nears the bottom of the band, it's usually (not always!) a time to buy; when it penetrates the top, it's usually time to sell.

The 5-day stochastic on the bottom is a check against the band, and vice versa. If the stock seems to be in a good buying position, and the stochastic indicator is also at a bottom, then things look fairly good and the decision to buy will usually be right. The converse is also true. How many times you want to pop in and out like this is a matter of your philosophy and your constitution. It certainly runs counter to the "buy and hold" theory. Not many people have the nerve for this kind of motion and emotion, but some absolutely love it.

Good-bye and Good Luck

In the appendix that follow, I have listed some useful numbers and addresses for you to gather more information, and after many requests to Morningstar, they have agreed to supply a list of more than 600 ADRs (American Depository Receipts) for foreign stocks actively traded in the U.S. This list is hard to put together, and I thank them for it.

With the disks and information provided in this book, you are in for a lot of fun, and hopefully some good profit as well. For still more assistance, I am going to start a bulletin board you can call, where you can ask questions of me and others who log in, as well as start discussions that should benefit everyone involved.

I will close with the immortal words of the late sports writer Red Smith: "The race is not always to the swift nor the battle to the strong. But that's the way to bet it."

THE LIST OF AMERICAN DEPOSITORY RECEIPTS

There are more than 600 foreign stocks in this list of ADRs and direct listings, each with its stock symbol and country of origin. This is about half the available total. ADR stands for American Depository Receipt, a piece of legal paper that is a receipt for stock registered in another country. A direct listing means simply that the foreign company has gone through the requirements for direct listing on that particular exchange—the New York Stock Exchange or some other. It has, in other words, agreed to the reporting rules required by that exchange. Typically, only very large companies will bother to do this, and while there are some advantages, such as being able to put up stock as collateral for loans, it does not mean that a directly listed company is financially more responsible or a safer buy than an ADR.

There are about 1,200 foreign stocks in all that can be bought and sold on U.S. exchanges or over the counter, but half of these are inactive. By inactive I don't mean that they only trade a few hundred shares a day—I mean that weeks and even months will go by with no trades at all. It is very difficult to buy such stocks and even more difficult to sell them. The process of separating the actively traded foreign stocks from the inactive ones was done by Morningstar, Inc., a Chicago-based mutual fund reporting firm, as a courtesy to our readers. They are considering doing this on a regular basis and selling such a list on disk. If you interested in that for the future you can contact them by calling 800/866-3472. The list is not expected to be substantially different from what you have here, but over a long period of time there will be changes.

COMPANY NAME	SYMBOL	ADR	EXCHANGE	INDUSTRY	COUNTRY
Apco Argentina	APAGF	Direct List	NASDAQ	Oil	Argentina
Banco de Galicia y Buenos Aires	BGALY	ADR	NASDAQ	Banks	Argentina
Compania Naviera Perez Companc	CNPC	ADR	OTC	Oil	Argentina
YPF	YPF	ADR	NYSE	Oil	Argentina
Agen	AGLTY	ADR	OTC	Health Care	Australia
Amcor	AMCRY	ADR	NASDAQ	Pulp & Paper	Australia
Ampolex	APLXY	ADR	OTC	Oil	Australia
Ashton Mining	ASHMY	ADR	OTC	Mining	Australia
Australia & New Zealand Banking	ANEWY	ADR	OTC	Banks	Australia
Australian Consolidated Press	ACPL	ADR	OTC	Media	Australia
Australian National Industries	ANNDY	ADR	OTC	Industrial Machinery	Australia
Boral	BORAY	ADR	NASDAQ	Building Materials	Australia
Bridge Oil	BROLY	ADR	OTC	Oil	Australia
Broken Hill Proprietary	BHP	ADR	NYSE	Nonferrous Metals	Australia

COMPANY NAME	SYMBOL	ADR	EXCHANGE	INDUSTRY	COUNTRY
Burns, Philip & Company	BPHCY	ADR	OTC	Food	Australia
CRA	CRADY	ADR	OTC	Mining	Australia
CSR	CSRLY	ADR	OTC	Building Materials	Australia
Central Norseman Gold	CNOGY	ADR	OTC	Gold Mining	Australia
Clyde Industries	CYDNY	ADR	OTC	Heavy Ind & Shipbuilding	Australia
Coca-Cola Amatil	CCLAY	ADR	OTC	Beverages	Australia
Coles Myer	CM	ADR	NYSE	Retailing/ Department Stores	Australia
Comalco	COM	ADR	OTC	Nonferrous Metals	Australia
Cortecs International	DLVRY	ADR	NASDAQ	Pharmaceuticals	Australia
Delta Gold	DLG	ADR	OTC	Gold Mining	Australia
Denehurst	DEN	ADR	OTC	Mining	Australia
Email	EML	ADR	OTC	Furniture/Home Furnishings	Australia
F.H. Faulding & Co	FHF	ADR	OTC	Pharmaceuticals	Australia
FAI Insurances	FAI	ADR	NYSE	Insurance	Australia
Foster's Brewing Group	FBWGY	ADR	OTC	Beverages	Australia
Gold Mines of Kalgoorlie	GMG	ADR	OTC	Mining	Australia
Goodman Fielder	GDM	ADR	OTC	Food	Australia
Gwalia Consolidated	GWB	ADR	OTC	Oil	Australia
James Hardie Industries	JHINY	ADR	OTC	Building Materials	Australia
Kidston Gold Mines	KSGMY	ADR	OTC	Mining	Australia
Mayne Nickless	MAYNY	ADR	OTC	Miscellaneous Transportation	Australia
McPherson's	MCP	ADR	OTC	Household Products	Australia
Memtec	MMTCY	ADR	NASDAQ	Industrial Machinery	Australia
Mt. Leyshon Gold Mines	LML	ADR	OTC	Mining	Australia
National Australia Bank	NAB	ADR	NYSE	Banks	Australia
Newcrest Mining	NWCMY	ADR	OTC	Mining	Australia

COMPANY NAME	SYMBOL	ADR	EXCHANGE	INDUSTRY	COUNTRY
News Corporation	NWS	ADR	NYSE	Media	Australia
Niugini Mining	NGIMY	ADR	OTC	Mining	Australia
Normandy Poseidon	NPL	ADR	OTC	Mining	Australia
North Broken Hill-Peko	NBHKY	ADR	OTC	Mining	Australia
Oil Search	OSL	ADR	OTC	Oil	Australia
Orbital Engine Corporation	OE	ADR	NYSE	Autos	Australia
Pacific Dunlop	PDLPY	ADR	NASDAQ	Multi-Industry	Australia
Palmer Tube Mills	PTMLY	ADR	NASDAQ	Building Materials	Australia
Pancontinental Mining	PAN	ADR	OTC	Mining	Australia
Pioneer International	PONNY	ADR	OTC	Building Materials	Australia
Placer Pacific	PLCAY	ADR	OTC	Mining	Australia
Poseidon Gold	PSGLY	ADR	OTC	Mining	Australia
S.A. Brewing Holdings	SABGY	ADR	OTC	Beverages	Australia
Samantha Gold	SMGOY	ADR	OTC	Mining	Australia
Santos	STOSY	ADR	NASDAQ	Oil	Australia
Sons Of Gwalia	SOGAY	ADR	OTC	Mining	Australia
Spargos Mining	SPA	ADR	OTC	Mining	Australia
TNT	TNTMY	ADR	OTC	Miscellaneous Transportation	Australia
Triad Minerals	TRD	ADR	OTC	Mining	Australia
Western Mining Corporation Holdings	WMC	ADR	NYSE	Mining	Australia
Westpac Banking	WBK	ADR	NYSE	Banks	Australia
Woodside Petroleum	WOPEY	ADR	OTC	Oil	Australia
EVN	EVNVY	ADR	OTC	Utilities	Austria
Veitsch-Radex	VMA	ADR	OTC	Mining	Austria
Gevaert Photo-Production	GPP	ADR	OTC	Multi-Industry	Belgium
Petrofina	PTRFY	ADR	OTC	Oil	Belgium
Aracruz Celulose	ARA	ADR	NYSE	Pulp & Paper	Brazil
CEMIG	CEMCY	ADR	OTC	Utilities	Brazil
Telebras	TBRAY	ADR	OTC	Utilities	Brazil

COMPANY NAME	SYMBOL	ADR	EXCHANGE	INDUSTRY	COUNTRY
Abitibi-Price	ABY	Direct List	NYSE	Pulp & Paper	Canada
Agnico-Eagle Mines	AEAGF	Direct List	NASDAQ	Gold Mining	Canada
Alcan Aluminum	AL	Direct List	NYSE	Nonferrous Metals	Canada
Alias Research	ADDDF	Direct List	NASDAQ	Software	Canada
American Barrick Resources	ABX	Direct List	NYSE	Gold Mining	Canada
BCE	BCE	Direct List	NYSE	Telecommun Equipment	Canada
Banister	BAN	Direct List	AMEX	Construction-General	Canada
Beta Well Service	BWS	Direct List	AMEX	Oil	Canada
Big Rock Brewery	BEERF	Direct List	NASDAQ	Beverages	Canada
BioChem Pharma	BCHXF	Direct List	NASDAQ	Pharmaceuticals	Canada
Biomira	BIOMF	Direct List	NASDAQ	Health Care	Canada
Bow Valley Energy	BVI	Direct List	AMEX	Oil	Canada
Brascan	BRSA	Direct List	AMEX	Multi-Industry	Canada
Breakwater Resources	BWRLF	Direct List	NASDAQ	Nonferrous Metals	Canada
Cam-net Comms Network	CWKTF	Direct List	NASDAQ	Utilities	Canada
Campbell Resources	CCH	Direct List	NYSE	Pharmaceuticals	Canada
Canadian Marconi	CMW	Direct List	AMEX	Defense & Aerospace	Canada
Canadian Occidental Petroleum	CXY	Direct List	AMEX	Oil	Canada
Canadian Pacific	CP	Direct List	NYSE	Railways	Canada
Canstar Sports	HKYIF	Direct List	NASDAQ	Recreation Products	Canada
Chieftain International	CID	Direct List	AMEX	Oil	Canada
Cineplex Odeon	CPX	Direct List	NYSE	Hotels & Leisure	Canada
Clearly Canadian Beverage	CLCDF	Direct List	NASDAQ	Beverages	Canada
Cognos	COGNF	Direct List	NASDAQ	Software	Canada
Cominco	CLT	Direct List	AMEX	Mining	Canada

COMPANY NAME	SYMBOL	ADR	EXCHANGE	INDUSTRY	COUNTRY
Compania Boliviana de Energia	BPWRF	Direct List	NASDAQ	Utilities	Canada
Consolidated Mercantile	CSLMF	Direct List	NASDAQ	Furniture/ Home Furnishings	Canada
Conversion Industries	CVD	Direct List	AMEX	Finance	Canada
Corel	COSFF	Direct List	NASDAQ	Software	Canada
Cornucopia Resources	CNPGF	Direct List	NASDAQ	Mining	Canada
Cott	COTTF	Direct List	NASDAQ	Beverages	Canada
Dakota Mining	DKT	Direct List	AMEX	Mining	Canada
Denovo	DNVOF	Direct List	NASDAQ	Electric Cable	Canada
Dickenson Mines	DMLA	Direct List	AMEX	Mining	Canada
Domtar	DTC	Direct List	NYSE	Pulp & Paper	Canada
Dreco Energy Services	DREAF	Direct List	NASDAQ	Mining	Canada
Echo Bay Mines	ECO	Direct List	AMEX	Mining	Canada
Elephant & Castle Group	PUBSF	Direct List	NASDAQ	Services-Misc	Canada
Enscor	ENCRF	Direct List	NASDAQ	Auto Parts & Assembly	Canada
Equinox Resources	EQXXF	Direct List	NASDAQ	Mining	Canada
Fahnestock Viner Holdings	FAHNF	Direct List	NASDAQ	Finance	Canada
Ford Motor Co. of Canada	FC	Direct List	AMEX	Autos	Canada
Glamis Gold	GLG	Direct List	NYSE	Mining	Canada
Golden Star Resources	GSR	Direct List	AMEX	Mining	Canada
Granges	GXL	Direct List	AMEX	Mining	Canada
Harvard International Technologies	HITTF	Direct List	NASDAQ	Industrial Machinery	Canada
Hemlo Gold Mines	HEM	Direct List	AMEX	Mining	Canada
Home Oil Company	HO	Direct List	AMEX	Oil	Canada
Horsham	HSM	Direct List	NYSE	Multi-Industry	Canada
Hyal Pharmaceutical	HYALF	Direct List	NASDAQ	Pharmaceuticals	Canada
Imperial Oil	IMO	Direct List	AMEX	Oil	Canada
Inco	N	Direct List	NYSE	Mining	Canada

COMPANY NAME	SYMBOL	ADR	EXCHANGE	INDUSTRY	COUNTRY
Inter-City Products	IPR	Direct List	AMEX	Industrial Machinery	Canada
Intera Information Technologies	IITCF	Direct List	NASDAQ	Services-Misc	Canada
International Absorbents	IABSF	Direct List	NASDAQ	Electric Cable	Canada
International Business Schools	IBSWF	Direct List	NASDAQ	Services-Misc	Canada
International Colin Energy	KCN	Direct List	AMEX	Oil	Canada
International Murex Technologies	MXX	Direct List	AMEX	Pharmaceuticals	Canada
Interprovincial Pipe Line System	IPPIF	Direct List	NASDAQ	Utilities	Canada
Intertan	ITN	Direct List	NYSE	Retailing-Specialty	Canada
Intertape Polymer Group	ITP	Direct List	AMEX	Chemical-Specialty	Canada
Ipsco	IPSCF	Direct List	NASDAQ	Steel	Canada
Jetform	FORMF	Direct List	NASDAQ	Software	Canada
Lac Minerals	LAC	Direct List	NYSE	Mining	Canada
Laidlaw	LDW	Direct List	NYSE	Electric Cable	Canada
Lawson Mardon Group	LMG	Direct List	AMEX	Pulp & Paper	Canada
Loewen Group	LWNGF	Direct List	NASDAQ	Chemicals - General	Canada
MTC Electronic Technologies	MTCEF	Direct List	NASDAQ	Telecommun Equipment	Canada
Macmillan Bloedel	MMBLF	Direct List	NASDAQ	Pulp & Paper	Canada
Magna International	MGA	Direct List	NYSE	Auto Parts & Assembly	Canada
Methanex	MEOHF	Direct List	NASDAQ	Telecommun Equipment	Canada
Mitel	MLT	Direct List	NYSE	Telecommun Equipment	Canada
Moore	MCL	Direct List	NYSE	Office Equipment/ Cameras	Canada

COMPANY NAME	SYMBOL	ADR	EXCHANGE	INDUSTRY	COUNTRY
NII Norsat International	NSATF	Direct List	NASDAQ	Telecommun Equipment	Canada
Newbridge Networks	NNCXF	Direct List	NASDAQ	Telecommun Equipment	Canada
Norcen Energy Resources	NCN	Direct List	AMEX	Mining	Canada
North American Vaccine	NVX	Direct List	AMEX	Health Care	Canada
North Canadian Oils	NCD	Direct List	AMEX	Oil	Canada
Northern Telecom	NT	Direct List	NYSE	Telecommun Equipment	Canada
Northgate Exploration	NGX	Direct List	NYSE	Mining	Canada
Nova	NVA	Direct List	NYSE	Oil	Canada
Nowsco Well Service	NWELF	Direct List	NASDAQ	Construction-Specialty	Canada
Ontario Store Fixtures	T.OSF	Direct List	NASDAQ	Furniture/ Home Furnishings	Canada
Pegasus Gold	PGU	Direct List	AMEX	Mining	Canada
Perle Systems	PERLF	Direct List	NASDAQ	Software	Canada
Petrolantic	PLANF	Direct List	NASDAQ	Oil	Canada
Philip Environmental	PENVF	Direct List	NASDAQ	Electric Cable	Canada
Placer Dome	PDG	Direct List	NYSE	Mining	Canada
Potash	POT	Direct List	NYSE	Mining	Canada
Prairie Oil Royalties	POY	Direct List	AMEX	Oil	Canada
Quebecor	POB	Direct List	AMEX	Media	Canada
Ranger Oil	RGO	Direct List	NYSE	Oil	Canada
Repap Enterprises	RMLPF	Direct List	NASDAQ	Pulp & Paper	Canada
Rigel Energy	RJL	Direct List	AMEX	Mining	Canada
Rio Algom	ROM	Direct List	AMEX	Mining	Canada
Rogers Cantel Mobile Comms	RCMIF	Direct List	NASDAQ	Telecommun Equipment	Canada
Royal Oak Mines	RYO	Direct List	AMEX	Mining	Canada
STN	STHIF	Direct List	NASDAQ	Utilities	Canada

COMPANY NAME	SYMBOL	ADR	EXCHANGE	INDUSTRY	COUNTRY
Sand Technology Systems Intl	SNDCF	Direct List	NASDAQ	Trading	Canada
Scurry-Rainbow Oil	SRB	Direct List	AMEX	Oil	Canada
Seagram	VO	Direct List	NYSE	Beverages	Canada
Serenpet	SRI	Direct List	AMEX	Oil	Canada
SHL Systemhouse	SHKIF	Direct List	NASDAQ	Telecommun Equipment	Canada
Softimage	SFTIF	Direct List	NASDAQ	Software	Canada
Softkey Software Products	SKEYF	Direct List	NASDAQ	Software	Canada
Spectrum Signal Processing	SSPIF	Direct List	NASDAQ	Electronic Components	Canada
Stake Technology	STKLF	Direct List	NASDAQ	Electric Cable	Canada
Tecnomatix Technologies	TCNOF	Direct List	NASDAQ	Software	Canada
Tee-Comm Electronics	TEN	Direct List	AMEX	Electronic Components	Canada
Total Petroleum (North America)	TPN	Direct List	AMEX	Oil	Canada
Tracer Petroleum	TCXXF	Direct List	NASDAQ	Oil	Canada
Transcanada Pipeline	TRP	Direct List	NYSE	Oil	Canada
United Dominion Industries	UDI	Direct List	NYSE	Industrial Machinery	Canada
Westcoast Energy	WE	Direct List	NYSE	Mining	Canada
Compania Cervecerias Unidas	CCUUY	ADR	NASDAQ	Food	Chile
Compania de Telefonos de Chile	CTC	ADR	NYSE	Utilities	Chile
Cristalerias de Chile	CGW	ADR	NYSE	Glass & Ceramics	Chile
Madeco	MAD	ADR	NYSE	Steel	Chile
Maderas y Sinteticos (MASISA)	MYS	ADR	NYSE	Pulp & Paper	Chile
Sociedad Quimica y Minera de Chile	SQM	ADR	NYSE	Chemical - Specialty	Chile

COMPANY NAME	SYMBOL	ADR	EXCHANGE	INDUSTRY	COUNTRY
Shanghai Erfangji	SHFGY	ADR	OTC	Industrial Machinery	China
Shanghai Petrochemical	SHI	ADR	NYSE	Chemicals - General	China
Den Danske Bank	DDB	ADR	OTC	Banks	Denmark
Novo Nordisk	NVO	ADR	NYSE	Pharmaceuticals	Denmark
Amer Group	AMRLY	ADR	OTC	Recreation Products	Finland
Cultor	CTRLY	ADR	OTC	Food	Finland
Instrumentarium	INMRY	ADR	NASDAQ	Health Care	Finland
Nokia	NAA	ADR	OTC	Electronics - Consumer	Finland
Alcatel Alsthom	ALA	ADR	NYSE	Telecommun Equipment	France
Canal Plus	CNPLY	ADR	OTC	Media	France
Clarins	CRASY	ADR	OTC	Household Products	France
Club Mediterranee	CLMDY	ADR	OTC	Hotels & Leisure	France
Compagnie de Suez	CSUZY	ADR	OTC	Multi-Industry	France
Groupe B.S.N.	BSNNY	ADR	OTC	Food	France
Havas	HAVSY	ADR	OTC	Media	France
L'Air Liquide	AIR	ADR	OTC	Chemicals - General	France
L'Oreal	ORE	ADR	OTC	Household Products	France
Moet Hennessy Louis Vuitton	LVMHY	ADR	NASDAQ	Beverages	France
Pernod Ricard	PDRDY	ADR	OTC	Beverages	France
Peugeot Citroen	PGTRY	ADR	OTC	Autos	France
Rhone-Poulenc	RP	ADR	NYSE	Chemical - Specialty	France
Schneider	SET	ADR	OTC	Construction - General	France
Societe Nationale Elf Aquitaine	ELF	ADR	NYSE	Oil	France

COMPANY NAME	SYMBOL	ADR	EXCHANGE	INDUSTRY	COUNTRY
Thomson-CSF	TCSFY	ADR	NASDAQ	Defense & Aerospace	France
Total	TOT	ADR	NYSE	Oil	France
Valeo	VAE	ADR	OTC	Autos	France
AEG	AEGXY	ADR	OTC	Electrical Machinery	Germany
BASF	BASFY	ADR	OTC	Chemicals - General	Germany
Bayer	BAYRY	ADR	OTC	Chemicals - General	Germany
Bayerische Vereinsbank	BAVNY	ADR	OTC	Banks	Germany
Berliner Handels-und Frankfurter Bank	BHFFY	ADR	OTC	Banks	Germany
Commerzbank	CRZBY	ADR	OTC	Banks	Germany
Continental	CGW	ADR	OTC	Tire & Rubber	Germany
Daimler-Benz	DAI	ADR	NYSE	Autos	Germany
Deutsche Bank	DBKAY	ADR	OTC	Banks	Germany
Deutsche Lufthansa	DLH	ADR	OTC	Airlines	Germany
Dresdner Bank	DRSDY	ADR	NASDAQ	Banks	Germany
Hoechst	HOEHY	ADR	OTC	Chemicals - General	Germany
Hoesch	HOO	ADR	OTC	Steel	Germany
Karstadt	KST	ADR	OTC	Retailing - Specialty	Germany
Mannesmann	MNSMY	ADR	OTC	Industrial Machinery	Germany
RWE	RWAGY	ADR	OTC	Utilities	Germany
Rosenthal	RAG	ADR	OTC	Glass & Ceramics	Germany
Siemens	SMAWY	ADR	OTC	Electrical Machinery	Germany
Thyssen	THY	ADR	OTC	Industrial Machinery	Germany
Volkswagen	VLKAY	ADR	OTC	Autos	Germany
Amoy Properties	APL	ADR	OTC	Real Estate	Hong Kong
Applied International Holdings	APP	ADR	OTC	Electronics - Consumer	Hong Kong

COMPANY NAME	SYMBOL	ADR	EXCHANGE	INDUSTRY	COUNTRY
Bank of East Asia	BEA	ADR	OTC	Banks	Hong Kong
C.P. Pokphand	CPPKY	ADR	OTC	Food - Commodity	Hong Kong
Cathay Pacific Airways	CPARY	ADR	OTC	Airlines	Hong Kong
Cheung Kong (Holdings)	CHEUY	ADR	OTC	Real Estate	Hong Kong
China Light and Power	CHLWY	ADR	OTC	Utilities	Hong Kong
Dairy Farm International Holdings	DFIHY	ADR	OTC	Food	Hong Kong
Evergo Holdings	EVE	ADR	OTC	Real Estate	Hong Kong
First Pacific	FPC	ADR	OTC	Multi-Industry	Hong Kong
Grand Hotel Holdings	GHH	ADR	OTC	Real Estate	Hong Kong
Great Wall Electronic	GWALY	ADR	NASDAQ	Electronics - Consumer	Hong Kong
Hang Lung Development	HANLY	ADR	OTC	Real Estate	Hong Kong
Hang Seng Bank	HSB	ADR	OTC	Banks	Hong Kong
Henderson Land Development	HLD	ADR	OTC	Real Estate	Hong Kong
Hong Kong Electric Holdings	HONGY	ADR	OTC	Utilities	Hong Kong
Hong Kong Telecommunications	HKT	ADR	NYSE	Utilities	Hong Kong
Hong Kong and China Gas	HKC	ADR	OTC	Utilities	Hong Kong
Hongkong Land Holdings	HKHGY	ADR	OTC	Real Estate	Hong Kong
Hopewell Holdings	HOWHY	ADR	OTC	Real Estate	Hong Kong
Hutchison Whampoa	HUWHY	ADR	OTC	Multi-Industry	Hong Kong
Hysan Development	HYS	ADR	OTC	Real Estate	Hong Kong
Jardine Matheson Holdings	JARLY	ADR	OTC	Multi-Industry	Hong Kong
Jardine Strategic Holdings	JDSHY	ADR	OTC	Multi-Industry	Hong Kong
Johnson Electric Holdings	JELCY	ADR	OTC	Electronic Components	Hong Kong
Mandarin Oriental International	MAORY	ADR	OTC	Hotels & Leisure	Hong Kong
New World Development	NEWDY	ADR	OTC	Real Estate	Hong Kong

COMPANY NAME	SYMBOL	ADR	EXCHANGE	INDUSTRY	COUNTRY
Peregrine Investments Holdings	PIHL	ADR	OTC	Securities	Hong Kong
Playmates International Holdings	PYMHY	ADR	OTC	Recreation Products	Hong Kong
Semi-Tech (Global)	SITGY	ADR	OTC	Multi-Industry	Hong Kong
Shun Tak Holdings	SHTGY	ADR	OTC	Miscellaneous Transportation	Hong Kong
Sino Land	SIN	ADR	OTC	Real Estate	Hong Kong
South China Morning Post (Holdings)	SCHPY	ADR	OTC	Media	Hong Kong
Sun Hung Kai & Company	SHK	ADR	OTC	Securities	Hong Kong
Sun Hung Kai Properties	SUHKY	ADR	OTC	Construction - Home Building	Hong Kong
Swire Pacific	SWIRY	ADR	OTC	Airlines	Hong Kong
TVE (Holdings)	TVE	ADR	OTC	Hotels & Leisure	Hong Kong
Television Broadcasts	TVB	ADR	OTC	Media	Hong Kong
Tommy Hilfiger	TOM	Direct List	NYSE	Apparel	Hong Kong
Wah Kwong Shipping Holdings	WKS	ADR	OTC	Marine Transportation	Hong Kong
Wharf Holdings	WARFY	ADR	OTC	Real Estate	Hong Kong
Winsor Industrial	WIC	ADR	OTC	Textiles	Hong Kong
P.T. Inti Indorayon Utama	PTI	ADR	OTC	Pulp & Paper	India
Allied Irish Banks	AIB	ADR	NYSE	Banks	Ireland
CRH	CRHCY	ADR	NASDAQ	Building Materials	Ireland
Elan	ELN	ADR	AMEX	Pharmaceuticals	Ireland
Waterford Wedgewood	WATFZ	ADR	NASDAQ	Glass & Ceramics	Ireland
4th Dimension Software	DDDDF	Direct List	NASDAQ	Software	Israel
American Israeli Paper Mills	AIP	Direct List	AMEX	Pulp & Paper	Israel
ETZ Lavud	ETZA	Direct List	AMEX	Building Materials	Israel
Electrochemical Industries (Frutarom)	EIF	Direct List	AMEX	Chemicals - General	Israel
Elscint	ELT	Direct List	NYSE	Health Care	Israel

COMPANY NAME	SYMBOL	ADR	EXCHANGE	INDUSTRY	COUNTRY
Laser Industries	LAS	Direct List	AMEX	Health Care	Israel
Scitex Corporation	SCIXF	Direct List	NASDAQ	Precision Equipment	Israel
Teva Pharmaceutical Industries	TEVIY	ADR	NASDAQ	Pharmaceuticals	Israel
Benetton Group	BNG	ADR	NYSE	Textiles	Italy
Fiat	FIA	ADR	NYSE	Autos	Italy
Fila Holding	FLH	ADR	NYSE	Apparel	Italy
Italcementi	ICF	ADR	OTC	Building Materials	Italy
La Rinascente	LSC	ADR	OTC	Retailing - Specialty	Italy
Luxottica Group	LUX	ADR	NYSE	Retailing - Specialty	Italy
Montedison	MNT	ADR	NYSE	Chemicals - General	Italy
Olivetti & Company	OLIVY	ADR	OTC	Software	Italy
Pirelli	PIR	ADR	OTC	Tire & Rubber	Italy
STET	STFEY	ADR	OTC	Telecommun Equipment	Italy
Aida Engineering	ADERY	ADR	OTC	Machine Tools	Japan
Ajinomoto	AJINY	ADR	OTC	Food	Japan
Akai Electric	AKELY	ADR	OTC	Electronics - Consumer	Japan
All Nippon Airways	ALNPY	ADR	OTC	Airlines	Japan
Alps Electric	ALPSY	ADR	OTC	Electronic Components	Japan
Amada	AMDLY	ADR	OTC	Machine Tools	Japan
Amway Japan	AJL	ADR	OTC	Household Products	Japan
Asahi Bank	ASB	ADR	OTC	Banks	Japan
Asahi Chemical Industry	ASHIY	ADR	OTC	Chemical - Specialty	Japan
Asahi Glass Company	ASGLY	ADR	OTC	Glass & Ceramics	Japan
Ashikaga Bank	AKGBY	ADR	OTC	Banks	Japan
Bank of Fukuoka	BOFLY	ADR	OTC	Banks	Japan

COMPANY NAME	SYMBOL	ADR	EXCHANGE	INDUSTRY	COUNTRY
Bank of Tokyo	BTKYY	ADR	OTC	Banks	Japan
Bank of Yokohama	BKJAY	ADR	OTC	Banks	Japan
Banyu Pharmaceutical	BNYUY	ADR	OTC	Pharmaceuticals	Japan
Bridgestone	BROCY	ADR	OTC	Tire & Rubber	Japan
Brother Industries	BRTRY	ADR	OTC	Electronics - Consumer	Japan
CSK	CSKKY	ADR	NASDAQ	Services - Misc	Japan
Calpis Food Industry	CPISY	ADR	OTC	Beverages	Japan
Canon	CANNY	ADR	NASDAQ	Office Equipment/ Cameras	Japan
Casio Computer	CSIOY	ADR	OTC	Electronics - Consumer	Japan
Dai Nippon Printing	DNP	ADR	OTC	Printing	Japan
Dai-ichi Kangyo Bank	DIK	ADR	OTC	Banks	Japan
Daibiru	DAC	ADR	OTC	Real Estate	Japan
Daiei	DAIEY	ADR	NASDAQ	Supermarket	Japan
Daiwa Danchi	DAN	ADR	OTC	Real Estate	Japan
Daiwa House Industry	DHI	ADR	OTC	Construction - Home Building	Japan
Daiwa Securities	DSC	ADR	OTC	Securities	Japan
Daiwa Seiko	DSI	ADR	OTC	Recreation Products	Japan
Ebara	EBA	ADR	OTC	Industrial Machinery	Japan
Eisai	EIS	ADR	OTC	Pharmaceuticals	Japan
Fuji Bank	FJB	ADR	OTC	Banks	Japan
Fuji Heavy Industries	FUH	ADR	OTC	Autos	Japan
Fuji Photo Film	FUJIY	ADR	NASDAQ	Recreation Products	Japan
Fujita	FJA	ADR	OTC	Construction - General	Japan
Furukawa Electric	FEK	ADR	OTC	Electric Cable	Japan
Hachijuni Bank	HJB	ADR	OTC	Banks	Japan

COMPANY NAME	SYMBOL	ADR	EXCHANGE	INDUSTRY	COUNTRY
Hino Motors	HIM	ADR	OTC	Autos	Japan
Hitachi Cable	HCL	ADR	OTC	Electric Cable	Japan
Hitachi Koki	HKK	ADR	OTC	Electrical Machinery	Japan
Hitachi Metals	HML	ADR	OTC	Steel	Japan
Hochiki	HOC	ADR	OTC	Electrical Machinery	Japan
Hokuriku Bank	HRB	ADR	OTC	Banks	Japan
Honda Motor	HMC	ADR	NYSE	Autos	Japan
Industrial Bank of Japan	IBJ	ADR	OTC	Banks	Japan
Isuzu Motors	ISUZY	ADR	OTC	Autos	Japan
Ito-Yokado	IYCOY	ADR	NASDAQ	Supermarket	Japan
Itochu	ITO	ADR	OTC	Trading	Japan
Japan Airlines	JAPNY	ADR	NASDAQ	Airlines	Japan
Japan Steel Works	JSW	ADR	OTC	Steel	Japan
Jusco	JUS	ADR	OTC	Supermarket	Japan
Kajima	KAJ	ADR	OTC	Construction - General	Japan
Kanebo	KAN	ADR	OTC	Textiles	Japan
Kao	KAO	ADR	OTC	Household Products	Japan
Kawasaki Steel	KSKSY	ADR	OTC	Steel	Japan
Kirin Brewery	KNBWY	ADR	NASDAQ	Beverages	Japan
Kobe Steel	KBSTY	ADR	OTC	Steel	Japan
Komatsu	KLE	ADR	OTC	Industrial Machinery	Japan
Konica	KON	ADR	OTC	Recreation Products	Japan
Kubota	KUB	ADR	NYSE	Industrial Machinery	Japan
Kumagai Gumi	KMA	ADR	OTC	Construction - General	Japan

COMPANY NAME	SYMBOL	ADR	EXCHANGE	INDUSTRY	COUNTRY
Kyocera	KYO	ADR	NYSE	Electronic Components	Japan
Makita	MKTAY	ADR	NASDAQ	Electrical Machinery	Japan
Marubeni	MAR	ADR	OTC	Trading	Japan
Marui	MAURY	ADR	OTC	Retailing - Department Stores	Japan
Matsushita Electric Industrial	MC	ADR	NYSE	Electronics - Consumer	Japan
Matsushita Electric Works	MAT	ADR	OTC	Electrical Machinery	Japan
Meiji Seika Kaisha	MSK	ADR	OTC	Food	Japan
Minebea	MBL	ADR	OTC	Electronic Components	Japan
Mitsubishi	MIC	ADR	OTC	Trading	Japan
Mitsubishi Bank	MBK	ADR	NYSE	Banks	Japan
Mitsubishi Chemical Machinery Mfg	MFG	ADR	OTC	Chemicals - General	Japan
Mitsubishi Estate	MIT	ADR	OTC	Real Estate	Japan
Mitsubishi Kasei	MCI	ADR	OTC	Chemicals - General	Japan
Mitsubishi Trust & Banking	MBA	ADR	OTC	Banks	Japan
Mitsui & Company	MITSY	ADR	NASDAQ	Trading	Japan
Mitsui Marine and Fire Insurance	TMF	ADR	OTC	Insurance	Japan
Mitsukoshi	MIK	ADR	OTC	Retailing - Department Stores	Japan
NKK	NKK	ADR	OTC	Steel	Japan
NSK	NSK	ADR	OTC	Steel	Japan
Nagoya Railroad	NGY	ADR	OTC	Miscellaneous Transportation	Japan
New Japan Securities	NJI	ADR	OTC	Securities	Japan
Nifco	NIF	ADR	OTC	Tire & Rubber	Japan

COMPANY NAME	SYMBOL	ADR	EXCHANGE	INDUSTRY	COUNTRY
Nikko Securities	NSC	ADR	OTC	Securities	Japan
Nikon	NIK	ADR	OTC	Office Equipment/ Cameras	Japan
Nintendo	NTDOY	ADR	OTC	Recreation Products	Japan
Nippon Kangyo Kakumaru Securities	NPP	ADR	OTC	Securities	Japan
Nippon Shinpan	NSP	ADR	OTC	Securities	Japan
Nippon Shokubai	NSL	ADR	OTC	Chemical - Specialty	Japan
Nippon Suisan Kaisha	NSU	ADR	OTC	Food - Commodity	Japan
Nippon Yusen	NYK	ADR	OTC	Marine Transportation	Japan
Nippondenso	NCL	ADR	OTC	Auto Parts & Assembly	Japan
Nissan Motor	NSANY	ADR	NASDAQ	Autos	Japan
Nisshin Steel	NSS	ADR	OTC	Steel	Japan
Nitto Denko	NIT	ADR	OTC	Electronic Components	Japan
Nomura Securities	NOM	ADR	OTC	Securities	Japan
Oji Paper	OJI	ADR	OTC	Pulp & Paper	Japan
Olympus Optical	OOC	ADR	OTC	Office Equipment/ Cameras	Japan
Omron	OMR	ADR	OTC	Factory Automation	Japan
Onoda Cement	OCC	ADR	OTC	Building Materials	Japan
Onward Kashiyama	ONW	ADR	OTC	Apparel	Japan
Pioneer Electronic	PIO	ADR	NYSE	Electronics - Consumer	Japan
Ricoh	RICOY	ADR	OTC	Office Equipment/ Cameras	Japan
Sakura Bank	SAK	ADR	OTC	Banks	Japan
Sanwa Bank	SBL	ADR	OTC	Banks	Japan

COMPANY NAME	SYMBOL	ADR	EXCHANGE	INDUSTRY	COUNTRY
Sanyo Electric	SANYY	ADR	NASDAQ	Electronics - Consumer	Japan
Sanyo Securities	SANSE	ADR	OTC	Securities	Japan
Secom	SEC	ADR	OTC	Electrical Machinery	Japan
Sega Enterprise	SEGNY	ADR	OTC	Electronics - Consumer	Japan
Sekisui House	SEK	ADR	OTC	Construction - Home Building	Japan
Seven-Eleven Japan	SEV	ADR	OTC	Supermarket	Japan
Sharp	SHP	ADR	OTC	Electronics - Consumer	Japan
Shiseido	SHS	ADR	OTC	Household Products	Japan
Shizuoka Bank	SZU	ADR	OTC	Banks	Japan
Showa Sangyo	SSC	ADR	OTC	Food - Commodity	Japan
Sony	SNE	ADR	NYSE	Electronics - Consumer	Japan
Sumitomo Bank	SMB	ADR	OTC	Banks	Japan
Sumitomo Electric Industries	SEI	ADR	OTC	Electric Cable	Japan
Sumitomo Metal Industries	SUM	ADR	OTC	Steel	Japan
Suruga Bank	SUR	ADR	OTC	Banks	Japan
TDK	TDK	ADR	NYSE	Electronic Components	Japan
TOA	TOA	ADR	OTC	Construction - General	Japan
Taisei	TAI	ADR	OTC	Construction - General	Japan
Taiyo Yuden	TYY	ADR	OTC	Electronics - Consumer	Japan
Teijin	TEI	ADR	OTC	Textiles	Japan
Teijin Seiki	TES	ADR	OTC	Industrial Machinery	Japan

COMPANY NAME	SYMBOL	ADR	EXCHANGE	INDUSTRY	COUNTRY
Tokai Bank	TKB	ADR	OTC	Banks	Japan
Tokio Marine & Fire Insurance	TKIOY	ADR	NASDAQ	Insurance	Japan
Tokyo Dome	TOK	ADR	OTC	Hotels & Leisure	Japan
Tokyo Land	TLC	ADR	OTC	Real Estate	Japan
Toppan Printing	TPP	ADR	OTC	Printing	Japan
Toray Industries	TOR	ADR	OTC	Textiles	Japan
Toto	TOO	ADR	OTC	Building Materials	Japan
Toyo Suisan Kaisha	TOS	ADR	OTC	Food	Japan
Toyobo	TYO	ADR	OTC	Textiles	Japan
Toyota Motor	TOYOY	ADR	NASDAQ	Autos	Japan
Tsubakimoto Precision Products	TSB	ADR	OTC	Industrial Machinery	Japan
Tsugami	TSU	ADR	OTC	Industrial Machinery	Japan
Victor Company of Japan	VCP	ADR	OTC	Electronics - Consumer	Japan
Wacoal	WACLY	ADR	NASDAQ	Apparel	Japan
Yamaichi Securities	YSC	ADR	OTC	Securities	Japan
Yamazaki Baking	YAM	ADR	OTC	Food	Japan
Yasuda Trust and Banking	YAS	ADR	OTC	Banks	Japan
Anangel-American Shipholdings	ASIPY	ADR	NASDAQ	Marine Transportation	Luxembourg
Amalgamated Steel Mills	ASM	ADR	OTC	Steel	Malaysia
Bandar Raya Developments	BROBY	ADR	OTC	Real Estate	Malaysia
Genting	GEN	ADR	OTC	Hotels & Leisure	Malaysia
Kuala Lumpur Kepong	KLK	ADR	OTC	Food - Commodity	Malaysia
Lion Land	LLB	ADR	OTC	Real Estate	Malaysia
Perlis Plantations	PPB	ADR	OTC	Food - Commodity	Malaysia
Resorts World	RWB	ADR	OTC	Hotels & Leisure	Malaysia
Selangor Properties	SEL	ADR	OTC	Real Estate	Malaysia
Sime Darby	SIDBY	ADR	OTC	Multi-Industry	Malaysia

COMPANY NAME	SYMBOL	ADR	EXCHANGE	INDUSTRY	COUNTRY
Apasco	AASAY	ADR	OTC	Building Materials	Mexico
Cemex	CMXBY	ADR	OTC	Building Materials	Mexico
Cifra	CFRAY	ADR	OTC	Retailing - Specialty	Mexico
Coca-Cola Femsa	KOF	ADR	NYSE	Beverages	Mexico
Consorcio G Grupo Dina	DIN	ADR	NYSE	Autos	Mexico
Controladora Commercial Mexicana	CCM	ADR	OTC	Supermarket	Mexico
Desc	DSF	ADR	OTC	Multi-Industry	Mexico
Empresas Ica-Sociedad Controladora	ICA	ADR	NYSE	Construction - General	Mexico
Empresas La Moderna	ELM	ADR	NYSE	Household Products	Mexico
Grupo Industrial Maseca	GRI	ADR	OTC	Supermarket	Mexico
Grupo Radio Centro	RC	ADR	NYSE	Media	Mexico
Grupo Sidek	GPOSY	ADR	OTC	Multi-Industry	Mexico
Grupo Simec	SIM	ADR	AMEX	Steel	Mexico
Grupo Synkro	GPSYY	ADR	OTC	Apparel	Mexico
Internacional De Ceramica	CER	ADR	OTC	Building Materials	Mexico
Servicios Financieros Quadrum	QDRMY	ADR	NASDAQ	Securities	Mexico
Telefonos de Mexico	TFONY	ADR	NASDAQ	Utilities	Mexico
Tolmex	TLMXY	ADR	OTC	Building Materials	Mexico
Transportacion Maritima Mexicana	TMMA	ADR	NYSE	Marine Transportation	Mexico
Tubos de Acero de Mexico	TAM	ADR	AMEX	Steel	Mexico
Vitro	VTO	ADR	NYSE	Building Materials	Mexico
ABN Amro Holding	ARBLY	ADR	OTC	Banks	Netherlands
Aegon	AEG	ADR	NYSE	Insurance	Netherlands
Affymax	AFMXF	Direct List	NASDAQ	Pharmaceuticals	Netherlands

COMPANY NAME	SYMBOL	ADR	EXCHANGE	INDUSTRY	COUNTRY
Akzo	AKZOY	ADR	NASDAQ	Chemicals - General	Netherlands
Amev	AMVNY	ADR	OTC	Insurance	Netherlands
DSM	DSMKY	ADR	OTC	Chemicals - General	Netherlands
Elsevier	ELNVY	ADR	OTC	Media	Netherlands
Heineken	HINKY	ADR	OTC	Beverages	Netherlands
Internationale Nederlanden Group	INLGY	ADR	OTC	Insurance	Netherlands
KLM Royal Dutch Airlines	KLM	ADR	NYSE	Airlines	Netherlands
Konink. Neder. Vlieg. Fokker	FOKKY	ADR	OTC	Defense & Aerospace	Netherlands
Koninklijke Ahold	AHLDY	ADR	NASDAQ	Supermarket	Netherlands
Koninklijke Bolswessanan	KNWSY	ADR	OTC	Food	Netherlands
Orthofix International	OFIXF	Direct List	NASDAQ	Health Care	Netherlands
Philips	PHG	ADR	NYSE	Electrical Machinery	Netherlands
Polygram	PLG	ADR	NYSE	Media	Netherlands
Royal Dutch Petroleum	RD	ADR	NYSE	Oil	Netherlands
Royal Nedlloyd Group	RNG	ADR	OTC	Marine Transportation	Netherlands
Schlumberger	SLB	Direct List	NYSE	Services - Misc	Netherlands
Singer Company	SEW	Direct List	NYSE	Electronics - Consumer	Netherlands

COMPANY NAME	SYMBOL	ADR	EXCHANGE	INDUSTRY	COUNTRY
Unilever	UN	ADR	NYSE	Food	Netherlands
Van Ommeren Ceteco	VMM	ADR	OTC	Marine Transportation	Netherlands
Wolters Kluwer	WTKWY	ADR	OTC	Media	Netherlands
Brierley Investment	BYILY	ADR	OTC	Multi-Industry	New Zealand
Fletcher Challenge	FTCHY	ADR	OTC	Multi-Industry	New Zealand
New Zealand Petroleum	NZPCY	ADR	NASDAQ	Oil	New Zealand
Telecom Corporation of New Zealand	NZT	ADR	NYSE	Telecommun Equipment	New Zealand
Hafslund Nycomed	HN	ADR	NYSE	Household Products	Norway
Norsk Data	NORKZ	ADR	OTC	Software	Norway
Norsk Hydro	NHY	ADR	NYSE	Chemicals - General	Norway
Petroleum Geo-Services	PGSAY	ADR	NASDAQ	Mining	Norway
Saga Petroleum	SGABY	ADR	OTC	Oil	Norway
Unitor Ships Services	USS	ADR	OTC	Marine Transportation	Norway
Vard	VARDY	ADR	OTC	Hotels & Leisure	Norway
Benguet	BE	Direct List	NYSE	Pharmaceuticals	Philippines
Banco Comercial Portugues	BPC	ADR	NYSE	Banks	Portugal
City Developments	CDEVY	ADR	OTC	Real Estate	Singapore
Creative Technology	CREAF	Direct List	NASDAQ	Electronic Components	Singapore
Cycle and Carriage	CYC	ADR	OTC	Autos	Singapore
Development Bank of Singapore	DEVBY	ADR	OTC	Banks	Singapore
GB Holdings	GBH	ADR	OTC	Hotels & Leisure	Singapore

COMPANY NAME	SYMBOL	ADR	EXCHANGE	INDUSTRY	COUNTRY
Hai Sun Hup Group	HISHF	ADR	OTC	Marine Transportation	Singapore
Inchcape	INC	ADR	OTC	Trading	Singapore
Keppel	KEP	ADR	OTC	Construction - General	Singapore
Malayan Credit	MLC	ADR	OTC	Securities	Singapore
Neptune Orient Lines	NPT	ADR	OTC	Marine Transportation	Singapore
Overseas Union Bank	OUB	ADR	OTC	Banks	Singapore
Sembawang Shipyards	SSL	ADR	OTC	Heavy Ind & Shipbuilding	Singapore
Singapore Land	SINPY	ADR	OTC	Real Estate	Singapore
United Overseas Bank	UOVEY	ADR	OTC	Banks	Singapore
United Overseas Land	UOL	ADR	OTC	Real Estate	Singapore
AE and CI	AECLY	ADR	OTC	Chemicals - General	South Africa
Anglovaal Holdings	ANAVY	ADR	OTC	Multi-Industry	South Africa
Asa Limited	ASA	Direct List	NYSE	Pharmaceuticals	South Africa
Barlow Rand	BRRAY	ADR	OTC	Multi-Industry	South Africa
Deelkraal Gold Mining Company	DLK	ADR	OTC	Mining	South Africa
Doornfontein Gold Mining	DORDY	ADR	OTC	Mining	South Africa
Driefontein Consolidated	DRFNY	ADR	NASDAQ	Mining	South Africa
Gold Fields of South Africa	GLDFY	ADR	NASDAQ	Mining	South Africa
Kloof Gold Mining Company	KLOFY	ADR	NASDAQ	Mining	South Africa
Leslie Gold Mines	LESGY	ADR	OTC	Mining	South Africa

COMPANY NAME	SYMBOL	ADR	EXCHANGE	INDUSTRY	COUNTRY
Loraine Gold Mines	LORAY	ADR	OTC	Mining	South Africa
Lydenburg Platinum	LYDPY	ADR	NASDAQ	Mining	South Africa
Middle Witwatersrand	MWW	ADR	OTC	Mining	South Africa
Palabora Mining Company	PAL	ADR	OTC	Mining	South Africa
Rembrandt Group	REM	ADR	OTC	Multi-Industry	South Africa
Rustenberg Platinum Holdings	RPATY	ADR	OTC	Mining	South Africa
Samancor	SMNCY	ADR	OTC	Chemicals - General	South Africa
Sasol	SASOY	ADR	NASDAQ	Oil	South Africa
Zandpan Gold Mining	ZGM	ADR	OTC	Mining	South Africa
Banco Bilbao Vizcaya	BBV	ADR	NYSE	Banks	Spain
Banco Central Hispanoamericano	BCM	ADR	NYSE	Banks	Spain
Banco Espanol de Credito (Banesto)	BNSTY	ADR	OTC	Banks	Spain
Banco de Santander	STD	ADR	NYSE	Banks	Spain
Compania Sevillana de Electricidad	COVDY	ADR	OTC	Utilities	Spain
Corporacion Mapfre	MAP	ADR	OTC	Insurance	Spain
Empresa Nacional de Electricidad	ELE	ADR	NYSE	Utilities	Spain
Repsol	REP	ADR	NYSE	Oil	Spain
Telefonica de Espana	TEF	ADR	NYSE	Utilities	Spain
AGA	AGABY	ADR	OTC	Chemicals - General	Sweden
Asea	ASEAY	ADR	NASDAQ	Electrical Machinery	Sweden

COMPANY NAME	SYMBOL	ADR	EXCHANGE	INDUSTRY	COUNTRY
Atlas Copco	ATLA	ADR	OTC	Industrial Machinery	Sweden
Electrolux	ELUXY	ADR	NASDAQ	Electronics - Consumer	Sweden
Ericsson Telephone Company	ERICY	ADR	NASDAQ	Telecommun Equipment	Sweden
Esselte	EBB	ADR	OTC	Services - Misc	Sweden
Gambro	GAMBY	ADR	NASDAQ	Pharmaceuticals	Sweden
SKF	SKFRY	ADR	NASDAQ	Steel	Sweden
Sandvik	SVI	ADR	OTC	Steel	Sweden
Volvo	VOLVY	ADR	NASDAQ	Autos	Sweden
BBC Brown Boveri	BBOVY	ADR	OTC	Electrical Machinery	Switzerland
CS Holding	CSHKY	ADR	OTC	Building Materials	Switzerland
Ciba-Geigy	CBGXY	ADR	OTC	Pharmaceuticals	Switzerland
Nestle	NSRGY	ADR	OTC	Food	Switzerland
Roche Holding	ROHHY	ADR	OTC	Pharmaceuticals	Switzerland
Sandoz	SDOZY	ADR	OTC	Pharmaceuticals	Switzerland
Advanced Info Service	AIS	ADR	OTC	Telecommun Equipment	Thailand
Asia Fiber Company	AFC	ADR	OTC	Textiles	Thailand
Shinawatra Computer & Communications	SHWCY	ADR	OTC	Telecommun Equipment	Thailand
Albert Fisher Group	AFHGY	ADR	OTC	Food	U.K.
Allied Lyons	ALLYY	ADR	OTC	Beverages	U.K.
Associated British Foods	ASBFY	ADR	OTC	Food	U.K.
Astec (BSR)	ASTCY	ADR	OTC	Electronics - Consumer	U.K.
Attwoods	A	ADR	NYSE	Electric Cable	U.K.
Automated Security (Holdings)	ASI	ADR	NYSE	Services - Misc	U.K.
B.A.T. Industries	BTI	ADR	AMEX	Trading	U.K.
BAA	BAAPY	ADR	OTC	Services - Misc	U.K.

COMPANY NAME	SYMBOL	ADR	EXCHANGE	INDUSTRY	COUNTRY
BET	BEP	ADR	NYSE	Services - Misc	U.K.
BOC Group	BOCNY	ADR	OTC	Chemicals - General	U.K.
BTR	BTRUY	ADR	OTC	Multi-Industry	U.K.
Barclays Bank	BCS	ADR	NYSE	Banks	U.K.
Bass	BAS	ADR	NYSE	Beverages	U.K.
Bespak	BSP	ADR	OTC	Pharmaceuticals	U.K.
Blenheim Exhibitions Group	BLE	ADR	OTC	Services - Misc	U.K.
Blue Circle Industries	BCLEY	ADR	OTC	Building Materials	U.K.
Body Shop International	BDSPY	ADR	OTC	Household Products	U.K.
Booker	BKERY	ADR	OTC	Food - Commodity	U.K.
Boots Company	BOOTY	ADR	OTC	Retailing - Specialty	U.K.
Bowater Industries	BWTRY	ADR	NASDAQ	Printing	U.K.
Brent Walker Group	BWG	ADR	OTC	Hotels & Leisure	U.K.
British Airways	BAB	ADR	NYSE	Airlines	U.K.
British Bio-Technology Group	BBIOY	ADR	NASDAQ	Pharmaceuticals	U.K.
British Gas	BRG	ADR	NYSE	Utilities	U.K.
British Petroleum	BP	ADR	NYSE	Oil	U.K.
British Steel	BST	ADR	NYSE	Steel	U.K.
British Telecommunications	BTY	ADR	NYSE	Telecommun Equipment	U.K.
Burmah Castrol	BURMY	ADR	NASDAQ	Chemicals - General	U.K.
Burton Group	BURUY	ADR	OTC	Retailing - Specialty	U.K.
CML Microsystems	CML	ADR	OTC	Electrical Machinery	U.K.
Cable And Wireless	CWP	ADR	NYSE	Telecommun Equipment	U.K.
Cadbury Schweppes	CADBY	ADR	NASDAQ	Food	U.K.
Carlton Communications	CCTVY	ADR	NASDAQ	Media	U.K.

COMPANY NAME	SYMBOL	ADR	EXCHANGE	INDUSTRY	COUNTRY
Challenger International	CSTIF	Direct List	NASDAQ	Recreation Products	U.K.
Chandler Insurance	CHANF	Direct List	NASDAQ	Insurance	U.K.
Charter Consolidated	CHRTY	ADR	OTC	Multi-Industry	U.K.
Chloride Group	CDGPY	ADR	OTC	Electrical Machinery	U.K.
Christian Salvesen	CSALY	ADR	OTC	Food	U.K.
Christies International	CTTDY	ADR	OTC	Services - Misc	U.K.
Coats Viyella	COATY	ADR	OTC	Textiles	U.K.
Corporate Service Group	CSG	ADR	OTC	Oil	U.K.
Courtaulds	COU	ADR	AMEX	Textiles	U.K.
DSG International	DSGIF	Direct List	NASDAQ	Household Products	U.K.
Danka Business Systems	DANKY	ADR	NASDAQ	Office Equipment/Cameras	U.K.
De La Rue Company	DLR	ADR	OTC	Services - Misc	U.K.
Dixons Group	DXN	ADR	OTC	Retailing - Specialty	U.K.
East Midlands Electricity	EMELY	ADR	OTC	Utilities	U.K.
Eastern Electricity	ESTNY	ADR	OTC	Utilities	U.K.
English China Clays	ENC	ADR	NYSE	Building Materials	U.K.
Enterprise Oil	ETP	ADR	NYSE	Oil	U.K.
Eurotunnel	ETNLY	ADR	OTC	Construction - General	U.K.
Fisons	FISNY	ADR	NASDAQ	Pharmaceuticals	U.K.
Futuremedia	FMDAY	ADR	NASDAQ	Media	U.K.
GKN	GKN	ADR	OTC	Autos	U.K.
General Electric Company	GNELY	ADR	OTC	Electrical Machinery	U.K.
Gestetner Holdings	GEZ	ADR	OTC	Retailing - Specialty	U.K.
Glaxo Holdings	GLX	ADR	NYSE	Pharmaceuticals	U.K.
Gold Greenlees Trott	GGTR	ADR	OTC	Media	U.K.

COMPANY NAME	SYMBOL	ADR	EXCHANGE	INDUSTRY	COUNTRY
Govett & Company	GOVTY	ADR	OTC	Securities	U.K.
Grand Metropolitan	GRM	ADR	NYSE	Food	U.K.
Great Universal Stores	GUS	ADR	OTC	Retailing - Specialty	U.K.
Guinness	GUI	ADR	OTC	Beverages	U.K.
Hanson	HAN	ADR	NYSE	Multi-Industry	U.K.
Hartstone Group	HSTEY	ADR	OTC	Retailing - Specialty	U.K.
Hillsdown Holdings	HDNHY	ADR	OTC	Food	U.K.
Horace Small Apparel	HSMAY	ADR	OTC	Textiles	U.K.
HSBC Holdings	HSBHY	ADR	OTC	Banks	U.K.
Huntingdon International Holdings	IITD	ADR	NYSE	Pharmaceuticals	U.K.
Imperial Chemical Industries	ICI	ADR	NYSE	Chemicals - General	U.K.
Kingfisher	KGFIY	ADR	OTC	Retailing - Specialty	U.K.
Ladbroke Group	LADGY	ADR	OTC	Hotels & Leisure	U.K.
Lasmo	LSO	ADR	NYSE	Oil	U.K.
Laura Ashley Holdings	LARAY	ADR	OTC	Retailing - Specialty	U.K.
Lep Group	LEPGY	ADR	NASDAQ	Miscellaneous Transportation	U.K.
London Electricity	LNDNY	ADR	OTC	Utilities	U.K.
London Finance and Investment	LFI	ADR	OTC	Securities	U.K.
London International Group	LONDY	ADR	NASDAQ	Pharmaceuticals	U.K.
Lonrho	LNRHY	ADR	OTC	Multi-Industry	U.K.
MB-Caradon	MBC	ADR	OTC	Printing	U.K.
Manweb	MANWY	ADR	OTC	Utilities	U.K.
Marks & Spencer	MSL	ADR	OTC	Retailing - Specialty	U.K.
Medeva	MDV	ADR	AMEX	Pharmaceuticals	U.K.
Micro Focus Group	MIFGY	ADR	NASDAQ	Software	U.K.

COMPANY NAME	SYMBOL	ADR	EXCHANGE	INDUSTRY	COUNTRY
Midlands Electricity	MIDEY	ADR	OTC	Utilities	U.K.
NFC	NFC	ADR	AMEX	Miscellaneous Transportation	U.K.
NMC Group	NMC	ADR	OTC	Pulp & Paper	U.K.
Nam Tai Electronics	NTAIF	ADR	NASDAQ	Electronics - Consumer	U.K.
National Power	NPWRY	ADR	OTC	Utilities	U.K.
National Westminster Bank	NW	ADR	NYSE	Banks	U.K.
Nobel Insurance	NOBLF	Direct List	NASDAQ	Insurance	U.K.
Northern Electric	NORLY	ADR	OTC	Utilities	U.K.
Norweb	NORWY	ADR	OTC	Utilities	U.K.
Peninsular and Oriental Steam Navigation	PIA	ADR	OTC	Marine Transportation	U.K.
Pentos	PNT	ADR	OTC	Retailing - Specialty	U.K.
Powergen	PWGNY	ADR	OTC	Utilities	U.K.
Premier Consolidated Oilfields	PCO	ADR	OTC	Oil	U.K.
Prudential Corporation	PRU	ADR	OTC	Insurance	U.K.
RTZ	RTZ	ADR	NYSE	Mining	U.K.
Racal Electronics	RCALY	ADR	OTC	Electrical Machinery	U.K.
Rank Organization	RANKY	ADR	NASDAQ	Hotels & Leisure	U.K.
Ratners Group	RATNY	ADR	OTC	Retailing - Specialty	U.K.
Redland	REDPY	ADR	OTC	Building Materials	U.K.
Reed International	RENEY	ADR	OTC	Media	U.K.
Reuters Holdings	RTRSY	ADR	NASDAQ	Media	U.K.
Rolls Royce	RYCEY	ADR	OTC	Defense & Aerospace	U.K.
Rothmans International	ROTHY	ADR	OTC	Multi-Industry	U.K.
Royal Bank of Scotland	RBSA	ADR	NYSE	Banks	U.K.
Saatchi & Saatchi	SAA	ADR	NYSE	Media	U.K.

COMPANY NAME	SYMBOL	ADR	EXCHANGE	INDUSTRY	COUNTRY
Sainsbury	JSA	ADR	OTC	Supermarket	U.K.
Scantronic Holdings	SCH	ADR	OTC	Electronics - Consumer	U.K.
Scottish Hydro-electric	SHYAY	ADR	OTC	Utilities	U.K.
Scottish Power	SPYAY	ADR	OTC	Utilities	U.K.
Sears	SER	ADR	OTC	Retailing - Specialty	U.K.
Sedgwick Group	SDW	ADR	OTC	Insurance	U.K.
Seeboard	SEEBY	ADR	OTC	Utilities	U.K.
Shell Transport & Trading	SC	ADR	NYSE	Oil	U.K.
Siebe	SIBEY	ADR	OTC	Electrical Machinery	U.K.
Smithkline Beecham Group	SBH	ADR	NYSE	Pharmaceuticals	U.K.
South Wales Electricity	SOWLY	ADR	OTC	Utilities	U.K.
South Western Electricity	SWSTY	ADR	OTC	Utilities	U.K.
Southern Electric	SOELY	ADR	OTC	Utilities	U.K.
T & N	TAN	ADR	OTC	Autos	U.K.
TI Group	TIGUY	ADR	OTC	Industrial Machinery	U.K.
Tarmac	TAA	ADR	OTC	Building Materials	U.K.
Tate and Lyle	TATYY	ADR	OTC	Food	U.K.
Tesco	TEO	ADR	OTC	Supermarket	U.K.
Thorn Emi	THC	ADR	OTC	Media	U.K.
Tiphook	TPH	ADR	NYSE	Miscellaneous Transportation	U.K.
Tomkins	TOMKY	ADR	NASDAQ	Multi-Industry	U.K.
Trafalgar House	THZ	ADR	OTC	Real Estate	U.K.
Transport Development Group	TDM	ADR	OTC	Miscellaneous Transportation	U.K.
Trinity International Holdings	TIH	ADR	OTC	Media	U.K.
Unigate	UNL	ADR	OTC	Food	U.K.
Unilever	UL	ADR	NYSE	Food	U.K.

COMPANY NAME	SYMBOL	ADR	EXCHANGE	INDUSTRY	COUNTRY
Unitech	UNT	ADR	OTC	Electronics - Consumer	U.K.
United Biscuits (Holdings)	UTBTY	ADR	OTC	Food	U.K.
United Newspapers	UNEWY	ADR	NASDAQ	Media	U.K.
Vickers	VPL	ADR	OTC	Autos	U.K.
Vodafone Group	VOD	ADR	NYSE	Telecommun Equipment	U.K.
WPP Group	WPPGY	ADR	NASDAQ	Media	U.K.
Wace Group	WACE	ADR	OTC	Media	U.K.
Wellcome	WEL	ADR	NYSE	Pharmaceuticals	U.K.
Wembley	WMB	ADR	OTC	Hotels & Leisure	U.K.
Whitbread and Company	WBR	ADR	OTC	Food	U.K.
Williams Holdings	WOD	ADR	OTC	Building Materials	U.K.
Willis Corroon Group	WCG	ADR	NYSE	Securities	U.K.
Yorkshire Electricity Group	YOREY	ADR	OTC	Utilities	U.K.
Ceramica Carabobo	CRCAY	ADR	OTC	Building Materials	Venezuela
Corimon	CRM	ADR	NYSE	Building Materials	Venezuela
Mhangura Copper Mines	MTD	ADR	OTC	Mining	Venezuela
Zambia Consolidated Copper Mines	ZCC	ADR	OTC	Mining	Zambia

Index

B

f

Here's a <u>free</u> way to get even more out of MetaStock.™

We've prepared a unique booklet to help you get the most out of your special edition of MetaStock.

The booklet is titled *Maximizing Your Investments With MetaStock*. And it's absolutely free. Just call us and we'll send your copy today.

It's filled with tips and ideas you can use right away with MetaStock SE™ to make better investment decisions.

- Get started with a Quick Tutorial
- Learn shortcuts, tips, and tricks
- See how to analyze your securities with technical analysis
- Locate a MetaStock User Group in your area
- Learn about MetaStock-compatible third-party products

- See how to use our extensive, free customer support network
- Learn about MetaStock features not included in MetaStock SE
- Get special discounts on upgrades and other EQUIS investment products

MetaStock SE and *Maximizing Your Investments With MetaStock* will help you reach your goal of becoming a successful investor.

You'll see why the readers of *Stocks & Commodities Magazine* recently voted MetaStock the #1 software program in its price category.

Investment software experts agree: "If you want to learn about technical analysis, this package is the place to start—and we guarantee that you'll never outgrow it. This may be the most well thought-out and easy-to-use package we reviewed." —*Worth Magazine, April 1994*

When you put your money on the line, you can trust MetaStock.

To order your FREE copy of *Maximizing Your Investments With MetaStock*, call Toll-Free
1-800-882-3040 ext. SE

EQUIS International • 3950 South 700 East, Suite 100 • Salt Lake City, Utah 84107 • 801-265-8886 • FAX: 801-265-3999 • CompuServe: GO EQUIS (Section 14) • Prodigy: Money Talk BB/Investment Tools/META   ©1994 EQUIS International, Inc. MetaStock and MetaStock SE are trademarks of EQUIS International. All other product names are trademarks of their respective companies.

" If you want to learn about technical analysis, this package is the place to start—and we guarantee that you'll never outgrow it. "

—*Worth Magazine, April 1994*

As a MetaStock SE™ user, you will have a full range of support services ready to use. Help is always available on CompuServe, Prodigy, or our Customer Support Hotline.

In addition, there's our quarterly newsletter, and one of the industry's largest user group communities.

That's one of the reasons why MetaStock is the world's best-selling technical analysis software.

**We'll Help You
Every Step Of The Way**

After 10 years of developing invest-

ment software, we're still totally committed to one thing—making software that helps you make money.

"Most users I checked loved the relationship they had with EQUIS. Some had gotten unsolicited callbacks to see how they were doing. EQUIS was a company on which they could rely." —*Stocks & Commodities Magazine, May 1994*

As you work with MetaStock SE, you'll see that we give you both top-notch investment software and top-notch service.

When you put your money on the line, you can trust MetaStock.

Order your FREE copy of
*Maximizing Your Investments
With MetaStock,*
an information-packed booklet
to help you get the most out of
MetaStock SE. Call Toll-Free:

1-800-882-3040 ext. SE

Call Today To Activate Your FREE
Telescan Investment Software
($199 value)
And receive 30 days FREE access to the Telescan Database

One call is all it takes to activate your Telescan Analyzer program and gain free trial access to the extensive Telescan database of stock market and financial information.

To activate your software, call: 1-800-324-4692

When you call, a Telescan Customer Service representative will give you:

- ➤ The local telephone number to dial to access the database
- ➤ Your User ID Number
- ➤ Your Password

You also have the option to receive a complete set of Telescan System documentation. To receive the documentation, you pay a one-time shipping and handling charge of $12.75.

Your 30-Day Free Trial Includes:

- ➤ Non-prime time access* to the Telescan historical database dating back to 1973. (Non-prime hours 6:00 p.m. to 7:00 a.m. your local time, plus weekends and some holidays)

- ➤ Free access to:
  S&P MarketScope™
  Hedged Options Trader newsletter
  Undervalued Growth newsletter

Toll-Free Customer Service is available to activate your software and answer any questions.
Monday – Friday 7:00 a.m. to Midnight
Saturday and Sunday 9:00 a.m. to 6:00 p.m.

* Long distance call required to access the Telescan database outside the continental United States.

Stock Market Screening,
Research and Analysis

Telescan Analyzer is the most powerful stock evaluation program on the market today.

With Telescan Analyzer you can:

➤ Access price and volume information dating back to 1973 on more than 77,000 stocks, bonds, mutual funds, options, futures, industry groups and market indexes.

➤ Retrieve on-line stock quotes for the NYSE, AMEX, NASDAQ and Canadian exchanges, updated on a 15-minute delay.

➤ Use more than 80 popular technical charting tools to pinpoint buy/sell decisions.

➤ View S&P MarketScope, Reuter's news wire, Zacks Estimate Service, Market Guide fact sheets, insider trading, quarterly earnings reports and much more.

➤ Access **Telescan Optimizer FREE ($100 value).** This profitability tester helps you optimize the time periods for most technical indicators and calculate the profitability for given indicator/time period combinations.

As a Telescan subscriber, you will receive:

➤ Bi-monthly newsletters featuring expert articles on investment strategies, news briefs on upcoming events and special offers.

➤ Invitations to exclusive regional Telescan investment seminars that will help you maximize the benefits of this powerful analysis tool.

As a Global Investment book purchaser you also receive a 20% discount on all other Telescan software products.

Call TODAY
to activate your free software
1-800-324-4692

PC REQUIREMENTS: IBM PC (286 or faster) or 100% compatible computer, MS DOS 3.1
or higher, 640K of memory, hard disk; CGA, EGA or VGA monitor, and a Hayes or
compatible modem. Contains optional mouse interface.

Tele*scan* ™
INCORPORATED

Dear Investor,

If you've installed the Windows On WallStreet Limited Edition that was enclosed in this book, we're sure you've discovered what thousands of other Windows On WallStreet customers have found, Windows On WallStreet is absolutely the #1 software solution that can help you pinpoint great trading opportunities, and increase your profits.

If you were impressed with this Limited Version of Windows On WallStreet, you simply won't believe the power of the *fully functional version!* Here are just a few of the many additional features that can help you ***discover the goldmines of the market:***

- ★ **A complete On-line Research System** for accessing fundamental information such as EPS, analysts earnings estimates, and a host of other fundamental information, all with the touch of a button!
- ★ **The Personal Investment Assistant™** automatically manages your daily investment chores. This hard working assistant will automatically download data, apply analysis, print charts (up to 100 per page) and much more all while you're away!
- ★ **Profit / System Testing** instantly shows you which indicators make money on your securities.
- ★ **User definable alerts** visually notify you of critical conditions that you specify.
- ★ **Custom indicators** allow you to add your own indicators and the latest indicators from the experts.
- ★ **Tracking of an UNLIMITED** number of securities (the Limited Version will only track 20).
- ★ **Downloading support** for additional data services such as CompuServe®, Dow Jones News/Retrieval®, and others.
- ★ **Reads other data formats** such as MetaStock, CompuTrac, TC2000, AIQ, CSI, and ASCII.

These and other additional features are worth their weight in gold!   *(over please)*

Upgrade NOW for Only $99!

WINDOWS ON WALL STREET

This special upgrade offer is being made to purchasers of *The Business Week Guide to Global Investments Using Electronic Tools.* We want to give every person who buys this book special treatment. In addition to upgrading to the fully functional version of Windows On WallStreet for only $99, Dial Data is making a special offer to buyers of this book who use Windows On WallStreet! This offer will save you a whopping $70 (see below).

That's not all! This offer also entitles you to a special deal on our *Investors PowerPack*! This power pack will get you started with historical data on 400 of the top Stocks and Mutual Funds, plus an incredible Trading System library that was developed by our analysts who have decades of experience in computerized trading! Order today and get the *Investors PowerPack* for only **$39.95.** Normally $69.95, that's a **43%** savings! The *Investors PowerPack* includes:

- ❏ Over 20 advanced trading systems including Multi-Indicator trading systems to strengthen their ability to generate profitable trading signals.
- ❏ Discounts on stock market/financial books and video tapes.
- ❏ 200 years of Mutual Fund Historical Data.
- ❏ 200 years of Historical Stock Data.

This is absolutely the best price on *Windows On WallStreet 2.1 and the Investors PowerPack we've ever offered.* We urge all serious investors to call now and order this special upgrade for Windows On WallStreet 2.1. It is simply the best investment you can make.

MarketArts Inc. Call toll free (800) 998-VIEW   International (214) 235-9594

DIAL / DATA
a division of TRACK DATA CORPORATION

FREE! FREE! FREE! FREE! FREE! FREE! FREE!
Receive first month free (B1 flat monthly fee plan... $35 value)
Plus no sign up fee! ($35 value) **A $70 value from Dial Data!**

Users of the *Windows On WallStreet Limited Edition* disk included in this book can get a full month of free data service from Dial Data. This means you can download stocks and indices and manage your portfolio, for an entire month, **FREE!** To receive your free month of service, call **Dial Data at (800) 275-5544** and tell the sales specialist that you're a *Windows On WallStreet Global Investments Edition* user. **Call Dial Data toll free at (800) 275-5544**

MarketArts Inc. 1810 N. Glenville Dr., Suite 124, Richardson, TX 75081 Ph: (214) 235-9594 Fax: (214) 783-6798

If you can find a better source of investment information, we'll post your bail.

With CompuServe, you get more inside information on international investments than with any other consumer information service. Quickly. Accurately. And, best of all, legally.

From beginning to end, CompuServe's there to help.

If you're looking to make an investment—or even if you're just browsing—you can begin by focusing on some likely opportunities. Our company libraries for the UK, Germany, and the rest of Europe, as well as D&B's Dun's Market Identifiers for the US, Canada, and international markets, will help to get you started.

Then, CompuServe will enable you to analyze those targets with a whole list of backgrounding services. Like Citibank's Global Report, featuring everything from market and industry news to real-time foreign exchange and fixed income prices.

Disclosure, a service that provides detailed SEC reports. Company Analyzer, which gives you individual company information. And MMS International, with monetary theory data, gives forecasts of central banking policies and operations, and economic reports. We are also a data source for MetaStock and Windows on WallStreet.

Talk over the alternatives.

You'll even be able to discuss your options with other members on CompuServe. In our financial forums, experts and beginners meet to exchange and discuss ideas, opportunities, and rumors. Our International Entrepreneurs Network and Investors' Forum are filled with helpful—and knowledge-able—people. And FundWatch Online by Money Magazine is a source of valu-able information—reporting on more than 1,900 professionally managed mutual funds.

Then, once you've got your eye on a likely prospect, check the price. On CompuServe, the current market value of stocks, options, and market indices are released as soon as the exchanges legally permit.

Finally, you can even make your investment through CompuServe, with online discount brokers like Quick & Reilly and E*Trade.

But there's more to life than investing.

CompuServe offers more than just financial services. When you join, you begin with the basics: more than 70 popular products and services for a low monthly fee of $8.95. With your basic membership, you can check out the latest news on the AP wire, exam-ine a satellite weather map, search for an entry in the encyclopedia, or even send an E-mail to a trading partner in Hong Kong. And you can do it all for the cost of a local phone call, any time of the day or night, from just about anywhere in the world.

From the basics, you can then move into a more advanced world of communication and information that features many of our financial services.

Free membership kit.

Join now, and you'll get a free membership kit ($49.95 value) that includes CompuServe Information Manager software, a $25 usage credit, a free month of basic services (an $8.95 value), and a subscription to our monthly *CompuServe Magazine*. All you have to do is call 1 800 522-4477, extension 106. Or mail in the attached coupon.

Either way, it'll be the one investment you make that's guaranteed to profit you.

CompuServe

The information service you won't outgrow.™

Please place this coupon in an envelope and mail to:

CompuServe
New Member Department
PO Box 20961
Columbus, OH 43220-9988

You're about to discover how a simple $4.^{95} investment can have a positive effect on your entire portfolio.

Please turn the page for details

The PRODIGY® service.

SOFTWARE AND ONE MONTH'S MEMBERSHIP FREE!

The investment resources it brings you are priceless. (Try membership free for one month—pay just $4.95 S&H for the software you need to get started.)

As soon as you connect with PRODIGY (all you need is a computer, a modem and regular phone line to do so) you're on the inside track to a world of valuable, unbiased investment information. PRODIGY delivers all the tools you need to make informed investment decisions. Get the top financial and company news almost as soon as it happens. Get current quotes on *your* portfolio, historical data, company charts and stock selection models. You can even access a daily digest of the important buy/sell recommendations from the newsletter writers and hotline services. Plan your next move or track a previous one using comprehensive databases of stock and mutual fund data. And when you see opportunity, trade online with a discount broker. They're all available online on demand. This is where Wall St. meets the digital highway—the most affordable and timesaving way to stay current and in control of your investments.

If you're in the market for a great way to manage and maximize your finances call PRODIGY today and begin *your* free month's membership. It could be the smartest $4.95 investment you ever make.

CALL 1 800 PRODIGY *ext.* 96
TO TRY A FREE MONTH OF MEMBERSHIP

The Internet is
for Investors.

FREE

FIVE HOUR
FREE TRIAL

Dial by modem, 1-800-365-4636

Press return a few times. At *Password*, enter BWGG2

Welcome to the Internet, made available to you by Delphi. As the only major online service to offer the full Internet, Delphi now makes it possible to track business trends faster than ever before. Thanks to Delphi, you'll be immediately apprised of what's happening - from commodities to mutual funds, and the NYSE to the Nikkei. To keep tabs on corporate SEC filings, the Internet on Delphi also gives you access to the EDGAR Dissemination Service. And, if you sign on now, you'll be treated to five hours of evening and weekend access to Delphi - absolutely FREE.

Log on and you'll instantly be part of a community of more than 20 million people. Jump into one of our discussion groups and meet thousands of business managers, from single proprietors to CEOs of the Fortune 500. Research thousands of companies. Become a member of the Usenet community, sharing intelligence worldwide on literally thousands of topics. Do it all and never get lost, because hundreds of online experts are available to answer your every question.

The last time we looked, the world's investments, markets, industries weren't standing still. We respectfully believe that you shouldn't either. Log on to Delphi. All you need to invest is the time.

DELPHI
INTERNET

GEnie®.
The most fun you can have with your computer on.

No other online service has more cool stuff to do, or more cool people to do it with than GEnie. Join dozens of awesome special interest RoundTables on everything from scuba diving to Microsoft to food and wine, download over 200,000 files, access daily stock quotes, talk to all those smart people on the Internet, play the most incredible multi-player games, and so much more you won't believe your eyes!

And GEnie has it all at a standard connect rate of just $3.00 an hour[1]! That's the lowest hourly connect rate of all the major online companies! Plus -- because you're a reader of the *Business Week Guide to Global Investments Using Electronic Tools* -- you get an even cooler deal[2]. When you sign up, we'll waive your first monthly subscription fee (an $8.95 value) and include ten additional hours of standard connect time (another $30.00 in savings). That's fourteen free hours during your first month -- *a $38.95 value!*

You can take advantage of this incredible offer immediately -- just follow the simple steps on the other side of this coupon.

To sign up for GEnie:

1. Set your communications software for half-duplex (local echo) at 300, 1200, or 2400 baud. Recommended communications parameters are 8 data bits, no parity, and 1 stop bit.

2. Dial toll-free in the U.S. at 1-800-638-8369 (or in Canada at 1-800-387-8330). Upon connection, type **HHH** (Please note that every time you use GEnie, you need to enter the HHH upon connection).

3. At the U#= message, type **JOINGENIE** and press <Return>.

4. At the offer prompt, enter **GAH225** to get this special offer.

5. Have a major credit card ready. In the U.S., you may also use your checking account number. (There is a $2.00 monthly fee for all checking accounts.) In Canada, VISA and MasterCard only.

Or, if you need more information, contact GEnie Client Services at 1-800-638-9636 from 9am to midnight, Monday through Friday, and from noon to 8pm Saturday and Sunday (all times are Eastern).

1 U.S. prices. Standard connect time is non-prime time: 6pm to 8am local time, Mon. - Fri., all day Sat. and Sun. and selected holidays.
2 The offer for ten additional hours applies to standard hourly connect charges only and must be used by the end of the billing period for your first month. Please see our GEnie brochure for more information on pricing and billing policies.

The disk comes with data on 15 stocks and indexes on board. To be able to load new data you should call Dial Data at 800/275-5544 and register for your free sign-up and month's trial use. Tell them you're a *Windows On WallStreet Global Investments Edition* user and they will sign you up. You should also call MarketArts at 800/998-8439 to register the program and be eligible for technical support.

NOTE: *If your computer can't read the Windows On WallStreet disk, please contact this book's publisher, Osborne/McGraw-Hill, at 800/227-0900 for a replacement disk. For any other problems with the installation procedure or for any other technical support help, please contact MarketArts at 214/783-6793.*

Copyright Information

EQUIS International® Copyright © 1994. MarketArts™, Telescan™, Telescan Analyzer™, and ProSearch™ are registered trademarks.

WARNING: BEFORE OPENING THE DISK PACKAGE, CAREFULLY READ THE TERMS AND CONDITIONS OF THE LIMITED WARRANTY BELOW.

LICENSING TERMS

The subscriber acknowledges that all information and/or programs provided are the exclusive property of Telescan, Inc., MarketArts Inc., or EQUIS International, or its licensor and are protected by copyright law. Any reproduction requires prior written approval of the respective Company.

LIMITED WARRANTY

Osborne/McGraw-Hill warrants the physical diskettes enclosed herein to be free of defects in materials and workmanship for a period of sixty days from the purchase date. If Osborne/McGraw-Hill receives written notification within the warranty period of defects in materials or workmanship, and such notification is determined by Osborne/McGraw-Hill to be correct, Osborne/McGraw-Hill will replace the defective diskettes.

The entire and exclusive liability and remedy for breach of this Limited Warranty shall be limited to replacement of defective diskettes and shall not include or extend to any claim for or right to cover any other damages, including but not limited to, loss of profit, data, or use of the software, or special, incidental, or consequential damages or other similar claims, even if Osborne/McGraw-Hill has been specifically advised of the possibility of such damages. In no event will Osborne/McGraw-Hill's liability for any damages to you or any other person ever exceed the lower of the suggested list price or actual price paid for the license to use the software, regardless of any form of the claim.

OSBORNE, A DIVISION OF MCGRAW-HILL, INC., SPECIFICALLY DISCLAIMS ALL OTHER WARRANTIES, EXPRESS OR IMPLIED, INCLUDING BUT NOT LIMITED TO, ANY IMPLIED WARRANTY OF MERCHANTABILITY OR FITNESS FOR A PARTICULAR PURPOSE. Specifically, Osborne/McGraw-Hill make no representation or warranty that the software is fit for any particular purpose and any implied warranty of merchantability is limited to the sixty-day duration of the Limited Warranty covering the physical diskettes only (and not the software) and is otherwise expressly and specifically disclaimed.

This limited warranty gives you specific legal rights; you may have others which may vary from state to state. Some states do not allow the exclusion of incidental or consequential damages, or the limitation on how long an implied warranty lasts, so some of the above may not apply to you.

About the Disks

Telescan

Telescan Analyzer is a high-performance investment tool with a powerful combination of investment research and analysis software. With Telescan Analyzer you can use more than 80 technical charting tools to help pinpoint buy/sell decisions and access more than 20 years of stock price and volume information. Before you install this disk you should call Telescan at 800/324-4692 and get a password, ID number, and phone number that will be used to download information from the system. Without the ID and password the program will not work. *This is a DOS program. If your computer starts out in Windows, you must exit Windows and you will then see a DOS prompt.*

To install the program, simply insert the Telescan disk in your floppy drive, make that the active drive, and type **install**. Press the ENTER key and the installation will proceed automatically. When it is finished you will see a new directory on your C drive; TELE30. To start the program, just type the letter **T**.

Your first job when the program comes up will be to click on the pull-down menu that says **System** and then click on the choice labeled **Logon Setup**. A screen will appear for entering the information you received from Telescan. Once that is entered the program is fully active.

NOTE: If your computer can't read the Telescan disk, please contact this book's publisher, Osborne/McGraw-Hill, at 800/227-0900 for a replacement disk. For any problems with the installaton procedure or for any other technical support help, please contact Telescan at 800/324-4692.

MetaStock

Your free copy of MetaStock SE is a special edition of the world's best-selling technical analysis software for the PC. With this easy-to-use program, you can chart and analyze any security. This version of MetaStock SE is also a DOS program, not Windows. If you are not already in DOS, exit Windows to return to the DOS prompt.

Insert the MetaStock disk in your floppy drive and make that the active drive. Type **install**. Everything will proceed automatically and you will end up with a new directory labeled MSSE on your C drive. (MSSE stands for "MetaStock Special Edition.") Type **MS** to start the program.

The disk will have data on closed-end funds and market indexes already on it. To register the program, find out how to update your data, and get a free instruction booklet mailed to you, call Equis International at 800/882-3040, ext SE.

NOTE: If your computer can't read the MetaStock disk, please contact this book's publisher, Osborne/McGraw-Hill, at 800/227-0900 for a replacement disk. For any problems with the installation procedure, please contact Equis International at 800/882-3040, ext. SE. For all other technical support, please call Equis at 801/265-9998.

Windows On WallStreet

This Windows-based investment program provides you with the tools that professional investors have used for years. Access online financial databases, chart your own portfolio, and use sophisticated graphing measures to time investments.

You must be in Windows to begin the installation procedure. Insert the Windows On WallStreet disk in your floppy drive and activate the File Manager in Windows. Click on the drive that holds the disk to make that the active drive. Double-click on the filename that says **setup**. The installation will proceed automatically. A tutorial and operating instructions are already on the disk. To run the program, double-click on the MarketArts icon and then double-click on the Windows On WallStreet icon.